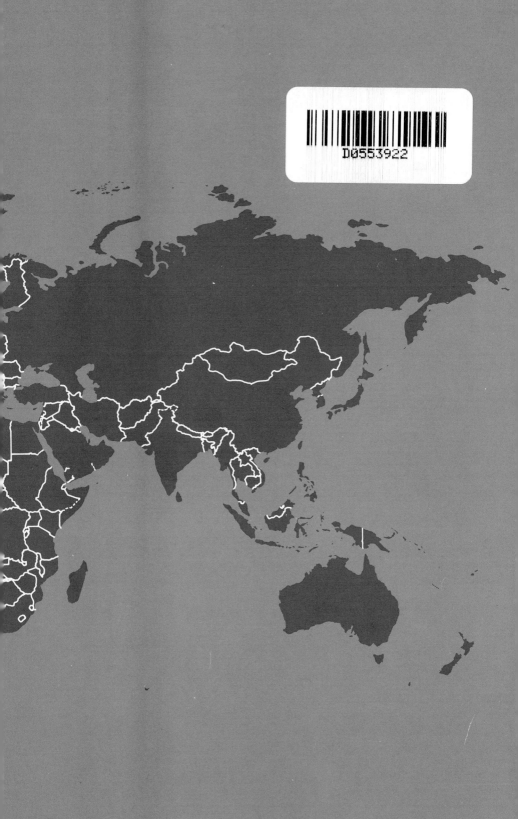

D0553922

Sudan
a country study

Federal Research Division
Library of Congress
Edited by
Helen Chapin Metz
Research Completed
June 1991

On the cover: An Nilain Mosque, at the site of the confluence of the Blue Nile and White Nile in Khartoum

Fourth Edition, First Printing, 1992.

Library of Congress Cataloging-in-Publication Data

Sudan : a country study / Federal Research Division, Library of
  Congress ; edited by Helen Chapin Metz. — 4th ed.
      p. cm. — (Area handbook series, ISSN 1057-5294) (DA
  pam ; 550-27)
      "Research completed June 1991."
      "Supersedes the 1982 edition of Sudan: a country study, edited
  by Harold D. Nelson"—T.p. verso.
      Includes bibliographical references (pp. 289-304) and index.
      ISBN 0-8444-0750-X
      1. Sudan.   I. Metz, Helen Chapin, 1928- . II. Library of
  Congress. Federal Research Division. III. Series. IV. Series: DA
  pam ; 550-27.
  DT154.6.S93   1992   92-21336
  962.4—dc20   CIP

Headquarters, Department of the Army
DA Pam 550-27

For sale by the Superintendent of Documents, U.S. Government Printing Office
Washington, D.C. 20402

Foreword

This volume is one in a continuing series of books prepared by the Federal Research Division of the Library of Congress under the Country Studies/Area Handbook Program sponsored by the Department of the Army. The last page of this book lists the other published studies.

Most books in the series deal with a particular foreign country, describing and analyzing its political, economic, social, and national security systems and institutions, and examining the interrelationships of those systems and the ways they are shaped by cultural factors. Each study is written by a multidisciplinary team of social scientists. The authors seek to provide a basic understanding of the observed society, striving for a dynamic rather than a static portrayal. Particular attention is devoted to the people who make up the society, their origins, dominant beliefs and values, their common interests and the issues on which they are divided, the nature and extent of their involvement with national institutions, and their attitudes toward each other and toward their social system and political order.

The books represent the analysis of the authors and should not be construed as an expression of an official United States government position, policy, or decision. The authors have sought to adhere to accepted standards of scholarly objectivity. Corrections, additions, and suggestions for changes from readers will be welcomed for use in future editions.

Louis R. Mortimer
Chief
Federal Research Division
Library of Congress
Washington, D.C. 20540

Acknowledgments

The authors wish to acknowledge the contributions of the writers of the 1982 edition of *Sudan: A Country Study*, edited by Harold D. Nelson. Their work provided general background for the present volume.

The authors are grateful to individuals in various government agencies and private institutions who gave of their time, research materials, and expertise in the production of this book. The individuals included Ralph K. Benesch, who oversees the Country Studies/Area Handbook Program for the Department of the Army. The authors also wish to thank members of the Federal Research Division staff who contributed directly to the preparation of the manuscript. These people included Sandra W. Meditz, who reviewed all graphic and textual material and served as liaison with the sponsoring agency, Marilyn Majeska, who managed editing and book production, and Joshua Sinai, who contributed additional research.

Also involved in preparing the text were editorial assistants Barbara Edgerton and Izella Watson; Ruth Nieland, who edited the chapters; Catherine Schwartzstein, who performed the prepublication editorial review; and Joan C. Cook, who compiled the index. Malinda B. Neale and Linda Peterson of the Library of Congress Composing Unit prepared the camera-ready copy under the supervision of Peggy Pixley.

Graphics were prepared by David P. Cabitto, and Tim L. Merrill reviewed map drafts. David P. Cabitto and Greenhorne and O'Mara prepared the final maps. Special thanks are owed to Marty Ittner, who prepared the illustrations on the title page of each chapter, and Wayne Horne, who did the cover art.

Finally, the authors acknowledge the generosity of many individuals and public and private agencies, especially the Embassy of the Republic of Sudan, who allowed their photographs to be used in this study.

Contents

List of Figures

Preface

This edition of *Sudan: A Country Study* replaces the previous edition, published in 1982. Like its predecessor, the present book attempts to treat in a compact and objective manner the dominant historical, social, economic, political, and national security aspects of contemporary Sudan. Sources of information included scholarly books, journals, and monographs; official reports and documents of governments and international organizations; and foreign and domestic newspapers and periodicals. Relatively up-to-date economic data were lacking.

Chapter bibliographies appear at the end of the book; brief comments on some of the more valuable sources for further reading appear at the conclusion of each chapter. Measurements are given in the metric system; a conversion table is provided to assist those who are unfamiliar with the metric system (see table 1, Appendix). The Glossary provides brief definitions of terms that may be unfamiliar to the general reader.

The transliteration of Arabic words and phrases posed a particular problem. For many of the words—such as Muhammad, Muslim, Quran, and shaykh—the authors followed a modified version of the system adopted by the United States Board on Geographic Names and the Permanent Committee on Geographic Names for British Official Use, known as the BGN/PCGN system; the modification entails the omission of all diacritical markings and hyphens. In numerous instances, however, the names of persons or places are so well known by another spelling that to have used the BGN/PCGN system may have created confusion. The reader will find Khartoum for the city rather than Al Khartum (the latter form is used for the state by that name), Roseires Dam rather than Ar Rusayris, and the Mahdi rather than Muhammad Ahmad ibn as Sayyid Abd Allah. Place-names pose another problem in that the government changed the administrative divisions of Sudan in February 1991. The country was then divided into nine states, generally with names and borders similar to the historical provinces of the colonial period and early independence. Readers will thus find Bahr al Ghazal and Kurdufan, for example, referred to either as states or as provinces depending on the context.

The body of the text reflects information available as of June 1991. Certain other portions of the text, however, have been updated. The Introduction discusses significant events that have occurred since the completion of research, and the Country Profile and Glossary include updated information as available.

Country Profile

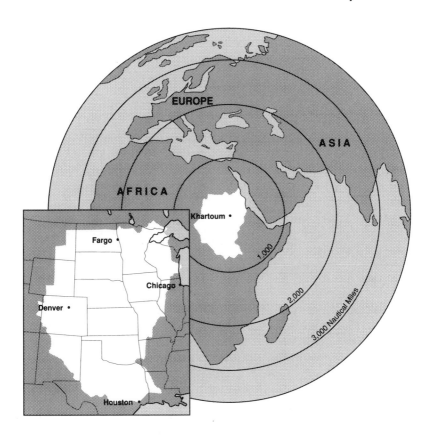

Country

Formal Name: Democratic Republic of Sudan.

Short Form: Sudan.

Term for Citizens: Sudanese.

Capital: Khartoum.

Date of Independence: January 1, 1956.

Geography

Size: Total area 2,505,813 square kilometers; land area 2,376,000 square kilometers; coastline 716 kilometers; largest country in Africa.

NOTE—The Country Profile contains updated information as available.

Topography: Plateau and plains predominate. Mountainous areas behind Red Sea coast, in far south, and in far west. Only interior highlands of consequence are Nuba Mountains west of White Nile River. All significant streams flow to White Nile and Blue Nile rivers, which join just north of Khartoum to form River Nile. Extensive swamps in south, especially along Bahr al Ghazal (southernmost part of White Nile).

Climate: Rainfall ranges from rare and occasional in far northern desert to relatively abundant and frequent (rainy seasons of six to nine months) in southern third of Sudan. In most years central third has enough rain for agriculture but lack of rain in 1980s and 1991 caused years of drought. Dust storms (often preceding rainstorms) common in north and northern parts of central Sudan, reducing visibility and causing much discomfort. Mean temperatures and daily maximums generally high; desert temperatures often quite cool at night.

Society

Population: Census of 1983 set population at 21.6 million people; July 1990 population estimate approximately 25 million. Annual growth rate between 2.8 and 3.1 percent. Half of population under eighteen years of age. About 20 percent of population urban, concentrated chiefly in three cities—Khartoum, Omdurman, and Khartoum North—constituting national capital area.

Languages: About 400 languages, but Arabic primary and official language. English common second language in south. Other languages include Bedawiye used by Beja and various dialects of Niger-Kurdufanian and Nilo-Saharan.

Ethnic Groups: Largest ethnic category in 1983 (nearly 40 percent of total, nearly 55 percent in north) comprises those considering themselves Arabs, but category internally split by regional and tribal loyalties and affiliation to various Muslim politico-religious groups. Major Muslim (but non-Arab) groups are Nubians in far north, nomadic Beja in northeast, and Fur in west. Southern non-Muslim groups include Dinka (more than 10 percent of total population and 40 percent in south), Nuer, and numerous smaller Nilotic and other ethnic groups.

Religion: More than half of total population Muslim, most living in north where Muslims constitute 75 percent or more of population. Relatively few Christians, most living in south. Most people in south and substantial minority in north adherents of various indigenous religions.

Education: Six-year primary education increasingly available, but in early 1990s the south and many northern communities still suffered from shortage of schools and teachers; many schools in south destroyed by civil war. Small proportion of primary school graduates continued in three-year junior secondary and upper secondary schools or attended technical schools. Most schools in urban locations; many lacked adequately trained teachers. Universities producing adequate numbers of highly educated graduates but Sudanese with skills relevant to largely agricultural economy still in short supply. Estimate of adult literacy about 30 percent.

Health: By 1991 civil war had destroyed most medical facilities in the south, and famine in 1980s and 1991 had serious impact on general health. Weak modern medical infrastructure suffering personnel shortages and urban-rural imbalance; most personnel and facilities concentrated in capital area. Malaria and gastrointestinal diseases prevalent through much of country; tuberculosis widespread in north but also occurs in south; schistosomiasis (snail fever) more restricted to territory near White Nile and Blue Nile rivers and adjacent irrigated areas; sleeping sickness spreading in south; acquired immune deficiency syndrome (AIDS) also increasing.

Economy

Salient Features: Government-dominated mixed economy. Modern agriculture sector and most of modern industry controlled by government corporations directly or through joint ventures; virtually all small- and medium-sized industry, most services, traditional agriculture, and handicrafts controlled privately. Civil war in south, massive influx of refugees from neighboring countries, and drought in 1980s and 1991 have hampered economic development. New economic recovery program announced June 1990 to end economic stagnation, develop agriculture, liberalize trade, abolish most government monopolies, progressively eliminate budget deficit, and develop energy resources.

Agriculture, Livestock, Fisheries, and Forestry: Agriculture and livestock raising provided livelihood for 61 percent of working population and roughly 95 percent of exports in early 1990s. Agriculture characterized by modern market-oriented sector of irrigated and mechanized rainfed farming concentrated in central part of country and large traditional sector engaged in subsistence activities elsewhere. Principal modern sector crops: cotton, sorghum, peanuts, sugarcane, wheat, sesame. Traditional sector crops: sorghum, millet, sesame, peanuts. Fisheries still largely subsistence occupation. Apart from gum arabic, a major export, forests used mainly for fuel.

Manufacturing: Public enterprises dominant in modern manufacturing activity, mainly foodstuffs, beverages, textiles. Output of government plants generally well below capacities because of raw materials shortages, power outages, lack of spare parts, and lack of competent managerial staff and skilled laborers. Three-quarters of large-scale modern manufacturing in Al Khartum State.

Mining: Contributed less than 1 percent to gross domestic product (GDP) in 1990. Most petroleum exploration operations ended in 1984 because of civil war in south and had not resumed as of mid-1991.

Energy: Chief sources of energy in 1992: domestic wood, charcoal, hydroelectric power, imported petroleum; large hydroelectric potential only partially exploited. Central area of country served by electric power grid; some towns elsewhere had local generating facilities.

Foreign Trade: Agricultural products (cotton, gum arabic, peanuts, sesame, livestock) dominate exports. Large trade deficit since late 1970s, accentuated by increased costs of petroleum imports. Main destinations of exports in 1986: Saudi Arabia, Japan, Britain, other European Community (EC) members. Main suppliers: Saudi Arabia (petroleum), Britain, other EC members, United States, Japan, China.

Transportation

Railroads: In 1991 government-owned Sudan Railways operated about 4,800 kilometers of 1.067-meter-gauge rail lines from Port Sudan to most major interior production and consumption centers except in far south. Also 716 kilometers of 1.6096-meter-gauge plantation line. Substantial loss of rail traffic to road transport after mid-1970s attributable to inefficient operations, but railroad still important for low-cost volume movement of agricultural exports and for inland delivery of heavy capital equipment, construction materials, and other goods for economic development.

Roads: In 1991 road system of between 20,000 and 25,000 kilometers, of which more than 2,000 kilometers paved or asphalted and about 3,700 kilometers gravel. Remaining roads fair-weather earth and sand tracks.

Inland Waterways: In 1991 about 1,750 kilometers navigable, but service on White Nile River in south largely discontinued by civil war.

Civil Aviation: Government-owned Sudan Airways in 1991 provided scheduled domestic air transport service to about twenty towns; international service by Sudan Airways and foreign airlines. Khartoum International principal airport; seven other airports had paved runways.

Marine Ports and Shipping: Port Sudan and Sawakin on Red Sea only deepwater ports; some modern port equipment available but most cargo handling manual. National merchant marine (ten ships of 122,200 deadweight tons in 1990) operated to Red Sea, Mediterranean, European ports.

Pipelines: Petroleum-products pipeline, 815 kilometers long, from Port Sudan to Khartoum; intermediate offtake point at Atbarah.

Government and Politics

Government: All executive and legislative powers vested in Revolutionary Command Council for National Salvation (RCC–NS), a fifteen-member body of military officers. RCC–NS chairman Lieutenant General Umar Hassan Ahmad al Bashir designated president of the republic and prime minister. RCC–NS appointed members of Council of Ministers, or cabinet, governors of states, and judges of courts. In mid-February 1992, Bashir announced formation of appointed 300-member Transitional National Assembly. No plans for new elections announced as of mid-1992. Government's authority in southern one-third of Sudan in mid-1992 concentrated around towns, a number of which had been retaken from the Sudanese People's Liberation Army (SPLA) during 1991–92 campaign.

Administrative Divisions: In 1991 RCC–NS decreed division of Sudan into nine states. Each state further subdivided into provinces and local government areas or districts.

Justice: Court system consisted of civil and special courts. Civil courts required to apply Islamic law, or sharia, but also permitted to consider customary law in reaching decisions. Apex of civil judicial system was High Court of Appeal. Lower courts consisted of state courts of appeal and at local level, major courts and magistrate's courts. Special courts, under military jurisdiction, dealt with offenses affecting national security or involving official corruption.

Politics: Although RCC–NS banned all political parties in 1989, it tolerated political activity by National Islamic Front (NIF), a coalition dominated by the Muslim Brotherhood. Leaders of other parties had reorganized abroad or in southern areas outside government control. Sudanese People's Liberation Movement (SPLM) drew support from predominantly non-Muslim and non-Arab population of the south.

Foreign Affairs: Prior to 1989 coup, Sudan had relatively close relations with Egypt, Saudi Arabia, and United States, and had history of tense relations with Libya. RCC–NS changed orientation of Sudan's foreign policy, particularly by supporting Iraq during Persian Gulf War of 1990–91. Saudi Arabia and Kuwait retaliated by suspending economic assistance, which constituted crucial component of government's budget.

National Security

Armed Forces: In 1991 Sudanese People's Armed Forces (SPAF) totaled approximately 71,500 personnel; army had about 65,000; air force and air defense command each had about 3,000; navy had about 500.

Major Tactical Units: SPAF organized into six regional commands having divisional structures. Main units: two armored brigades, one mechanized infantry brigade, one airborne brigade, one air assault brigade, seventeen infantry brigades, three artillery regiments, two antiaircraft artillery brigades, and one engineering regiment. Strengths of brigades, battalions, and companies varied greatly. Air force organized into two fighter-ground attack squadrons and two fighter squadrons, of which only one functioning, plus transport squadron, unarmed helicopter squadron, and training aircraft. Air defense command equipped with radar-directed antiaircraft guns and Soviet SA–2 missiles. Naval forces, under army command, had some functioning river patrol boats but little or no capacity to patrol Red Sea coast. Much of armed forces equipment nonoperational because of poor maintenance and lack of spare parts.

Civil War: Since 1983 armed rebellion has been conducted by forces of Sudan People's Liberation Army (SPLA) with estimated strength of 50,000 to 60,000 in 1991. SPLA controlled most rural areas of the south, government forces holding major towns. In 1991–92 government forces launched campaign and captured many SPLA-held centers. SPLA armed with light weapons, shoulder-fired antiaircraft missiles, some artillery and rocket launchers, and a few armored vehicles. Government forces assisted by tribal militia groups, which were guilty of many atrocities against civilians in the south. Government also organized in 1989 paramilitary body called Popular Defence Forces that participated in 1991–92 campaign in the south.

Military Assistance: Most military equipment supplied by Soviet Union, 1968–71; limited cooperation with Soviet Union continued until 1977. Egypt and China subsequently became prominent suppliers. In early 1980s, United States became principal source of aid, notably aircraft, tanks, armored vehicles, and artillery. United States aid sharply reduced in 1983 and formally terminated in 1989.

Defense Costs: Official data unavailable; defense budget estimated at US$610 million in 1989, constituting 7.2 percent of gross national product.

Internal Security Forces: National police (Sudan Police Force) totaled about 30,000. State Security Organisation main instrument of domestic intelligence and internal security until 1985. After 1989 military coup, separate Islamic-oriented security bodies formed to suppress opposition to regime.

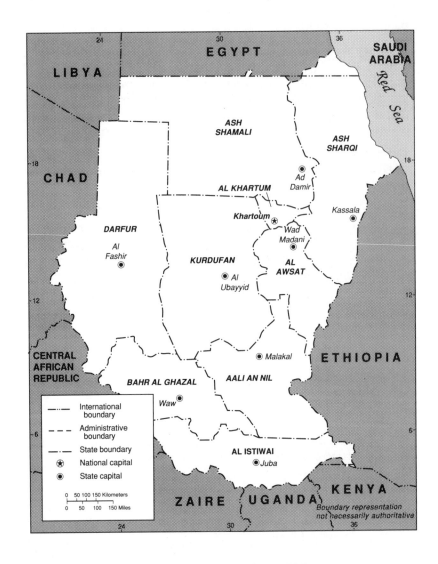

Figure 1. Administrative Divisions of Sudan, 1991

Introduction

SUDAN, LIKE MANY AFRICAN COUNTRIES, consists of numerous ethnic groups. Unlike most states, however, Sudan has two distinct divisions: the north, which is largely Arab and Muslim, and the south, which consists predominantly of black Nilotic peoples, some of whom are members of indigenous faiths and others who are Christians. British policy during the Anglo-Egyptian condominium (1899–1955) intensified the rift because Britain established separate administrations for the two areas and forbade northerners to enter the south. In the 1990s, many southerners continued to fear being ruled by northerners, who lacked familiarity with their beliefs and ethnic traditions and sought to impose northern institutions on them.

Given its proximity to Egypt and the centrality of the Nile River that both countries share, it is not surprising that culturally Egypt has influenced Sudan significantly, especially the northern part of the country. Ancient Cush, located in present-day northern Sudan, was strongly influenced by Egypt for about 1,000 years beginning ca. 2700 B.C. Although the Hyksos kings of Egypt temporarily broke off contact, Cush subsequently was incorporated into Egypt's New Kingdom as a province about 1570 B.C. and remained under Egyptian control until about 1100 B.C. In a move that reversed the pattern of Egyptian dominance, a Cushite king conquered Upper Egypt in 730 B.C.; in 590 B.C., however, the Cushite capital was sacked by the Egyptians and the court moved farther south along the Nile to Meroe.

By the sixth century A.D., Meroe had broken up into three kingdoms collectively referred to as Nubia. The people of Nubia adopted Christianity and were ministered to largely by Egyptian clergy. The kingdoms reached their peak in the ninth and tenth centuries. Prior to the coming of Islam, the people had contact with the Arabs primarily in the form of trade. Sudan became known as a source of ivory, gold, gems, aromatic gum, and cattle, all products that were transported to markets in Egypt and Arabia. Following the Muslim conquest of the area, in 1276 the Mamluk rulers of Egypt gave Nubia to a Muslim overlord. The Nubians themselves converted to Islam only gradually; a majority of them remained Christian until the fifteenth or sixteenth century. During the sixteenth century, the Muslim religious brotherhoods spread through northern Nubia, and the Ottoman Empire exerted its jurisdiction through military leaders whose rule endured for three centuries.

In 1820 Muhammad Ali, who ruled Egypt on behalf of the Ottomans, sent 4,000 troops to Sudan to clear the area of Mamluks. The invasion resulted in Ottoman-Egyptian rule of Sudan from 1821 to 1885; the rule was accompanied by the introduction of secular courts and a large bureaucracy. The 1880s saw the rise of the Mahdist movement, consisting of disciples of Muhammad Ahmad ibn as Sayyid Abd Allah, a Sudanese who proclaimed himself the Mahdi or "guided one," and launched a jihad against the Ottoman rulers. Britain perceived the Mahdists as a threat to stability in the region and sent first Charles George Gordon and then Herbert Kitchener to Sudan to assert British control. The British conquest led to the establishment of the Anglo-Egyptian condominium and, initially, to military rule of Sudan, followed by civilian administration. Britain largely ignored southern Sudan until after World War I, leaving Western missionary societies to establish schools and medical facilities in the area.

After World War I, Sudanese nationalism, which favored either independence or union with Egypt, gathered popular support. Recognizing the inevitable, Britain signed a self-determination agreement with Sudan in 1952, followed by the Anglo-Egyptian accord in 1953 that set up a three-year transition period to self-government. Sudan proclaimed its independence January 1, 1956. The country had two short-lived civilian coalition governments before a coup in November 1958 brought in a military regime under Major General Ibrahim Abbud and a collective body known as the Supreme Council of the Armed Forces. Abbud's government sought to arabize the south and in 1964 expelled all Western missionaries. Northern repression of the south led to open civil war in the mid-1960s and the rise of various southern resistance groups, the most powerful of which was the Anya Nya guerrillas, who sought autonomy. Civilian rule returned to Sudan between 1964 and 1969, and political parties reappeared. In the 1965 elections, Muhammad Ahmad Mahjub became prime minister, succeeded in June 1966 by Sadiq al Mahdi, a descendant of the Mahdi. In the 1968 elections, no party had a clear majority, and a coalition government took office under Mahjub as prime minister.

In May 1969, the Free Officers' Movement led by Jaafar an Nimeiri staged a coup and established the Revolutionary Command Council (RCC). In July 1971, a short-lived procommunist military coup occurred, but Nimeiri quickly regained control, was elected to a six-year term as president, and abolished the RCC. Meanwhile in the south, Joseph Lagu, a Christian, had united several opposition elements under the Southern Sudan Liberation Movement. In March 1972, the southern resistance movement concluded an agreement with the Nimeiri regime at Addis Ababa, and a cease-fire followed. A Constituent Assembly was created in August 1972 to draft a constitution at a time when the growing opposition to military rule was reflected in strikes and student unrest. Despite this dissent, Nimeiri was reelected for another six-year term in 1977.

During the early stages of his new term, Nimeiri worked toward reconciliation with the south. As the south became stronger, however, he considered it a threat to his regime; and in June 1983, having abolished the Southern Regional Assembly, he redivided the southern region into its three historical provinces. The Sudanese People's Liberation Movement (SPLM) and the Sudanese People's Liberation Army (SPLA), founded in 1983, opposed this division. They intensified their opposition following the imposition of Muslim sharia law throughout the country, and the civil war in the south broke out again with renewed vigor. In early 1985, while Nimeiri was returning from a visit to the United States, a general strike occurred that the government could not quell, followed by a successful military coup led by Lieutenant General Abd ar Rahman Siwar adh Dhahab. A Transitional Military Council was created, but the government proved incapable of establishing a national political consensus or of dealing with the deteriorating economic situation and the famine threatening southern and western Sudan. In March 1986, in the Koka Dam Declaration, the government and the SPLM called for a Sudan free from "discrimination and disparity" and the repeal of the sharia.

Sadiq al Mahdi formed what proved to be a weak coalition government following the April 1986 elections. An agreement with the SPLM was signed by Sadiq al Mahdi's coalition partners at Addis Ababa in November 1988; the agreement called for a cease-fire and freezing the application of the sharia. Sadiq al Mahdi's failure to end the civil war in the south or improve the economic and famine situations led to the overthrow of the government at the end of June 1989 by Colonel Umar Hassan Ahmad al Bashir.

Sudan's economic straits reflected its position as Africa's largest nation geographically, but one possessed of large areas of desert and semidesert east and west of the Nile and in the south the world's largest swamp, As Sudd, which led to tropical rain forests in the southernmost area. As a result, although the Nile itself with its tributaries—the Blue Nile and the White Nile, which joined at Khartoum—constituted a vital communications link for the country and a source of water for agriculture, the cultivable area of Sudan was somewhat limited. Moreover, in years of drought the agriculturally productive sector declines appreciably, causing the likelihood of severe famine.

In accordance with the focal role played by the Nile, about one-third of Sudan's 1990 estimated population of 25 million lived around Khartoum and in Al Awsat State (see fig. 1). The latter included the rich agricultural region of Al Jazirah, south of Khartoum between the Blue Nile and the White Nile. Although only one-fifth of the population lived in urban areas, two-thirds of the total population resided within 300 kilometers of Khartoum. About 600 ethnic groups speaking around 400 languages were represented. Arabic was the official language of the country, with English spoken widely in the south. Ethnic statistics for the 1990s were lacking, but in 1983 Arabs constituted about two-fifths of the total population, representing the majority in the north where the next largest group was the Nile Nubians. Much of the remainder of Sudan's population consisted of non-Muslim Nilotic peoples living in southern Sudan or in the hilly areas west of the Blue Nile or near the Ethiopian border. Among the largest of these ethnic groups were the Dinka and the Nuer, followed by the Shilluk. Many of these groups migrated with their herds, seeking areas of rainfall, and therefore it was difficult to establish their numbers accurately.

In the early 1990s, agriculture and livestock raising provided the major sources of livelihood for about four-fifths of the population. Wherever possible, Nile waters were used for irrigation, and the government has sponsored a number of irrigation projects. Commercial crops such as cotton, peanuts, sugarcane, sorghum, and sesame were grown, and gum arabic was obtained from *Acacia senegal* trees. Most of these products along with livestock destined primarily for Saudi Arabia also represented Sudan's major exports.

Manufacturing concentrated on food-processing enterprises and textiles, as well as some import substitution industries such as cement, chemicals, and fertilizers. Industry, however, contributed less than one-tenth to gross domestic product (GDP—see Glossary) in the early 1990s, in comparison with agriculture's more than three-tenths contribution. Sudan was among the world's poorest countries according to the World Bank (see Glossary), with an annual per capita income of US$310 in FY (fiscal year—see Glossary) 1991.

Several factors accounted for the relative economic insignificance of the industrial sector. Historically, during the colonial period, Britain had discouraged industrialization, preferring to keep Sudan as a source of raw materials and a market for British manufactured goods. Following independence, a paucity of development programs as well as better employment opportunities in the Persian Gulf states contributed to a shortage of skilled workers. In the early 1990s, Sudan also had limited energy sources—only small amounts of petroleum in the south between Kurdufan State and Bahr al Ghazal

State and only a few dams producing hydroelectric power. In addition, transportation facilities were limited; there existed only a sketchy network of railroads and roads, many of the latter being impassable in the rainy season. Inland waterways could also be difficult to use because of low water, cataracts, or swamps. The lack of a good transportation network hindered not only the marketing of produce and consumer goods but also the processing of such minerals as gold, chrome, asbestos, gypsum, mica, and uranium. The lack of capital accumulation also limited financial resources and necessitated funding by the government, which itself had inadequate revenues. Some northern Sudanese hoped that the rise of Islamic banks might result in more capital being invested in private industrial development, especially after the World Bank refused to extend further loans to the country.

Sudan's problems with the World Bank occurred initially in 1984. The World Bank cited Sudan's large external debt—in June 1992 the debt was about US$15.3 billion, of which approximately two-thirds represented payment arrears—and its failure to take steps to restructure its economy as reasons for denying credit. The large debt resulted primarily from the nationalization of major sectors of the economy in the 1970s and the use of funds borrowed from abroad to finance enterprises with low productivity. The government needed to use its revenues to meet the losses of these enterprises. In addition, the civil war, the prolonged drought, widespread malnutrition, famine, and the hundreds of thousands of refugees further sapped the economy.

Not until June 1990 did the government act to reform the economy by instituting a three-year (FY 1991–93) National Economic Salvation Program. The program aimed to reduce the budget deficit, privatize nationalized enterprises, heighten the role of the private sector, and remove controls on prices, profits, and exports. In October 1991, other steps toward economic reform included devaluing the official exchange rate from £Sd4.5 to £Sd15 (for value of the Sudanese pound—see Glossary) to the United States dollar and reducing subsidies on sugar and petroleum products. In February 1992, in a further liberalization of the economy, all price controls were removed and official exchange rates devalued to £Sd90 to the United States dollar. Officials hoped that these measures would not cause the inflation rate, which was about 115 percent per year as of March 1992, to worsen. In a further move designed to curb inflation, Sudan instituted a new currency, the dinar, worth ten Sudanese pounds, in May 1992.

Although the World Bank refused to authorize new loans for Sudan, in July 1991 the Bank granted Sudan US$16 million for the Emergency Drought Recovery Project. In addition, in the spring of 1992 Sudan received an agricultural credit of US$42 million from the African Development Bank and some bilateral aid from Iran and Libya. Like the World Bank, the United States and the European Community had suspended loans to Sudan but had provided some humanitarian assistance; the value of United States humanitarian aid in 1991 was estimated to exceed US$150 million. Nevertheless, the drought, the famine, and the massive influx into the north of refugees from the south as a result of the civil war caused the country's already precarious economy to deteriorate further and complicated the government's ability to rule.

Since the military coup of June 30, 1989, the constitution had been suspended, political parties banned, and the legislative assembly dissolved. For practical purposes, in mid-1992 Bashir made political decisions in his capacity as president or head of state, prime minister, commander in chief, and chairman of the legislative body created by the 1989 coup, the Revolutionary Command Council for National Salvation (RCC-NS). The RCC-NS consisted of fifteen members who had carried out the coup along with Bashir. Several members had ties to the National Islamic Front (NIF), the political arm of the Muslim Brotherhood, an Islamist (sometimes seen as fundamentalist) activist group.

Although political parties were illegal under the Bashir government, the NIF represented the equivalent of a party. The nature of the relationship between Bashir and the NIF was not clear. Some well informed Western observers considered Bashir to be a tool of the NIF in spreading its Islamist programs and its strong advocacy of the imposition of the sharia. Other observers believed that Bashir was using the NIF for his own purposes. The leading figure in the NIF was Hassan Abd Allah at Turabi, an Oxford-educated Muslim religious scholar and lawyer, who strongly advocated the spread of Islamism in the Muslim world. As Turabi was ending his tour of the United States and Canada in the spring of 1992, he was attacked in Ottawa in late May by a Sudanese opponent of the NIF and was seriously injured. Although by late July Turabi had resumed meetings with government and Islamic officials and speeches to Muslim groups in Khartoum and in London, the effects of his impaired health on the NIF, the RCC-NS, and the political scene were uncertain in mid-August.

In addition to their legislative functions, members of the RCC-NS shared with Bashir and members of the Council of Ministers functions traditionally associated with the executive branch, such as heading government ministries. The Council of Ministers included civilians as well as military officers and in practice was subordinate to the RCC–NS. In April 1991, probably in response to growing criticism of its authoritarian rule, the RCC–NS convened a constitutional conference. However, major opposition groups boycotted the conference. As on previous occasions, the principal intractable problem proved to be the inability of Muslims and non-Muslims to agree on the role of Islamic law as the basis of the legal system at both the national and local levels.

Another vexing problem historically was the relationship of regional and local governmental bodies to the national government. The Nimeiri regime had created a pyramidal structure with councils at various levels. The councils were theoretically elective, but in practice the only legal party at the time, the Sudan Socialist Union, dominated them. In February 1991, the RCC–NS introduced a federal structure, creating nine states that resembled the nine provinces of Sudan's colonial and early independence years. The states were subdivided into provinces and local government areas, with officials at all levels appointed by the RCC–NS. Although the governors of the three southern states were southerners, power lay in the hands of the deputy governors who were Muslim members of the NIF and who controlled finance, trade, and cooperatives. Below them the most important ministerial posts in the southern states also were held by Muslims, including the post of minister of education, culture, youth, guidance, and information.

In a further step, in mid-February 1992, Bashir announced the formation of an appointed 300-member Transitional National Assembly to include all RCC–NS members, federal cabinet ministers, and state governors. Bashir also indicated in March that, beginning in May, popular conferences based on religious values would be held in the north and in "secure areas" of the south to elect chairmen and members of such conferences. The election process would create a "general mobilization of all political institutions." Although the agendas for conferences over the succeeding ten-year period would be based on national issues set by the head of state and local issues raised by the governors, the government touted the process as one that would "fulfill the revolution's promise to hand over full power to the people." The proposed conference committees were somewhat reminiscent of the popular committees established by the Popular Defence Act of October 1989. Initially, these popular committees had the function of overseeing rationing, but their mandate was broadened to include powers such as arresting enemies of the state.

The control exerted by the RCC–NS over various parts of the country varied. For example, western Sudan, especially Darfur, enjoyed considerable autonomy, which at times approached anarchy, as a result of the various armed ethnic groups and the refugee population that existed within it. The situation was even more confused in the south, where until 1991 the government had controlled the major centers and the SPLM occupied the smaller towns and rural areas. The government launched a military campaign in 1991–92 that succeeded in recapturing many military posts that had served as SPLM and SPLA strongholds. The government's success resulted in part from the acquisition of substantial military equipment financed by Iran, including weapons and aircraft bought from China. Another reason for the successes of the government forces was the split that occurred in August 1991 within the SPLA between John Garang's Torit faction (mainly Dinka from southern Al Istiwai) and the Nasir group (mainly Nuer and other non-Dinka from northern Al Istiwai). The two groups launched military attacks against each other, thereby not only destroying their common front against the government but also killing numerous civilians. The Nasir group had defected from the main SPLA body and tried unsuccessfully to overthrow Garang because of the SPLA's human rights violations, Garang's authoritarian leadership style, and his favoritism toward his ethnic group, the Dinka. Abortive peace talks with representatives of both groups as well as the government were held in Abuja, Nigeria, in May and early June 1992. (In December 1989, former United States president Jimmy Carter had attempted without success to mediate peace talks between the government and the SPLA.) The Torit faction sought a secular state and an end to the sharia; the Nasir group wanted self-determination or independence for southern Sudan. During the talks, both groups agreed to push for self-determination, but when the government rejected this proposal, they decided instead to discuss Nigeria's power-sharing plan.

A major basis of southern dissidence was strong opposition to the imposition of the sharia—the SPLA had vowed not to lay down its arms until the sharia was abrogated. The other source of concern was the fear of northern pressure to arabize the education system (the Bashir regime had declared Arabic the language of instruction in the south in early 1992), government offices, and society in general. These fears had led to the civil war, which, with a respite between 1972 and 1983, had been ongoing since 1955.

The Bashir government's need for assistance in pursuing the war in the south determined to a large degree Sudan's foreign policy in the 1990s. Bashir recognized that the measures taken in the south, which outside observers termed human rights abuses, had alienated the West. Historically, the West had been the source of major financial support for Sudan. Furthermore, Sudan's siding with Iraq in the 1991 Persian Gulf War had antagonized Saudi Arabia and Kuwait, principal donors for Sudan's military and economic needs in the preceding several decades.

Bashir therefore turned to Iran, especially for military aid, and, to a lesser extent, to Libya. Iranian president Ali Akbar Hashemi Rafsanjani visited Sudan in December 1991, accompanied by several cabinet ministers. The visit led to an Iranian promise of military and economic assistance. Details of the reported aid varied, but in July 1992, in addition to the provision of 1 million tons of oil annually for military and civil consumption, aid was thought to include the financing of Sudanese weapons and aircraft purchases from China in the amount of at least US$300 million. Some accounts alleged that 3,000 Iranian soldiers had also arrived in January 1992 to engage in the war in the south and that Iran had been granted use of Port Sudan facilities and permission to establish a communications monitoring station in the area; however, these reports were not verified as of mid-August 1992.

The only other country with which Sudan had close relations in the early 1990s was Libya. Following an economic agreement the two countries signed in July 1990, head of state Muammar al Qadhafi paid an official visit to Khartoum in October. Bashir paid a return visit to Libya in November 1991. Libyan officials arrived in Khartoum for talks on unity, primarily economic unity, in January 1992.

While the government was cultivating relations with Iran and Libya, the SPLM and SPLA were seeking other sources of aid in Africa. They had lost their major source of support when the government of Mengistu Haile Mariam in Ethiopia was overthrown in May 1991. The SPLM and SPLA subsequently sought help from Kenya, Uganda, and several other African countries, thereby creating tensions between those nations and the Bashir regime. Furthermore, Sudan's relations with Egypt had soured in 1991 as a result of the Bashir government's failure to support Egypt's position in the Persian Gulf War. One manifestation of the deteriorating relations occurred in April 1992 when Sudan became involved in a border confrontation with Egypt. The disagreement resulted from an oil concession Sudan had granted to a subsidiary of Canada's International Petroleum Corporation for exploration of a 38,400-square-kilometer area onshore and offshore near Halaib on the Red Sea coast, an area also claimed by Egypt.

Initially, Sudan's military was seen as being free from specific ethnic or religious identification and thus in a position to accomplish what civilians could not, namely to resolve economic problems and to bring peace to the south. Such hopes proved futile, however.

The growing civil war in the south and the strength of the SPLA and the SPLM posed tremendous problems for the military and for the internal security forces. The civil war was extremely costly; according to one Sudanese government estimate, it cost approximately US$1 million per day. Furthermore, it disrupted the economy—Bashir stated in February 1992 that the loss of oil revenues alone since 1986 had amounted to more than US$6 billion. In addition, based on United States Department of State estimates in late 1991, war had displaced as many as 4.5 million Sudanese.

To counter the SPLA, the government armed various non-Arab southern ethnic groups as militias as early as 1985. In addition, in October 1989 the Bashir government created a new paramilitary body, the Popular Defence Forces (PDF) to promote the Islamist aims of the government and the NIF. Although the Bashir regime prominently featured the PDF's participation in the 1991–92 campaign in the south, informed observers believed the PDF's role lacked military significance.

In view of the ongoing civil war, internal security was a major concern of the Bashir regime, which reportedly had been the object of coup attempts in 1990, 1991, and 1992. In this regard, the government faced problems on several fronts. There was the outright dissidence or rebellion of several southern ethnic groups. There was also the creation in January 1991 of an opposition abroad in the form of a government in exile. This body, called the National Democratic Alliance, was headed by Lieutenant General Fathi Ahmad Ali, formerly commander of the armed forces under Sadiq al Mahdi. There also was increasing opposition in the north on the part of Sudanese who favored a secular state, including professional persons, trade union leaders, and other modernizers. Such persons opposed the application of Islamic *hudud* punishments, the growing restrictions on the activities and dress of women, and the increasing authoritarianism of the government as reflected, for example, in the repression of criticism through censorship, imprisonment, and death sentences. On a wider scale Sudanese in the north staged protests in February 1992 against the price increases on staples after price supports were removed.

As a result of the repressive measures taken by the government and the actions of armed government militias in the south as well as retaliatory measures of the SPLA forces, the human rights group Africa Watch estimated that at least 500,000 civilian deaths had occurred between 1986 and the end of 1989. The overall number of deaths between 1983 and mid-1992 was far greater, an outcome not only of the civil war, but also of the famine and drought in the late 1980s and early 1990s. In late 1989, the government, which has considered famine relief efforts a highly political issue, ended its cooperation with relief efforts from abroad because it feared such measures were strengthening southern resistance. The pressure of world public opinion, however, obliged Sudan to allow relief efforts to resume in 1990.

The United Nations (UN) World Food Programme (WFP) had initiated Operation Lifeline Sudan (OLS) in March 1989, which had delivered more than 110,000 tons of food aid to southern Sudan before it was obliged by renewed hostilities to close down operations in October 1989. OLS II was launched in late March 1990, via the UN and the International Committee of the Red Cross, to bring in food flights via Kenya and Uganda. In the spring of 1990, WFP indicated it was helping 4.2 million people in Sudan: 1.8 million refugees in Khartoum; 1.4 million people in rural areas of the south; 600,000 who had sought refuge in southern towns; and 400,000 in the "transition zone" in Darfur and Kurdufan, between the north and the south.

In addition to these sources of suffering, the government, beginning in the 1980s, had undertaken campaigns to destroy the Dinka and the Fur and Zaghawa ethnic groups in Darfur. As of 1991, the Bashir regime was also using armed militias to undertake depopulation campaigns against the Nuba in southern Kurdufan. Moreover, the government had to deal with the return in 1991 of Sudanese citizens and their families who had been working in Iraq and Kuwait; according to estimates of the International Labour Organisation, such persons numbered at least 150,000. Finally, during the period from late November 1991 to early 1992, the government forcibly uprooted more than 400,000 non-Arab southern squatters, who had created shanty towns in the outskirts of Khartoum, and transported them to the desert about fifty kilometers away, creating an international outcry.

In summary, in August 1992 the Bashir government found itself in a very difficult position. Although the country's economic problems had begun to be addressed, the economic situation remained critical. At the peace negotiations in Abuja, slight progress had been made toward ending the civil war in the south, but the central concerns about imposition of the sharia and arabization had not been resolved. Moreover, the regime appeared to be facing growing dissension, not only in the south but from elements in the north as well. These considerations raised serious questions about the stability of the Bashir government.

August 14, 1992   Helen Chapin Metz

Chapter 1. Historical Setting

Tomb of the Mahdi in Omdurman

THROUGHOUT ITS HISTORY SUDAN has been divided between its Arab heritage, identified with northern Sudan, and its African heritage to the south. The two groups are divided along linguistic, religious, racial, and economic lines, and the cleavage has generated ethnic tensions and clashes. Moreover, the geographical isolation of Sudan's southern African peoples has prevented them from participating fully in the country's political, economic, and social life. Imperial Britain acknowledged the north-south division by establishing separate administrations for the two regions. Independent Sudan further reinforced this cleavage by treating African southerners as a minority group.

Another major factor that has affected Sudan's evolution is the country's relationship with Egypt. As early as the eighth millennium B.C., there was contact between Sudan and Egypt. Modern relations between the two countries began in 1820, when an Egyptian army under Ottoman command invaded Sudan. In the years following this invasion, Egypt expanded its area of control in Sudan down the Red Sea coast and toward East Africa's Great Lakes region. The sixty-four-year period of Egyptian rule, which ended in 1885, left a deep mark on Sudan's political and economic systems. The emergence of the Anglo-Egyptian condominium in 1899 reinforced the links between Cairo and Khartoum. After Sudan gained independence in 1956, Egypt continued to exert influence over developments in Sudan.

Similarly, the period of British control (1899–1955) has had a lasting impact on Sudan. In addition to pacifying and uniting the country, Britain sought to modernize Sudan by using technology to facilitate economic development and by establishing democratic institutions to end authoritarian rule. Even in 1991, many of Sudan's political and economic institutions owed their existence to the British.

Lastly, Sudan's postindependence history has been shaped largely by the southern civil war. This conflict has retarded the country's social and economic development, encouraged political instability, and led to an endless cycle of weak and ineffective military and civilian governments. The conflict appeared likely to continue to affect Sudan's people and institutions for the rest of the twentieth century.

Early History

Archaeological excavation of sites on the Nile above Aswan has

3

confirmed human habitation in the river valley during the Paleolithic period that spanned more than 60,000 years of Sudanese history. By the eighth millennium B.C., people of a Neolithic culture had settled into a sedentary way of life there in fortified mud-brick villages, where they supplemented hunting and fishing on the Nile with grain gathering and cattle herding. Contact with Egypt probably occurred at a formative stage in the culture's development because of the steady movement of population along the Nile River. Skeletal remains suggest a blending of negroid and Mediterranean populations during the Neolithic period (eighth to third millennia B.C.) that has remained relatively stable until the present, despite gradual infiltration by other elements.

Cush

Northern Sudan's, or Nubia's, earliest record comes from Egyptian sources, which described the land upstream from the first cataract, called Cush, as "wretched." For more than 2,000 years after the Old Kingdom (ca. 2700–2180 B.C.), Egyptian political and economic activities determined the course of the central Nile region's history. Even during intermediate periods when Egyptian political power in Cush waned, Egypt exerted a profound cultural and religious influence on the Cushite people.

Over the centuries, trade developed. Egyptian caravans carried grain to Cush and returned to Aswan with ivory, incense, hides, and carnelian (a stone prized both as jewelry and for arrowheads) for shipment downriver. Egyptian traders particularly valued gold and slaves, who served as domestic servants, concubines, and soldiers in the pharaoh's army. Egyptian military expeditions penetrated Cush periodically during the Old Kingdom. Yet there was no attempt to establish a permanent presence in the area until the Middle Kingdom (ca. 2100–1720 B.C.), when Egypt constructed a network of forts along the Nile as far south as Samnah, in northern Sudan, to guard the flow of gold from mines in Wawat.

Around 1720 B.C., Asian nomads called Hyksos invaded Egypt, ending the Middle Kingdom. Links with Cush were severed, and forts along the Nile were destroyed. To fill the vacuum left by the Egyptian withdrawal, a culturally distinct indigenous kingdom emerged at Karmah, near present-day Dunqulah. After Egyptian power revived during the New Kingdom (ca. 1570–1100 B.C.), the pharaoh Ahmose I incorporated Cush as an Egyptian province governed by a viceroy. Although Egypt's administrative control of Cush extended down only to the fourth cataract, Egyptian sources list tributary districts reaching to the Red Sea and upstream to the confluence of the Blue Nile and White Nile rivers. Egyptian authorities ensured the loyalty of local chiefs by drafting their children to serve as pages at the pharaoh's court. Egypt also expected tribute in gold and slaves from local chiefs.

Once Egypt had established political control over Cush, officials and priests joined military personnel, merchants, and artisans and settled in the region. The ancient Egyptian language became widely used in everyday activities. The Cushite elite adopted Egyptian gods and built temples like that dedicated to the sun god Amon at Napata, near present-day Kuraymah. The temples remained centers of official religious worship until the coming of Christianity to the region in the sixth century. When Egyptian influence declined or succumbed to foreign domination, the Cushite elite regarded themselves as champions of genuine Egyptian cultural and religious values.

By the eleventh century B.C., the authority of the New Kingdom dynasties had diminished, allowing divided rule in Egypt, and ending Egyptian control of Cush. There is little information about the region's activities over the next 300 years. In the eighth century B.C., however, Cush reemerged as an independent kingdom ruled from Napata by an aggressive line of monarchs who gradually extended their influence into Egypt. About 750 B.C., a Cushite king called Kashta conquered Upper Egypt and became ruler of Thebes until approximately 740 B.C. His successor, Painkhy, subdued the delta, reunited Egypt under the Twenty-fifth Dynasty, and founded a line of kings who ruled Cush and Thebes for about a hundred years. The dynasty's intervention in the area of modern Syria caused a confrontation between Egypt and Assyria. When the Assyrians in retaliation invaded Egypt, Taharqa (688–663 B.C.), the last Cushite pharaoh, withdrew and returned the dynasty to Napata, where it continued to rule Cush and extended its dominions to the south and east.

Meroe

Egypt's succeeding dynasty failed to reassert control over Cush. In 590 B.C., however, an Egyptian army sacked Napata, compelling the Cushite court to move to a more secure location at Meroe near the sixth cataract. For several centuries thereafter, the Meroitic kingdom developed independently of Egypt, which passed successively under Persian, Greek, and, finally, Roman domination. During the height of its power in the second and third centuries B.C., Meroe extended over a region from the third cataract in the north to Sawba, near present-day Khartoum, in the south.

The pharaonic tradition persisted among a line of rulers at Meroe, who raised stelae to record the achievements of their reigns

5

and erected pyramids to contain their tombs. These objects and the ruins of palaces, temples, and baths at Meroe attest to a centralized political system that employed artisans' skills and commanded the labor of a large work force. A well-managed irrigation system allowed the area to support a higher population density than was possible during later periods. By the first century B.C., the use of hieroglyphs gave way to a Meroitic script that adapted the Egyptian writing system to an indigenous, Nubian-related language spoken later by the region's people. Meroe's succession system was not necessarily hereditary; the matriarchal royal family member deemed most worthy often became king. The queen mother's role in the selection process was crucial to a smooth succession. The crown appears to have passed from brother to brother (or sister) and only when no siblings remained from father to son.

Although Napata remained Meroe's religious center, northern Cush eventually fell into disorder as it came under pressure from the Blemmyes, predatory nomads from east of the Nile. However, the Nile continued to give the region access to the Mediterranean world. Additionally, Meroe maintained contact with Arab and Indian traders along the Red Sea coast and incorporated Hellenistic and Hindu cultural influences into its daily life. Inconclusive evidence suggests that metallurgical technology may have been transmitted westward across the savanna belt to West Africa from Meroe's iron smelteries.

Relations between Meroe and Egypt were not always peaceful. In 23 B.C., in response to Meroe's incursions into Upper Egypt, a Roman army moved south and razed Napata. The Roman commander quickly abandoned the area, however, as too poor to warrant colonization.

In the second century A.D., the Nobatae occupied the Nile's west bank in northern Cush. They are believed to have been one of several well-armed bands of horse- and camel-borne warriors who sold protection to the Meroitic population; eventually they intermarried and established themselves among the Meroitic people as a military aristocracy. Until nearly the fifth century, Rome subsidized the Nobatae and used Meroe as a buffer between Egypt and the Blemmyes. Meanwhile, the old Meroitic kingdom contracted because of the expansion of Axum, a powerful trading state in modern Ethiopia to the east. About A.D. 350, an Axumite army captured and destroyed Meroe city, ending the kingdom's independent existence.

Christian Nubia

By the sixth century, three states had emerged as the political and cultural heirs of the Meroitic kingdom. Nobatia in the north,

Tombs in the north at Meroe of kings who ruled ca. 300–200 B.C.
Temple of Naqa, southwest of Meroe
Courtesy Robert O. Collins

also known as Ballanah, had its capital at Faras, in what is now Egypt; the central kingdom, Muqurra, was centered at Dunqulah, the old city on the Nile about 150 kilometers south of modern Dunqulah; and Alwa, in the heartland of old Meroe in the south, had its capital at Sawba. In all three kingdoms, warrior aristocracies ruled Meroitic populations from royal courts where functionaries bore Greek titles in emulation of the Byzantine court.

The earliest references to Nubia's successor kingdoms are contained in accounts by Greek and Coptic authors of the conversion of Nubian kings to Christianity in the sixth century. According to tradition, a missionary sent by Byzantine empress Theodora arrived in Nobatia and started preaching the gospel about 540. It is possible that the conversion process began earlier, however, under the aegis of Coptic missionaries from Egypt, who in the previous century had brought Christianity to the area. The Nubian kings accepted the Monophysite Christianity practiced in Egypt and acknowledged the spiritual authority of the Coptic patriarch of Alexandria over the Nubian church. A hierarchy of bishops named by the Coptic patriarch and consecrated in Egypt directed the church's activities and wielded considerable secular power. The church sanctioned a sacerdotal kingship, confirming the royal line's legitimacy. In turn the monarch protected the church's interests. The queen mother's role in the succession process paralleled that of Meroe's matriarchal tradition. Because women transmitted the right to succession, a renowned warrior not of royal birth might be nominated to become king through marriage to a woman in line of succession.

The emergence of Christianity reopened channels to Mediterranean civilization and renewed Nubia's cultural and ideological ties to Egypt. The church encouraged literacy in Nubia through its Egyptian-trained clergy and in its monastic and cathedral schools. The use of Greek in liturgy eventually gave way to the Nubian language, which was written using an indigenous alphabet that combined elements of the old Meroitic and Coptic scripts. Coptic, however, often appeared in ecclesiastical and secular circles. Additionally, early inscriptions have indicated a continuing knowledge of colloquial Greek in Nubia as late as the twelfth century. After the seventh century, Arabic gained importance in the Nubian kingdoms, especially as a medium for commerce.

The Christian Nubian kingdoms, which survived for many centuries, achieved their peak of prosperity and military power in the ninth and tenth centuries. However, Muslim Arab invaders, who in 640 had conquered Egypt, posed a threat to the Christian Nubian kingdoms. Most historians believe that Arab pressure forced

Nobatia and Muqurra to merge into the kingdom of Dunqulah sometime before 700. Although the Arabs soon abandoned attempts to reduce Nubia by force, Muslim domination of Egypt often made it difficult to communicate with the Coptic patriarch or to obtain Egyptian-trained clergy. As a result, the Nubian church became isolated from the rest of the Christian world.

The Coming of Islam

The coming of Islam eventually changed the nature of Sudanese society and facilitated the division of the country into north and south. Islam also fostered political unity, economic growth, and educational development among its adherents; however, these benefits were restricted largely to urban and commercial centers.

The spread of Islam began shortly after the Prophet Muhammad's death in 632. By that time, he and his followers had converted most of Arabia's tribes and towns to Islam (literally, submission), which Muslims maintained united the individual believer, the state, and society under God's will. Islamic rulers, therefore, exercised temporal and religious authority. Islamic law (sharia—see Glossary), which was derived primarily from the Quran, encompassed all aspects of the lives of believers, who were called Muslims ("those who submit" to God's will).

Within a generation of Muhammad's death, Arab armies had carried Islam north and east from Arabia into North Africa. Muslims imposed political control over conquered territories in the name of the caliph (the Prophet's successor as supreme earthly leader of Islam). The Islamic armies won a major North African victory in 643 in Tripoli (in modern Libya). However, the Muslim subjugation of all of North Africa took about seventy-five years. The Arabs invaded Nubia in 642 and again in 652, when they laid siege to the city of Dunqulah and destroyed its cathedral. The Nubians put up a stout defense, however, causing the Arabs to accept an armistice and withdraw their forces.

The Arabs

Contacts between Nubians and Arabs long predated the coming of Islam, but the arabization of the Nile Valley was a gradual process that occurred over a period of nearly 1,000 years. Arab nomads continually wandered into the region in search of fresh pasturage, and Arab seafarers and merchants traded in Red Sea ports for spices and slaves. Intermarriage and assimilation also facilitated arabization. After the initial attempts at military conquest failed, the Arab commander in Egypt, Abd Allah ibn Saad, concluded the first in a series of regularly renewed treaties with the

9

Nubians that, with only brief interruptions, governed relations between the two peoples for more than 600 years. So long as Arabs ruled Egypt, there was peace on the Nubian frontier; however, when non-Arabs acquired control of the Nile Delta, tension arose in Upper Egypt.

The Arabs realized the commercial advantages of peaceful relations with Nubia and used the treaty to ensure that travel and trade proceeded unhindered across the frontier. The treaty also contained security arrangements whereby both parties agreed that neither would come to the defense of the other in the event of an attack by a third party. The treaty obliged both to exchange annual tribute as a goodwill symbol, the Nubians in slaves and the Arabs in grain. This formality was only a token of the trade that developed between the two, not only in these commodities but also in horses and manufactured goods brought to Nubia by the Arabs and in ivory, gold, gems, gum arabic, and cattle carried back by them to Egypt or shipped to Arabia.

Acceptance of the treaty did not indicate Nubian submission to the Arabs, but the treaty did impose conditions for Arab friendship that eventually permitted Arabs to achieve a privileged position in Nubia. For example, provisions of the treaty allowed Arabs to buy land from Nubians south of the frontier at Aswan. Arab merchants established markets in Nubian towns to facilitate the exchange of grain and slaves. Arab engineers supervised the operation of mines east of the Nile in which they used slave labor to extract gold and emeralds. Muslim pilgrims en route to Mecca traveled across the Red Sea on ferries from Aydhab and Sawakin, ports that also received cargoes bound from India to Egypt.

Traditional genealogies trace the ancestry of most of the Nile Valley's mixed population to Arab tribes that migrated into the region during this period. Even many non-Arabic-speaking groups claim descent from Arab forebears. The two most important Arabic-speaking groups to emerge in Nubia were the Jaali and the Juhayna (see Ethnic Groups, ch. 2). Both showed physical continuity with the indigenous pre-Islamic population. The former claimed descent from the Quraysh, the Prophet Muhammad's tribe. Historically, the Jaali have been sedentary farmers and herders or townspeople settled along the Nile and in Al Jazirah. The nomadic Juhayna comprised a family of tribes that included the Kababish, Baqqara, and Shukriya. They were descended from Arabs who migrated after the thirteenth century into an area that extended from the savanna and semidesert west of the Nile to the hill country east of the Blue Nile. Both groups formed a series of tribal shaykhdoms that succeeded the crumbling Christian Nubian kingdoms and that were in frequent conflict with one another and with neighboring non-Arabs. In some instances, as among the Beja, the indigenous people absorbed Arab migrants who settled among them. Beja ruling families later derived their legitimacy from their claims of Arab ancestry.

Although not all Muslims in the region were Arabic-speaking, acceptance of Islam facilitated the arabizing process. There was no policy of proselytism, however, and forced conversion was rare. Islam penetrated the area over a long period of time through intermarriage and contacts with Arab merchants and settlers. Exemption from taxation in regions under Muslim rule also proved a powerful incentive to conversion.

The Decline of Christian Nubia

Until the thirteenth century, the Nubian kingdoms proved their resilience in maintaining political independence and their commitment to Christianity. In the early eighth century and again in the tenth century, Nubian kings led armies into Egypt to force the release of the imprisoned Coptic patriarch and to relieve fellow Christians suffering persecution under Muslim rulers. In 1276, however, the Mamluks (Arabic for "owned"), who were an elite but frequently disorderly caste of soldier-administrators composed largely of Turkish, Kurdish, and Circassian slaves, intervened in a dynastic dispute, ousted Dunqulah's reigning monarch and delivered the crown and silver cross that symbolized Nubian kingship to a rival claimant (see The Rule of the Kashif, this ch.). Thereafter, Dunqulah became a satellite of Egypt.

Because of the frequent intermarriage between Nubian nobles and the kinswomen of Arab shaykhs, the lineages of the two elites merged and the Muslim heirs took their places in the royal line of succession. In 1315 a Muslim prince of Nubian royal blood ascended the throne of Dunqulah as king. The expansion of Islam coincided with the decline of the Nubian Christian church. A "dark age" enveloped Nubia in the fifteenth century during which political authority fragmented and slave raiding intensified. Communities in the river valley and savanna, fearful for their safety, formed tribal organizations and adopted Arab protectors. Muslims probably did not constitute a majority in the old Nubian areas until the fifteenth or sixteenth century.

The Rule of the Kashif

For several centuries Arab caliphs had governed Egypt through the Mamluks. In the thirteenth century, the Mamluks seized control of the state and created a sultanate that ruled Egypt until the early sixteenth century. Although they repeatedly launched military expeditions that weakened Dunqulah, the Mamluks did not directly rule Nubia. In 1517 the Turks conquered Egypt and incorporated the country into the Ottoman Empire as a *pashalik* (province).

Ottoman forces pursued fleeing Mamluks into Nubia, which had been claimed as a dependency of the Egyptian *pashalik*. Although they established administrative structures in ports on the Red Sea coast, the Ottomans exerted little authority over the interior. Instead, the Ottomans relied on military *kashif* (leaders), who controlled their virtually autonomous fiefs as agents of the pasha in Cairo, to rule the interior. The rule of the *kashif*, many of whom were Mamluks who had made their peace with the Ottomans, lasted 300 years. Concerned with little more than tax collecting and slave trading, the military leaders terrorized the population and constantly fought among themselves for title to territory.

The Funj

At the same time that the Ottomans brought northern Nubia into their orbit, a new power, the Funj, had risen in southern Nubia and had supplanted the remnants of the old Christian kingdom of Alwa. In 1504 a Funj leader, Amara Dunqas, founded the Black Sultanate (As Saltana az Zarqa) at Sannar. The Black Sultanate eventually became the keystone of the Funj Empire. By the mid-sixteenth century, Sannar controlled Al Jazirah and commanded the allegiance of vassal states and tribal districts north to the third cataract and south to the swampy grasslands along the Nile.

The Funj state included a loose confederation of sultanates and dependent tribal chieftaincies drawn together under the suzerainty of Sannar's *mek* (sultan). As overlord, the *mek* received tribute, levied taxes, and called on his vassals to supply troops in time of war. Vassal states in turn relied on the *mek* to settle local disorders and to resolve internal disputes. The Funj stabilized the region and interposed a military bloc between the Arabs in the north, the Ethiopians in the east, and the non-Muslim blacks in the south.

The sultanate's economy depended on the role played by the Funj in the slave trade. Farming and herding also thrived in Al Jazirah and in the savanna. Sannar apportioned tributary areas into tribal homelands (each one termed a *dar;* pl., *dur*), where the *mek* granted the local population the right to use arable land. The diverse groups that inhabited each *dar* eventually regarded themselves as units of tribes. Movement from one *dar* to another entailed a change in tribal identification. (Tribal distinctions in these areas in modern Sudan can be traced to this period.) The *mek* appointed a chieftain (*nazir;* pl., *nuzzar*) to govern each *dar. Nuzzar* administered *dur* according to customary law, paid tribute to the *mek,* and collected taxes. The *mek* also derived income from crown lands set aside for his use in each *dar.*

At the peak of its power in the mid-seventeenth century, Sannar repulsed the northward advance of the Nilotic Shilluk people up the White Nile and compelled many of them to submit to Funj authority. After this victory, the *mek* Badi II Abu Duqn (1642–81) sought to centralize the government of the confederacy at Sannar. To implement this policy, Badi introduced a standing army of slave soldiers that would free Sannar from dependence on vassal sultans for military assistance and would provide the *mek* with the means to enforce his will. The move alienated the dynasty from the Funj warrior aristocracy, which in 1718 deposed the reigning *mek* and placed one of its own ranks on the throne of Sannar. The mid-eighteenth century witnessed another brief period of expansion when the Funj turned back an Ethiopian invasion, defeated the Fur, and took control of much of Kurdufan. But civil war and the demands of defending the sultanate had overextended the warrior society's resources and sapped its strength.

Another reason for Sannar's decline may have been the growing influence of its hereditary viziers (chancellors), chiefs of a non-Funj tributary tribe who managed court affairs. In 1761 the vizier Muhammad Abu al Kaylak, who had led the Funj army in wars, carried out a palace coup, relegating the sultan to a figurehead role. Sannar's hold over its vassals diminished, and by the early nineteenth century more remote areas ceased to recognize even the nominal authority of the *mek.*

The Fur

Darfur was the Fur homeland. Renowned as cavalrymen, Fur clans frequently allied with or opposed their kin, the Kanuri of Borno, in modern Nigeria. After a period of disorder in the sixteenth century, during which the region was briefly subject to Borno, the leader of the Keira clan, Sulayman Solong (1596–1637), supplanted a rival clan and became Darfur's first sultan. Sulayman Solong decreed Islam to be the sultanate's official religion. However, large-scale religious conversions did not occur until the reign of Ahmad Bakr (1682–1722), who imported teachers, built mosques, and compelled his subjects to become Muslims. In the eighteenth century, several sultans consolidated the dynasty's hold on Darfur, established a capital at Al Fashir, and contested the Funj for control of Kurdufan.

The sultans operated the slave trade as a monopoly. They levied taxes on traders and export duties on slaves sent to Egypt, and took a share of the slaves brought into Darfur. Some household slaves advanced to prominent positions in the courts of sultans, and the power exercised by these slaves provoked a violent reaction among the traditional class of Fur officeholders in the late eighteenth century. The rivalry between the slave and traditional elites caused recurrent unrest throughout the next century.

The Turkiyah, 1821–85

As a *pashalik* of the Ottoman Empire, Egypt had been divided into several provinces, each of which was placed under a Mamluk bey (governor) reponsible to the pasha, who in turn answered to the Porte, the term used for the Ottoman government referring to the Sublime Porte, or high gate, of the grand vizier's building. In approximately 280 years of Ottoman rule, no fewer than 100 pashas succeeded each other. In the eighteenth century, their authority became tenuous as rival Mamluk beys became the real power in the land. The struggles among the beys continued until 1798 when the French invasion of Egypt altered the situation. Combined British and Turkish military operations forced the withdrawal of French forces in 1801, introducing a period of chaos in Egypt. In 1805 the Ottomans sought to restore order by appointing Muhammad Ali as Egypt's pasha.

With the help of 10,000 Albanian troops provided by the Ottomans, Muhammad Ali purged Egypt of the Mamluks. In 1811 he launched a seven-year campaign in Arabia, supporting his suzerain, the Ottoman sultan, in the suppression of a revolt by the Wahhabi, an ultraconservative Muslim sect. To replace the Albanian soldiers, Muhammad Ali planned to build an Egyptian army with Sudanese slave recruits.

Although a part of present-day northern Sudan was nominally an Egyptian dependency, the previous pashas had demanded little more from the *kashif* who ruled there than the regular remittance of tribute; that changed under Muhammad Ali. After he had defeated the Mamluks in Egypt, a party of them escaped and fled south. In 1811 these Mamluks established a state at Dunqulah as a base for their slave trading. In 1820 the sultan of Sannar informed Muhammad Ali that he was unable to comply with the demand to expel the Mamluks. In response the pasha sent 4,000 troops to invade Sudan, clear it of Mamluks, and reclaim it for Egypt. The pasha's forces received the submission of the *kashif*, dispersed the Dunqulah Mamluks, conquered Kurdufan, and accepted Sannar's surrender from the last Funj sultan, Badi IV. The Jaali Arab tribes offered stiff resistance, however.

Initially, the Egyptian occupation of Sudan was disastrous. Under the new government established in 1821, which was known as the Turkiyah or Turkish regime, soldiers lived off the land and exacted exorbitant taxes from the population. They also destroyed many ancient Meroitic pyramids searching for hidden gold. Furthermore, slave trading increased, causing many of the inhabitants of the fertile Al Jazirah, heartland of Funj, to flee to escape the slave traders. Within a year of the pasha's victory, 30,000 Sudanese slaves went to Egypt for training and induction into the army. However, so many perished from disease and the unfamiliar climate that the remaining slaves could be used only in garrisons in Sudan.

As the military occupation became more secure, the government became less harsh. Egypt saddled Sudan with a parasitic bureaucracy, however, and expected the country to be self-supporting. Nevertheless, farmers and herders gradually returned to Al Jazirah. The Turkiyah also won the allegiance of some tribal and religious leaders by granting them a tax exemption. Egyptian soldiers and Sudanese *jahidiyah* (slave soldiers; literally, fighters), supplemented by mercenaries recruited in various Ottoman domains, manned garrisons in Khartoum, Kassala, Al Ubayyid, and at several smaller outposts. The Shaiqiyah, Arabic speakers who had resisted Egyptian occupation, were defeated and allowed to serve the Egyptian rulers as tax collectors and irregular cavalry under their own shaykhs. The Egyptians divided Sudan into provinces, which they then subdivided into smaller administrative units that usually corresponded to tribal territories. In 1835 Khartoum became the seat of the *hakimadar* (governor general); many garrison towns also developed into administrative centers in their respective regions. At the local level, shaykhs and traditional tribal chieftains assumed administrative responsibilities.

In the 1850s, the *pashalik* revised the legal systems in Egypt and Sudan, introducing a commercial code and a criminal code administered in secular courts. The change reduced the prestige of the qadis (Islamic judges) whose sharia courts were confined to dealing with matters of personal status. Even in this area, the courts lacked credibility in the eyes of Sudanese Muslims because they conducted hearings according to the Ottoman Empire's Hanafi school of law rather than the stricter Maliki school customary in the area.

The Turkiyah also encouraged a religious orthodoxy favored in the Ottoman Empire. The government undertook a mosque-building program and staffed religious schools and courts with teachers and judges trained at Cairo's Al Azhar University. The government favored the Khatmiyyah, a traditional religious order, because its leaders preached cooperation with the regime. But Sudanese Muslims condemned the official orthodoxy as decadent because it had rejected many popular beliefs and practices.

Until its gradual suppression in the 1860s, the slave trade was the most profitable undertaking in Sudan and was the focus of Egyptian interests in the country. The government encouraged economic development through state monopolies that had exported slaves, ivory, and gum arabic. In some areas, tribal land, which had been held in common, became the private property of the shaykhs and was sometimes sold to buyers outside the tribe.

Muhammad Ali's immediate successors, Abbas I (1849-54) and Said (1854-63), lacked leadership qualities and paid little attention to Sudan, but the reign of Ismail (1863-79) revitalized Egyptian interest in the country. In 1865 the Ottoman Empire ceded the Red Sea coast and its ports to Egypt. Two years later, the Ottoman sultan granted Ismail the title of khedive (sovereign prince). Egypt organized and garrisoned the new provinces of Upper Nile, Bahr al Ghazal, and Equatoria and, in 1874, conquered and annexed Darfur. Ismail named Europeans to provincial governorships and appointed Sudanese to more responsible government positions. Under prodding from Britain, Ismail took steps to complete the elimination of the slave trade in the north of present-day Sudan. The khedive also tried to build a new army on the European model that no longer would depend on slaves to provide manpower. However, this modernization process caused unrest. Army units mutinied, and many Sudanese resented the quartering of troops among the civilian population and the use of Sudanese forced labor on public projects. Efforts to suppress the slave trade angered the urban merchant class and the Baqqara Arabs, who had grown prosperous by selling slaves.

There is little documentation for the history of the southern Sudanese provinces until the introduction of the Turkiyah in the north in the early 1820s and the subsequent extension of slave raiding into the south. Information about their peoples before that time is based largely on oral history. According to these traditions, the Nilotic peoples—the Dinka, Nuer, Shilluk, and others—first entered southern Sudan sometime before the tenth century. During the period from the fifteenth century to the nineteenth century, tribal migrations, largely from the area of Bahr al Ghazal, brought these peoples to their modern locations. Some, like the Shilluk, developed a centralized monarchical tradition that enabled them to preserve their tribal integrity in the face of external pressures in the nineteenth and twentieth centuries. The non-Nilotic Azande people, who entered southern Sudan in the sixteenth century, established the region's largest state. In the eighteenth century, the militaristic Avungara people entered and quickly imposed their authority over the poorly organized and weaker Azande. Avungara power remained largely unchallenged until the arrival of the British at the end of the nineteenth century. Geographic barriers protected the southerners from Islam's advance, enabling them to retain their social and cultural heritage and their political and religious institutions. During the nineteenth century, the slave trade brought southerners into closer contact with Sudanese Arabs and resulted in a deep hatred for the northerners.

Slavery had been an institution of Sudanese life throughout history, but southern Sudan, where slavery flourished particularly, was originally considered an area beyond Cairo's control. Because Sudan had access to Middle East slave markets, the slave trade in the south intensified in the nineteenth century and continued after the British had suppressed slavery in much of sub-Saharan Africa. Annual raids resulted in the capture of countless thousands of southern Sudanese and the destruction of the region's stability and economy. The horrors associated with the slave trade generated European interest in Sudan.

Until 1843 Muhammad Ali maintained a state monopoly on slave trading in Egypt and the *pashalik*. Thereafter, authorities sold licenses to private traders who competed with government-conducted slave raids. In 1854 Cairo ended state participation in the slave trade, and in 1860, in response to European pressure, Egypt prohibited the slave trade. However, the Egyptian army failed to enforce the prohibition against the private armies of the slave traders. The introduction of steamboats and firearms enabled slave traders to overwhelm local resistance and prompted the creation of southern "bush empires" by Baqqara Arabs.

Ismail implemented a military modernization program and proposed to extend Egyptian rule to the southern region. In 1869 British explorer Sir Samuel Baker received a commission as governor of Equatoria Province, with orders to annex all territory in the White Nile's basin and to suppress the slave trade. In 1874 Charles George Gordon, a British officer, succeeded Baker. Gordon disarmed many slave traders and hanged those who defied him. By the time he became Sudan's governor general in 1877, Gordon had weakened the slave trade in much of the south.

Unfortunately, Ismail's southern policy lacked consistency. In 1871 he had named a notorious Arab slave trader, Rahman Mansur az Zubayr, as governor of the newly created province of Bahr al

Ghazal. Zubayr used his army to pacify the province and to eliminate his competition in the slave trade. In 1874 he invaded Darfur after the sultan had refused to guard caravan routes through his territory. Zubayr then offered the region as a province to the khedive. Later that year, Zubayr defied Cairo when it attempted to relieve him of his post, and he defeated an Egyptian force that sought to oust him. After he became Sudan's governor general, Gordon ended Zubayr's slave trading, disbanded his army, and sent him back to Cairo.

The Mahdiyah, 1884–98

Developments in Sudan during this period cannot be understood without reference to the British position in Egypt. In 1869 the Suez Canal opened and quickly became Britain's economic lifeline to India and the Far East. To defend this waterway, Britain sought a greater role in Egyptian affairs. In 1873 the British government therefore supported a program whereby an Anglo-French debt commission assumed responsibility for managing Egypt's fiscal affairs. This commission eventually forced Khedive Ismail to abdicate in favor of his more politically acceptable son, Tawfiq (1877–92).

After the removal, in 1877, of Ismail, who had appointed him to the post, Gordon resigned as governor general of Sudan in 1880. His successors lacked direction from Cairo and feared the political turmoil that had engulfed Egypt. As a result, they failed to continue the policies Gordon had put in place. The illegal slave trade revived, although not enough to satisfy the merchants whom Gordon had put out of business. The Sudanese army suffered from a lack of resources, and unemployed soldiers from disbanded units troubled garrison towns. Tax collectors arbitrarily increased taxation.

In this troubled atmosphere, Muhammad Ahmad ibn as Sayyid Abd Allah, a *faqir* or holy man who combined personal magnetism with religious zealotry, emerged, determined to expel the Ottomans and restore Islam to its primitive purity. The son of a Dunqulah boatbuilder, Muhammad Ahmad had become the disciple of Muhammad ash Sharif, the head of the Sammaniyah order. Later, as a shaykh of the order, Muhammad Ahmad spent several years in seclusion and gained a reputation as a mystic and teacher. In 1880 he became a Sammaniyah leader.

Muhammad Ahmad's sermons attracted an increasing number of followers. Among those who joined him was Abdallahi ibn Muhammad, a Baqqara from southern Darfur. His planning capabilities proved invaluable to Muhammad Ahmad, who revealed himself as Al Mahdi al Muntazar ("the awaited guide in the right path,'' usually seen as the Mahdi), sent from God to redeem the faithful and prepare the way for the second coming of the Prophet Isa (Jesus). The Mahdist movement demanded a return to the simplicity of early Islam, abstention from alcohol and tobacco, and the strict seclusion of women.

Even after the Mahdi proclaimed a jihad, or holy war, against the Turkiyah, Khartoum dismissed him as a religious fanatic. The government paid more attention when his religious zeal turned to denunciation of tax collectors. To avoid arrest, the Mahdi and a party of his followers, the Ansar, made a long march to Kurdufan, where he gained a large number of recruits, especially from the Baqqara. From a refuge in the area, he wrote appeals to the shaykhs of the religious orders and won active support or assurances of neutrality from all except the pro-Egyptian Khatmiyyah. Merchants and Arab tribes that had depended on the slave trade responded as well, along with the Hadendowa Beja, who were rallied to the Mahdi by an Ansar captain, Usman Digna.

Early in 1882, the Ansar, armed with spears and swords, overwhelmed a 7,000-man Egyptian force not far from Al Ubayyid and seized their rifles and ammunition. The Mahdi followed up this victory by laying siege to Al Ubayyid and starving it into submission after four months. The Ansar, 30,000 men strong, then defeated an 8,000-man Egyptian relief force at Sheikan. Next the Mahdi captured Darfur and imprisoned Rudolf Slatin, an Austrian in the khedive's service, who later became the first Egyptian-appointed governor of Darfur Province.

The advance of the Ansar and the Beja rising in the east imperiled communications with Egypt and threatened to cut off garrisons at Khartoum, Kassala, Sannar, and Sawakin and in the south. To avoid being drawn into a costly military intervention, the British government ordered an Egyptian withdrawal from Sudan. Gordon, who had received a reappointment as governor general, arranged to supervise the evacuation of Egyptian troops and officials and all foreigners from Sudan.

After reaching Khartoum in February 1884, Gordon realized that he could not extricate the garrisons. As a result, he called for reinforcements from Egypt to relieve Khartoum. Gordon also recommended that Zubayr, an old enemy whom he recognized as an excellent military commander, be named to succeed him to give disaffected Sudanese a leader other than the Mahdi to rally behind. London rejected this plan. As the situation deteriorated, Gordon argued that Sudan was essential to Egypt's security and that to allow the Ansar a victory there would invite the movement to spread elsewhere.

Increasing British popular support for Gordon eventually forced
Prime Minister William Gladstone to mobilize a relief force under
the command of Lord Garnet Joseph Wolseley. A "flying column"
sent overland from Wadi Halfa across the Bayyudah Desert bogged
down at Abu Tulayh (commonly called Abu Klea), where the
Hadendowa Beja—the so-called Fuzzy Wuzzies—broke the British line. An advance unit that had gone ahead by river when the
column reached Al Matammah arrived at Khartoum on January 28, 1885, to find the town had fallen two days earlier. The Ansar
had waited for the Nile flood to recede before attacking the poorly
defended river approach to Khartoum in boats, slaughtering the
garrison, killing Gordon, and delivering his head to the Mahdi's
tent. Kassala and Sannar fell soon after, and by the end of 1885
the Ansar had begun to move into the southern region. In all Sudan,
only Sawakin, reinforced by Indian army troops, and Wadi Halfa
on the northern frontier remained in Anglo-Egyptian hands (see
fig. 2).

The Mahdiyah (Mahdist regime) imposed traditional Islamic
laws. Sudan's new ruler also authorized the burning of lists of
pedigrees and books of law and theology because of their association with the old order and because he believed that the former
accentuated tribalism at the expense of religious unity.

The Mahdiyah has become known as the first genuine Sudanese
nationalist government. The Mahdi maintained that his movement
was not a religious order that could be accepted or rejected at will,
but that it was a universal regime, which challenged man to join
or to be destroyed. The Mahdi modified Islam's five pillars to support the dogma that loyalty to him was essential to true belief (see
Islamic Movements and Religious Orders, ch. 2). The Mahdi also
added the declaration "and Muhammad Ahmad is the Mahdi of
God and the representative of His Prophet" to the recitation of
the creed, the *shahada*. Moreover, service in the jihad replaced the
hajj, or pilgrimage to Mecca, as a duty incumbent on the faithful.
Zakat (almsgiving) became the tax paid to the state. The Mahdi
justified these and other innovations and reforms as responses to
instructions conveyed to him by God in visions.

The Khalifa

Six months after the capture of Khartoum, the Mahdi died of
typhus. The task of establishing and maintaining a government
fell to his deputies—three caliphs chosen by the Mahdi in emulation of the Prophet Muhammad. Rivalry among the three, each
supported by people of his native region, continued until 1891, when
Abdallahi ibn Muhammad, with the help primarily of the Baqqara

Arabs, overcame the opposition of the others and emerged as un-challenged leader of the Mahdiyah. Abdallahi—called the Khalifa (successor)—purged the Mahdiyah of members of the Mahdi's family and many of his early religious disciples.

Originally, the Mahdiyah was a jihad state, run like a military camp. Sharia courts enforced Islamic law and the Mahdi's precepts, which had the force of law. After consolidating his power, the Khalifa instituted an administration and appointed Ansar (who were usually Baqqara) as amirs over each of the several provinces. The Khalifa also ruled over rich Al Jazirah. Although he failed to restore this region's commercial well-being, the Khalifa organized workshops to manufacture ammunition and to maintain river steamboats.

Regional relations remained tense throughout much of the Mahdiyah period, largely because of the Khalifa's commitment to using the jihad to extend his version of Islam throughout the world. For example, the Khalifa rejected an offer of an alliance against the Europeans by Ethiopia's negus (king), Yohannes IV. In 1887 a 60,000-man Ansar army invaded Ethiopia, penetrated as far as Gonder, and captured prisoners and booty. The Khalifa then refused to conclude peace with Ethiopia. In March 1889, an Ethiopian force, commanded by the king, marched on Qallabat; however, after Yohannes IV fell in battle, the Ethiopians withdrew. Abd ar Rahman an Nujumi, the Khalifa's best general, invaded Egypt in 1889, but British-led Egyptian troops defeated the Ansar at Tushkah. The failure of the Egyptian invasion ended the Ansar's invincibility. The Belgians prevented the Mahdi's men from conquering Equatoria, and in 1893 the Italians repulsed an Ansar attack at Akordat (in present-day Eritrea) and forced the Ansar to withdraw from Ethiopia.

Reconquest of Sudan

In 1892 Herbert Kitchener (later Lord Kitchener) became sirdar, or commander, of the Egyptian army and started preparations for the reconquest of Sudan. The British decision to occupy Sudan resulted in part from international developments that required the country be brought under British supervision. By the early 1890s, British, French, and Belgian claims had converged at the Nile headwaters. Britain feared that the other colonial powers would take advantage of Sudan's instability to acquire territory previously annexed to Egypt. Apart from these political considerations, Britain wanted to establish control over the Nile to safeguard a planned irrigation dam at Aswan.

Figure 2. The Mahdist State, 1881–98

In 1895 the British government authorized Kitchener to launch a campaign to reconquer Sudan. Britain provided men and matériel while Egypt financed the expedition. The Anglo-Egyptian Nile Expeditionary Force included 25,800 men, 8,600 of whom were British. The remainder were troops belonging to Egyptian units that included six battalions recruited in southern Sudan. An armed river flotilla escorted the force, which also had artillery support. In preparation for the attack, the British established army headquarters at

Wadi Halfa and extended and reinforced the perimeter defenses around Sawakin. In March 1896, the campaign started; in September, Kitchener captured Dunqulah. The British then constructed a rail line from Wadi Halfa to Abu Hamad and an extension parallel to the Nile to transport troops and supplies to Barbar. Anglo-Egyptian units fought a sharp action at Abu Hamad, but there was little other significant resistance until Kitchener reached Atbarah and defeated the Ansar. After this engagement, Kitchener's soldiers marched and sailed toward Omdurman, where the Khalifa made his last stand.

On September 2, 1898, the Khalifa committed his 52,000-man army to a frontal assault against the Anglo-Egyptian force, which was massed on the plain outside Omdurman. The outcome never was in doubt, largely because of superior British firepower. During the five-hour battle, about 11,000 Mahdists died whereas Anglo-Egyptian losses amounted to 48 dead and fewer than 400 wounded.

Mopping-up operations required several years, but organized resistance ended when the Khalifa, who had escaped to Kurdufan, died in fighting at Umm Diwaykarat in November 1899. Many areas welcomed the downfall of his regime. Sudan's economy had been all but destroyed during his reign, and the population had declined by approximately one-half because of famine, disease, persecution, and warfare. Moreover, none of the country's traditional institutions or loyalties remained intact. Tribes had been divided in their attitudes toward Mahdism, religious brotherhoods had been weakened, and orthodox religious leaders had vanished.

The Anglo-Egyptian Condominium, 1899–1955

In January 1899, an Anglo-Egyptian agreement restored Egyptian rule in Sudan but as part of a condominium, or joint authority, exercised by Britain and Egypt. The agreement designated territory south of the twenty-second parallel as the Anglo-Egyptian Sudan. Although it emphasized Egypt's indebtedness to Britain for its participation in the reconquest, the agreement failed to clarify the juridical relationship between the two condominium powers in Sudan or to provide a legal basis for continued British presence in the south. Britain assumed responsibility for governing the territory on behalf of the khedive.

Article II of the agreement specified that "the supreme military and civil command in Sudan shall be vested in one officer, termed the Governor-General of Sudan. He shall be appointed by Khedival Decree on the recommendation of Her Britannic Majesty's Government and shall be removed only by Khedival Decree with the consent of Her Britannic Majesty's Government.'' The British governor general, who was a military officer, reported to the Foreign Office through its resident agent in Cairo. In practice, however, he exercised extraordinary powers and directed the condominium government from Khartoum as if it were a colonial administration. Sir Reginald Wingate succeeded Kitchener as governor general in 1899. In each province, two inspectors and several district commissioners aided the British governor (*mudir*). Initially, nearly all administrative personnel were British army officers attached to the Egyptian army. In 1901, however, civilian administrators started arriving in Sudan from Britain and formed the nucleus of the Sudan Political Service. Egyptians filled middle-level posts while Sudanese gradually acquired lower-level positions.

In the condominium's early years, the governor general and provincial governors exercised great latitude in governing Sudan. After 1910, however, an executive council, whose approval was required for all legislation and for budgetary matters, assisted the governor general. The governor general presided over this council, which included the inspector general; the civil, legal, and financial secretaries; and two to four other British officials appointed by the governor general. The executive council retained legislative authority until 1948.

After restoring order and the government's authority, the British dedicated themselves to creating a modern government in the condominium. Jurists adopted penal and criminal procedural codes similar to those in force in British India. Commissions established land tenure rules and adjusted claims in dispute because of grants made by successive governments. Taxes on land remained the basic form of taxation, the amount assessed depending on the type of irrigation, the number of date palms, and the size of herds; however, the rate of taxation was fixed for the first time in Sudan's history. The 1902 Code of Civil Procedure continued the Ottoman separation of civil law and sharia, but it also created guidelines for the operation of sharia courts as an autonomous judicial division under a chief qadi appointed by the governor general. Religious judges and other sharia court officials were invariably Egyptian.

There was little resistance to the condominium. Breaches of the peace usually took the form of intertribal warfare, banditry, or revolts of short duration. For example, Mahdist uprisings occurred in February 1900, in 1902–3, in 1904, and in 1908. In 1916 Abd Allah as Suhayni, who claimed to be the Prophet Isa, launched an unsuccessful jihad.

The problem of the condominium's undefined borders was a greater concern. A 1902 treaty with Ethiopia fixed the southeastern

Portrait of Herbert Kitchener, commander of the Anglo-Egyptian army that reconquered Sudan in the 1890s
Courtesy Robert O. Collins

boundary with Sudan. Seven years later, an Anglo-Belgian treaty determined the status of the Lado Enclave in the south, establishing a border with the Belgian Congo (present-day Zaire). The western boundary proved more difficult to resolve. Darfur was the only province formerly under Egyptian control that was not soon recovered under the condominium. When the Mahdiyah disintegrated, Sultan Ali Dinar reclaimed Darfur's throne, which had been lost to the Egyptians in 1874 and, with British approval, held the throne under Ottoman suzerainty on condition that he pay annual tribute to the khedive. When World War I broke out, Ali Dinar proclaimed his loyalty to the Ottoman Empire and responded to the Porte's call for a jihad against the Allies. Britain, which had declared a protectorate over Egypt in 1914, sent a small force against Ali Dinar, who died in subsequent fighting. In 1916 the British annexed Darfur to Sudan and terminated the Fur sultanate (see fig. 3).

During the condominium period, economic development occurred only in the Nile Valley's settled areas. In the first two decades of condominium rule, the British extended telegraph and rail lines to link key points in northern Sudan but services did not reach more remote areas. Port Sudan opened in 1906, replacing Sawakin as the country's principal outlet to the sea. In 1911 the Sudanese government and the private Sudan Plantations Syndicate launched the Gezira Scheme (Gezira is also seen as Jazirah) to provide a source of high-quality cotton for Britain's textile industry (see Irrigated Agriculture, ch. 3). An irrigation dam near Sannar, completed in 1925, brought a much larger area in Al Jazirah under cultivation. Planters sent cotton by rail from Sannar to Port Sudan for shipment abroad. The Gezira Scheme made cotton the mainstay of the country's economy and turned the region into Sudan's most densely populated area.

In 1922 Britain renounced the protectorate and approved Egypt's declaration of independence. However, the 1923 Egyptian constitution made no claim to Egyptian sovereignty over Sudan. Subsequent negotiations in London between the British and the new Egyptian government foundered on the Sudan question. Nationalists who were inflamed by the failure of the talks rioted in Egypt and Sudan, where a minority supported union with Egypt. In November 1924, Sir Lee Stack, governor general of Sudan and sirdar, was assassinated in Cairo. Britain ordered all Egyptian troops, civil servants, and public employees withdrawn from Sudan. In 1925 Khartoum formed the 4,500-man Sudan Defence Force (SDF) under Sudanese officers to replace Egyptian units.

Sudan was relatively quiet in the late 1920s and 1930s. During this period, the colonial government favored indirect rule, which allowed the British to govern through indigenous leaders. In Sudan, the traditional leaders were the shaykhs—of villages, tribes, and districts—in the north and tribal chiefs in the south. The number of Sudanese recognizing them and the degree of authority they held varied considerably. The British first delegated judicial powers to shaykhs to enable them to settle local disputes and then gradually allowed the shaykhs to administer local governments under the supervision of British district commissioners.

The mainstream of political development, however, occurred among local leaders and among Khartoum's educated elite. In their view, indirect rule prevented the country's unification, exacerbated tribalism in the north, and served in the south to buttress a less-advanced society against Arab influence. Indirect rule also implied government decentralization, which alarmed the educated elite who had careers in the central administration and envisioned an eventual transfer of power from British colonial authorities to their class. Although nationalists and the Khatmiyyah opposed indirect rule, the Ansar, many of whom enjoyed positions of local authority, supported the concept.

Britain's Southern Policy

From the beginning of the Anglo-Egyptian condominium, the British sought to modernize Sudan by applying European technology to its underdeveloped economy and by replacing its authoritarian institutions with ones that adhered to liberal English traditions. However, southern Sudan's remote and undeveloped provinces— Equatoria, Bahr al Ghazal, and Upper Nile—received little official attention until after World War I, except for efforts to suppress tribal warfare and the slave trade. The British justified this policy by claiming that the south was not ready for exposure to the modern world. To allow the south to develop along indigenous lines, the British, therefore, closed the region to outsiders. As a result, the south remained isolated and backward. A few Arab merchants controlled the region's limited commercial activities and Arab bureaucrats administered whatever laws existed. Christian missionaries, who operated schools and medical clinics, provided limited social services in southern Sudan.

The earliest Christian missionaries were the Verona Fathers, a Roman Catholic religious order that had established southern missions before the Mahdiyah. Other missionary groups active in the south included Presbyterians from the United States and the Anglican Church Missionary Society. There was no competition among these missions, largely because they maintained separate areas of influence. The government eventually subsidized the mission schools that educated southerners. Because mission graduates usually succeeded in gaining posts in the provincial civil service, many northerners regarded them as tools of British imperialism. The few southerners who received higher training attended schools in the British East African colonies (present-day Kenya, Uganda, and Tanzania) rather than in Khartoum, thereby exacerbating the north-south division.

British authorities treated the three southern provinces as a separate region. The colonial administration, as it consolidated its southern position in the 1920s, detached the south from the rest of Sudan for all practical purposes. The period's "closed door" ordinances, which barred northern Sudanese from entering or working in the south, reinforced this separate development policy. Moreover, the British gradually replaced Arab administrators and expelled Arab merchants, thereby severing the south's last economic contacts with the north. The colonial administration also discouraged the spread of Islam, the practice of Arab customs, and the wearing of Arab dress. At the same time, the British attempted to revitalize African customs and tribal life that the slave trade had disrupted. Finally, a 1930 directive stated that blacks in the southern provinces were to be considered a people distinct from northern Muslims and that the region should be prepared for eventual integration with the British East African colonies.

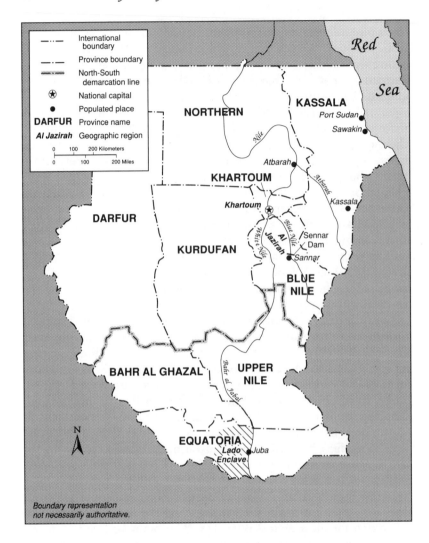

Figure 3. Anglo-Egyptian Sudan, 1899–1955

Although potentially a rich agricultural zone, the south's economic development suffered because of the region's isolation. Moreover, a continual struggle went on between British officials in the north and south, as those in the former resisted recommendations that northern resources be diverted to spur southern economic development. Personality clashes between officials in the two branches in the Sudan Political Service also impeded the south's growth. Those individuals who served in the southern provinces tended to be military officers with previous Africa experience on secondment to the colonial service. They usually were distrustful of Arab influence and were committed to keeping the south under British control. By contrast, officials in the northern provinces tended to be Arabists, often drawn from the diplomatic and consular service. Whereas northern provincial governors conferred regularly as a group with the governor general in Khartoum, their three southern colleagues met to coordinate activities with the governors of the British East African colonies.

Rise of Sudanese Nationalism

Sudanese nationalism, as it developed after World War I, was an Arab and Muslim phenomenon with its support base in the northern provinces. Nationalists opposed indirect rule and advocated a centralized national government in Khartoum responsible for both regions. Nationalists also perceived Britain's southern policy as artificially dividing Sudan and preventing its unification under an arabized and Islamic ruling class.

Ironically, however, a non-Arab led Sudan's first modern nationalist movement. In 1921 Ali Abd al Latif, a Muslim Dinka and former army officer, founded the United Tribes Society that called for an independent Sudan in which power would be shared by tribal and religious leaders. Three years later, Ali Abd al Latif's movement, reconstituted as the White Flag League, organized demonstrations in Khartoum that took advantage of the unrest that followed Stack's assassination. Ali Abd al Latif's arrest and subsequent exile in Egypt sparked a mutiny by a Sudanese army battalion, the suppression of which succeeded in temporarily crippling the nationalist movement.

In the 1930s, nationalism reemerged in Sudan. Educated Sudanese wanted to restrict the governor general's power and to obtain Sudanese participation in the council's deliberations. However, any change in government required a change in the condominium agreement. Neither Britain nor Egypt would agree to a modification. Moreover, the British regarded their role to be the protection of the Sudanese from Egyptian domination. The nationalists feared that the eventual result of friction between the condominium powers might be the attachment of northern Sudan to Egypt and southern Sudan to Uganda and Kenya. Although they settled most of their differences in the 1936 Treaty of Alliance, which set a timetable for the end of British military occupation, Britain and Egypt failed to agree on Sudan's future status.

Nationalists and religious leaders were divided on the issue of whether Sudan should apply for independence or for union with

29

Egypt. The Mahdi's son, Abd ar Rahman al Mahdi, emerged as a spokesman for independence in opposition to Ali al Mirghani, the Khatmiyyah leader, who favored union with Egypt. Coalitions supported by each of these leaders formed rival wings of the nationalist movement. Later, radical nationalists and the Khatmiyyah created the Ashigga, later renamed the National Unionist Party (NUP), to advance the cause of Sudanese-Egyptian unification. The moderates favored Sudanese independence in cooperation with Britain and together with the Ansar established the Umma Party.

The Road to Independence

As World War II approached, the SDF assumed the mission of guarding Sudan's frontier with Italian East Africa (present-day Ethiopia). During the summer of 1940, Italian forces invaded Sudan at several points and captured Kassala. However, the SDF prevented a further advance on Port Sudan. In January 1941, the SDF, expanded to 20,000 troops, retook Kassala and participated in the British offensive that routed the Italians in Eritrea and liberated Ethiopia. Some Sudanese units later contributed to the British Eighth Army's North Africa victory.

In the immediate postwar years, the condominium government made a number of significant changes. In 1942 the Graduates' General Conference, a quasi-nationalist movement formed by educated Sudanese, presented the government with a memorandum that demanded a pledge of self-determination after the war to be preceded by abolition of the "closed door" ordinances, an end to the separate curriculum in southern schools, and an increase in the number of Sudanese in the civil service. The governor general refused to accept the memorandum but agreed to a government-supervised transformation of indirect rule into a modernized system of local government. Sir Douglas Newbold, governor of Kurdufan Province in the 1930s and later the executive council's civil secretary, advised the establishment of parliamentary government and the administrative unification of north and south. In 1948, over Egyptian objections, Britain authorized the partially elected consultative Legislative Assembly representing both regions to supersede the advisory executive council.

The pro-Egyptian NUP boycotted the 1948 Legislative Assembly elections. As a result, pro-independence groups dominated the Legislative Assembly. In 1952 leaders of the Umma-dominated legislature negotiated the Self-Determination Agreement with Britain. The legislators then enacted a constitution that provided for a prime minister and council of ministers responsible to a bicameral parliament. The new Sudanese government would have responsibility in all areas except military and foreign affairs, which remained in the British governor general's hands. Cairo, which demanded recognition of Egyptian sovereignty over Sudan, repudiated the condominium agreement in protest and declared its reigning monarch, Faruk, king of Sudan.

After seizing power in Egypt and overthrowing the Faruk monarchy in late 1952, Colonel Muhammad Naguib broke the deadlock on the problem of Egyptian sovereignty over Sudan. Cairo previously had linked discussions on Sudan's status to an agreement on the evacuation of British troops from the Suez Canal. Naguib separated the two issues and accepted the right of Sudanese self-determination. In February 1953, London and Cairo signed an Anglo-Egyptian accord, which allowed for a three-year transition period from condominium rule to self-government. During the transition phase, British and Egyptian troops would withdraw from Sudan. At the end of this period, the Sudanese would decide their future status in a plebiscite conducted under international supervision. Naguib's concession seemed justified when parliamentary elections held at the end of 1952 gave a majority to the pro-Egyptian NUP, which had called for an eventual union with Egypt. In January 1954, a new government emerged under NUP leader Ismail al Azhari.

The South and the Unity of Sudan

During World War II, some British colonial officers questioned the economic and political viability of the southern provinces as separate from northern Sudan. Britain also had become more sensitive to Arab criticism of the southern policy. In 1946 the Sudan Administrative Conference determined that Sudan should be administered as one country. Moreover, the conference delegates agreed to readmit northern administrators to southern posts, abolish the trade restrictions imposed under the "closed door" ordinances, and allow southerners to seek employment in the north. Khartoum also nullified the prohibition against Muslim proselytizing in the south and introduced Arabic in the south as the official administration language.

Some southern British colonial officials responded to the Sudan Administrative Conference by charging that northern agitation had influenced the conferees and that no voice had been heard at the conference in support of retaining the separate development policy. These British officers argued that northern domination of the south would result in a southern rebellion against the government. Khartoum therefore convened a conference at Juba to allay the fears of southern leaders and British officials in the south and to assure them that a postindependence government would safeguard southern political and cultural rights.

Despite these promises, an increasing number of southerners expressed concern that northerners would overwhelm them. In particular, they resented the imposition of Arabic as the official language of administration, which deprived most of the few educated English-speaking southerners of the opportunity to enter public service. They also felt threatened by the replacement of trusted British district commissioners with unsympathetic northerners. After the government had replaced several hundred colonial officials with Sudanese, only four of whom were southerners, the southern elite abandoned hope of a peaceful, unified, independent Sudan.

The hostility of southerners toward the northern Arab majority surfaced violently when southern army units mutinied in August 1955 to protest their transfer to garrisons under northern officers. The rebellious troops killed several hundred northerners, including government officials, army officers, and merchants. The government quickly suppressed the revolt and eventually executed seventy southerners for sedition. But this harsh reaction failed to pacify the south, as some of the mutineers escaped to remote areas and organized resistance to the Arab-dominated government of Sudan.

Independent Sudan

The Azhari government temporarily halted progress toward self-determination for Sudan, hoping to promote unity with Egypt. Although his pro-Egyptian NUP had won a majority in the 1953 parliamentary elections, Azhari realized that popular opinion had shifted against union with Egypt. As a result, Azhari, who had been the major spokesman for the ''unity of the Nile Valley,'' reversed the NUP's stand and supported Sudanese independence. On December 19, 1955, the Sudanese parliament, under Azhari's leadership, unanimously adopted a declaration of independence; on January 1, 1956, Sudan became an independent republic. Azhari called for the withdrawal of foreign troops and requested that the condominium powers sponsor a plebiscite in advance of the scheduled date.

The Politics of Independence

Sudan achieved independence without the rival political parties having agreed on the form and content of a permanent constitution. Instead, the Constituent Assembly adopted a document known as the Transitional Constitution, which replaced the governor general as head of state with a five-member Supreme Commission that

*As Sudd, the world's largest swamp, found in south-central Sudan
along the White Nile River
Courtesy Robert O. Collins*

was elected by a parliament composed of an indirectly elected Senate and a popularly elected House of Representatives. The Transitional Constitution also allocated executive power to the prime minister, who was nominated by the House of Representatives and confirmed in office by the Supreme Commission.

Although it achieved independence without conflict, Sudan inherited many problems from the condominium. Chief among these was the status of the civil service. The government placed Sudanese in the administration and provided compensation and pensions for British officers of the Sudan Political Service who left the country; it retained those who could not be replaced, mostly technicians and teachers. Khartoum achieved this transformation quickly and with a minimum of turbulence, although southerners resented the replacement of British administrators in the south with northern Sudanese. To advance their interests, many southern leaders concentrated their efforts in Khartoum, where they hoped to win constitutional concessions. Although determined to resist what they perceived to be Arab imperialism, they were opposed to violence. Most southern representatives supported provincial autonomy and warned that failure to win legal concessions would drive the south to rebellion.

The parliamentary regime introduced plans to expand the country's education, economic, and transportation sectors. To achieve these goals, Khartoum needed foreign economic and technical assistance, to which the United States made an early commitment. Conversations between the two governments had begun in mid-1957, and the parliament ratified a United States aid agreement in July 1958. Washington hoped this agreement would reduce Sudan's excessive reliance on a one-crop (cotton) economy and would facilitate the development of the country's transportation and communications infrastructure.

The prime minister formed a coalition government in February 1956, but he alienated the Khatmiyyah by supporting increasingly secular government policies. In June some Khatmiyyah members who had defected from the NUP established the People's Democratic Party (PDP) under Mirghani's leadership. The Umma and the PDP combined in parliament to bring down the Azhari government. With support from the two parties and backing from the Ansar and the Khatmiyyah, Abd Allah Khalil put together a coalition government.

Major issues confronting Khalil's coalition government included winning agreement on a permanent constitution, stabilizing the south, encouraging economic development, and improving relations with Egypt. Strains within the Umma-PDP coalition hampered the government's ability to make progress on these matters. The Umma, for example, wanted the proposed constitution to institute a presidential form of government on the assumption that Abd ar Rahman al Mahdi would be elected the first president. Consensus was lacking about the country's economic future. A poor cotton harvest followed the 1957 bumper cotton crop, which Sudan had been unable to sell at a good price in a glutted market. This downturn depleted Sudan's reserves and caused unrest over government-imposed economic restrictions. To overcome these problems and finance future development projects, the Umma called for greater reliance on foreign aid. The PDP, however, objected to this strategy because it promoted unacceptable foreign influence in Sudan. The PDP's philosophy reflected the Arab nationalism espoused by Gamal Abdul Nasser, who had replaced Egyptian leader Naguib in 1954. Despite these policy differences, the Umma-PDP coalition lasted for the remaining year of the parliament's tenure. Moreover, after the parliament adjourned, the two parties promised to maintain a common front for the 1958 elections.

The electorate gave a plurality in both houses to the Umma and an overall majority to the Umma-PDP coalition. The NUP, however, won nearly one-quarter of the seats, largely from urban centers and from Gezira Scheme agricultural workers. In the south, the vote represented a rejection of the men who had cooperated with the government—voters defeated all three southerners in the preelection cabinet—and a victory for advocates of autonomy within a federal system. Resentment against the government's taking over mission schools and against the measures used in suppressing the 1955 mutiny contributed to the election of several candidates who had been implicated in the rebellion.

After the new parliament convened, Khalil again formed an Umma-PDP coalition government. Unfortunately, factionalism, corruption, and vote fraud dominated parliamentary deliberations at a time when the country needed decisive action with regard to the proposed constitution and the future of the south. As a result, the Umma-PDP coalition failed to exercise effective leadership.

Another issue that divided the parliament concerned Sudanese-United States relations. In March 1958, Khalil signed a technical assistance agreement with the United States. When he presented the pact to parliament for ratification, he discovered that the NUP wanted to use the issue to defeat the Umma-PDP coalition and that many PDP delegates opposed the agreement. Nevertheless, the Umma, with the support of some PDP and southern delegates, managed to obtain approval of the agreement.

Factionalism and bribery in parliament, coupled with the government's inability to resolve Sudan's many social, political, and economic problems, increased popular disillusion with democratic government. Specific complaints included Khartoum's decision to sell cotton at a price above world market prices. This policy resulted in low sales of cotton, the commodity from which Sudan derived most of its income. Restrictions on imports imposed to take pressure off depleted foreign exchange reserves caused consternation among town dwellers who had become accustomed to buying foreign goods. Moreover, rural northerners also suffered from an embargo that Egypt placed on imports of cattle, camels, and dates from Sudan. Growing popular discontent caused many antigovernment demonstrations in Khartoum. Egypt also criticized Khalil and suggested that it might support a coup against his government. Meanwhile, reports circulated in Khartoum that the Umma and the NUP were near agreement on a new coalition that would exclude the PDP and Khalil.

On November 17, 1958, the day parliament was to convene, a military coup occurred. Khalil, himself a retired army general, planned the preemptive coup in conjunction with leading Umma members and the army's two senior generals, Ibrahim Abbud and Ahmad Abd al Wahab, who became leaders of the military regime.

Abbud immediately pledged to resolve all disputes with Egypt, including the long-standing problem of the status of the Nile River. Abbud abandoned the previous government's unrealistic policies regarding the sale of cotton. He also appointed a constitutional commission, headed by the chief justice, to draft a permanent constitution. Abbud maintained, however, that political parties only served as vehicles for personal ambitions and that they would not be reestablished when civilian rule was restored.

The Abbud Military Government, 1958–64

The coup removed political decision making from the control of the civilian politicians. Abbud created the Supreme Council of the Armed Forces to rule Sudan. This body contained officers affiliated with the Ansar and the Khatmiyyah. Abbud belonged to the Khatmiyyah, whereas Abd al Wahab was a member of the Ansar. Until Abd al Wahab's removal in March 1959, the Ansar were the stronger of the two groups in the government.

The regime benefited during its first year in office from successful marketing of the cotton crop. Abbud also profited from the settlement of the Nile waters dispute with Egypt and the improvement of relations between the two countries. Under the military regime, the influence of the Ansar and the Khatmiyyah lessened. The strongest religious leader, Abd ar Rahman al Mahdi, died in early 1959. His son and successor, the elder Sadiq al Mahdi, failed to enjoy the respect accorded his father. When Sadiq died two years later, Ansar religious and political leadership divided between his brother, Imam Al Hadi al Mahdi, and his son, the younger Sadiq al Mahdi.

Despite the Abbud regime's early successes, opposition elements remained powerful. In 1959 dissident military officers made three attempts to displace the Abbud government and to establish a ''popular government.'' Although the courts sentenced the leaders of these attempted coups to life imprisonment, discontent in the military continued to hamper the government's performance. In particular, the Sudanese Communist Party (SCP), which supported the attempted coups, gained a reputation as an effective antigovernment organization. To compound its problems, the Abbud regime lacked dynamism and the ability to stabilize the country. Its failure to place capable civilian advisers in positions of authority, to launch a credible economic and social development program, and to gain the army's support created an atmosphere that encouraged political turbulence.

Abbud's southern policy proved to be his undoing. The government suppressed expressions of religious and cultural differences and bolstered attempts to arabize society. In February 1964, for example, Abbud ordered the mass explusion of foreign missionaries from the south. He then closed parliament to cut off outlets for southern complaints. Southern leaders had renewed in 1963 the armed struggle against the Sudanese government that had continued sporadically since 1955. The rebellion was spearheaded from 1963 by guerrilla forces known as the Anya Nya (the name of a poisonous concoction).

Return to Civilian Rule, 1964–69

Recognizing its inability to quell growing southern discontent, the Abbud regime asked the civilian sector to submit proposals for a solution to the southern problem. However, criticism of government policy quickly went beyond the southern issue and included Abbud's handling of other problems, such as the economy and education. Government attempts to silence these protests, which were centered in the University of Khartoum, brought a reaction not only from teachers and students but also from Khartoum's civil servants and trade unionists. The so-called October Revolution of 1964 centered around a general strike that spread throughout the country. Strike leaders identified themselves as the National Front for Professionals. Along with some former politicians, they formed the leftist United National Front (UNF), which made contact with dissident army officers.

After several days of rioting that resulted in many deaths, Abbud dissolved the government and the Supreme Council of the Armed Forces. UNF leaders and army commanders who planned the transition from military to civilian rule selected a nonpolitical senior civil servant, Sirr al Khatim al Khalifa, as prime minister to head a transitional government.

The new civilian regime, which operated under the 1956 Transitional Constitution, tried to end political factionalism by establishing a coalition government. There was continued popular hostility to the reappearance of political parties, however, because of their divisiveness during the Abbud regime. Although the new government allowed all parties, including the SCP, to operate, only five of fifteen posts in Khatim's cabinet went to party politicians. The prime minister gave two positions to nonparty southerners and the remaining eight to members of the National Front for Professionals, which included several communists.

Eventually two political parties emerged to represent the south. The Sudan African National Union (SANU), founded in 1963 and led by William Deng and Saturino Lahure, a Roman Catholic priest, operated among refugee groups and guerrilla forces. The

37

Southern Front, a mass organization led by Stanislaus Paya-sama that had worked underground during the Abbud regime, functioned openly within the southern provinces. After the collapse of government-sponsored peace conferences in 1965, Deng's wing of SANU—known locally as SANU-William—and the Southern Front coalesced to take part in the parliamentary elections. SANU remained active in parliament for the next four years as a voice for southern regional autonomy within a unified state. Exiled SANU leaders balked at Deng's moderate approach and formed the Azania Liberation Front based in Kampala, Uganda.

Anya Nya leaders remained aloof from political movements. The guerrillas were fragmented by ethnic and religious differences. Additionally, conflicts surfaced within Anya Nya between older leaders who had been in the bush since 1955, and younger, better educated men like Joseph Lagu, a former Sudanese army captain, who eventually became a strong guerrilla leader, largely because of his ability to get arms from Israel.

The government scheduled national elections for March 1965 and announced that the new parliament's task would be to prepare a new constitution. The deteriorating southern security situation prevented elections from being conducted in that region, however, and the political parties split on the question of whether elections should be held in the north as scheduled or postponed until the whole country could vote. The PDP and SCP, both fearful of losing votes, wanted to postpone the elections, as did southern elements loyal to Khartoum. Their opposition forced the government to resign. The president of the reinstated Supreme Commission, who had replaced Abbud as chief of state, directed that the elections be held wherever possible. The PDP rejected this decision and boycotted the elections.

The 1965 election results were inconclusive. Apart from a low voter turnout, there was a confusing overabundance of candidates on the ballots. As a result, few of those elected won a majority of the votes cast. The Umma captured 75 out of 158 parliamentary seats while its NUP ally took 52 of the remainder. The two parties formed a coalition cabinet in June headed by Umma leader Muhammad Ahmad Mahjub, whereas Azhari, the NUP leader, became the Supreme Commission's permanent president and chief of state.

The Mahjub government had two goals: progress toward solving the southern problem and the removal of communists from positions of power. The army launched a major offensive to crush the rebellion and in the process augmented its reputation for brutality among the southerners. Many southerners reported government atrocities against civilians, especially at Juba and Waw. Sudanese army troops also burned churches and huts, closed schools, and destroyed crops and cattle. To achieve his second objective, Mahjub succeeded in having parliament approve a decree that abolished the SCP and deprived the eleven communists of their seats.

In October 1965, the Umma-NUP coalition collapsed because of a disagreement over whether Mahjub, as prime minister, or Azhari, as president, should conduct Sudan's foreign relations. Mahjub continued in office for another eight months but resigned in July 1966 after a parliamentary vote of censure, which resulted in a split in the Umma. The traditional wing led by Mahjub, under the Imam Al Hadi al Mahjub's spiritual leadership, opposed the party's majority. The latter group professed loyalty to the imam's nephew, the younger Sadiq al Mahdi, who was the Umma's official leader and who rejected religious sectarianism. Sadiq became prime minister with backing from his own Umma wing and from NUP allies.

The Sadiq al Mahdi government, supported by a sizable parliamentary majority, sought to reduce regional disparities by organizing economic development. Sadiq al Mahdi also planned to use his personal rapport with southern leaders to engineer a peace agreement with the insurgents. He proposed to replace the Supreme Commission with a president and a southern vice president and called for the approval of autonomy for the southern provinces.

The educated elite and segments of the army opposed Sadiq al Mahdi because of his gradualist approach to Sudan's political, economic, and social problems. Leftist student organizations and the trade unions demanded the creation of a socialist state. Although these elements lacked widespread popular support, they represented an influential portion of educated public opinion. Their resentment of Sadiq increased when he refused to honor a Supreme Court ruling that overturned legislation banning the SCP and ousting communists elected to parliamentary seats. In December 1966, a coup attempt by communists and a small army unit against the government failed. The government subsequently arrested many communists and army personnel.

In March 1967, the government held elections in thirty-six constituencies in pacified southern areas. The Sadiq al Mahdi wing of the Umma won fifteen seats, the federalist SANU ten, and the NUP five. Despite this apparent boost in his support, however, Sadiq's position in parliament had become tenuous because of concessions he promised to the south in order to bring an end to the civil war. The Umma traditionalist wing opposed Sadiq al Mahdi

because of his support for constitutional guarantees of religious freedom and his refusal to declare Sudan an Islamic state. When the
traditionalists and the NUP withdrew their support, his government fell. In May 1967, Mahjub became prime minister and head
of a coalition government whose cabinet included members of his
wing of the Umma, of the NUP, and of the PDP. In December
1967, the PDP and the NUP formed the Democratic Unionist Party
(DUP) under Azhari's leadership.

By early 1968, widening divisions in the Umma threatened the
survival of the Mahjub government. Sadiq al Mahdi's wing held
a majority in parliament and could thwart any government action.
Mahjub therefore dissolved parliament. However, Sadiq refused
to recognize the legitimacy of the prime minister's action. As a
result, two governments functioned in Khartoum—one meeting
in the parliament building and the other on its lawn—both of which
claimed to represent the legislature's will. The army commander
requested clarification from the Supreme Court regarding which
of them had authority to issue orders. The court backed Mahjub's
dissolution; the government scheduled new elections for April.

Although the DUP won 101 of 218 seats, no single party controlled a parliamentary majority. Thirty-six seats went to the Umma
traditionalists, thirty to the Sadiq wing, and twenty-five to the two
southern parties—SANU and the Southern Front. The SCP secretary general, Abd al Khaliq Mahjub, also won a seat. In a major
setback, Sadiq lost his own seat to a traditionalist rival.

Because it lacked a majority, the DUP concluded an alliance with
Umma traditionalists, who received the prime ministership for their
leader, Muhammad Ahmad Mahjub, and four other cabinet posts.
The coalition's program included plans for government reorganization, closer ties with the Arab world, and renewed economic development efforts, particularly in the southern provinces. The
Muhammad Ahmad Mahjub government also accepted military, technical, and economic aid from the Soviet Union. Sadiq
al Mahdi's wing of the Umma formed the small parliamentary opposition. When it refused to participate in efforts to complete the
draft constitution, already ten years overdue, the government
retaliated by closing the opposition's newspaper and clamping down
on pro-Sadiq demonstrations in Khartoum.

By late 1968, the two Umma wings agreed to support the Ansar
chief Imam Al Hadi al Mahdi in the 1969 presidential election.
At the same time, the DUP announced that Azhari also would seek
the presidency. The communists and other leftists aligned themselves behind the presidential candidacy of former Chief Justice

Babikr Awadallah, whom they viewed as an ally because he had ruled against the government when it attempted to outlaw the SCP.

The Nimeiri Era, 1969-85

On May 25, 1969, several young officers, calling themselves the Free Officers' Movement, seized power. At the conspiracy's core were nine officers led by Colonel Jaafar an Nimeiri, who had been implicated in plots against the Abbud regime. Nimeiri's coup preempted plots by other groups, most of which involved army factions supported by the SCP, Arab nationalists, or conservative religious groups. He justified the coup on the grounds that civilian politicians had paralyzed the decision-making process, had failed to deal with the country's economic and regional problems, and had left Sudan without a permanent constitution.

Revolutionary Command Council

The coup leaders, joined by Awadallah, the former chief justice who had been privy to the coup, constituted themselves as the ten-member Revolutionary Command Council (RCC), which possessed collective executive authority under Nimeiri's chairmanship. On assuming control, the RCC proclaimed the establishment of a "democratic republic" dedicated to advancing independent "Sudanese socialism." The RCC's first acts included the suspension of the Transitional Constitution, the abolition of all government institutions, and the banning of political parties. The RCC also nationalized many industries, businesses, and banks. Furthermore, Nimeiri ordered the arrest of sixty-three civilian politicians and forcibly retired senior army officers.

Awadallah, appointed prime minister to form a new government to implement RCC policy directives, wanted to dispel the notion that the coup had installed a military dictatorship. He presided over a twenty-one-member cabinet that included only three officers from the RCC, among them its chairman, Nimeiri, who was also defense minister. The cabinet's other military members held the portfolios for internal security and communications. Nine members of the Awadallah regime were allegedly communists, including one of the two southerners in the cabinet, John Garang, minister of supply and later minister for southern affairs. Others identified themselves as Marxists. Since the RCC lacked political and administrative experience, the communists played a significant role in shaping government policies and programs. Despite the influence of individual SCP members, the RCC claimed that its cooperation with the party was a matter of convenience.

41

In November 1969, after he claimed the regime could not survive without communist assistance, Awadallah lost the prime ministership. Nimeiri, who became head of a largely civilian government in addition to being chief of state, succeeded him. Awadallah retained his position as RCC deputy chairman and remained in the government as foreign minister and as an important link with leftist elements.

Conservative forces, led by the Ansar, posed the greatest threat to the RCC. Imam Al Hadi al Mahdi had withdrawn to his Aba Island stronghold (in the Nile, near Khartoum) in the belief that the government had decided to strike at the Ansar movement. The imam had demanded a return to democratic government, the exclusion of communists from power, and an end to RCC rule. In March 1970, hostile Ansar crowds prevented Nimeiri from visiting the island for talks with the imam. Fighting subsequently erupted between government forces and as many as 30,000 Ansar. When the Ansar ignored an ultimatum to surrender, army units with air support assaulted Aba Island. About 3,000 people died during the battle. The imam escaped only to be killed while attempting to cross the border into Ethiopia. The government exiled Sadiq al Mahdi to Egypt, where Nasser promised to keep him under guard to prevent him from succeeding his uncle as head of the Ansar movement.

After neutralizing this conservative opposition, the RCC concentrated on consolidating its political organization to phase out communist participation in the government. This strategy prompted an internal debate within the SCP. The orthodox wing, led by party secretary general Abd al Khaliq Mahjub, demanded a popular front government with communists participating as equal partners. The National Communist wing, on the other hand, supported cooperation with the government.

Soon after the army had crushed the Ansar at Aba Island, Nimeiri moved against the SCP. He ordered the deportation of Abd al Khaliq Mahjub. Then, when the SCP secretary general returned to Sudan illegally after several months abroad, Nimeiri placed him under house arrest. In March 1971, Nimeiri indicated that trade unions, a traditional communist stronghold, would be placed under government control. The RCC also banned communist-affiliated student, women's, and professional organizations. Additionally, Nimeiri announced the planned formation of a national political movement called the Sudan Socialist Union (SSU), which would assume control of all political parties, including the SCP. After this speech, the government arrested the SCP's central committee and other leading communists.

The SCP, however, retained a covert organization that was not damaged in the sweep. Before further action could be taken against the party, the SCP launched a coup against Nimeiri. The coup occurred on July 19, 1971, when one of the plotters, Major Hisham al Atta, surprised Nimeiri and the RCC meeting in the presidential palace and seized them along with a number of pro-Nimeiri officers. Atta named a seven-member revolutionary council, in which communists ranked prominently, to serve as the national government. Three days after the coup, however, loyal army units stormed the palace, rescued Nimeiri, and arrested Atta and his confederates. Nimeiri, who blamed the SCP for the coup, ordered the arrest of hundreds of communists and dissident military officers. The government subsequently executed some of these individuals and imprisoned many others.

Having survived the SCP-inspired coup, Nimeiri reaffirmed his commitment to establishing a socialist state. A provisional constitution, published in August 1971, described Sudan as a "socialist democracy" and provided for a presidential form of government to replace the RCC. A plebiscite the following month elected Nimeiri to a six-year term as president.

The Southern Problem

The origins of the civil war in the south date back to the 1950s. On August 18, 1955, the Equatoria Corps, a military unit composed of southerners, mutinied at Torit. Rather than surrender to Sudanese government authorities, many mutineers disappeared into hiding with their weapons, marking the beginning of the first war in southern Sudan. By the late 1960s, the war had resulted in the deaths of about 500,000 people. Several hundred thousand more southerners hid in the bush or escaped to refugee camps in neighboring countries.

By 1969 the rebels had developed foreign contacts to obtain weapons and supplies. Israel, for example, trained Anya Nya recruits and shipped weapons via Ethiopia and Uganda to the rebels. Anya Nya also purchased arms from Congolese rebels and international arms dealers with monies collected in the south and from among southern Sudanese exile communities in the Middle East, Western Europe, and North America. The rebels also captured arms, equipment, and supplies from government troops.

Militarily, Anya Nya controlled much of the southern countryside while government forces occupied the region's major towns. The guerrillas operated at will from remote camps. However, rebel units were too small and scattered to be highly effective in any single area. Estimates of Anya Nya personnel strength ranged from 5,000 to 10,000.

Government operations against the rebels declined after the 1969 coup. However, when negotiations failed to result in a settlement, Khartoum increased troop strength in the south to about 12,000 in 1969, and intensified military activity throughout the region. Although the Soviet Union had concluded a US$100 million to US$150 million arms agreement with Sudan in August 1968, which included T-55 tanks, armored personnel carriers, and aircraft, the nation had not delivered any equipment to Khartoum by May 1969. During this period, Sudan obtained some Soviet-manufactured weapons from Egypt, most of which went to the Sudanese air force. By the end of 1969, however, the Soviet Union had shipped unknown quantities of 85mm antiaircraft guns, sixteen MiG-21s, and five Antonov-24 transport aircraft. Over the next two years, the Soviet Union delivered an impressive array of equipment to Sudan, including T-54, T-55, T-56, and T-59 tanks; and BTR-40 and BTR-152 light armored vehicles (see Foreign Military Assistance, ch. 5).

In 1971 Joseph Lagu, who had become the leader of southern forces opposed to Khartoum, proclaimed the creation of the Southern Sudan Liberation Movement (SSLM). Anya Nya leaders united behind him, and nearly all exiled southern politicians supported the SSLM. Although the SSLM created a governing infrastructure throughout many areas of southern Sudan, real power remained with Anya Nya, with Lagu at its head.

Despite his political problems, Nimeiri remained committed to ending the southern insurgency. He believed he could stop the fighting and stabilize the region by granting regional self-government and undertaking economic development in the south. By October 1971, Khartoum had established contact with the SSLM. After considerable consultation, a conference between SSLM and Sudanese government delegations convened at Addis Ababa, Ethiopia, in February 1972. Initially, the two sides were far apart, the southerners demanding a federal state with a separate southern government and an army that would come under the federal president's command only in response to an external threat to Sudan. Eventually, however, the two sides, with the help of Ethiopia's Emperor Haile Selassie, reached an agreement.

The Addis Ababa accords guaranteed autonomy for a southern region—composed of the three provinces of Equatoria (present-day Al Istiwai), Bahr al Ghazal, and Upper Nile (present-day Aali an Nil)—under a regional president appointed by the national president on the recommendation of an elected Southern Regional

Blue Nile at the border with Ethiopia
Courtesy Robert O. Collins

Assembly. The High Executive Council or cabinet named by the regional president would be responsible for all aspects of government in the region except such areas as defense, foreign affairs, currency and finance, economic and social planning, and inter-regional concerns, authority over which would be retained by the national government in which southerners would be represented. Southerners, including qualified Anya Nya veterans, would be incorporated into a 12,000-man southern command of the Sudanese army under equal numbers of northern and southern officers. The accords also recognized Arabic as Sudan's official language and English as the south's principal language, which would be used in administration and would be taught in the schools.

Although many SSLM leaders opposed the settlement, Lagu approved its terms and both sides agreed to a cease-fire. The national government issued a decree legalizing the agreement and creating an international armistice commission to ensure the well-being of returning southern refugees. Khartoum also announced an amnesty, retroactive to 1955. The two sides signed the Addis Ababa accords on March 27, 1972, which was thereafter celebrated as National Unity Day.

Political Developments

After the settlement in the south, Nimeiri attempted to mend fences with northern Muslim religious groups. The government undertook administrative decentralization, popular with the Ansar, that favored rural over urban areas, where leftist activism was most evident. Khartoum also reaffirmed Islam's special position in the country, recognized the sharia as the source of all legislation, and released some members of religious orders who had been incarcerated. However, a reconciliation with conservative groups, which had organized outside Sudan under Sadiq al Mahdi's leadership and were later known as the National Front, eluded Nimeiri.

In August 1972, Nimeiri sought to consolidate his position by creating a Constituent Assembly to draft a permanent constitution. He then asked for the government's resignation to allow him to appoint a cabinet whose members were drawn from the Constituent Assembly. Nimeiri excluded individuals who had opposed the southern settlement or who had been identified with the SSU's pro-Egyptian faction.

In May 1973, the Constituent Assembly promulgated a draft constitution. This document provided for a continuation of presidential government, recognized the SSU as the only authorized political organization, and supported regional autonomy for the south. The constitution also stipulated that voters were to choose members for the 250-seat People's Assembly from an SSU-approved slate. Although it cited Islam as Sudan's official religion, the constitution admitted Christianity as the faith of a large number of Sudanese citizens (see Christianity, ch. 2). In May 1974, voters selected 125 members for the assembly; SSU-affiliated occupational and professional groups named 100; and the president appointed the remaining 25.

Discontent with Nimeiri's policies and the increased military role in government escalated as a result of food shortages and the southern settlement, which many Muslim conservatives regarded as surrender. In 1973 and 1974 there were unsuccessful coup attempts against Nimeiri. Muslims and leftist students also staged strikes against the government. In September 1974, Nimeiri responded to this unrest by declaring a state of emergency, purging the SSU, and arresting large numbers of dissidents. Nimeiri also replaced some cabinet members with military personnel loyal to him.

Conservative opposition to Nimeiri coalesced in the National Front, formed in 1974. The National Front included people from Sadiq's wing of Umma; the NUP; and the Islamic Charter Front, then the political arm of the Muslim Brotherhood, an Islamic activist movement. Their activity crystallized in a July 1976 Ansar-inspired coup attempt. Government soldiers quickly restored order by killing more than 700 rebels in Khartoum and arresting scores of dissidents, including many prominent religious leaders. Despite this unrest, in 1977 Sudanese voters reelected Nimeiri for a second six-year term as president.

National Reconciliation

Following the 1976 coup attempt, Nimeiri and his opponents adopted more conciliatory policies. In early 1977, government officials met with the National Front in London, and arranged for a conference between Nimeiri and Sadiq al Mahdi in Port Sudan. In what became known as the "national reconciliation," the two leaders signed an eight-point agreement that readmitted the opposition to national life in return for the dissolution of the National Front. The agreement also restored civil liberties, freed political prisoners, reaffirmed Sudan's nonaligned foreign policy, and promised to reform local government. As a result of the reconciliation, the government released about 1,000 detainees and granted an amnesty to Sadiq al Mahdi. The SSU also admitted former supporters of the National Front to its ranks. Sadiq renounced multiparty politics and urged his followers to work within the regime's one-party system.

The first test of national reconciliation occurred during the February 1978 People's Assembly elections. Nimeiri authorized returning exiles who had been associated with the old Umma Party, the DUP, and the Muslim Brotherhood to stand for election as independent candidates. These independents won 140 of 304 seats, leading many observers to applaud Nimeiri's efforts to democratize Sudan's political system. However, the People's Assembly elections marked the beginning of further political decline. The SSU's failure to sponsor official candidates weakened party discipline and prompted many assembly deputies who also were SSU members to claim that the party had betrayed them. As a result, an increasing number of assembly deputies used their offices to advance personal rather than national interests.

The end of the SSU's political monopoly, coupled with rampant corruption at all levels of government, cast increasing doubt on Nimeiri's ability to govern Sudan. To preserve his regime, Nimeiri adopted a more dictatorial leadership style. He ordered the State Security Organisation to imprison without trial thousands of opponents and dissidents (see Security Organizations, ch. 5). Nimeiri also dismissed or transferred any minister or senior military officer who appeared to be developing his own power base. Nimeiri selected replacements based on their loyalty to him rather than on their abilities. This strategy caused the president to lose touch with popular feeling and the country's deteriorated political situation.

On June 5, 1983, Nimeiri sought to counter the south's growing political power by redividing the Southern Region into the three old provinces of Bahr al Ghazal, Al Istiwai, and Aali an Nil; he had suspended the Southern Regional Assembly almost two years earlier. The southern-based Sudanese People's Liberation Movement (SPLM) and its military wing, the Sudanese People's Liberation Army (SPLA), which emerged in mid-1983, unsuccessfully opposed this redivision and called for the creation of a new united Sudan.

Within a few months, in September 1983 Nimeiri proclaimed the sharia as the basis of the Sudanese legal system. Nimeiri's decrees, which became known as the September Laws, were bitterly resented both by secularized Muslims and by the predominantly non-Muslim southerners. The SPLM denounced the sharia and the executions and amputations ordered by religious courts. Meanwhile, the security situation in the south had deteriorated so much that by the end of 1983 it amounted to a resumption of the civil war.

In early 1985, antigovernment discontent resulted in a general strike in Khartoum. Demonstrators opposed rising food, gasoline, and transport costs. The general strike paralyzed the country. Nimeiri, who was on a visit to the United States, was unable to suppress the rapidly growing demonstrations against his regime.

The Transitional Military Council

The combination of the south's redivision, the introduction throughout the country of the sharia, the renewed civil war, and growing economic problems eventually contributed to Nimeiri's downfall. On April 6, 1985, a group of military officers, led by Lieutenant General Abd ar Rahman Siwar adh Dhahab, overthrew Nimeiri, who took refuge in Egypt. Three days later, Dhahab authorized the creation of a fifteen-man Transitional Military Council (TMC) to rule Sudan. During its first few weeks in power, the TMC suspended the constitution; dissolved the SSU, the secret police, and the parliament and regional assemblies; dismissed regional governors and their ministers; and released hundreds of political detainees from Kober Prison. Dhahab also promised to negotiate an end to the southern civil war and to relinquish power to a civilian government in twelve months. The general populace welcomed and supported the new regime. Despite the TMC's energetic beginning, it soon became evident that Dhahab lacked the skills to resolve Sudan's economic problems, restore peace to the south, and establish national unity.

By the time Dhahab seized power, Sudan's economy was in shambles. The country's international debt was approximately US$9 billion. Agricultural and industrial projects funded by the International Monetary Fund (IMF—see Glossary) and the World Bank (see Glossary) remained in the planning stages. Most factories operated at less than 50 percent of capacity, and agricultural output had dropped by 50 percent since 1960. Moreover, famine threatened vast areas of southern and western Sudan.

The TMC lacked a realistic strategy to resolve these problems. The Dhahab government refused to accept IMF economic austerity measures. As a result, the IMF, which influenced nearly all bilateral and multilateral donors, in February 1986, declared Sudan bankrupt. Efforts to attract a US$6 billion twenty-five-year investment from the Arab Fund for Economic and Social Development failed when Sudan mismanaged an initial US$2.3 billion investment. A rapid expansion of the money supply and the TMC's inability to control prices caused a soaring inflation rate. Although he appealed to forty donor and relief agencies for emergency food shipments, Dhahab was unable to prevent famine from claiming an estimated 400,000 to 500,000 lives. He also failed to end hostilities in the south, which constituted the major drain on Sudan's limited resources.

Shortly after taking power, Dhahab adopted a conciliatory approach toward the south. Among other things, he declared a unilateral cease-fire, called for direct talks with the SPLM, and offered an amnesty to rebel fighters. The TMC recognized the need for special development efforts in the south and proposed a national conference to review the southern problem. However, Dhahab's refusal to repeal the sharia negated these overtures and convinced SPLM leader John Garang that the Sudanese government still wanted to subjugate the south.

Despite this gulf, both sides continued to work for a peaceful resolution of the southern problem. In March 1986, the Sudanese government and the SPLM produced the Koka Dam Declaration, which called for a Sudan "free from racism, tribalism, sectarianism and all causes of discrimination and disparity." The declaration also demanded the repeal of the sharia and the opening of a constitutional conference. All major political parties and organizations, with the exception of the Democratic Unionist Party (DUP) and the National Islamic Front (NIF), supported the Koka Dam Declaration. To avoid a confrontation with the DUP and the NIF, Dhahab decided to leave the sharia question to the new civilian government. Meanwhile, the SPLA kept up the military pressure on the Sudanese government, especially in Aali an Nil, Bahr al Ghazal, and Al Istiwai provinces.

The TMC's greatest failure concerned its inability to form a national political consensus. In late April 1985, negotiations between the TMC and the Alliance of Professional and Trade Unions resulted in the establishment of a civilian cabinet under the direction of Dr. Gazuli Dafalla. The cabinet, which was subordinate to the TMC, devoted itself to conducting the government's daily business and to preparing for the election. Although it contained three southerners who belonged to the newly formed Southern Sudanese Political Association, the cabinet failed to win the loyalty of most southerners, who believed the TMC only reflected the policies of the deposed Nimeiri. As a result, Sudan remained a divided nation.

The other factor that prevented the emergence of a national political consensus concerned party factionalism. After sixteen years of one-party rule, most Sudanese favored the revival of the multiparty system. In the aftermath of Nimeiri's overthrow, approximately forty political parties registered with the TMC and announced their intention to participate in national politics. The political parties ranged from those committed to revolutionary socialism to those that supported Islamism. Of these latter, the NIF had succeeded the Islamic Charter Front as the main vehicle for the Muslim Brotherhood's political aspirations. However, policy disagreements over the sharia, the southern civil war, and the country's future direction contributed to the confusion that characterized Sudan's national politics.

In this troubled atmosphere, Dhahab sanctioned the promised April 1986 general election, which the authorities spread over a twelve-day period and postponed in thirty-seven southern constituencies because of the civil war. The Umma Party, headed by Sadiq al Mahdi, won ninety-nine seats. The DUP, which was led after the April 1985 uprising by Khatmiyyah leader Muhammad Uthman al Mirghani, gained sixty-four seats. Dr. Hassan Abd Allah at Turabi's NIF obtained fifty-one seats. Regional political parties from the south, the Nuba Mountains, and the Red Sea Hills won lesser numbers of seats. The Sudanese Communist Party (SCP) and other radical parties failed to score any significant victories.

Sadiq al Mahdi and Coalition Governments

In June 1986, Sadiq al Mahdi formed a coalition government with the Umma, the DUP, the NIF, and four southern parties. Unfortunately, however, Sadiq proved to be a weak leader and incapable of governing Sudan. Party factionalism, corruption, personal rivalries, scandals, and political instability characterized the Sadiq regime. After less than a year in office, Sadiq al Mahdi dismissed the government because it had failed to draft a new penal code to replace the sharia, reach an agreement with the IMF, end the civil war in the south, or devise a scheme to attract remittances from Sudanese expatriates. To retain the support of the DUP and the southern political parties, Sadiq formed another ineffective coalition government.

Instead of removing the ministers who had been associated with the failures of the first coalition government, Sadiq al Mahdi retained thirteen of them, of whom eleven kept their previous portfolios. As a result, many Sudanese rejected the second coalition government as being a replica of the first. To make matters worse, Sadiq and DUP leader Mirghani signed an inadequate memorandum of understanding that fixed the new government's priorities as affirming the application of the sharia to Muslims, consolidating the Islamic banking system, and changing the national flag and national emblem. Furthermore, the memorandum directed the government to remove Nimeiri's name from all institutions and dismiss all officials appointed by Nimeiri to serve in international and regional organizations. As expected, antigovernment elements criticized the memorandum for not mentioning the civil war, famine, or the country's disintegrating social and economic conditions.

In August 1987, the DUP brought down the government because Sadiq al Mahdi opposed the appointment of a DUP member, Ahmad as Sayid, to the government. For the next nine months, Sadiq and Mirghani failed to agree on the composition of another coalition government. During this period, Sadiq moved closer to the NIF. However, the NIF refused to join a coalition government that included leftist elements. Moreover, Turabi indicated that the formation of a coalition government would depend on numerous factors, the most important of which were the resignation or dismissal of those serving in senior positions in the central and regional governments, the lifting of the state of emergency reimposed in July 1987, and the continuation of the Constituent Assembly.

Because of the endless debate over these issues, it was not until May 15, 1988, that a new coalition government emerged headed by Sadiq al Mahdi. Members of this coalition included the Umma, the DUP, the NIF, and some southern parties. As in the past, however, the coalition quickly disintegrated because of political bickering among its members. Major disagreements included the NIF's demand that it be given the post of commissioner of Khartoum, the inability to establish criteria for the selection of regional governors, and the NIF's opposition to the replacement of senior military officers and the chief of staff of the executive branch.

In November 1988, another more explosive political issue emerged when Mirghani and the SPLM signed an agreement in Addis Ababa that included provisions for a cease-fire, the freezing of the sharia, the lifting of the state of emergency, and the abolition of all foreign political and military pacts. The two sides also proposed to convene a constitutional conference to decide Sudan's political future. The NIF opposed this agreement because of its stand on the sharia. When the government refused to support the agreement, the DUP withdrew from the coalition. Shortly thereafter armed forces commander in chief Lieutenant General Fathi Ahmad Ali presented an ultimatum, signed by 150 senior military officers, to Sadiq al Mahdi demanding that he make the coalition government more representative and that he announce terms for ending the civil war.

On March 11, 1989, Sadiq al Mahdi responded to this pressure by dissolving the government. The new coalition included the Umma, the DUP, and representatives of southern parties and the trade unions. The NIF refused to join the coalition because it was not committed to enforcing the sharia. Sadiq claimed his new government was committed to ending the southern civil war by implementing the November 1988 DUP–SPLM agreement. He also promised to mobilize government resources to bring food relief to famine areas, reduce the government's international debt, and build a national political consensus. Sadiq's inability to live up to these promises eventually caused his downfall. On June 30, 1989, Colonel (later Lieutenant General) Umar Hassan Ahmad al Bashir overthrew Sadiq and established the Revolutionary Command Council for National Salvation to rule Sudan. Bashir's commitment to imposing the sharia on the non-Muslim south and to seeking a military victory over the SPLA, however, seemed likely to keep the country divided for the foreseeable future and hamper resolution of the same problems faced by Sadiq al Mahdi. Moreover, the emergence of the NIF as a political force made compromise with the south more unlikely.

* * *

Interested readers may consult several books for a better understanding of Sudan's history. Useful surveys include P.M. Holt's and M.W. Daly's, *A History of the Sudan;* Peter Woodward's, *Sudan, 1898–1989;* and Kenneth Henderson's *Sudan Republic.* Richard Hill's *Egypt in the Sudan, 1820–1881* assesses Egypt's nineteenth century conquest and occupation of Sudan. For an excellent analysis of the British period, see M.W. Daly's *Empire on the Nile* and *Imperial Sudan.* The postindependence period is discussed in Mansour Khalid's *The Government They Deserve;* and Gabriel Warburg's *Islam, Nationalism, and Communism in a Traditional Society.* Apart from these books, the *Sudan Notes and Records* journal is essential for studying Sudan's historical development.

Over the past few years, there has been an increase in the literature about southern Sudan. Many of Robert Collins's studies are particularly useful, including *Land Beyond the Rivers; Shadows in the Grass;* and *The Waters of the Nile.* Two sympathetic assessments of southern Sudan's relationship to Khartoum are Dunstan M. Wai's, *The African-Arab Conflict in the Sudan* and Abel Alier's, *Southern Sudan.* For an Arab viewpoint, Mohamed Omer Beshir's *The Southern Sudan: Background to Conflict* and *The Southern Sudan: From Conflict to Peace* are pertinent. (For further information and complete citations, see Bibliography.)

Chapter 2. The Society and Its Environment

Dinka spearfisherman contemplates the White Nile as a food source.

THE FIRST AND OVERWHELMING impression of Sudan is its physical vastness and ethnic diversity, elements that have shaped its regional history from time immemorial. The country encompasses virtually every geographical feature, from the harsh deserts of the north to the rain forests rising on its southern borders. Like most African countries, Sudan is defined by boundaries that European powers determined at the end of the nineteenth century. The British colonial administration in Sudan, established in 1899, emphasized indirect rule by tribal shaykhs (see Glossary) and chiefs, although tribalism had been considerably weakened as an administrative institution during the Mahdist period (1884–98). This loosening of loyalties exacerbated problems in governmental structure and administration and in the peoples' identification as Sudanese. To this day, loyalty remains divided among family, clan, ethnic group, and religion, and it is difficult to forge a nation because the immensity of the land permits many of Sudan's ethnic and tribal groups to live relatively undisturbed by the central government.

The Nile is the link that runs through Sudan and influences the lives of Sudan's people, even though many of them farm and herd far from the Nile or its two main tributaries, the Blue Nile and the White Nile. Not only do nomads come to the river to water their herds and cultivators to drain off its waters for their fields, but the Nile facilitates trade, administration, and urbanization. Consequently, the confluence of the Blue Nile and the White Nile became the administrative center of a vast hinterland because the area commanded the river, its commerce, and its urban society. This location enabled the urban elites to control the scattered and often isolated population of the interior while enjoying access to the peoples of the outside world.

Although linked by dependence on the Nile, Sudan's population is divided by ethnic, linguistic, and religious differences. Many Sudanese in the north claim Arab descent and speak Arabic, but Sudanese Arabs are highly differentiated. Over many generations, they have intermingled in varying degrees with the indigenous peoples. Arabic is Sudan's official language (with Arabic and English the predominant languages in the south), but beyond Khartoum and its two neighboring cities of Omdurman and Khartoum North a variety of languages is spoken. A more unifying factor is Islam, which has spread widely among the peoples of northern Sudan. But, once again, the Sunni (see Glossary) Muslims of northern

Sudan form no monolithic bloc. Some, especially in the urban centers, are strictly orthodox Muslims, whereas others, mostly in the rural areas, are attracted more to Sufism, Islamic mysticism, in their search for Allah. Within this branch and tendency of Islam are a host of religious sects with their own Islamic rituals and syncretistic adaptations.

The Sudanese of the south are of African origin. Islam has made only modest inroads among these followers of traditional religions and of Christianity, which was spread in the twentieth century by European missionaries, and Arabic has not replaced the diverse languages of the south. The differences between north and south have usually engendered hostility, a clash of cultures that in the last 150 years has led to seemingly endless violence. The strong regional and cultural differences have inhibited nation building and have caused the civil war in the south that has raged since independence, except for a period of peace between 1972 and 1983. The distrust between Sudanese of the north and those of the south—whether elite or peasants—has deepened with the long years of hostilities. And the cost of war has drained valuable national resources at the expense of health, education, and welfare in both regions.

Physical Setting

Sudan is Africa's largest country, embracing 2,505,813 square kilometers of northeast and central Africa. It consists of a huge plain bordered on three sides by mountains: to the east the Red Sea Hills, to the west Jabal Marrah, and on the southern frontier the Didinga Hills and the Dongotona and Imatong mountains. Jutting up abruptly in the south-central region of this vast plain are the isolated Nuba Mountains and Ingessana Hills, and far to the southeast, the lone Boma Plateau near the Ethiopian border. Spanning eighteen degrees of latitude, the plain of the Sudan (see Glossary) includes from north to south significant regions with distinctive characters—northern Sudan, western Sudan, the central clay plains, eastern Sudan, the southern clay plains, the Jabal Hadid, or Ironstone Plateau, and the southern hill masses (see fig. 4).

Geographical Regions

Northern Sudan, lying between the Egyptian border and Khartoum, has two distinct parts, the desert and the Nile Valley. To the east of the Nile lies the Nubian Desert; to the west, the Libyan Desert. They are similar—stony, with sandy dunes drifting over the landscape. There is virtually no rainfall in these deserts, and in the Nubian Desert there are no oases. In the west there are a

few small watering holes, such as Bir an Natrun. Here the water table reaches the surface to form wells that provide water for nomads, caravans, and administrative patrols, although insufficient to support an oasis and inadequate to provide for a settled population. Flowing through the desert is the Nile Valley, whose alluvial strip of habitable land is no more than two kilometers wide and whose productivity depends on the annual flood.

Western Sudan is a generic term describing the regions known as Darfur and Kurdufan that comprise 850,000 square kilometers. Traditionally, this area has been regarded as a single regional unit despite the physical differences. The dominant feature throughout this immense area is the absence of perennial streams; thus, people and animals must remain within reach of permanent wells. Consequently, the population is sparse and unevenly distributed. Western Darfur is an undulating plain dominated by the volcanic massif of Jabal Marrah towering 900 meters above the Sudanic plain; the drainage from Jabal Marrah onto the plain can support a settled population. Western Darfur stands in stark contrast to northern and eastern Darfur, which are semidesert with little water either from the intermittent streams known as wadis or from wells that normally go dry during the winter months. Northwest of Darfur and continuing into Chad lies the unusual region called the *jizzu* (see Glossary), where sporadic winter rains generated from the Mediterranean frequently provide excellent grazing into January or even February. The southern region of western Sudan is known as the *qoz* (see Glossary), a land of sand dunes that in the rainy season is characterized by a rolling mantle of grass and has more reliable sources of water with its bore holes and *hafri* (sing., *hafr*— see Glossary) than does the north. A unique feature of western Sudan is the Nuba Mountain range of southeast Kurdufan in the center of the country, a conglomerate of isolated dome-shaped, sugarloaf hills that ascend steeply and abruptly from the great Sudanic plain. Many hills are isolated and extend only a few square kilometers, but there are several large hill-masses with internal valleys that cut through the mountains high above the plain.

Sudan's third distinct region is the central clay plains that stretch eastward from the Nuba Mountains to the Ethiopian frontier, broken only by the Ingessana Hills, and from Khartoum in the north to the far reaches of southern Sudan. Between the Dindar and the Rahad rivers, a low ridge slopes down from the Ethiopian highlands to break the endless skyline of the plains, and the occasional hill stands out in stark relief. The central clay plains provide the backbone of Sudan's economy because they are productive where settlements cluster around available water. Furthermore, in the heartland of the central clay plains lies the *jazirah* (see Glossary), the land between the Blue Nile and the White Nile (literally in Arabic "peninsula") where the great Gezira Scheme (also seen as Jazirah Scheme) was developed. This project grows cotton for export and has traditionally produced more than half of Sudan's revenue and export earnings.

Northeast of the central clay plains lies eastern Sudan, which is divided between desert and semidesert and includes Al Butanah, the Qash Delta, the Red Sea Hills, and the coastal plain. Al Butanah is an undulating land between Khartoum and Kassala that provides good grazing for cattle, sheep, and goats. East of Al Butanah is a peculiar geological formation known as the Qash Delta. Originally a depression, it has been filled with sand and silt brought down by the flash floods of the Qash River, creating a delta above the surrounding plain. Extending 100 kilometers north of Kassala, the whole area watered by the Qash is a rich grassland with bountiful cultivation long after the river has spent its waters on the surface of its delta. Trees and bushes provide grazing for the camels from the north, and the rich moist soil provides an abundance of food crops and cotton.

Northward beyond the Qash lie the more formidable Red Sea Hills. Dry, bleak, and cooler than the surrounding land, particularly in the heat of the Sudan summer, they stretch northward into Egypt, a jumbled mass of hills where life is hard and unpredictable for the hardy Beja inhabitants. Below the hills sprawls the coastal plain of the Red Sea, varying in width from about fifty-six kilometers in the south near Tawkar to about twenty-four kilometers near the Egyptian frontier. The coastal plain is dry and barren. It consists of rocks, and the seaward side is thick with coral reefs.

The southern clay plains, which can be regarded as an extension of the northern clay plains, extend all the way from northern Sudan to the mountains on the Sudan-Uganda frontier, and in the west from the borders of Central African Republic eastward to the Ethiopian highlands. This great Nilotic plain is broken by several distinctive features. First, the White Nile bisects the plain and provides large permanent water surfaces such as lakes Fajarial, No, and Shambe. Second, As Sudd, the world's largest swamp, provides a formidable expanse of lakes, lagoons, and aquatic plants, whose area in high flood waters exceeds 30,000 square kilometers, approximately the area of Belgium. So intractable was this *sudd* (see Glossary) as an obstacle to navigation that a passage was not discovered until the mid-nineteenth century. Then as now, As Sudd with its extreme rate of evaporation consumes on average more than half the waters that come down the White Nile from the equatorial lakes. These waters also create a flood plain known as the *toic* that provides grazing when the flood waters retreat to the permanent swamp and sluggish river, the Bahr al Jabal, as the White Nile is called here.

The land rising to the south and west of the southern clay plain is referred to as the Ironstone Plateau (Jabal Hadid), a name derived from its laterite soils and increasing elevation. The plateau rises from the west bank of the Nile, sloping gradually upward to the Congo-Nile watershed. The land is well watered, providing rich cultivation, but the streams and rivers that come down from the watershed divide and erode the land before flowing on to the Nilotic plain to flow into As Sudd. Along the streams of the watershed are the gallery forests, the beginnings of the tropical rain forests that extend far into Zaire. To the east of the Jabal Hadid and the Bahr al Jabal rise the foothills of the mountain ranges along the Sudan-Uganda border—the Imatong, Didinga, and Dongotona—which rise to more than 3,000 meters. These mountains form a stark contrast to the great plains to the north that dominate Sudan's geography.

Soils

The country's soils can be divided geographically into three categories: the sandy soils of the northern and west central areas, the clay soils of the central region, and the laterite soils of the south. Less extensive and widely separated, but of major economic importance, is a fourth group consisting of alluvial soils found along the lower reaches of the White Nile and Blue Nile rivers, along the main Nile to Lake Nubia, in the delta of the Qash River in the Kassala area, and in the Baraka Delta in the area of Tawkar near the Red Sea in Ash Sharqi State.

Agriculturally, the most important soils are the clays in central Sudan that extend from west of Kassala through Al Awsat and southern Kurdufan. Known as cracking soils because of the practice of allowing them to dry out and crack during the dry months to restore their permeability, they are used in the areas of Al Jazirah and Khashm al Qirbah for irrigated cultivation. East of the Blue Nile, large areas are used for mechanized rainfed crops. West of the White Nile, these soils are used by traditional cultivators to grow sorghum, sesame, peanuts, and (in the area around the Nuba Mountains) cotton. The southern part of the clay soil zone lies in the broad floodplain of the upper reaches of the White Nile and its tributaries, covering most of Aali an Nil and upper Bahr al Ghazal states. Subject to heavy rainfall during the rainy season, the floodplain proper is inundated for four to six months. The large swampy area, As Sudd, is permanently flooded, and adjacent areas are flooded for one or two months. In general this area is poorly suited to crop production, but the grasses it supports during dry periods are used for grazing.

The sandy soils in the semiarid areas south of the desert in northern Kurdufan and northern Darfur states support vegetation used for grazing. In the southern part of these states and the western part of southern Darfur are the so-called *qoz* sands. Livestock raising is this area's major activity, but a significant amount of crop cultivation, mainly of millet, also occurs. Peanuts and sesame are grown as cash crops. The *qoz* sands are the principal area from which gum arabic is obtained through tapping of *Acacia senegal* (known locally as *hashab*). This tree grows readily in the region, and cultivators occasionally plant *hashab* trees when land is returned to fallow.

The laterite soils of the south cover most of western Al Istiwai and Bahr al Ghazal states. They underlie the extensive moist woodlands found in these provinces. Crop production is scattered, and the soils, where cultivated, lose fertility relatively quickly; even the richer soils are usually returned to bush fallow within five years.

Hydrology

Except for a small area in northeastern Sudan where wadis discharge the sporadic runoff into the Red Sea or rivers from Ethiopia flow into shallow, evaporating ponds west of the Red Sea Hills, the entire country is drained by the Nile and its two main tributaries, the Blue Nile (Al Bahr al Azraq) and the White Nile (Al Bahr al Abyad). The longest river in the world, the Nile flows for 6,737 kilometers from its farthest headwaters in central Africa to the Mediterranean. The importance of the Nile has been recognized since biblical times; for centuries the river has been a lifeline for Sudan.

The Blue Nile flows out of the Ethiopian highlands to meet the White Nile at Khartoum. The Blue Nile is the smaller of the two; its flow usually accounts for only one-sixth of the total. In August, however, the rains in the Ethiopian highlands swell the Blue Nile until it accounts for 90 percent of the Nile's total flow. Several dams have been constructed to regulate the river's flow—the Roseires Dam (Ar Rusayris), about 100 kilometers from the Ethiopian border; the Meina al Mak Dam at Sinjah; and the largest, the forty-meter-high Sennar Dam constructed in 1925 at Sannar. The Blue Nile's two main tributaries, the Dindar and the Rahad, have headwaters in the Ethiopian highlands and discharge water into the Blue

Nile only during the summer high-water season. For the remainder of the year, their flow is reduced to pools in their sandy riverbeds. The White Nile flows north from central Africa, draining Lake Victoria and the highland regions of Uganda, Rwanda, and Burundi. At Bor, the great swamp of the Nile, As Sudd begins. The river has no well-defined channel here; the water flows slowly through a labyrinth of small spillways and lakes choked with papyrus and reeds. Much water is lost to evaporation. To provide for water transportation through this region and to speed the river's flow so that less water evaporates, Sudan, with French help, began building the Jonglei Canal (also seen as Junqali Canal) from Bor to a point just upstream from Malakal. However, construction was suspended in 1984 because of security problems caused by the civil war in the south.

South of Khartoum, the British built the Jabal al Auliya Dam in 1937 to store the water of the White Nile and then release it in the fall when the flow from the Blue Nile slackens. Much water from the reservoir has been diverted for irrigation projects in central Sudan, however, and much of the remainder evaporates. Hence the overall flow released downstream is not great.

The White Nile has several substantial tributaries that drain southern Sudan. In the southwest, the Bahr al Ghazal drains a basin larger in area than France. Although the drainage area is extensive, evaporation takes most of the water from the slow-moving streams in this region, and the discharge of the Bahr al Ghazal into the White Nile is minimal. In southeast Sudan, the Sobat River drains an area of western Ethiopia and the hills near the Sudan-Uganda border. The Sobat's discharge is considerable; at its confluence with the White Nile just south of Malakal, the Sobat accounts for half the White Nile's water.

Above Khartoum, the Nile flows through desert in a large S-shaped pattern to empty into Lake Nasser behind the Aswan High Dam in Egypt. The river flows slowly above Khartoum, dropping little in elevation although five cataracts hinder river transport at times of low water. The Atbarah River, flowing out of Ethiopia, is the only tributary north of Khartoum, and its waters reach the Nile for only the six months between July and December. During the rest of the year, the Atbarah's bed is dry, except for a few pools and ponds.

Climate

Although Sudan lies within the tropics, the climate ranges from arid in the north to tropical wet-and-dry in the far southwest. Temperatures do not vary greatly with the season at any location; the most significant climatic variables are rainfall and the length of the dry season. Variations in the length of the dry season depend on which of two air flows predominates, dry northeasterly winds from the Arabian Peninsula or moist southwesterly winds from the Congo River basin.

From January to March, the country is under the influence of the dry northeasterlies. There is practically no rainfall countrywide except for a small area in northwestern Sudan where the winds have passed over the Mediterranean and bring occasional light rains. By early April, the moist southwesterlies have reached southern Sudan, bringing heavy rains and thunderstorms. By July the moist air has reached Khartoum, and in August it extends to its usual northern limits around Abu Hamad, although in some years the humid air may even reach the Egyptian border. The flow becomes weaker as it spreads north. In September the dry northeasterlies begin to strengthen and to push south, and by the end of December they cover the entire country. Yambio, close to the border with Zaire, has a nine-month rainy season (April–December) and receives an average of 1,142 millimeters of rain each year; Khartoum has a three-month rainy season (July–September) with an annual average rainfall of 161 millimeters; Atbarah receives showers in August that produce an annual average of only 74 millimeters.

In some years, the arrival of the southwesterlies and their rain in central Sudan can be delayed, or they may not come at all. If that happens, drought and famine follow. The decades of the 1970s and 1980s saw the southwesterlies frequently fail, with disastrous results for the Sudanese people and economy.

Temperatures are highest at the end of the dry season when cloudless skies and dry air allow them to soar. The far south, however, with only a short dry season, has uniformly high temperatures throughout the year. In Khartoum, the warmest months are May and June, when average highs are 41°C and temperatures can reach 48°C. Northern Sudan, with its short rainy season, has hot daytime temperatures year round, except for winter months in the northwest where there is precipitation from the Mediterranean in January and February. Conditions in highland areas are generally cooler, and the hot daytime temperatures during the dry season throughout central and northern Sudan fall rapidly after sunset. Lows in Khartoum average 15°C in January and have dropped as low as 6°C after the passing of a cool front in winter.

The haboob, a violent dust storm, can occur in central Sudan when the moist southwesterly flow first arrives (May through July). The moist, unstable air forms thunderstorms in the heat of the afternoon. The initial downflow of air from an approaching storm produces a huge yellow wall of sand and clay that can temporarily reduce visibility to zero.

Population

Population information for Sudan has been limited, but in 1990 it was clear that the country was experiencing a high birth rate and a high, but declining, death rate. Infant mortality was high, but Sudan was expected to continue its rapid population growth, with a large percentage of its people under fifteen years of age, for some time to come. The trends indicated an overall low population density. However, with famine affecting much of the country, internal migration by hundreds of thousands of people was on the increase. The United Nations High Commissioner for Refugees reported that in early 1991, approximately 1,800,000 people were displaced in the northern states, of whom it was estimated that 750,000 were in Al Khartum State, 30,000 each in Kurdufan and Al Awsat states, 300,000 each in Darfur and Ash Sharqi states, and 150,000 in Ash Shamali State. Efforts were underway to provide permanent sites for about 800,000 of these displaced people. The civil war and famine in the south were estimated to have displaced up to 3.5 million southern Sudanese by early 1990.

In addition to uncertainties concerning the number of refugees, population estimates were complicated by census difficulties. Since independence there have been three national censuses, in 1955–56, 1973, and 1983. The first was inadequately prepared and executed. The second was not officially recognized by the government, and thus its complete findings have never been released. The third census was of better quality, but some of the data has never been analyzed because of inadequate resources.

The 1983 census put the total population at 21.6 million with a growth rate between 1956 and 1983 of 2.8 percent per year (see table 2, Appendix). In 1990, the National Population Committee and the Department of Statistics put Sudan's birth rate at 50 births per 1,000 and the death rate at 19 per 1,000, for a rate of increase of 31 per 1,000 or 3.1 percent per year. This is a staggering increase. When compared with the world average of 1.8 percent per year and the average for developing countries of 2.1 percent per annum, this percentage made Sudan one of the world's fastest growing countries. The 1983 population estimate was thought to be too low, but even accepting it and the pre-1983 growth rate of 2.8 percent, Sudan's population in 1990 would have been well over 25 million. At the estimated 1990 growth rate of 3.1 percent, the population would double in twenty-two years. Even if the lower estimated rate were sustained, the population would reach 38.6 million by 2003 and 50.9 million by 2013.

Both within Sudan and among the international community, it was commonly thought that with an average population density of nine persons per square kilometer, population density was not a major problem. This assumption, however, failed to take into account that much of Sudan was uninhabitable and that its people were unevenly distributed, with about 33 percent of the nation's population occupying 7 percent of the land and concentrated around Khartoum and in Al Awsat. In fact, 66 percent of the population lived within 300 kilometers of Khartoum (see table 3, Appendix). In 1990 the population of the Three Towns (Khartoum, Omdurman, and Khartoum North) was unknown because of the constant influx of refugees, but estimates of 3 million, well over half the urban dwellers in Sudan, may not have been unrealistic. Nevertheless, only 20 percent of Sudanese lived in towns and cities; 80 percent still lived in rural areas.

The birth rate between the 1973 census and the 1987 National Population Conference appeared to have remained constant at from 48 to 50 births per 1,000 population. The fertility rate (the average number of children per woman) was estimated at 6.9 in 1983. Knowledge of family planning remained minimal. During the period, the annual death rate fell from 23 to 19 per 1,000, and the estimated life expectancy rose from 43.5 years to 47 years.

For more than a decade the gross domestic product (GDP—see Glossary) of Sudan had not kept pace with the increasing population, a trend indicating that Sudan would have difficulty in providing adequate services for its people. Moreover, half the population were under eighteen years of age and therefore were primarily consumers not producers. Internal migration caused by civil war and famine created major shifts in population distribution, producing overpopulation in areas that could provide neither services nor employment. Furthermore, Sudan has suffered a continuous "brain drain" as its finest professionals and most skilled laborers emigrated, while simultaneously there has been an influx of more than 1 million refugees, who not only lacked skills but required massive relief. Droughts in the 1970s, 1980s, and 1990s have undermined Sudan's food production, and the country would have to double its production to feed its expected population within the next generation. In the absence of a national population policy to deal with these problems, they were expected to worsen.

Moreover, throughout Sudan continuous environmental degradation accompanied the dearth of rainfall. Experts estimated that desertification caused by deforestation and drought had allowed the Sahara to advance southward at the rate of ten kilometers per year. About 7.8 million Sudanese were estimated to be at risk from famine in early 1991, according to the United Nations World Food Programme and other agencies. The Save the Children Fund estimated that the famine in Darfur would cost the lives of "tens of thousands" of people in the early 1990s. Analysts believed that the lack of rainfall combined with the ravages of war would result in massive numbers of deaths from starvation in the 1990s.

Ethnicity

Sudan's ethnic and linguistic diversity remained one of the most complex in the world in 1991. Its nearly 600 ethnic groups spoke more than 400 languages and dialects, many of them intelligible to only a small number of individuals. In the 1980s and 1990s some of these small groups became absorbed by larger groups, and migration often caused individuals reared in one tongue to converse only in the dominant language of the new area. Such was the case with migrants to the Three Towns. There Arabic was the lingua franca despite the use of English by many of the elite. Some linguistic groups had been absorbed by accommodation, others by conflict. Most Sudanese were, of necessity, multilingual. Choice of language played a political role in the ethnic and religious cleavage between the northern and southern Sudanese. English was associated with being non-Muslim, as Arabic was associated with Islam. Thus language was a political instrument and a symbol of identity.

Language

Language differences have served as a partial basis for ethnic classification and as symbols of ethnic identity. Such differences have been obstacles to the flow of communication in a state as linguistically fragmented as Sudan. These barriers have been overcome in part by the emergence of some languages as lingua francas and by a considerable degree of multilingualism in some areas.

Most languages spoken in Africa fall into four language superstocks. Three of them—Afro-Asiatic, Niger-Kurdufanian, and Nilo-Saharan—are represented in Sudan. Each is divided into groups that are in turn subdivided into sets of closely related languages. Two or more major groups of each superstock are represented in Sudan, which has been historically both a north-south and an east-west migration crossroad.

The most widely spoken language in the Sudan is Arabic, a member of the Semitic branch of the Afro-Asiatic language family. Cushitic, another major division of the Afro-Asiatic language, is represented by Bedawiye (with several dialects), spoken by the

69

largely nomadic Beja. Chadic, a third division, is represented by its most important single language, Hausa, a West African tongue used by the Hausa themselves and employed by many other West Africans in Sudan as a lingua franca.

Niger-Kurdufanian is first divided into Niger-Congo and Kurdufanian. The widespread Niger-Congo language group includes many divisions and subdivisions of languages. Represented in Sudan are Azande and several other tongues of the Adamawa-Eastern language division, and Fulani of the West Atlantic division. The Kurdufanian stock comprises only thirty to forty languages spoken in a limited area of Sudan, the Nuba Mountains and their environs.

The designation of a Nilo-Saharan superstock has not been fully accepted by linguists, and its constituent groups and subgroups are not firmly fixed, in part because many of the languages have not been well studied. Assuming the validity of the category and its internal divisions, however, eight of its nine major divisions and many of their subdivisions are well represented in Sudan, where roughly seventy-five languages, well over half of those named in the 1955–56 census, could be identified as Nilo-Saharan. Many of these languages are used only by small groups of people. Only six or seven of them were spoken by 1 percent or more of Sudan's 1956 population. Perhaps another dozen were the home languages of 0.5 to 1 percent. Many other languages were used by a few thousand or even a few hundred people.

The number of languages and dialects in Sudan is assumed to be about 400, including languages spoken by an insignificant number of people. Moreover, languages of smaller ethnic groups tended to disappear when the groups assimilated with more dominant ethnic units.

Several lingua francas have emerged and many peoples have become genuinely multilingual, fluent in a native language spoken at home, a lingua franca, and perhaps other languages. Arabic is the primary lingua franca in Sudan, given its status as the country's official language and as the language of Islam. Arabic, however, has several different forms, and not all who master one are able to use another. Among the varieties noted by scholars are classical Arabic, the language of the Quran (although generally not a spoken language and only used for printed work); Modern Standard Arabic, derived from classical Arabic and used by the educated in conversation; and at least two kinds of colloquial Arabic in the Sudan—that spoken in roughly the eastern half of the country and called Sudanese colloquial Arabic and that spoken in western Sudan, closely akin to the colloquial Arabic spoken in Chad. There are other colloquial forms. A pidgin called Juba Arabic is peculiar to southern Sudan. Although some Muslims might become acquainted with classical Arabic in the course of rudimentary religious schooling, very few except the most educated know it except by rote.

Modern Standard Arabic is in principle the same everywhere in the Arab world and presumably permits communication among educated persons whose mother tongue is one or another form of colloquial Arabic. Despite its international character, however, Modern Standard Arabic varies from country to country. It has been, however, the language used in Sudan's central government, the press, and Radio Omdurman. The latter also broadcast in classical Arabic. One observer, writing in the early 1970s, noted that Arabic speakers (and others who had acquired the language informally) in western Sudan found it easier to understand the Chadian colloquial Arabic used by Chad Radio than the Modern Standard Arabic used by Radio Omdurman. This might also be the case elsewhere in rural Sudan where villagers and nomads speak a local dialect of Arabic.

Despite Arabic's status as the official national language, English was acknowledged as the principal language in southern Sudan in the late 1980s. It was also the chief language at the University of Khartoum and was the language of secondary schools even in the north before 1969. The new policy for higher education announced by the Sudanese government in 1990 indicated that Arabic would be the language of instruction in all institutions of higher learning.

Nevertheless, in the south, the first two years of primary school were taught in the local language. Thereafter, through secondary school, either Arabic or English could become the medium of instruction (English and Arabic were regarded as of equal importance); the language not used as a medium was taught as a subject. In the early 1970s, when this option was established, roughly half the general secondary classes (equivalent to grades seven through nine) were conducted in Arabic and half in English in Bahr al Ghazal and Al Istiwai provinces. In early 1991, with about 90 percent of the southern third of the country controlled by the Sudanese People's Liberation Army (SPLA), the use of Arabic as a medium of instruction in southern schools remained a political issue, with many southerners regarding Arabic as an element in northern cultural domination.

Juba (or pidgin) Arabic, developed and learned informally, had been used in southern towns, particularly in Al Istiwai, for some time and had spread slowly but steadily throughout the south, but not always at the expense of English. The Juba Arabic used in the marketplace and even by political figures addressing ethnically mixed urban audiences could not be understood by northern Sudanese.

Ethnic Groups

The definition and boundaries of ethnic groups depend on how people perceive themselves and others. Language, cultural characteristics, and common ancestry may be used as markers of ethnic identity or difference, but they do not always define groups of people. Thus, the people called Atuot and the much larger group called Nuer speak essentially the same language, share many cultural characteristics, and acknowledge a common ancestry, but each group defines itself and the other as different. Identifying ethnic groups in Sudan is made more complicated by the multifaceted character of internal divisions among Arabic-speaking Muslims, the largest population that might be considered a single ethnic group.

The distinction between Sudan's Muslim and non-Muslim people has been of considerable importance in the country's history and provides a preliminary ordering of the ethnic groups. It does not, however, correspond in any simple way to distinctions based on linguistic, cultural, or racial criteria nor to social or political solidarity. Ethnic group names commonly used in Sudan and by foreign analysts are not always used by the people themselves. This fact is particularly true for non-Arabs known by names coined by Arabs or by the British, who based the names on terms used by Arabs or others not of the group itself. Thus, the Dinka and the Nuer, the largest groups in southern Sudan, call themselves, respectively, Jieng and Naath.

Muslim Peoples

Arabs

In the early 1990s, the largest single category among the Muslim peoples consisted of those speaking some form of Arabic. Excluded were a small number of Arabic speakers originating in Egypt and professing Coptic Christianity. In 1983 the people identified as Arabs constituted nearly 40 percent of the total Sudanese population and nearly 55 percent of the population of the northern provinces. In some of these provinces (Al Khartum, Ash Shamali, Al Awsat), they were overwhelmingly dominant. In others (Kurdufan, Darfur), they were less so but made up a majority. By 1990 Ash Sharqi State was probably largely Arab. It should be emphasized, however, that the acquisition of Arabic as a second language did not necessarily lead to the assumption of Arab identity.

Despite common language, religion, and self-identification, Arabs did not constitute a cohesive group. They were highly differentiated in their modes of livelihood and ways of life. Besides the major distinction dividing Arabs into sedentary and nomadic, there was an old tradition that assigned them to tribes, each said to have a common ancestor.

The two largest of the supratribal categories in the early 1990s were the Juhayna and the Jaali (or Jaalayin). The Juhayna category consisted of tribes considered nomadic, although many had become fully settled. The Jaali encompassed the riverine, sedentary peoples from Dunqulah to just north of Khartoum and members of this group who had moved elsewhere. Some of its groups had become sedentary only in the twentieth century. Sudanese saw the Jaali as primarily indigenous peoples who were gradually arabized. Sudanese thought the Juhayna were less mixed, although some Juhayna groups had become more diverse by absorbing indigenous peoples. The Baqqara, for example, who moved south and west and encountered the Negroid peoples of those areas were scarcely to be distinguished from them.

A third supratribal division of some importance was the Kawahla, consisting of thirteen tribes of varying size. Of these, eight tribes and segments of the other five were found north and west of Khartoum. There people were more heavily dependent on pastoralism than were the segments of the other five tribes, who lived on either side of the White Nile from south of Khartoum to north of Kusti. This cluster of five groups (for practical purposes independent tribes) exhibited a considerable degree of self-awareness and cohesion in some circumstances, although that had not precluded intertribal competition for local power and status.

The *ashraf* (sing., *sharif*), who claim descent from the Prophet Muhammad, were found in small groups (lineages) scattered among other Arabs. Most of these lineages had been founded by religious teachers or their descendants. A very small group of descendants of the Funj Dynasty also claimed descent from the Umayyads, an early dynasty of caliphs based in present-day Syria. That claim had little foundation, but it served to separate from other Arabs a small group living on or between the White Nile and the Blue Nile. The term *ashraf* was also applied in Sudan to the family of Muhammad Ahmad ibn as Sayyid Abd Allah, known as the Mahdi (1848–85; see The Mahdiyah, ch. 1).

The division into Jaali and Juhayna did not appear to have a significant effect on the ways in which individuals and groups regarded each other. Conflicts between tribes generally arose from competition for good grazing land, or from the competing demands of nomadic and sedentary tribes on the environment. Among nomadic and recently sedentary Arabs, tribes and subtribes competed for local power (see The Social Order, this ch.).

Membership in tribal and subtribal units is generally by birth, but individuals and groups may also join these units by adoption, clientship, or a decision to live and behave in a certain way. For example, when a sedentary Fur becomes a cattle nomad, he is perceived as a Baqqara. Eventually the descendants of such newcomers are regarded as belonging to the group by birth.

Tribal and subtribal units divide the Arab ethnic category vertically, but other distinctions cut across Arab society and its tribal and subtribal components horizontally by differences of social status and power. Still another division is that of religious associations (see Islamic Movements and Religious Orders, this ch.).

Nubians

In the early 1990s, the Nubians were the second most significant Muslim group in Sudan, their homeland being the Nile River valley in far northern Sudan and southern Egypt. Other, much smaller groups speaking a related language and claiming a link with the Nile Nubians have been given local names, such as the Birqid and the Meidab in Darfur State (see fig. 5). Almost all Nile Nubians speak Arabic as a second language; some near Dunqulah have been largely arabized and are referred to as Dunqulah.

In the mid-1960s, in anticipation of the flooding of their lands after the construction of the Aswan High Dam, 35,000 to 50,000 Nile Nubians resettled at Khashm al Qirbah on the Atbarah River in what was then Kassala Province. It is not clear how many Nubians remained in the Nile Valley. Even before the resettlement, many had left the valley for varying lengths of time to work in the towns, although most sought to maintain a link with their traditional homeland. In the 1955–56 census, more Nile Nubians were counted in Al Khartum Province than in the Nubian country to the north. A similar pattern of work in the towns was apparently followed by those resettled at Khashm al Qirbah. Many Nubians there retained their tenancies, having kin oversee the land and hiring non-Nubians to work it. The Nubians, often with their families, worked in Khartoum, the town of Kassala, and Port Sudan in jobs ranging from domestic service and semi-skilled labor to teaching and civil service, which required literacy. Despite their knowledge of Arabic and their devotion to Islam, Nubians retained a considerable self-consciousness and tended to maintain tightly knit communities of their own in the towns.

Beja

The Beja probably have lived in the Red Sea Hills since ancient times. Arab influence was not significant until a millennium or so ago, but it has since led the Beja to adopt Islam and genealogies that link them to Arab ancestors, to arabize their names, and to include many Arabic terms in their language. Although some Arabs figure in the ancestry of the Beja, the group is mostly descended from an indigenous population, and they have not become generally arabized. Their language (Bedawiye) links them to Cushitic-speaking peoples farther south.

In the 1990s, most Beja belonged to one of four groups—the Bisharin, the Amarar, the Hadendowa, and the Bani Amir. The largest group was the Hadendowa, but the Bisharin had the most territory, with settled tribes living on the Atbarah River in the far south of the Beja range and nomads living in the north. A good number of the Hadendowa were also settled and engaged in agriculture, particularly in the coastal region near Tawkar, but many remained nomads. The Amarar, living in the central part of the Beja range, seemed to be largely nomads, as were the second largest group, the Bani Amir, who lived along the border with northern Ethiopia. The precise proportion of nomads in the Beja population in the early 1990s was not known, but it was far greater relatively than the nomadic component of the Arab population. The Beja were characterized as conservative, proud, and aloof even toward other Beja and very reticent in relations with strangers. They were long reluctant to accept the authority of central governments.

Fur

The Fur, ruled until 1916 by an independent sultanate and oriented politically and culturally to peoples in Chad, were a sedentary, cultivating group long settled on and around the Jabal Marrah. Although the ruling dynasty and the peoples of the area had long been Muslims, they have not been arabized. Livestock has played a small part in the subsistence of most Fur. Those who acquired a substantial herd of cattle could maintain it only by living like the neighboring Baqqara Arabs, and those who persisted in this pattern eventually came to be thought of as Baqqara.

Zaghawa

Living on the plateau north of the Fur were the seminomadic people calling themselves Beri and known to the Arabs as Zaghawa. Large numbers of the group lived in Chad. Herders of cattle, camels, sheep, and goats, the Zaghawa also gained a substantial part of their livelihood by gathering wild grains and other products.

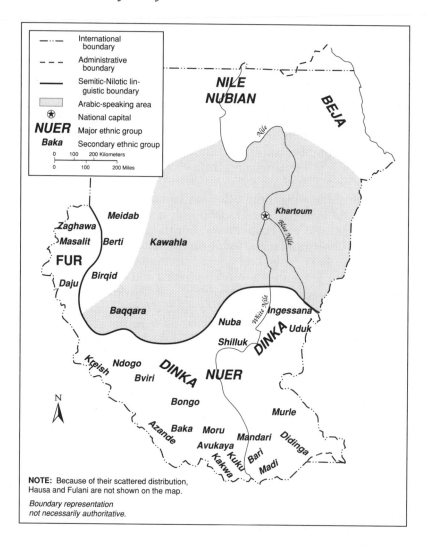

Figure 5. Principal Ethnolinguistic Groups, 1991

Cultivation had become increasingly important but remained risky, and the people reverted to gathering in times of drought. Converted to Islam, the Zaghawa nevertheless retain much of their traditional religious orientation.

Masalit, Daju, and Berti

Of other peoples living in Darfur in the 1990s who spoke Nilo-Saharan languages and were at least nominally Muslim, the most important were the Masalit, Daju, and Berti. All were primarily cultivators living in permanent villages, but they practiced animal husbandry in varying degrees. The Masalit, living on the Sudan-Chad border, were the largest group. Historically under a minor sultanate, they were positioned between the two dominant sultanates of the area, Darfur and Wadai (in Chad). A part of the territory they occupied had been formerly controlled by the Fur, but the Masalit gradually encroached on it in the first half of the twentieth century in a series of local skirmishes carried out by villages on both sides, rather than by the sultanates. In 1990–91 much of Darfur was in a state of anarchy, with many villages being attacked. There were many instances in which Masalit militias attacked Fur and other villages (see Western Sudan, ch. 4).

The Berti consisted of two groups. One lived northeast of Al Fashir; the other had migrated to eastern Darfur and western Kurdufan provinces in the nineteenth century. The two Berti groups did not seem to share a sense of common identity and interest. Members of the western group, in addition to cultivating subsistence crops and practicing animal husbandry, gathered gum arabic for sale in local markets. The Berti tongue had largely given way to Arabic as a home language.

The term Daju was a linguistic designation that was applied to a number of groups scattered from western Kurdufan and southwestern Darfur states to eastern Chad. These groups called themselves by different names and exhibited no sense of common identity.

West Africans

Living in Sudan in 1990 were nearly a million people of West African origin. Together, West Africans who have become Sudanese nationals and resident nonnationals from West Africa made up 6.5 percent of the Sudanese population. In the mid-1970s, West Africans had been estimated at more than 10 percent of the population of the northern provinces. Some were descendants of persons who had arrived five generations or more earlier; others were recent immigrants. Some had come in self-imposed exile, unable to accommodate to the colonial power in their homeland. Others had been pilgrims to Mecca, settling either en route or on their return. Many came over decades in the course of the great dispersion of the nomadic Fulani; others arrived, particularly after World War II, as rural and urban laborers or to take up land as peasant cultivators.

Nearly 60 percent of people included in the West African category were said to be of Nigerian origin (locally called Borno after the

Nigerian emirate that was their homeland). Given Hausa dominance in northern Nigeria and the widespread use of their language there and elsewhere, some non-Hausa might also be called Hausa and describe themselves as such. But the Hausa themselves, particularly those long in Sudan, preferred to be called Takari. The Fulani, even more widely dispersed throughout West Africa, may have originated in states other than Nigeria. Typically, the term applied to the Fulani in Sudan was Fallata, but Sudanese also used that term for other West Africans.

The Fulani nomads were found in many parts of central Sudan from Darfur to the Blue Nile, and they occasionally competed with indigenous populations for pasturage. In Darfur groups of Fulani origin adapted in various ways to the presence of the Baqqara tribes. Some retained all aspects of their culture and language. A few had become much like Baqqara in language and in other respects, although they tended to retain their own breeds of cattle and ways of handling them. Some of the Fulani groups in the eastern states were sedentary, descendants of sedentary Fulani of the ruling group in northern Nigeria.

Non-Muslim Peoples

In the 1990s, most of Sudan's diverse non-Muslim peoples lived in southern Sudan, but a number of small groups resided in the hilly areas south of the Blue Nile on or near the border with Ethiopia. Another cluster of peoples commonly called the Nuba, but socially and culturally diverse, lived in the Nuba Mountains of southern Kurdufan State.

Nilotes

Nilote is a common name for many of the peoples living on or near the Bahr al Jabal and its tributaries. The term refers to people speaking languages of one section of the Nilotic subbranch of the Eastern Sudanic branch of Nilo-Saharan and sharing a myth of common origin. They are marked by physical similarity and many common cultural features. Many had a long tradition of cattlekeeping, including some for whom cattle were no longer of practical importance. Because of their adaptation to different climates and their encounters, peaceful and otherwise, with other peoples, there was also some diversity among the Nilotes.

Despite the civil war and famine, the Nilotes still constituted more than three-fifths of the population of southern Sudan in 1990. One group—the Dinka—made up roughly two-thirds of the total category, 40 percent or more of the population of the area and more than 10 percent of Sudan's population. The Dinka were widely

*A Shilluk, member of a leading southern ethnic group,
prepares to launch his canoe.
Courtesy Robert O. Collins*

79

distributed over the northern portion of the southern region, particularly in Aali an Nil and Bahr al Ghazal. The next largest group, only one-fourth to one-third the size of the Dinka, were the Nuer. The Shilluk, the third largest group, had only about one-fourth as many people as the Nuer, and the remaining Nilotic groups were much smaller.

The larger and more dispersed the group, however, the more internally varied it had become. The Dinka and Nuer, for example, did not develop a centralized government encompassing all or any large part of their groups. The Dinka are considered to have as many as twenty-five tribal groups. The Nuer have nine or ten separately named groups.

Armed conflict between and within ethnic groups continued well into the twentieth century. Sections of the Dinka fought sections of the Nuer and each other. Other southern groups also expanded and contracted in the search for cattle and pasturage. The Nuer absorbed some of the Dinka, and some present-day sections of the Nuer have significant Dinka components.

Relations among various southern groups were affected in the nineteenth century by the intrusion of Ottomans, Arabs, and eventually the British. Some ethnic groups made their accommodation with the intruders and others did not, in effect pitting one southern ethnic group against another in the context of foreign rule. For example, some sections of the Dinka were more accommodating to British rule than were the Nuer. These Dinka treated the resisting Nuer as hostile, and hostility developed between the two groups as result of their differing relationships to the British. The granting of Sudanese independence in 1956, and the adoption of certain aspects of Islamic law, or the sharia, by the central government in 1983 greatly influenced the nature of relations among these groups in modern times.

The next largest group of Nilotes, the Shilluk (self-named Collo), were not dispersed like the Dinka and the Nuer, but settled mainly in a limited, uninterrupted area along the west bank of the Bahr al Jabal, just north of the point where it becomes the White Nile proper. A few lived on the eastern bank. With easy access to fairly good land along the Nile, they relied much more heavily on cultivation and fishing than the Dinka and the Nuer did, and they had fewer cattle. The Shilluk had truly permanent settlements and did not move regularly between cultivating and cattle camps.

Unlike the larger groups, the Shilluk, in the Upper Nile, were traditionally ruled by a single politico-religious head (*reth*), believed to become at the time of his investiture as king the representative, if not the reincarnation, of the mythical hero Nyiking, putative founder of the Shilluk. The administrative and political powers of the *reth* have been the subject of some debate, but his ritual status was clear enough: his health was believed to be closely related to the material and spiritual welfare of the Shilluk. It is likely that the territorial unity of the Shilluk and the permanence of their settlements contributed to the centralization of their political and ritual structures. In the late 1980s, the activities against the SPLA by the armed militias supported by the government seriously alienated the Shilluk in Malakal.

Bari, Kuku, Kakwa, and Mandari

Several peoples living mainly to the south and east of the Nilotes spoke languages of another section of the Nilotic subbranch of Eastern Sudanic. Primary among them were the Bari and the closely related Kuku, Kakwa, and Mandari. The Bari and Mandari, who lived near the Nilotes, had been influenced by them and had sometimes been in conflict with them in the past. The more southerly Kuku and Kakwa lived in the highlands, where cultivation was more rewarding than cattle-keeping or where cattle diseases precluded herding.

Murle, Didinga, and Others

Two other tribes, the Murle and the Didinga, spoke Eastern Sudanic languages of subbranches other than Nilotic. The Murle had dwelt in southern Ethiopia in the nineteenth century and some were still there in the 1990s. Others had moved west and had driven out the local Nilotes, whom they reportedly regarded with contempt, and had acquired a reputation as warriors. Under environmental pressure, the Murle raided other groups in the late 1970s and early 1980s.

Along the mountainous border with Ethiopia in Al Awsat State lived several small heterogeneous groups. Some, like the Uduk, spoke languages of the Koman division of Nilo-Saharan and were believed to have been in the area since antiquity. Others, like the Ingessana, were refugees driven into the hills by the expansion of other groups. Most of these peoples straddling the Sudan-Ethiopia border had experienced strife with later-arriving neighbors and slave-raiding by the Arabs. All adapted by learning the languages of more dominant groups.

Azande

In western Al Istiwai and Bahr al Ghazal states lived a number of small, sometimes fragmented groups. The largest of these groups were the Azande, who comprised 7 to 8 percent of the population of southern Sudan and were the dominant group in western Al Istiwai.

The Azande had emerged in the eighteenth and nineteenth centuries when groups of hunters, divided into aristocrats and commoners, entered the northeastern part of present-day Zaire (and later southwestern Sudan) and conquered the peoples already there. Although the aristocrats provided ruling kings and nobles, they did not establish an inclusive, centralized state. The means of succession to kingship, however, encouraged Azande expansion. A man succeeded to his father's throne only when he had vanquished those of his brothers who chose to compete for it. The brothers— princes without land or people but with followers looking for the fruits of conquest—would find and rule hitherto unconquered groups. Thus, the Azande became a heterogeneous people.

Their earlier military and political successes notwithstanding, the Azande in the twentieth century were poor, largely dependent on cultivation (hunting was no longer a feasible source of food), and afflicted by sleeping sickness. The British colonial authorities instituted a project, known as the Azande Scheme, involving cotton growing and resettlement in an effort to deal with these problems. The program failed, however, for a variety of reasons, including an inadequate understanding of Azande society, economy, and values on the part of the colonial planners. Azande society deteriorated still further, a deterioration reflected in a declining birth rate. Azande support of the Anya Nya guerrilla groups, as well as conflicts with the Dinka, also served to worsen the Azande's situation. In the early 1980s, there was talk of resurrecting a revised Azande project but the resumption of the civil war in 1983 prevented progress.

Bviri and Ndogo

Several other groups of cultivators in southwestern Sudan spoke languages closely akin to that of the Azande but lacked a dominant group. The most important seemed to be the Bviri. They and a smaller group called Ndogo spoke a language named after the latter; other, smaller communities spoke dialects of that tongue. These communities did not share a sense of common ethnic identity, however.

Others

The other groups in southwestern Sudan spoke languages of the central branch of Nilo-Saharan and were scattered from the western Bahr al Ghazal (the Kreish) to central Al Istiwai (the Moru and the Avukaya) to eastern Al Istiwai (the Madi). In between, in Al

An Azande chief in the south standing near a hut being completed
for his new wife
Courtesy Robert O. Collins

Istiwai, were such peoples as the Bongo and the Baka. The languages of Moru and Madi were so close, as were aspects of their cultures, that they were sometimes lumped together. The same was true of the Bongo and the Baka, but there was no indication that either pair constituted a self-conscious ethnic group.

Nuba

Living in the Nuba Mountains of southern Kurdufan State were perhaps three dozen small groups collectively called the Nuba but varying considerably in their culture and social organization. For example, some were patrilineally organized, others adhered to matrilineal patterns, and a very few—the southeastern Nuba—had both patrilineal and matrilineal groupings in the same community. The Kurdufanian languages these people spoke were not generally mutually intelligible except for those of some adjacent communities.

Despite the arabization of the people around them, only small numbers of Nuba had adopted Arabic as a home language, and even fewer had been converted to Islam. Some had, however, served in the armed forces and police. Most remained cultivators; animal husbandry played only a small part in their economy.

83

Migration

One of the most important and complicating factors in defining ethnicity is the dramatic increase in the internal migration of Sudanese within the past twenty years. It has been estimated that in 1973 alone well over 10 percent of the population moved away from their ethnic groups to mingle with other Sudanese in the big agricultural projects or to work in other provinces. Most of the migrants sought employment in the large urban areas, particularly in the Three Towns, which attracted 30 percent of all internal migrants. The migrants were usually young; 60 percent were between the ages of fifteen and forty-four. Of that number, 46 percent were females. The number of migrants escalated greatly in the latter 1980s because of drought and famine, the civil war in the south, and Chadian raiders in the west. Thus, as in the past, the migrants left their ethnic groups for economic, social, and psychological reasons, but now with the added factor of personal survival.

Another ethnic group involved in migration was that of the Falasha, who were Ethiopian Jews. In January 1985, it was revealed that the Sudanese government had cooperated with Ethiopia, Israel, and the United States in transporting several thousand Falasha through Sudan to Israel. Their departure occurred initially on a small scale in 1979 and 1982 and in larger numbers between 1983 and 1985. In Sudan the Falasha had been placed in temporary refugee settlements and reception centers organized by the Sudanese government.

In addition to the problems of employment, housing, and services that internal migration created, it had an enormous impact on ethnicity. Although migrants tended to cluster with their kinsfolk in their new environments, the daily interaction with Sudanese from many other ethnic groups rapidly eroded traditional values learned in the villages. In the best of circumstances, this erosion might lead to a new sense of national identity as Sudanese, but the new communities often lacked effective absorptive mechanisms and were weak economically. Ethnic divisions were thus reinforced, and at the same time social anomie was perpetuated.

Refugees from other countries, like internal migrants, were a factor that further complicated ethnic patterns. In 1991 Sudan was host to about 763,000 refugees from neighboring countries, such as Ethiopia and Chad. Included among the refugees were about 175,000 soldiers, most of whom fled following the overthrow of the Ethiopian government in May 1991. Over the past several years, approximately 426,000 Sudanese had fled their country, becoming refugees in Kenya and Ethiopia. Many of them began returning to Sudan in June 1991. Incoming refugees were at first hospitably received but they gradually came to be regarded as unwelcome visitors. The refugees required many social services, a need only partially met by international humanitarian agencies, which also had to care for Sudanese famine victims. The presence of foreign refugees, who had little prospect of returning to their own countries, thus created not only social but also political instability.

Regionalism and Ethnicity

The long war in Sudan had a profound effect not only on ethnic groups but also on political action and attitudes. With the exception of a fragile peace established by negotiations between southern Sudanese insurgents (the Anya Nya) and the Sudan government at Addis Ababa in 1972, and lasting until the resumption of the conflict in 1983, southern Sudan has been a battlefield. The conflict has deeply eroded traditional ethnic patterns in the region, and it has extended northward, spreading incalculable political and economic disruption. It has, moreover, caused the dislocation and often the obliteration of the smaller, less resistant ethnic groups.

The north-south distinction and the hostility between the two regions were grounded in religious conflict as well as a conflict between peoples of differing culture and language. The language and culture of the north were based on Arabic and the Islamic faith, whereas the south had its own diverse, mostly non-Arabic languages and cultures. It was with few exceptions non-Muslim, and its religious character was indigenous (traditional or Christian). Adequate contemporary data were lacking, but in the early 1990s possibly no more than 10 percent of southern Sudan's population was Christian. Nevertheless, given the missions' role in providing education in the south, most educated persons in the area, including the political elite, were nominally Christians (or at least had Christian names). Several African Roman Catholic priests figured in southern leadership, and the churches played a significant role in bringing the south's plight to world attention in the civil war period (see The Southern Problem, ch. 1). Sudan's Muslim Arab rulers thus considered Christian mission activity to be an obstacle to the full arabization and Islamization of the south.

Occasionally, the distinction between north and south has been framed in racial terms. The indigenous peoples of the south are blacks, whereas those of the north are of Semitic stock. Northern populations fully arabized in language and culture, such as the Baqqara, however, could not be distinguished physically from some of the southern and western groups. Many sedentary Arabs descended from the pre-Islamic peoples of that area who were black, as were the Muslim but nonarabized Nubians and the Islamized peoples of Darfur.

It is not easy to generalize about the importance of physical attributes in one group's perceptions of another. But physical appearance often has been taken as an indicator of cultural, religious, and linguistic status or orientation. Arabs were also likely to see southerners as members of the population from which they once took slaves and to use the word for slave, *abd,* as a pejorative in referring to southerners.

North-south hostilities predate the colonial era. In the nineteenth century and earlier, Arabs saw the south as a source of slaves and considered its peoples inferior by virtue of their paganism if not their color. Organized slave raiding ended in the late nineteenth century, but the residue of bitterness remained among southerners, and the Arab view of southerners as pagans persisted.

During British rule, whatever limited accommodation there may have been between Arabs and Africans was neither widespread nor deep enough to counteract a longer history of conflict between these peoples. At the same time, for their own reasons, the colonial authorities discouraged integration of the ethnically different north and south (see Britain's Southern Policy, ch. 1).

Neither Arab attitudes of superiority nor British dominance in the south led to loss of self-esteem among southerners. A number of observers have remarked that southern peoples, particularly Nilotes, such as the Dinka, Nuer, and Shilluk, naturally object to the assumption by the country's Arab rulers that the southern peoples ought to be prepared to give up their religious orientation and values.

Interethnic tensions also have occurred in the north. Disaffection in Darfur with the Arab-dominated Khartoum government led in the late 1980s to Darfur becoming a virtually autonomous province. There has also been a history of regionally based political movements in the area. The frustrations of a budding elite among the Fur, the region's largest ethnic group, and Fur-Arab competition may account for that disaffection and for Darfur regionalism. After World War II, many educated Fur made a point of mastering Arabic in the hope that they could make their way in the Arab-dominated political, bureaucratic, and economic world; they did not succeed in their quest. Further, by the late 1960s, as cash crops were introduced, land and labor were becoming objects of commercial transactions. As this happened, the Arabs and the Fur competed for scarce resources and, given their greater prominence and power, the Arabs were regarded by the Fur as exploiters.

The discovery of oil in the late 1970s (not appreciably exploited by 1991 because of the civil war leading to the departure of Chevron Overseas Petroleum Corporation personnel) added another resource and further potential for conflict. Opposition to the imposition by Nimeiri of the sharia in 1983, and the later attempts at Islamization of the country in the late 1980s, as well as the government's poor handling of the devastating famine of 1990 deeply alienated the Fur from the national government.

There were other tensions in northern Sudan generated not by traditional antipathies but by competition for scarce resources. For example, there was a conflict between the Rufaa al Huj, a group of Arab pastoralists living in the area between the Blue Nile and the White Nile, and Fallata (Fulani) herders. The movements of the Fallata intersected with the seasonal migrations of the Rufaa al Huj. Here ethnic differences aggravated but did not cause competition.

The reluctance of southern groups to accept Arab domination did not imply southern solidarity. The opportunities for power and wealth in the new politics and bureaucracy in southern Sudan were limited; some groups felt deprived of their shares by an ethnic group in power. Moreover, ethnic groups at one time or another competed for more traditional resources, contributing to a heritage of hostility toward one another.

In the early 1990s, one of the main sources of ethnic conflict in the south was the extent to which the Dinka dominated southern politics and controlled the allocation of rewards, whether of government posts or of other opportunities. In the 1955–56 census, the Dinka constituted a little more than 40 percent of the total population of the three provinces that in 1990 constituted southern Sudan: Bahr al Ghazal, Aali an Nil, and Al Istiwai. Because no other group approached their number, if their proportion of the regional total had not changed appreciably, the Dinka would be expected to play a large part in the new politics of southern Sudan. Some of the leading figures in the south, such as Abel Alier, head of southern Sudan's government until 1981, and SPLA leader John Garang, were Dinka (although the SPLA made an effort to shed its Dinka image by cultivating supporters in other groups). It is not known whether the twenty-five Dinka tribal groups were equally represented in the alleged Dinka predominance. Some groups, such as the Nuer, a comparable Nilotic people and traditional rivals of the Dinka, had been deprived of leadership opportunities in colonial times because they were considered intractable, were then not numerous, and lived in inaccessible areas (various small groups in Bahr al Ghazal and northern Aali an Nil provinces). In contrast, some small groups in Al Istiwai Province had easier access to education and hence to political participation because of nearby missions. The first graduating class of the university in Juba, for example, had many more Azande students from Al Istiwai Province than from Bahr al Ghazal and Aali an Nil.

The Social Order

Local ethnic communities remained in the early 1990s the fundamental societies in rural Sudan, whether they were fully settled, semisedentary, or nomadic. Varying in size but never very large, such communities formerly interacted with others of their kind in hostile or symbiotic fashion, raiding for cattle, women, and slaves or exchanging products and sometimes intermarrying. In many cases, particularly in the north, local communities were incorporated into larger political systems, paying taxes to the central authority and adapting their local political arrangements to the needs of the central government. Even if they were not incorporated into major tribes or groups, many people considered themselves part of larger groupings, such as the Juhayna, the Jaali, or the Dinka, which figured in a people's system of ideas and myths but not their daily lives. In the north the Muslim religious orders were important. They brought religion to the people, and their leaders acted as mediators between local communities. Despite these connections, however, the local village or nomadic community was the point of reference for most individuals.

Most of these communities were based on descent, although occupation of a common territory became increasingly important in long-settled communities. Descent groups varied in hierarchical arrangement. In some, the people were essentially equal. In others, various lineages held political power, with their members filling certain offices. Lineage groups might also control religious ritual in the community. On the one hand, people who held ritual or political offices often had privileged access to economic resources. On the other hand, many communities granted formal or informal authority to those who were already wealthy and who used their wealth generously and with tactical skill.

Theoretically, descent-group societies are cohesive units whose members act according to group interests. In practice, however, individuals often had their own interests, and these interests sometimes became paramount. An individual might, however, use the ideal of descent-group solidarity to justify his behavior, and an ambitious person might use the descent-group framework to organize support for himself. Sudanese communities always have experienced a good deal of change, either because of forces like the Muslim orders, or as a result of dynamics within the groups themselves, like the expansion of Nuer communities.

The Anglo-Egyptian condominium (1899–1955) weakened the role of hitherto autonomous communities and created a more stable social order. Warfare and raiding between communities largely ended. Leadership in raids was no longer a way to acquire wealth and status. Although many local communities remained subsistence oriented, they became more aware of the world economy. Their members were introduced to new resources and opportunities, however scarce, that reoriented their notions of power, status, and wealth and of the ways they were acquired. If one invested in a truck rather than in a camel and engaged in trading rather than herding, one's relationship to kin and community changed.

The central authorities—links with the world economy and with services like education and communications—were located in the cities and large towns. Urban centers therefore became the sources of change in the condominium era, and it was there that new occupations emerged. These new occupations had not yet changed the social strata, however.

In rural areas several large-scale development projects were introduced, resulting in major rearrangements of communities and authority structures. The most significant example was the Gezira Scheme, located between the Blue Nile and the White Nile, and considered the world's largest single-management farming enterprise (about 790 hectares were covered by the project). The scheme involved small-scale farmer tenants producing cotton under the administration of the Sudan Gezira Board, a state subsidiary.

Northern Arabized Communities

Distinctions may be drawn among long-settled arabized communities, those settled in the past half century, and those—the minority—that remained nomadic. Recently settled groups might still participate in nomadic life or have close connections with nomadic kin.

Formerly, where long-settled and nomadic or beduin communities came in contact with each other, relations were hostile or cool, reflecting earlier competition for resources. More recently, a degree of mutual dependency had developed, usually involving exchanges of foodstuffs.

Along the White Nile and between the White Nile and Blue Nile, sections of nomadic tribes had become sedentary. This transition occurred either because of the opportunities for profitable cultivation or because nomads had lost their animals and turned to cultivation until they could recoup their fortunes and return to nomadic life. Having settled, some communities found sedentary life more materially rewarding. Sometimes nomads lacking livestock worked for sedentary Arabs, and where employer and employee were of the same or similar tribes, the relationship could be close. It was understood that when such a laborer acquired enough livestock, he would return to nomadic life. In other cases, a fully settled former nomad with profitable holdings allowed his poorer kin to maintain his livestock, both parties gaining from the transaction.

Arab nomads in Sudan in the early 1990s were generally camel or cattle herders. They might own sheep and goats also for economic reasons, but these animals were not otherwise valued. Typically, camel herders migrated to the more arid north, whereas cattle herders traveled farther south where camel herding was not feasible.

The ancestors of the Baqqara tribes began as nomadic camel herders. When they moved south to raid for slaves, they found camel travel inappropriate and took cattle as well as people from the southerners. They have been cattle herders since the eighteenth century. Their environment permitted cultivation also, and most Baqqara grew some of their food. Camel herders, in contrast, rarely sowed a crop, although they might gather wild grain and obtain grains from local cultivators.

In the 1990s, the communities of arabized nomads were similar. In principle, all units from the smallest to the largest were based on patrilineal descent. The largest entity was the tribe. A tribe was divided into sections, and each of these, into smaller units. If a tribe were small, it became a *naziriyah* (administrative unit—see Glossary); if large, its major sections became *naziriyat*. The sections below the *naziriyah* became *umudiyat* (sing., *umudiyah*—see Glossary). Below that were lineages, often headed by a shaykh, which had no formal position in the administrative hierarchy. The smallest unit, which the Baqqara called *usrah*, was likely to consist of a man, his sons, their sons, and any daughters who had not yet married. (Patrilineal cousins were preferred marriage partners.) The *usrah* and the women who married into it constituted an extended family.

All divisions had rights to all tribal territory for grazing purposes as long as they stayed clear of cultivated land; however, through frequent use, tribal sections acquired rights to specific areas for gardens. Members of an *usrah*, for example, returned year after year to the same land, which they regarded as their home.

The constant subdividing of lineages gave fluidity to nomadic society. Tribal sections seceded, moved away, and joined with others for various reasons. The composition and size of even the smallest social units varied according to the season of the year and the natural environment. Individuals, families, and larger units usually moved in search of a more favorable social environment, but also because of quarrels, crowding, or personal attachments. The size and composition of various groups, and ultimately of the tribe itself, depended on the amount of grazing land available and on the policies and personalities of the leaders.

Traditionally, a man rich in cattle always had been sure to attract followers. The industry, thrift, and hardiness needed to build a large herd have been considered highly desirable qualities. At the same time, a rich man would be expected to be generous. If he lived up to that expectation, his fame would spread, and he would attract more followers. But wealth alone did not gain a nomad power beyond the level of a camp or several related camps. Ambition, ability to manipulate, hardheaded shrewdness, and attention to such matters as the marriage of his daughters to possible allies were also required.

In the precondominium era, leaders of various sections of a tribe had prestige but relatively little authority, in part because those who did not like them could leave. The colonial authorities stabilized the floating power positions in the traditional system. For purposes of taxation, justice, and public order, the new government needed representative authorities over identifiable groups. Locality could not serve as a basis in a nomadic society, so the government settled on the leaders of patrilineal descent groups and gave them a formal power they had previously lacked.

Among the nomadic Kababish camel herders (a loose confederation of tribes fluctuating in size, composition, and location), the definition of the tribe as a single unit by the colonial authorities and the appointment of an ambitious and capable individual as *nazir* led to a major change in social structure. Tribal sections and subsections were gradually eroded, leaving the individual household as the basic unit, ruled by the *nazir* and his primitive bureaucracy. The ruling lineage developed a concept of aristocracy, became very wealthy, and in effect spoke for its people in all contexts.

The administrative structure of the *naziriyah* and *umudiyah* ended shortly after the establishment of President Jaafar an Nimeiri's government in 1969, but the families of those who had held formal authority retained a good deal of local power. This authority or administrative structure was officially revived in 1986 by the coalition government of Sadiq al Mahdi.

Of continuing importance in economic and domestic matters and often in organizing political factions were minimal lineages, each comprehending three (at best four) generations. The social status of these lineages depended on whether they stemmed from old settler families or from newer ones. In villages composed of families or lineages of several tribes, marriage would likely take place within the tribe.

A class structure existed within villages. Large holdings were apt to be in the hands of merchants or leaders of religious brotherhoods, whose connections were wider and who did not necessarily live in the villages near their land. Although no longer nomadic, the ordinary villager preferred not to cultivate the land himself, however. Before the abolition of slavery, slaves did much of the work. Even after emancipation some ex-slaves or descendants of slaves remained as servants of their former masters or their descendants. Some villagers hired West Africans to do their work. Ex-slaves and seminomads or gypsies (*halabi,* usually smiths) living near the village were looked down on, and marriage with them by members of other classes was out of the question. A descendant of slaves could acquire education and respect, but villagers did not consider him a suitable partner for their daughters. Slave women had formerly been taken as concubines by villagers, but it was not clear that they were acceptable as wives.

Landholders in government-sponsored projects did not own the property but were tenants of the government. The tenants might be displaced Nubians, settled non-Arab nomads—as in Khashm al Qirbah—settled or nomadic Arabs, or West Africans. Many of these people used hired labor, either West Africans or nomads temporarily without livestock. In many instances, the original tenant remained a working farmer even if he used wage labor. In others, however, the original tenant might leave management in the hands of a kinsman and either live as a nomad or work and live in a city, a lifestyle typical of Nubians.

Although all settled communities were linked to the government, the projects involved a much closer relation between officials and villagers because officials managed the people as well as the enterprise. In effect, however, officials were outsiders, dominating the community but not part of it. They identified with the civil service rather than the community.

West Africans working in Arab settled communities formed cohesive communities of their own, and their relations with Arab tenants appeared to be restricted to their work agreements, even though both groups were Muslims. Cotton cultivation, practiced on most of the farms, was labor intensive, and because available labor was often scarce, particularly during the picking season, the West African laborers could command good wages. Their wages were set by agreements between the tenants who held the land and the headmen of the West African communities, and these agreements tended to set the wage scale for Arab laborers as well.

In the White Nile area, more recently settled by nomadic groups, aspects of nomadic social organization persisted through the condominium era. As among the nomads, leadership went to those who used their wealth generously and judiciously to gain the support of their lineages. In this case, however, wealth often took the form of grain rather than livestock. Most major lineages had such leaders, and those that did not were considered at a disadvantage. In addition to the wealthy, religious leaders (shaykhs) also had influence in these communities, particularly as mediators, in contrast to secular leaders who were often authoritarian.

The establishment of the *naziriyah* and *umudiyah* system tended to fix leadership in particular families, but there were often conflicts over which members should hold office. In the case of the Kawahla tribes of the White Nile, the ruling family tended to settle these differences in order to maintain its monopoly of important positions, and it took on the characteristics of a ruling lineage. Other lineages, however, tended to decline in importance as the system of which they had been a part changed. The ruling lineage made a point of educating its sons, so that they could find positions in business or in government. Although the Nimeiri government abolished the older system of local government, it appears that the former ruling lineage continued to play a leading role in the area.

Southern Communities

In preindependence Sudan, most southern communities were small, except for the large conglomerate of Nilotes, Dinka, and Nuer who dominated the Bahr al Ghazal and the Aali an Nil provinces and the Azande people of Al Istiwai Province. During the condominium, the colonial administration imposed stronger local authority on the communities. It made local leaders chiefs or headmen and gave them executive and judicial powers—tempered by local councils, usually of elders—to administer their people, under the scrutiny of a British district commissioner. As in the north, the relatively fluid relationships and boundaries among southern Sudanese became more stabilized.

There is no systematic record of how independence, civil war, and famine have affected the social order of southern peoples. The gradual incorporation of southerners into the national system—if only as migrant laborers and as local craftpeople—and increased opportunities for education have, however, affected social arrangements, ideas of status, and political views.

An educated elite had emerged in the south, and in 1991, some members of this elite were important politicians and administrators at the regional and national levels; however, other members had emigrated to escape northern discrimination. How the newer elite was linked to the older one was not clear. Secular chieftainships had been mostly gifts of the colonial authorities, but the sons of chiefs took advantage of their positions to get a Western education and to create family ties among local and regional elites.

Southern Sudan's development of an elite based on education and government office was facilitated by the absence of an indigenous trading and entrepreneurial class, who might have challenged the educated elite. Southern merchants were mostly Arabs or others of nonsouthern origin. In addition, the south lacked the equivalent of the northern Muslim leaders of religious orders, who also might have claimed a share of influence. Instead of several elites owing their status and power to varied sources and constituencies, the south developed an elite that looked for its support to persons of its own ethnic background and to those who identified with the south's African heritage. It was difficult to assess in the early 1990s, however, whether the civil war still allowed any elite southerners to gain much advantage.

In traditional Nilotic society clans were of two kinds. One kind, a minority but a large one, consisted of clans whose members had religious functions and furnished the priests of subtribes, sections, and sometimes of tribes. These priests have been called chiefs or masters of the fishing spear, a reference to the ritual importance of that instrument. Clans of the other kind were warrior groupings. The difference was one of function rather than rank. A spearmaster prayed for his people going to war or in other difficult situations and mediated between quarreling groups. He could function as a leader, but his powers lay in persuasion, not coercion. A spearmaster with a considerable reputation for spiritual power was deferred to on many issues. In rare cases—the most important was that of the Shilluk—one of the ritual offices gained influence over an entire people, and its holder was assigned the attributes of a divine king.

A special religious figure—commonly called a prophet—has arisen among some of the Nilotic peoples from time to time. Such prophets, thought to be possessed by a sky spirit, often had much wider influence than the ritual officeholders, who were confined to specific territorial segments. They gained substantial reputations as healers and used those reputations to rally their people against other ethnic groups and sometimes against the Arabs and the Europeans. The condominium authorities considered prophets subversive even when their message did not apparently oppose authority and hence suppressed them.

Another social pattern common to the Nilotes was the age-set system. Traditionally, males were periodically initiated into sets according to age; with the set, they moved through a series of stages, assuming and shedding rights and responsibilities as the group advanced in age. The system was closely linked to warfare and raiding, which diminished during the condominium. In modern times the civil war and famine further undermined the system, and its remnants seemed likely to fade as formal education became more accessible.

Historically, the Dinka have been the most populous Nilotic people, so numerous that social and political patterns varied from one tribal group to another. Among the Dinka, the tribal group was composed of a set of independent tribes that settled in a continuous area. The tribe, which ranged in size from 1,000 to 25,000 persons, traditionally had only two political functions. First, it controlled and defended the dry season pastures of its constituent subtribes; second, if a member of the tribe killed another member, the issue would be resolved peacefully. Homicide committed by someone outside the tribe was avenged, but not by the tribe as a whole. The colonial administration, seeking equitable access to adequate pasturage for all tribes, introduced a different system and thus eliminated one of the tribe's two responsibilities. In post-independence Sudan, the handling of homicide as a crime against the state made the tribe's second function also irrelevant. The utilization and politicization of ethnic groups as units of local government have supported the continuation of tribal structures into the 1990s; however, the tribal chiefs lacked any traditional functions, except as sage advisers to their people in personal and family matters. In the contemporary period, some attempts have been made to transform these ethnic tribal structures in order to produce a national or at least a greater subnational identity. For instance, in the early formation of the Sudanese People's Liberation Movement (SPLM), one of the main ideological tenets was the need to produce a new nonnorthern riverine area solidarity based on the mobilization of diverse ethnic groups in deprived areas. Although its success has been limited, to achieve this new sense of solidarity it has attempted to recruit not only southerners, but also the Fur, Funj, Nuba, and Beja communities.

The subtribes were the largest significant political segments, and they were converted into subchiefdoms by the colonial government. Although the subchiefs were stripped of most of their administrative authority during the Nimeiri regime (1969–85) and replaced by loyal members of the Sudan Socialist Union, the advice of subchiefs was sought on local matters. Thus, a three-tiered system was created: the traditional authorities, the Sudanese civil service, and the political bureaucrats from Khartoum. During the 1980s, this confused system of administration dissolved into virtual anarchy as a result of the replacement of one regime by another, civil war, and famine. In the south, however, the SPLM created new local administrative structures in areas under its control. In general, thus, although severely damaged, the traditional structure of Nilotic society remained relatively unchanged. Loyalties to one's rural ethnic community were deeply rooted and were not forgotten even by those who fled for refuge to northern urban centers.

Urban and National Elites

In this regionally and ethnically differentiated country, peoples and communities have been identified as Sudanese only by virtue of orientation to and control by a common government. They seemed not to share significant elements of a common value system, and economic ties among them were tenuous. If a national society and elites were emerging, it was in the Three Towns constituting the national capital area. It was in Khartoum, Khartoum North, and Omdurman that the national politicians, high-level bureaucrats, senior military, educated professionals, and wealthy merchants and entrepreneurs lived, worked, and socialized. Even those who had residences elsewhere maintained second homes in Omdurman.

These elites had long recognized the usefulness of maintaining a presence in the capital area, invariably living in Omdurman, a much more Arab city than Khartoum. The other, truly urban elites also tended to live in Omdurman, but the concentration of northern Sudan's varied elites in one city did not necessarily engender a common social life. As in many Arab and African cities, much of Omdurman's population lived in separate if not wholly isolated quarters.

Two components of the elite structure were not dominantly urban, however, although they were represented in the cities. These were the heads of important religious groups, whose constituencies and sources of power and wealth were largely rural, and what may be termed tribal elites, who carried some weight on the national level by virtue of their representing regional or sectional interests.

To the extent that the elites were Muslim and Arab—most were both—they shared a religion and language, but they were otherwise marked by differences in interest and outlook. Even more divergent were the southerners. Most elite southerners were non-Muslims, few spoke Arabic fluently, and they were regarded—

and saw themselves—not primarily as a professional or bureaucratic elite, but as a regional one. Many were said to prefer a career in the south to a post in Khartoum. These southern elites exercised political power directly or gave significant support to those who did. But so diverse and sometimes conflicting were their interests and outlooks that they did not constitute a cohesive class.

Changing Sudanese society had not developed a consensus on what kinds of work, talents, possessions, and background were more worthy than others and therefore conferred higher status. There had long been merchants, entrepreneurs, and religious leaders in Sudan. The latter had a special status, but wealth and the influence and power it generated had come to carry greater status in the Sudan of 1991 than did religious position. The educated secular elite was a newer phenomenon, and some deference was given its members by other elites. In the Muslim north, the educated ranged from devotees of Islamic activism to Islamic reformers and a few avowed secularists. Despite the respect generally given the educated, those at either extreme were likely to make members of other elites uncomfortable.

The younger, larger generation of the educated elite were not all offspring of the older, smaller educated elite. Many were sons (and sometimes daughters) of businessmen, wealthy landowners, and the tribal elite. It had not been established where the interests of first-generation educated persons lay, whether with a growing educated elite or with their families of very different backgrounds. A peculiar feature of the educated Sudanese was the fact that large numbers lived outside Sudan for years at a time, working in Middle Eastern oil-producing states, Europe, or North America. Some of their earnings came back to Sudan, but it was not clear that they had much to do with the formation or characteristics of a specifically Sudanese elite.

Tribal and ethnic elites carried weight in specific localities and might be significant if the states were to achieve substantial autonomy; however, their importance on the national scene was questionable.

Socializing and intermarriage among members of the different elites would have been significant in establishing a cohesive upper class. But that had not happened yet, and movement in that direction had suffered a severe blow when the government of Colonel Umar Hassan Ahmad al Bashir that came to power on June 30, 1989, imprisoned and executed leaders of the elite. Until the Bashir government displaced it in favor of Islamists, the elite regarded itself as the arbiter of social acceptance into the company of those riverine Arab families who had long lived in the Omdurman-Khartoum area, had substantial income from landholding, and had participated in the higher reaches of government during the condominium or engaged in the professions of medicine, law, and the university. Men from these families were well educated. Few engaged in business, which tended to be in the hands of families of at least partial Egyptian ancestry.

Beginning in the late 1960s, northern Muslims of non-Egyptian background began to acquire substantial wealth as businessmen, often as importers and exporters. By the early 1980s, perhaps twenty of them were millionaires. These men had been relatively young when they began their entrepreneurial activity, and unlike members of the older elite families, they were not well educated. By the late 1970s and early 1980s, however, many of these businessmen had started sending their children to Britain or the United States for their education. Reflecting trends in other societies, whereas the sons of the older elite had been educated mainly for government careers, by the 1980s business education was increasingly emphasized. In contrast to the more secular elites in the professions, the civil service, and the military, however, many members of these newer economic elites gravitated toward religion and the Muslim Brotherhood.

Typically, the older elite intermarried and excluded those whose backgrounds they did not know, even if the families were wealthy and successful in business, religion, or education. Gradually, after independence, Arabic speakers of other sedentary families acquired higher education, entered the bureaucracy or founded lucrative businesses, and began to participate to a limited degree in the social circle of the older families. The emphasis on "good family" persisted, however, in most marriages. Sedentary Arabs were acceptable, as were some persons of an older mixture of Arab and Nile Nubian ancestry, for example, the people around Dunqulah. But southern and western Sudanese—even if Muslims—and members of nomadic groups (particularly the darker Baqqara Arabs) were not. A southern Sudanese man might be esteemed for his achievements and other qualities, but he was not considered an eligible husband for a woman of a sedentary Arab family. There were some exceptions, as there had been decades ago, but they were generally perceived as such.

Women and the Family

In Sudan, the extended family provided social services. Traditionally, the family was responsible for the old, the sick, and the mentally ill, although many of these responsibilities had been eroded by urbanization. Whether in rural or urban society, however, the burden of these social services fell upon the women.

Except for a small number of liberated, educated young women from families of the elite, women remained within the household and were segregated at all festivities, eating after the men. This was particularly the case with Muslim households. Men entertained in their own quarters, and males of an extended family ate together. In a small family, the husband ate alone or, more frequently, took his bowl to join his male neighbors.

A young university couple might live much as in the West, in a house without relatives, and might live, eat, and entertain together. Nevertheless, traditional patterns were deeply rooted, and the husband would often be away visiting his male friends in the market and cafés. At home a servant helped with the children. Although the educated young married or unmarried woman had greater mobility because of her job, she was not exempt from the traditional restrictions and the supremacy of the Muslim husband. She was aware that her education and job were not a license to trespass upon male-dominated social norms.

In some respects, the uneducated woman had greater freedom so long as it was with her peers; for even among well-to-do families, a young woman was restricted to her household and female friends until transferred to similar seclusion in the house of her husband. Paradoxically, this segregation could create a spirit of independence, particularly among educated women, for there were a host of aunts, cousins, and grandmothers to look after the children and allow the mothers to work outside the home. Nevertheless, social traditions governed the way of life of Sudanese women. The segregation and subordination of women in Sudanese society should not obscure the fact that women dominated the household just as their men commanded public life. The home and the rearing of children were their domains—so long as they upheld male-oriented social norms.

Two traditional customs among Sudanese women had an enormous impact upon their private and social relationships—the *zar* cult and female "circumcision." *Zar* was the name given to the ceremony conducted only by women practitioners required to pacify evil spirits and to cleanse women of afflictions caused by demons or jinn. *Zar* cults were numerous throughout Muslim Africa. Illnesses, including depression, infertility, and other organic and psychological disorders, were attributed to possession by hostile spirits. Although *zar* ceremonies varied widely, they not only freed the one possessed but were great social occasions where women could communicate together as men did within male circles.

Female circumcision, or infibulation (excising the external genitalia and sewing the vagina shut) was widely practiced throughout Muslim Africa, and especially among Sudan's northern Arab population. Enormous pressure was put on the twelve-year-old or younger girl, as well as older women and their families, to observe these ceremonies and practices.

The issue of female circumcision was controversial, however, because of the physical and psychological problems it caused women. Midwives performed the operations, which often led to shock, hemorrhage, and septicemia. They created innumerable obstetrical problems before and after childbirth and throughout life. Despite international conferences, legislation, and efforts to eradicate these practices, however, in the early 1990s they appeared to be on the increase, not only in Sudan but in Africa, generally. At the same time, the adoption of Western medicine by growing educated classes was increasingly promoting awareness of the harmful effects of infibulation on women; the spread of Islam, however, inhibited the eradication of this practice.

In southern Sudan, the role of women differed dramatically from that in the north. Although women were subordinate to men, they enjoyed much greater freedom within southern Sudan's societies. Female circumcision was not practiced and no *zar* cult existed, although the spirits were regularly consulted about private and public affairs through practitioners. Women had greater freedom of movement and, indeed, participated to a limited degree in the councils of lineage. Husbands consulted their wives on matters pertaining to public affairs. Many women also played important roles in the mediation of disputes.

Religious Life

Somewhat more than half Sudan's population was Muslim in the early 1990s. Most Muslims, perhaps 90 percent, lived in the north, where they constituted 75 percent or more of the population. Data on Christians was less reliable; estimates ranged from 4 to 10 percent of the population. At least one-third of the Sudanese were still attached to the indigenous religions of their forebears. Most Christian Sudanese and adherents of local religious systems lived in southern Sudan. Islam had made inroads into the south, but more through the need to know Arabic than a profound belief in the tenets of the Quran. The SPLM, which in 1991 controlled most of southern Sudan, opposed the imposition of the sharia (Islamic law).

Islam: Tenets and Practice

Sudanese Muslims are adherents of the Sunni branch of Islam, sometimes called orthodox, by far the larger of the two major branches; the other branch is Shia (see Glossary), which is not represented in Sudan. Sunni Islam in Sudan is not marked by a uniform body of belief and practice, however. Some Muslims opposed aspects of Sunni orthodoxy, and rites having a non-Islamic origin were widespread, being accepted as if they were integral to Islam, or sometimes being recognized as separate. Moreover, Sunni Islam in Sudan (as in much of Africa) has been characterized by the formation of religious orders or brotherhoods, each of which made special demands on its adherents.

Sunni Islam requires of the faithful five fundamental obligations that constitute the five pillars of Islam. The first pillar, the *shahada* or profession of faith, is the affirmation "There is no god but God (Allah) and Muhammad is his prophet." It is the first step in becoming a Muslim and a significant part of prayer. The second obligation is prayer at five specified times of the day. The third enjoins almsgiving. The fourth requires fasting during daylight hours in the month of Ramadan. The fifth requires a pilgrimage to Mecca for those able to perform it, to participate in the special rites that occur during the twelfth month of the lunar calendar.

Most Sudanese Muslims who are born to the faith meet the first requirement. Conformity to the second requirement is more variable. Many males in the cities and larger towns manage to pray five times a day—at dawn, noon, midafternoon, sundown, and evening. Only one of these prayer times occurs during the usual working day of an urban dweller. A cultivator or pastoralist may find it more difficult to meet the requirements. Regular prayer is considered the mark of a true Muslim; it is usually accomplished individually or in small groups. Congregational prayer takes place at the Friday mosque when Muslims (usually men, but occasionally women separately located) gather, not only for the noon prayer, but also to hear readings and a sermon by the local imam (see Glossary). Muslims fast during the ninth month of the Muslim calendar, Ramadan, the time during which the first revelations to Muhammad occurred. It is a period during which most Muslims must abstain from eating, drinking, smoking, and sexual activity during the daylight hours. The well-to-do perform little work during this period, and many businesses close or operate on reduced schedules. Because the months of the lunar calendar revolve through the solar year, Ramadan occurs during various seasons over a period of a decade or so. In the early 1990s, observance appeared to be widespread, especially in urban areas and among sedentary Sudanese Muslims.

Historically, in the Muslim world almsgiving meant both a special tax for the benefit of the poor and voluntary giving to the needy, but its voluntary aspect alone survives. Alms may be given at any time, but there are specific occasions in the Islamic year or in the life of the donor when they are more commonly dispensed. Gifts, whether of money or food, may be made on such occasions as the feasts that end Ramadan and the pilgrimage to Mecca, or in penance for some misdeed. These offerings and others are typically distributed to poor kin and neighbors.

The pilgrimage to Mecca is less costly and arduous for the Sudanese than it is for many Muslims. Nevertheless, it takes time (or money if travel is by air), and the ordinary Sudanese Muslim has generally found it difficult to accomplish, rarely undertaking it before middle age. Some have joined pilgrimage societies into which members pay a small amount monthly and choose one of their number when sufficient funds have accumulated to send someone on the pilgrimage. A returned pilgrim is entitled to use the honorific title *hajj* or *hajjih* for a woman.

Another ceremony commonly observed is the great feast Id al Adha (also known as Id al Kabir), representing the sacrifice made during the last days of the pilgrimage. The centerpiece of the day is the slaughter of a sheep, which is distributed to the poor, kin, neighbors, and friends, as well as the immediate family.

Islam imposes a standard of conduct encouraging generosity, fairness, and honesty. Sudanese Arabs, especially those who are wealthy, are expected by their coreligionists to be generous.

In accordance with Islamic law, most Sudanese Muslims do not eat pork or shellfish. Conformity to the prohibitions on gambling and alcohol is less widespread. Usury is also forbidden by Islamic law, but Islamic banks have developed other ways of making money available to the public (see Islamic Banking, ch. 3).

Sunni Islam insists on observance of the sharia, which governs not only religious activity narrowly conceived but also daily personal and social relationships. In principle, the sharia stems not from legislative enactment or judicial decision but from the Quran and the hadith—the accepted sayings of Muhammad. That principle has given rise to the conventional understanding, advocated by Islamists, that there is no distinction between the religious and the secular in a truly Islamic society. Until 1983 modern criminal and civil, including commercial, law generally prevailed in Sudan. In the north, however, the sharia was expected to govern what is usually called family and personal law, i.e., matters such as marriage, divorce, and inheritance. In the towns and in some sedentary communities sharia was accepted, but in other sedentary communities and among nomads local custom was likely to prevail—particularly with respect to inheritance (see The Legal System, ch. 4).

In September 1983, Nimeiri imposed the sharia throughout the land, eliminating the civil and penal codes by which the country had been governed in the twentieth century. Traditional Islamic punishments were imposed for theft, adultery, homicide, and other crimes. The zealousness with which these punishments were carried out contributed to the fall of Nimeiri. Nevertheless, no successor government, including that of Bashir, has shown inclination to abandon the sharia.

Islam is monotheistic and insists that there can be no intercessors between an individual and God. Nevertheless, Sudanese Islam includes a belief in spirits as sources of illness or other afflictions and in magical ways of dealing with them. The imam of a mosque is a prayer leader and preacher of sermons. He may also be a teacher and in smaller communities combines both functions. In the latter role, he is called a *faqih* (pl., *fuqaha*), although a *faqih* need not be an imam. In addition to teaching in the local Quranic school (*khalwa*—see Glossary), the *faqih* is expected to write texts (from the Quran) or magical verses to be used as amulets and cures. His blessing may be asked at births, marriages, deaths, and other important occasions, and he may participate in wholly non-Islamic harvest rites in some remote places. All of these functions and capacities make the *faqih* the most important figure in popular Islam. But he is not a priest. His religious authority is based on his putative knowledge of the Quran, the sharia, and techniques for dealing with occult threats to health and well-being. The notion that the words of the Quran will protect against the actions of evil spirits or the evil eye is deeply embedded in popular Islam, and the amulets prepared by the *faqih* are intended to protect their wearers against these dangers.

In Sudan as in much of African Islam, the cult of the saint is of considerable importance, although some Muslims would reject it. The development of the cult is closely related to the presence of the religious orders; many who came to be considered saints on their deaths were founders or leaders of religious orders who in their lifetimes were thought to have *baraka,* a state of blessedness implying an indwelling spiritual power inherent in the religious office. *Baraka* intensifies after death as the deceased becomes a *wali* (literally friend of God, but in this context translated as saint). The tomb and other places associated with the saintly being become the loci of the person's *baraka,* and in some views he or she becomes the guardian spirit of the locality. The intercession of the *wali* is sought on a variety of occasions, particularly by those seeking cures or by barren women desiring children. A saint's annual holy day is the occasion of a local festival that may attract a large gathering.

Better-educated Muslims in Sudan may participate in prayer at a saint's tomb but argue that prayer is directed only to God. Many others, however, see the saint not merely as an intercessor with and an agent of God, but also as a nearly autonomous source of blessing and power, thereby approaching popular as opposed to orthodox Islam.

Islamic Movements and Religious Orders

Islam made its deepest and longest lasting impact in Sudan through the activity of the Islamic religious brotherhoods or orders. These orders emerged in the Middle East in the twelfth century in connection with the development of Sufism, a mystical current reacting to the strongly legalistic orientation of orthodox Islam. The orders first came to Sudan in the sixteenth century and became significant in the eighteenth. Sufism seeks for its adherents a closer personal relationship with God through special spiritual disciplines. The exercises (*dhikr*) include reciting prayers and passages of the Quran and repeating the names, or attributes, of God while performing physical movements according to the formula established by the founder of the particular order. Singing and dancing may be introduced. The outcome of an exercise, which lasts much longer than the usual daily prayer, is often a state of ecstatic abandon.

A mystical or devotional way (sing., *tariqa;* pl., *turuq*) is the basis for the formation of particular orders, each of which is also called a *tariqa*. The specialists in religious law and learning initially looked askance at Sufism and the Sufi orders, but the leaders of Sufi orders in Sudan have won acceptance by acknowledging the significance of the sharia and not claiming that Sufism replaces it.

The principal *turuq* vary considerably in their practice and internal organization. Some orders are tightly organized in hierarchical fashion; others have allowed their local branches considerable autonomy. There may be as many as a dozen *turuq* in Sudan. Some are restricted to that country; others are widespread in Africa or the Middle East. Several *turuq,* for all practical purposes independent, are offshoots of older orders and were established by men who altered in major or minor ways the *tariqa* of the orders to which they had formerly been attached.

The oldest and most widespread of the *turuq* is the Qadiriyah founded by Abd al Qadir al Jilani in Baghdad in the twelfth century and introduced into Sudan in the sixteenth. The Qadiriyah's principal rival and the largest *tariqa* in the western part of the country was the Tijaniyah, a sect begun by Ahmad at Tijani in Morocco, which eventually penetrated Sudan in about 1810 via the western Sahel (see Glossary). Many Tijani became influential in Darfur, and other adherents settled in northern Kurdufan. Later on, a class of Tijani merchants arose as markets grew in towns and trade expanded, making them less concerned with providing religious leadership. Of greater importance to Sudan was the *tariqa* established by the followers of Sayyid Ahmad ibn Idris, known as Al Fasi, who died in 1837. Although he lived in Arabia and never visited Sudan, his students spread into the Nile Valley establishing indigenous Sudanese orders, the Majdhubiyah, the Idrisiyah, and the Khatmiyyah.

Much different in organization from the other brotherhoods is the Khatmiyyah (or Mirghaniyah after the name of the order's founder). Established in the early nineteenth century by Muhammad Uthman al Mirghani, it became the best organized and most politically oriented and powerful of the *turuq* in eastern Sudan (see The Turkiyah, 1821–85, ch. 1). Mirghani had been a student of Sayyid Ahmad ibn Idris and had joined several important orders, calling his own order the seal of the paths (Khatim at Turuq— hence Khatmiyyah). The salient features of the Khatmiyyah are the extraordinary status of the Mirghani family, whose members alone may head the order; loyalty to the order, which guarantees paradise; and the centralized control of the order's branches.

The Khatmiyyah had its center in the southern section of Ash Sharqi State and its greatest following in eastern Sudan and in portions of the riverine area. The Mirghani family were able to turn the Khatmiyyah into a political power base, despite its broad geographical distribution, because of the tight control they exercised over their followers. Moreover, gifts from followers over the years have given the family and the order the wealth to organize politically. This power did not equal, however, that of the Mirghani's principal rival, the Ansar, or followers of the Mahdi, whose present-day leader was Sadiq al Mahdi, the great-grandson of Muhammad Ahmad ibn as Sayyid Abd Allah, al Mahdi, who drove the Egyptian administration from Sudan in 1885.

Most other orders were either smaller or less well organized than the Khatmiyyah. Moreover, unlike many other African Muslims, Sudanese Muslims did not all seem to feel the need to identify with one or another *tariqa*, even if the affiliation were nominal. Many Sudanese Muslims preferred more political movements that sought to change Islamic society and governance to conform to their own visions of the true nature of Islam.

One of these movements, Mahdism, was founded in the late nineteenth century. It has been likened to a religious order, but it is not a *tariqa* in the traditional sense. Mahdism and its adherents, the Ansar, sought the regeneration of Islam, and in general were critical of the *turuq*. Muhammad Ahmad ibn as Sayyid Abd Allah, a *faqih,* proclaimed himself to be Al Mahdi al Muntazar ("the awaited guide in the right path," usually seen as the Mahdi), the messenger of God and representative of the Prophet Muhammad, not simply a charismatic and learned teacher, an assertion that became an article of faith among the Ansar. He was sent, he said, to prepare the way for the second coming of the Prophet Isa (Jesus) and the impending end of the world. In anticipation of Judgment Day, it was essential that the people return to a simple and rigorous, even puritanical Islam (see The Mahdiyah, 1884–98, ch. 1). The idea of the coming of a Mahdi has roots in Sunni Islamic traditions. The issue for Sudanese and other Muslims was whether Muhammad Ahmad was in fact the Mahdi.

In the century since the Mahdist uprising, the neo-Mahdist movement and the Ansar, supporters of Mahdism from the west, have persisted as a political force in Sudan. Many groups, from the Baqqara cattle nomads to the largely sedentary tribes on the White Nile, supported this movement. The Ansar were hierarchically organized under the control of Muhammad Ahmad's successors, who have all been members of the Mahdi family (members of the *ashraf*). The ambitions and varying political perspectives of different members of the family have led to internal conflicts, and it appeared that Sadiq al Mahdi, putative leader of the Ansar since the early 1970s, did not enjoy the unanimous support of all Mahdists. Mahdist family political goals and ambitions seemed to have taken precedence over the movement's original religious mission. The modern-day Ansar were thus loyal more to the political descendants of the Mahdi than to the religious message of Mahdism.

A movement that spread widely in Sudan in the 1960s, responding to the efforts to secularize Islamic society, was the Muslim Brotherhood (Al Ikhwan al Muslimin), founded by Hasan al Banna in Egypt in the 1920s. Originally it was conceived as a religious revivalist movement that sought to return to the fundamentals of Islam in a way that would be compatible with the technological innovations introduced from the West. Disciplined, highly motivated, and well financed, the Muslim Brotherhood, known as the Brotherhood, became a powerful political force during the 1970s and 1980s, although it represented only a small minority of Sudanese. In the government that was formed in June 1989, following a bloodless coup d'état, the Brotherhood exerted influence through its political expression, the National Islamic Front (NIF) party, which included several cabinet members among its adherents (see Political Groups, ch. 4).

Christianity

Christianity was most prevalent among the peoples of Al Istiwai State—the Madi, Moru, Azande, and Bari. The major churches in the Sudan were the Roman Catholic and the Anglican. Southern communities might include a few Christians, but the rituals and world view of the area were not in general those of traditional Western Christianity. The few communities that had formed around mission stations had disappeared with the dissolution of the missions in 1964. The indigenous Christian churches in Sudan, with external support, continued their mission, however, and had opened new churches and repaired those destroyed in the continuing civil conflict. Originally, the Nilotic peoples were indifferent to Christianity, but in the latter half of the twentieth century many people in the educated elite embraced its tenets, at least superficially. English and Christianity have become symbols of resistance to the Muslim government in the north, which has vowed to destroy both. Unlike the early civil strife of the 1960s and 1970s, the insurgency in the 1980s and the 1990s has taken on a more religiously confrontational character.

Indigenous Religions

Each indigenous religion is unique to a specific ethnic group or part of a group, although several groups may share elements of belief and ritual because of common ancestry or mutual influence. The group serves as the congregation, and an individual usually belongs to that faith by virtue of membership in the group. Believing and acting in a religious mode is part of daily life and is linked to the social, political, and economic actions and relationships of the group. The beliefs and practices of indigenous religions in Sudan are not systematized, in that the people do not generally attempt to put together in coherent fashion the doctrines they hold and the rituals they practice.

The concept of a high spirit or divinity, usually seen as a creator and sometimes as ultimately responsible for the actions of lesser spirits, is common to most Sudanese groups. Often the higher divinity is remote, and believers treat the other spirits as autonomous, orienting their rituals to these spirits rather than to the high god. Such spirits may be perceived as forces of nature or as manifestations of ancestors. Spirits may intervene in people's lives, either because individuals or groups have transgressed the norms

107

of the society or because they have failed to pay adequate attention to the ritual that should be addressed to the spirits.

The Nilotes generally acknowledge an active supreme deity, who is therefore the object of ritual, but the beliefs and rituals differ from group to group. The Nuer, for example, have no word corresponding solely and exclusively to God. The word sometimes so translated refers not only to the universal governing spirit but also to ancestors and forces of nature whose spirits are considered aspects of God. It is possible to pray to one spirit as distinct from another but not as distinct from God. Often the highest manifestation of spirit, God, is prayed to directly. God is particularly associated with the winds, the sky, and birds, but these are not worshiped. The Dinka attribute any remarkable occurrence to the direct influence of God and will sometimes mark the occasion with an appropriate ritual. Aspects of God (the universal spirit) are distinguished, chief of which is Deng (rain). For the Nuer, the Dinka, and other Nilotes, human beings are as ants to God, whose actions are not to be questioned and who is regarded as the judge of all human behavior.

Cattle play a significant role in Nilotic rituals. Cattle are sacrificed to God as expiatory substitutes for their owners. The function is consistent with the significance of cattle in all aspects of Nilotic life. Among the Nuer, for example, and with some variations among the Dinka, cattle are the foundation of family and community life, essential to subsistence, marriage payments, and personal pride. The cattle shed is a shrine and meeting place, the center of the household; a man of substance, head of a family, and a leading figure in the community is called a "bull." Every man and the spirits themselves have ox names that denote their characteristic qualities. These beliefs and institutions give meaning to the symbolism of the rubbing of ashes on a sacrificial cow's back in order to transfer the burden of the owner's sins to the animal.

The universal god of the Shilluk is more remote than that of the Nuer and Dinka and is addressed through the founder of the Shilluk royal clan. Nyiking, considered both man and god, is not clearly distinguished from the supreme deity in ritual, although the Shilluk may make the distinction in discussing their beliefs. The king (*reth*) of the Shilluk is regarded as divine, an idea that has never been accepted by the Nuer and Dinka.

All of the Nilotes and other peoples as well pay attention to ancestral spirits, the nature of the cult varying considerably as to the kinds of ancestors who are thought to have power in the lives of their descendants. Sometimes it may be the founding ancestors of the group whose spirits are potent. In many cases it is the recently deceased ancestors who are active and must be placated.

Of the wide range of natural forces thought to be activated by spirits, perhaps the most common is rain. Although southern Sudan does not suffer as acutely as northern Sudan from lack of rain, there has sometimes been a shortage, particularly during the 1970s and 1980s and in 1990; this shortage has created hardship, famine, and death amidst the travail of civil war. For this reason, rituals connected with rain have become important in many ethnic groups, and ritual specialists concerned with rain or thought to incarnate the spirit of rain are important figures.

The distinction between the natural and the supernatural that has emerged in the Western world is not relevant to the traditional religions. Spirits may have much greater power than human beings, but their powers are perceived not as altering the way the world commonly works but as explaining occurrences in nature or in the social world.

Some men and women are also thought to have extraordinary powers. How these powers are believed to be acquired and exercised varies from group to group. In general, however, some people are thought to have inherited the capacity to harm others and to have a disposition to do so. Typically they are accused of inflicting illnesses on specific individuals, frequently their neighbors or kin. In some groups, it is thought that men and women who have no inherent power to harm may nevertheless do damage to others by manipulating images of the victim or items closely associated with that person.

Occasionally an individual may be thought of as a sorcerer. When illness or some other affliction strikes in a form that is generally attributed to a sorcerer, there are ways (typically some form of divination) of confirming that witchcraft was used and identifying the sorcerer.

The notions of sorcery are not limited to the southern Sudanese, but are to be found in varying forms among peoples, including nomadic and other Arabs, who consider themselves Muslims. A specific belief widespread among Arabs and other Muslim peoples is the notion of the evil eye. Although a physiological peculiarity of the eye (walleye or cross-eye) may be considered indicative of the evil eye, any persons expressing undue interest in the private concerns of another may be suspected of inflicting deliberate harm by a glance. Unlike most witchcraft, where the perpetrator is known by and often close to the victim, the evil eye is usually attributed to strangers. Children are thought to be the most vulnerable.

Ways exist to protect oneself against sorcery or the evil eye. Many magico-religious specialists—diviners and sorcerers—deal with these matters in Sudanese societies. The diviner is able to determine whether witchcraft or sorcery is responsible for the affliction and to discover the source. He also protects and cures by providing amulets and other protective devices for a fee or by helping a victim punish (in occult fashion) the sorcerer in order to be cured of the affliction. If it is thought that an evil spirit has possessed a person, an exorcist may be called in. In some groups these tasks may be accomplished by the same person; in others the degree of specialization may be greater. In northern Sudan among Muslim peoples, the *faqih* may spend more of his time as diviner, dispenser of amulets, healer, and exorcist than as Quranic teacher, imam of a mosque, or mystic.

Education

The public and private education systems inherited by the government after independence were designed more to provide civil servants and professionals to serve the colonial administration than to educate the Sudanese. Moreover, the distribution of facilities, staff, and enrollment was biased in favor of the needs of the administration and a Western curriculum. Schools tended to be clustered in the vicinity of Khartoum and to a lesser extent in other urban areas, although the population was predominantly rural. This concentration was found at all levels but was most marked for those in situations beyond the four-year primary schools where instruction was in the vernacular. The north suffered from shortages of teachers and buildings, but education in the south was even more inadequate. During the condominium, education in the south was left largely to the mission schools, where the level of instruction proved so poor that as early as the mid-1930s the government imposed provincial education supervisors upon the missionaries in return for the government subsidies that they sorely needed. The civil war and the ejection of all foreign missionaries in February 1964 further diminished education opportunities for southern Sudanese.

Since World War II, the demand for education has exceeded Sudan's education resources. At independence in 1956, education accounted for only 15.5 percent of the Sudanese budget, or £Sd45 million (for value of the Sudanese pound—see Glossary), to support 1,778 primary schools (enrollment 208,688), 108 intermediate schools (enrollment 14,632), and 49 government secondary schools (enrollment 5,423). Higher education was limited to the University of Khartoum, except for less than 1,000 students sent

Anglican mission school at Yei, southern Sudan
Courtesy Robert O. Collins

abroad by wealthy parents or on government scholarships. The
adult literacy rate in 1956 was 22.9 percent, and, despite the efforts of successive governments, by 1990 it had risen only to about
30 percent in the face of a rapidly expanding population.

The philosophy and curriculum beyond primary school followed
the British educational tradition. Although all students learned
Arabic and English in secondary and intermediate schools, the language of instruction at the University of Khartoum was English.
Moreover, the increasing demand for intermediate, secondary, and
higher education could not be met by Sudanese teachers alone, at
least not by the better educated ones graduated from the elite
teacher-training college at Bakht ar Ruda. As a result, education
in Sudan continued to depend upon expensive foreign teachers.

When the Nimeiri-led government took power in 1969, it considered the education system inadequate for the needs of social and
economic development. Accordingly, an extensive reorganization
was proposed, which would eventually make the new six-year
elementary education program compulsory and would pay much
more attention to technical and vocational education at all levels.
Previously, primary and intermediate schools had been preludes
to secondary training, and secondary schools prepared students for
the university. The system produced some well-trained university

111

graduates, but little was done to prepare for technical work or skilled labor the great bulk of students who did not go as far as the university or even secondary school.

By the late 1970s, the government's education system had been largely reorganized. There were some preprimary schools, mainly in urban areas. The basic system consisted of a six-year curriculum in primary schools and a three-year curriculum in junior secondary schools. From that point, qualified students could go on to one of three kinds of schools: the three-year upper secondary, which prepared students for higher education; commercial and agricultural technical schools; and teacher-training secondary schools designed to prepare primary-school teachers. The latter two institutions offered four-year programs. Postsecondary schools included universities, higher technical schools, intermediate teacher-training schools for junior secondary teachers, and higher teacher-training schools for upper-secondary teachers (see table 4, Appendix).

Of the more than 5,400 primary schools in 1980, less than 14 percent were located in southern Sudan, which had between 20 and 33 percent of the country's population. Many of these southern schools were established during the Southern Regional administration (1972–81). The renewal of the civil war in mid-1983 destroyed many schools, although the SPLA operated schools in areas under its control. Nevertheless, many teachers and students were among the refugees fleeing the ravages of war in the south.

In the early 1980s, the number of junior (also called general) secondary schools was a little more than one-fifth the number of primary schools, a proportion roughly consistent with that of general secondary to primary-school population (260,000 to 1,334,000). About 6.5 percent of all general secondary schools were in the south until 1983.

There were only 190 upper-secondary schools in the public system in 1980, but it was at this level that private schools of varying quality proliferated, particularly in the three cities of the capital area. Elite schools could recruit students who had selected them as a first choice, but the others took students whose examination results at the end of junior secondary school did not gain them entry to the government's upper secondary schools.

In 1980, despite the emphasis on technical education proposed by the government and encouraged by various international advisory bodies, there were only thirty-five technical schools in Sudan, less than one-fifth the number of academic upper secondary schools. In 1976–77 eight times as many students entered the academic stream as entered the technical schools, creating a profound imbalance in the marketplace. Moreover, prospective employers often found technical school graduates inadequately trained, a consequence of sometimes irrelevant curricula, low teacher morale, and lack of equipment. Performance may also have suffered because of the low morale of students, many of whom tended to see this kind of schooling as second choice at best, a not surprising view given the system's past emphasis on academic training and the low status of manual labor, at least among much of the Arab population. The technical schools were meant to include institutions for training skilled workers in agriculture, but few of the schools were directed to that end, most of them turning out workers more useful in the urban areas.

The hope for universal and compulsory education had not been realized by the early 1980s, but as a goal it led to a more equitable distribution of facilities and teachers in rural areas and in the south. During the 1980s, the government established more schools at all levels and with them, more teacher-training schools, although these were never sufficient to provide adequate staff. But the process was inherently slow and was made slower by limited funds and by the inadequate compensation for staff; teachers who could find a market for their skills elsewhere, including places outside Sudan, did not remain teachers within the Sudanese system.

The proliferation of upper-level technical schools has not dealt with what most experts saw as Sudan's basic education problem: providing a primary education to as many Sudanese children as possible. Establishing more primary schools was, in this view, more important that achieving equity in the distribution of secondary schools. Even more important was the development of a primary-school curriculum that was geared to Sudanese experience and took into account that most of those who completed six years of schooling did not go further. The realistic assumption was that Sudan's resources were limited and that expenditures on the postprimary level limited expenditures on the primary level, leaving most Sudanese children with an inadequate education. In the early 1990s, this situation had not significantly changed.

In the mid-1970s, there were four universities, eleven colleges, and twenty-three institutes in Sudan. The universities were in the capital area, and all of the institutions of higher learning were in the northern provinces. Colleges were specialized degree-granting institutions. Institutes granted diplomas and certificates for periods of specialized study shorter than those commonly demanded at universities and colleges. These postsecondary institutions and universities had provided Sudan with a substantial number of well-educated persons in some fields but left it short of technical personnel and specialists in sciences relevant to the country's largely rural character.

By 1980 two new universities had opened, one in Al Awsat Province at Wad Madani, the other in Juba in Al Istiwai Province, and in 1981 there was talk of opening a university in Darfur, which was nearly as deprived of educational facilities as the south. By 1990 some institutes had been upgraded to colleges, and many had become part of an autonomous body called the Khartoum Institute of Technical Colleges (also referred to as Khartoum Polytechnic). Some of its affiliates were outside the capital area, for example, the College of Mechanical Engineering at Atbarah, northeast of Khartoum, and Al Jazirah College of Agriculture and Natural Resources at Abu Naamah in Al Awsat.

The oldest university was the University of Khartoum, which was established as a university in 1956. In 1990 it enrolled about 12,000 students in degree programs ranging from four to six years in length. Larger but less prestigious was the Khartoum branch of the University of Cairo with 13,000 students. The size of the latter and perhaps its lack of prestige reflected the fact that many if not most of its students worked to support themselves and attended classes in the afternoon and at night, although some day classes were introduced in 1980. At the Khartoum branch only tuition was free, whereas all costs at the fully residential University of Khartoum were paid for by the government. At the Institute of Higher Technical Studies, which had 4,000 students in 1990, tuition was free, and a monthly grant helped to defray but did not fully cover other expenses. The smallest of the universities in the capital area was the specialized Islamic University of Omdurman, which existed chiefly to train Muslim religious judges and scholars.

The University of Juba, established in 1977, graduated its first class in 1981. It was intended to provide education for development and for the civil service for southern Sudan, although it was open to students from the whole country. In its first years, it enrolled a substantial number of civil servants from the south for further training, clearly needed in an area where many in the civil service had had little educational opportunity in their youth. After the outbreak of hostilities in the south in 1983, the university was moved to Khartoum, a move that had severely curtailed its instructional programs, but the university continued to operate again in Juba in the late 1980s. Al Jazirah College of Agriculture and Natural Resources was also intended to serve the country as a whole, but its focus was consistent with its location in the most significant agricultural area in Sudan.

Of particular interest was the dynamic growth and expansion of Omdurman Ahlia University. It was established by academics, professionals, and businesspeople in 1982 upon the hundredth anniversary of the founding of the city of Omdurman and was intended to meet the ever-growing demand for higher education and training. The university was to be nongovernmental, job oriented, and self-supporting. Support came mainly from private donations, foreign foundations, and the government, which approved the allotment of thirty acres of prime land on the western outskirts of Omdurman for the campus. Its curriculum, taught in English and oriented to job training pertinent to the needs of Sudan, had attracted more than 1,800 students by 1990. Its emphasis on training in administration, environmental studies, physics and mathematics, and library science had proven popular.

Girls' Education

Traditionally, girls' education was of the most rudimentary kind, frequently provided by a *khalwa,* or religious school, in which Quranic studies were taught. Such basic schools did not prepare girls for the secular learning mainstream, from which they were virtually excluded. Largely through the pioneering work of Shaykh Babikr Badri, the government had provided five elementary schools for girls by 1920. Expansion was slow, however, given the bias for boys and the conservatism of Sudanese society, with education remaining restricted to the elementary level until 1940. It was only in 1940 that the first intermediate school for girls, the Omdurman Girls' Intermediate School, opened. By 1955, ten intermediate schools for girls were in existence. In 1956, the Omdurman Secondary School for Girls, with about 265 students, was the only girls' secondary school operated by the government. By 1960, 245 elementary schools for girls had been established, but only 25 junior secondary or general schools and 2 upper-secondary schools. There were no vocational schools for girls, only a Nurses' Training College with but eleven students, nursing not being regarded by many Sudanese as a respectable vocation for women. During the 1960s and 1970s, girls' education made considerable gains under the education reforms that provided 1,086 primary schools, 268 intermediate schools, and 52 vocational schools for girls by 1970, when girls' education claimed approximately one-third of the total school resources available. Although by the early 1990s the numbers had increased in the north but not in the war-torn south, the ratio had remained approximately the same.

This slow development of girls' education was the product of the country's tradition. Parents of Sudanese girls tended to look upon girls' schools with suspicion if not fear that they would corrupt the morals of their daughters. Moreover, preference was given to sons, who by education could advance themselves in society to the pride and profit of the family. This girls could not do; their value was enhanced not at school but at home, in preparation for marriage and the dowry that accompanied the ceremony. The girl was a valuable asset in the home until marriage, either in the kitchen or in the fields. Finally, the lack of schools has discouraged even those who desired elementary education for their daughters.

This rather dismal situation should not obscure the successful efforts of schools such as the Ahfad University College in Omdurman, founded by Babikr Badri as an elementary school for girls in the 1920s. By 1990 it had evolved as the premier women's university college in Sudan with an enrollment of 1,800. It had a mixture of academic and practical programs, such as those that educated women to teach in rural areas.

Education Reform

The revolutionary government of General Bashir announced sweeping reforms in Sudanese education in September 1990. In consultation with leaders of the Muslim Brotherhood and Islamic teachers and administrators, who were the strongest supporters of his regime, Bashir proclaimed a new philosophy of education. He allocated £Sd400 million for the academic year 1990–91 to carry out these reforms and promised to double the sum if the current education system could be changed to meet the needs of Sudan.

The new education philosophy was to provide a frame of reference for the reforms. Education was to be based on the permanence of human nature, religious values, and physical nature. The reform could be accomplished only by a Muslim curriculum, which in all schools, colleges, and universities would consist of two parts: an obligatory and an optional course of study. The obligatory course to be studied by every student was to be based on revealed knowledge concerning all disciplines. All the essential elements of the obligatory course would be drawn from the Quran and the recognized books of the hadith. The optional course of study would permit the student to select certain specializations according to individual aptitudes and inclinations. Whether the government could carry out such sweeping reforms throughout the country in the face of opposition from within the Sudanese education establishment and the dearth of resources for implementing such an ambitious project remained to be seen. Membership in the Popular Defence Forces, a paramilitary body allied to the National Islamic Front, became a requirement for university admission. By early 1991,

*Hospital at Li Yubu, near the border with Central African Republic,
cares for lepers and victims of sleeping sickness.
Leprosy patients outside the bush dispensary
Courtesy Robert O. Collins*

117

Bashir had decreed that the number of university students be doubled and that Arabic replace English as the language of instruction in universities. He dismissed about seventy faculty members at the University of Khartoum who opposed his reforms.

Health

The high incidence of debilitating and sometimes fatal diseases that persisted in the 1980s and had increased dramatically by 1991 reflected difficult ecological conditions and inadequate diets. The diseases resulting from these conditions were hard to control without substantial capital inputs, a much more adequate health care system, and the education of the population in preventive medicine.

By 1991 health care in Sudan had all but disintegrated. The civil war in southern Sudan destroyed virtually all southern medical facilities except those that the SPLA had rebuilt to treat their own wounded and the hospitals in the three major towns—Malakal, Waw, and Juba—controlled by government forces. These facilities were virtually inoperable because of the dearth of the most basic medical supplies. A similar situation existed in northern Sudan, where health care facilities, although not destroyed by war, had been rendered almost impotent by the economic situation. Sudan lacked the hard currency to buy the most elementary drugs, such as antimalarials and antibiotics, and the most basic equipment, such as syringes. Private medical care in the principal towns continued to function but was also hampered by the dearth of pharmaceuticals. In addition, the Bashir government harassed the private sector, particularly the Sudan Medical Association, which was dissolved and many of its members jailed. Compounding the rapid decline in health care have been the years of famine during most of the 1980s, culminating in the great famine of 1991, which was caused by drought and widespread crop failures in Bahr al Ghazal State and in Darfur and Kurdufan. The famine was so widespread that, according to various estimates, 1.5 million to 7 million Sudanese would perish.

Widespread malnutrition also made the people more vulnerable to the many debilitating and fatal diseases present in Sudan. The most common illnesses were malaria, prevalent throughout the country; various forms of dysentery or other intestinal diseases, also widely prevalent; and tuberculosis, more common in the north but also found in the south. More restricted geographically but affecting substantial portions of the population in the areas of occurrence were schistosomiasis (snail fever), found in the White Nile and Blue Nile areas and in irrigated zones between the two Niles, and trypanosomiasis (sleeping sickness), originally limited to the southern borderlands but spreading rapidly in the 1980s in the forested regions of southern Sudan. It was estimated that by 1991 nearly 250,000 persons had been affected by sleeping sickness. Not uncommon were such diseases as cerebrospinal meningitis, measles, whooping cough, infectious hepatitis, syphilis, and gonorrhea.

Even in years of normal rainfall, many Sudanese in the rural areas suffered from temporary undernourishment on a seasonal basis, a situation that worsened when drought, locusts, or other disasters struck crops or animals. More dangerous was malnutrition among children, defined as present when a child's body weight was less than 80 percent of the expected body weight for the age. The weight criterion in effect stood for a complex of nutritional deficiencies that might lead directly to death or make the child susceptible to diseases from which he or she could not recover. A Sudanese government agency estimated that half the population under fifteen—roughly one-fourth of the total population—suffered from malnutrition in the early 1980s. This figure increased substantially during the famine of 1991.

Acquired immune deficiency syndrome (AIDS) was present in Sudan, primarily in the southern states bordering Uganda and Zaire, where the disease had reached epidemic proportions. There had been a steady increase in AIDS in Khartoum because of the hundreds of thousands of people emigrating to the capital to escape the civil war and famine. The use of unsterile syringes and untested blood by health care providers clearly contributed to its spread. In spite of the increase in the spread of AIDS, the Sudanese government in 1991 lacked a coherent national AIDS control policy.

In the late 1970s and early 1980s, the government undertook programs to deal with specific diseases in limited areas, with help from the World Health Organization and other sources. It also initiated more general approaches to the problems of health maintenance in rural areas, particularly in the south. These efforts began against a background of inadequate and unequal distribution of medical personnel and facilities, and events of the late 1980s and early 1990s caused an almost complete breakdown in health care. In 1982 there were nearly 2,200 physicians in Sudan, or roughly one for each 8,870 persons. Most physicians were concentrated in urban areas in the north, as were the major hospitals, including those specializing in the treatment of tuberculosis, eye disorders, and mental illness. In 1981 there were 60 physicians in the south for a population of roughly 5 million, or one for approximately 83,000 persons. In 1976 there were 2,500 medical assistants, the crucial participants in a system that could not assume the availability of an adequate number of physicians in the foreseeable future. After three years of training and three to four years of supervised hospital experience, medical assistants were expected to be able to diagnose common endemic diseases and to provide simple treatments and vaccinations. There were roughly 12,800 nurses in 1982 and about 7,000 midwives, trained and working chiefly in the north.

In principle, medical consultation and therapeutic drugs were free. There were, however, private clinics and pharmacies, and they were said to be growing in number in the capital area in the late 1970s and early 1980s. The ever worsening shortage of medical personnel and of pharmaceuticals had, however, limited the effectiveness of free treatment. In urban areas, physicians and medical assistants could be seen only after a long wait at the hospitals or clinics at which they served. In rural areas, extended travel as well as long waits were common. In urban and rural areas, the drugs prescribed were often not obtainable from hospital pharmacies. In the Khartoum area, they could be obtained at considerable cost from private pharmacies. In addition to the problems of cost, however, were those posed by difficulties of transportation and inadequate storage facilities. In the south, especially during the rainy season, the roads were often impassable. There and elsewhere, the refrigeration necessary for many pharmaceuticals was not available. All of these difficulties were compounded by inadequacies of stock rotation and inspection. Members of the country's elite overcame these problems by taking advantage of medical treatment abroad.

In the mid-1970s, the Ministry of Health began a national program to provide primary health care with emphasis on preventive medicine. The south was expected to be the initial beneficiary of the program, given the dearth of health personnel and facilities there, but other areas were not to be ignored. The basic component in the system was the primary health care center staffed by community health workers and expected to serve about 4,000 persons. Community health care workers received six months of formal training followed by three months of practical work at an existing center, after which they were assigned to a new center. Refresher courses were also planned. The workers were to provide health care information and certain medicines and would refer cases they could not deal with to dispensaries and hospitals. In principle, there would be one dispensary for every 24,000 persons. Of the forty primary health care centers and dispensaries to be completed by 1984, about half were in place by 1981. In addition, local (district) hospitals were to be improved. The program in the south was supported by the Federal Republic of Germany (West Germany), which also provided medical advisers. In 1981 the program

Doctors at a bush dispensary inspecting a pneumonia patient outside his hut
Courtesy Robert O. Collins

was most advanced in eastern Al Istiwai Province, but it was too early to assess the effects on the health of the people, and the program had virtually disappeared by 1991.

Two local programs for the control of endemic disease were also undertaken in the late 1970s and early 1980s. One was in the area of the Gezira Scheme, where it was estimated that 50 to 70 percent of the people suffered from schistosomiasis, a health problem aggravated by the presence of malaria and dysentery. The Blue Nile Health Care Project, a ten-year program inaugurated in early 1980, was intended to deal with all of these waterborne diseases simultaneously. Because people bathed in and drank the water in the irrigation canals, which were contaminated by human waste, a major change in their habits was required, as well as the provision of healthful drinking water and sanitary facilities that did not drain into the canals. Diarrheal diseases were to be treated with rehydration salts that should diminish considerably the very high rate of infant deaths. As of 1991, the persistent civil war and the collapse of the Sudanese economy made the inauguration of these projects doubtful. Other programs to provide relief to disease and famine victims in Sudan were organized by foreign aid agencies such as the United Nations World Food Programme, the Save the Children Fund, Oxford Committee for Famine Relief, and the

French medical group, Médecins sans Frontières (Doctors Without Borders). Sudan in 1991 faced serious problems in providing its people with adequate health care as well as education and an acceptable standard of living.

* * *

Extensively detailed and systematic analyses of contemporary Sudanese society or any large segment of it were not available as of 1991. The Bashir government's systematic purge of the civil service, the professional associations, the academic community, and the trade unions disrupted and curtailed the flow of statistics and information from ministries and other government and nongovernmental organizations. Such research material has also been impeded by the civil war in southern Sudan and the recurring famines. Nevertheless, many monographs have been written on specific Sudanese subjects ranging from anthropology to zoology.

As a description of the physical and geographical nature of Sudan, K.M. Barbour's *The Republic of the Sudan: A Regional Geography* remains the standard work, supplemented by J.M.G. Lebon's *Land Use in the Sudan.* Because the Nile flows are crucial to Sudan, they have been extensively studied, producing a voluminous literature. Information on this subject is synthesized in two works: John Waterbury, *Hydropolitics and the Nile Valley* and Robert O. Collins, *The Waters of the Nile: Hydropolitics and the Jonglei Canal, 1900–1988.*

Interpretations of the population situation by several authors are found in *Population of the Sudan: A Joint Project on Mapping and Analyzing the 1983 Census Data* and in articles in the *Sudan Journal of Population Studies.*

Most ethnic studies are monographs that describe a particular ethnic group. Those include Edward E. Evans-Pritchard's *The Nuer* and Francis Mading Deng's *The Dinka of the Sudan.* For a more recent and sensitive treatment of ethnicity in Sudan, see articles in *The Middle East Journal,* autumn 1990; the perceptive novel by Francis Mading Deng, *Cry of the Owl;* and Abel Alier's *Southern Sudan: Too Many Agreements Dishonoured.*

Anne Cloudsley's *Women of Omdurman: Life, Love, and the Cult of Virginity,* Asma El Dareer's *Woman, Why Do You Weep? Circumcision and Its Consequences,* and Hanny Lightfoot Klein's *Prisoners of Ritual: An Odyssey into Female Genital Circumcision in Africa* are perhaps the three most informative studies of women's role in Sudan.

Although it is somewhat outdated (he does not discuss the Muslim Brotherhood, which appeared in Sudan only in the 1950s), J. Spencer Trimingham's *Islam in the Sudan* remains the best reference on orthodox Islam and the Sufi brotherhoods. Anthropologist

Godfrey Lienhardt's *Divinity and Experience: The Religion of the Dinka* explores the importance of religion among the largest ethnic group in Sudan.

The history of education in southern Sudan is covered in Lilian Passmore Sanderson and Neville Sanderson's *Education, Religion, and Politics in Southern Sudan, 1899-1964*. To assess the contemporary reordering of the education system, one should examine M. Abdalghaffar Othman's *Current Philosophies, Patterns, and Issues in Higher Education*.

The two standard historical studies of the Sudan Medical Service are Ahmed Bayoumi's *The History of Sudan Health Services* and Herbert Chavasse Squire's *The Sudan Medical Service*. (For further information and complete citations, see Bibliography.)

Chapter 3. The Economy

Worker picking cotton, one of Sudan's leading exports

THE ECONOMY OF SUDAN continued to be in disarray in mid-1991. The principal causes of the disorder have been the violent, costly civil war, an inept government, an influx of refugees from neighboring countries as well as internal migration, and a decade of below normal annual rainfall with the concomitant failure of staple food and cash crops.

The economic and political upheavals that characterized Sudan in the 1980s have made statistical material either difficult to obtain or unreliable. Prices and wages in the marketplace fluctuated constantly, as did the government's revenue. Consequently, information concerning Sudan's economy tends to be more historical than current.

In the 1970s, economic growth had been stimulated by a large influx of capital from Saudi Arabia and Kuwait, invested with the expectation that Sudan would become "the breadbasket" of the Arab world, and by large increments of foreign aid from the United States and the European Community (EC). Predictions of continuing economic growth were sustained by loans from the World Bank (see Glossary) and generous contributions from such disparate countries as Norway, Yugoslavia, and China. Sudan's greatest economic resource was its agriculture, to be developed in the vast arable land that either received sufficient rainfall or could be irrigated from the Nile. By 1991 Sudan had not yet claimed its full water share (18.5 billion cubic meters) under the 1959 Nile Waters Agreement between Egypt and Sudan.

Sudan's economic future in the 1970s was also energized by the Chevron Overseas Petroleum Corporation's discovery of oil on the borderlands between the provinces of Kurdufan and Bahr al Ghazal. Concurrently, the most thoroughly researched hydrological project in the Third World, the Jonglei Canal (also seen as Junqali Canal), was proceeding ahead of schedule, planned not only to provide water for northern Sudan and Egypt, but also to improve the life of the Nilotic people living in the canal area. New, large agricultural projects had been undertaken in sugar at Kinanah and cotton at Rahad. Particularly in southern Sudan, where the Addis Ababa accords of March 27, 1972, had seemingly ended the insurgency, a sense of optimism and prosperity prevailed, dashed, however, when the civil war resumed in 1983. The Khartoum government controlled these development projects, but entrepreneurs could make fortunes through the intricate network of kinship and political relations that has traditionally driven Sudan's social and economic machinery.

In the early 1970s, public enterprises dominated the modern sector, including much of agriculture and most of large-scale industry, transport, electric power, banking, and insurance. This situation resulted from the private sector's inability to finance major development and from an initial government policy after the 1969 military coup to nationalize the financial sector and part of existing industry. Private economic activities were relegated to modern small- and medium-scale industry. The private sector dominated road transport and domestic commerce and virtually controlled traditional agriculture and handicrafts.

In the 1980s, however, Sudan underwent severe political and economic upheavals that shook its traditional institutions and its economy. The civil war in the south resumed in 1983, at a cost of more than £Sd11 million per day (for value of the Sudanese pound—see Glossary). The main participant in the war against the government was the Sudanese People's Liberation Army (SPLA), the armed wing of the Sudanese People's Liberation Movement (SPLM), under John Garang's leadership. The SPLA made steady gains against the Sudanese army until by 1991 it controlled nearly one-third of the country.

The dearth of rainfall in the usually productive regions of the Sahel (see Glossary) and southern Sudan added to the country's economic problems. Refugees, both Sudanese and foreigners from Eritrea, Ethiopia, Uganda, and Chad, further strained the Sudanese budget. International humanitarian agencies have rallied to Sudan's aid, but the government rejected their help.

When Jaafar an Nimeiri was overthrown in April 1985, his political party disappeared, as did his elaborate security apparatus. The military transitional government and the democratically elected coalition government of Sadiq al Mahdi that succeeded the exiled Nimeiri failed to address the country's economic problems. Production continued to decline as a result of mismanagement and natural disasters. The national debt grew at an alarming rate because Sudan's resources were insufficient to service it. Not only did the SPLA shut down Chevron's prospecting and oil production, but it also stopped work on the Jonglei Canal.

On June 30, 1989, a military coup d'état led by Colonel (later Lieutenant General) Umar al Bashir overthrew the government of Sadiq al Mahdi. Ideologically tied to the Muslim Brotherhood and dependent for political support on the Brotherhood's party, the National Islamic Front, the Bashir regime has methodically purged those agencies that dealt primarily with the economy—the civil service, the trade unions, the boards of publicly owned enterprises, the Ministry of Finance and Economic Planning, and the central bank. Under Bashir's government, Sudan's economy has been further strained by the most severe famine of this century, the continuation of the war in the south, and a foreign policy that has left Sudan economically, if not politically, isolated from the world community.

Economic Development

Historically, the colonial government was not interested in balanced economic growth and instead concentrated its development efforts on irrigated agriculture and the railroad system throughout the Anglo-Egyptian condominium (see The Anglo-Egyptian Condominium, 1899–1955, ch. 1). Incidental government investment had gone mainly into ad hoc projects, such as the construction of cotton gins and oilseed-pressing mills as adjuncts of the irrigation program. A limited amount of rainfed mechanized farming, similarly on an ad hoc basis, had also been developed during World War II. After the war, two development programs—actually lists of proposed investments—were drawn up for the periods 1946–50 and 1951–55. These plans appear to have been a belated effort to broaden the country's economic base in preparation for eventual Sudanese independence. Both programs were seriously hampered by a lack of experienced personnel and materials and had little real impact. Independently, the private sector had expanded irrigated agriculture, and some small manufacturing operations had been started, but only three larger industrial enterprises (meat and cement plants and a brewery) had been constructed, all between 1949 and 1952. As a result, at independence the new Sudanese government's principal development inheritance was the vast irrigated Gezira Scheme (also seen as Jazirah Scheme) and Sudan Railways.

Not until 1960 did the new government attempt to prepare a national development plan. Since that time, three plans have been formulated, none of which has been carried through to completion. Work on the first of these, the Ten-Year Plan of Economic and Social Development, for the fiscal years (FY—see Glossary) 1961–70, began in late 1960, but the plan was not formally adopted until September 1962, well over a year after its scheduled starting date. The total ten-year investment was set at £Sd565 million, at the time equivalent to more than US$1.6 billion. The private sector was expected to provide 40 percent of the amount. Unfortunately, the goals were overly ambitious, and the government had few experienced planners. The plan as prepared was not adhered

to, and implementation was actually carried out through investment programs that were drawn up annually and funded through
the development budget. Projects not in the original plan were frequently included. Investment was at a high rate in the first years,
well beyond projections, and a number of major undertakings had
been completed by mid-plan, including the Khashm al Qirbah and
Manaqil irrigation projects, a sugar factory at the former site,
another at Al Junayd irrigation project, and the Roseires (also called
Ar Rusayris) Dam.

As the 1960s progressed, a lack of funds threatened the continuation of development activities. Government current expenditure
had increased much faster than receipts, in part because of the intensification of the civil war in the south, and government surpluses
to finance development vanished. At the same time, there was a
shortfall in foreign investment capital. The substantial foreign
reserves held at the beginning of the plan period were depleted,
and the government resorted to deficit financing and foreign borrowing. The situation had so deteriorated by 1967 that implementation of the Ten-Year Plan was abandoned. Sudan's international
credit worthiness became open to question.

Despite major financial problems, real economic gains were
nevertheless made during the Ten-Year Plan, and per capita income rose from the equivalent of US$86 in 1960 to about US$104
at the end of the decade. Late in the 1960s, the government prepared a new plan covering FY 1968 to FY 1972. This plan was
discarded after the military coup led by Nimeiri in May 1969. Instead, the government adopted the Five-Year Plan of Economic
and Social Development, 1970–74. This plan, prepared with the
assistance of Soviet planning personnel, sought to achieve the major
goals of the May revolution (creation of an independent national
economy; steady growth of prosperity; and further development
of cultural, education, and health services) through socialist development.

During the plan's first two years, expenditures remained low,
affected largely by uncertainties that stemmed from the civil war.
After the war ceased in early 1972, the government felt that the
plan failed to provide for transportation improvements and large-
scale productive projects. In 1973, the government therefore established the Interim Action Program, which extended the original
plan period through FY 1976. New objectives included the removal of transportation bottlenecks, attainment of self-sufficiency
in the production of several agricultural and industrial consumer
items, and an increase in agricultural exports. To accomplish these
goals, proposed public sector investment increased from £Sd215

million to £Sd463 million (however, actual expenditures during the five years, excluding technical assistance, were £Sd250 million). Private sector projected investment was estimated at £Sd170 million originally, but the nationalizations carried out in 1970 and 1971 discouraged private investment in productive undertakings. Foreign private capital investment became negligible, and domestic private capital was put mostly into areas considered less subject to takeover, such as service enterprises, housing, traditional agriculture, and handicrafts (see Manufacturing, this ch.). The denationalizations since 1972 resulted in increased private foreign investment in development. The final investment total during the first five years was considerably above the original plan projection. The plan failed to achieve its goal of a 7.6 percent annual growth rate in gross domestic product (GDP—see Glossary), however, and was extended to 1977.

From FY 1973, after introduction of the Interim Action Program, through 1977, development expenditures grew to more than 1 billion Sudanese pounds. The government initiated several irrigation projects at Rahad, Satit southeast of Khashm al Qirba, Ad Damazin, and Kinanah; and established factories at Sannar, Kinanah, at Shandi on the Nile northeast of Khartoum, Kusti, Kaduqli, Nyala, and Rabak on the White Nile south of Khartoum. Roads between Khartoum and Port Sudan were paved with tarmacadam and excavation began on the Jonglei Canal. The original plan called for almost half of investment to be provided by surpluses in the central government budget. Although this assumption appeared highly optimistic in view of the modest surpluses attained during the last half of the 1960s, tax revenues did increase as projected.

Earnings from public corporations, however, fell short of projections, and growth in government current expenditures greatly exceeded revenue growth. As a result, not only were there no surpluses in the public sector, but the government had to borrow from the Bank of Sudan to cover the current expenditure account. Foreign capital, although abundant, also did not equal the spending on development, and, contrary to the expectations of the plan's drafters, the government had to resort to domestic borrowing to proceed with project implementation.

In early 1977, the government published the successor Six-Year Plan of Economic and Social Development, 1977–82. Its goals and projections also appeared optimistic because of the worsening domestic economic situation, which was marked by growing inflation. The inflation stemmed in large part from deficit development financing (printing money), increasing development costs because of worldwide price rises, and rising costs for external capital. During the plan's second year, FY 1978, there was no economic growth as the deficit development financing in the mid- and late 1970s led Sudan into a deepening economic crisis. At the same time, external debt pressures mounted, and Sudan failed to meet its scheduled payments (see Foreign Trade and Balance of Payments, this ch.). A substantial cutback in further development expenditures became unavoidable. The result was an abandonment of Six-Year Plan projections, a restriction of expenditures generally to the completion of projects under way, improvement of the performance of existing operational projects, elimination of transport constraints, and a series of short-term "rolling" programs that particularly emphasized exports.

In October 1983, the government announced a three-year public investment program, but efforts to Islamize the economy in 1984 impeded its implementation, and after the Nimeiri overthrow in April 1985, the program was suspended (see table 5, Appendix). In August 1987, an economic recovery program was initiated. This program was followed, beginning in October 1988, by a three-year recovery program to reform trade policy and regulate the exchange rate, reduce the budget deficit and subsidies, and encourage exports and privatization. There was little possibility for early economic recovery offered by the military government of Colonel Umar al Bashir that took office on June 30, 1989. The government's economic policies proposed to Islamize the banking system, but foreign business interests viewed this measure as a disincentive to do business in Sudan because no interest would be paid on new loans. Furthermore, Islamic banks and other economic supporters of the regime were to be granted disproportionate influence over the economy, a policy that led to widespread resentment among other sectors. Finally, the government did not go far enough to satisfy the International Monetary Fund (IMF—see Glossary) or other major creditors that it had sufficiently reduced subsidies on basic commodities, thus reducing its budget deficit. Bashir had announced an economic recovery program in mid-1990, but in 1991 its results were still awaited.

The late 1970s had seen corruption become widespread. Although always present, corruption never had been a major characteristic of the Sudanese economic scene. The enormous sums that poured into Sudan in the late 1970s from the Arab oil-exporting countries, the United States, and the European Community, however, provided opportunities for the small clique that surrounded Nimeiri to enrich themselves. This corruption fell into three principal categories: embezzlement of public funds, most of which left the country; agricultural acquisition schemes; and investment in the mercantile sphere.

The most common ways of embezzling public funds were acquiring liquid assets from banks or government agencies, selling the state's assets, selling state land, and smuggling. The siphoning off of liquid assets usually required the connivance of a high government official. Between 1975 and 1982, more than 800 cases were reported of embezzlement of, on the average, more than £Sd1,000. In one case, principal bank officials embezzled £Sd3 million; another bank made a loan of £Sd200 million to a businessman whose business was fictitious.

State property sold by embezzlers included gasoline and medicines. State officials also sold real estate in residential areas at below the market price. An impressive residence would then be built on the property for rental to diplomatic officials or executives of multinational companies. In the past, small operators penetrating the vast and unpatrolled borders of Sudan had carried out smuggling, but in the late 1980s it became a vast and sophisticated business. Of the smuggling operations uncovered, one involved £Sd2.5 million in cloth, another £Sd1 million in matches, and a third £Sd0.5 million in automobiles.

Another highly profitable form of corruption was the selling of state farmlands, each about 30,000 *feddans* (1 *feddan* is equivalent to 0.42 hectare). Mechanized Farming Corporation (MFC) officials sold large numbers of *feddans* at low prices to senior officials in Khartoum; many of the latter exploited the land for profit at the expense of the peasantry and caused profound ecological deterioration.

As corruption ran rampant during the late 1970s until Nimeiri was overthrown, commercial companies, particularly in the export-import trade, profited through their influence on public policy and through special permits they received. The Islamic institutions that dominated Sudanese banking facilitated this corruption (see Islamic Banking, this ch.). These banks, of which the most important was the Faisal Islamic Bank, possessed privileges not enjoyed by Sudanese national banks, such as exemption from taxation and the right to transfer profits abroad. An example of the combination of political power and financial capital was the Islamic Development Company. Established in 1983 as a limited shareholding company with an authorized capitalization of US$1 billion, the company was chartered to invest in agriculture, industry, services, construction, and Islamic banks. In practice, it concentrated on the export-import trade, where high profits could be made quickly and easily, in contrast to the slow returns of agricultural development projects. The board of directors consisted of ten persons, four Sudanese and six foreign nationals, mostly Saudis, including a son of the late King Faisal ibn Abd al Aziz Al Saud. Of the Sudanese, three belonged to the National Islamic Front, and the fourth was the son of the leader of the Khatmiyyah, a Muslim religious group associated with the National Unionist Party. All had connections with Islamic banks and the Sudanese parliament. Their purpose was to strengthen the Islamist movement's economic power by tying their commercial enterprise to the state in order to achieve a privileged position in the marketplace. They accomplished this aim by granting shares valued at US$100,000 to founding members and to prominent persons, ranging from the republic's president to wealthy Muslim businessmen.

In spite of the growth of the Islamic banking movement, between 1978 and 1985, agricultural and industrial production had declined in per capita terms. Imports during much of the 1980s were three times the level of exports. By 1991 the value of the Sudanese pound against the dollar had sunk to less than 10 percent of its 1978 value, and the country's external debt had risen to US$13 billion, the interest on which could be paid only by raising new loans.

Two reasons for this decline were the droughts and accompanying famine occurring in the 1980s and 1991, and the influx of more than 1 million refugees from Eritrea, Ethiopia, Chad, and Uganda, in addition to the persons displaced by the continuing war in southern Sudan who were estimated to number between 1.5 million and 3.5 million. Nevertheless, the decline in Sudan's agricultural and industrial production had begun before these calamities. Few development projects were completed on time and those that were failed to achieve projected production. After 1978 the GDP steadily fell so that the vast sums of money borrowed could not be repaid by increased productivity. Sudan found itself in a cycle of increasing debt and declining production.

These economic problems had two fundamental causes. First, in planning little thought was given to the impact of any one project on the whole economy and even less to the burden such huge projects would place on a fragile infrastructure. Some ministries undertook projects by unilaterally negotiating loans without reference to the Central Planning Agency. Second, remittances by Sudanese laborers in the Persian Gulf (thousands of workers were based in Kuwait and Iraq, until many of them were expelled) placed a stress on Sudan's economy because the government was forced to relax its stringent currency controls to induce these workers to repatriate their earnings. Such funds were largely invested in consumer goods and housing, rather than in development projects.

Foreign Aid

Foreign capital has played a major role in development. The great reliance on it and the general ease with which it was acquired were major factors contributing to the severe financial problems that beset the country after the mid-1970s. Sudan obtained public sector loans for development from a wide variety of international agencies and individual governments. Until the mid-1970s, the largest single source had been the World Bank, including the International Development Association (IDA) and the International Finance Corporation (IFC). By 1975 the World Bank and its organs had furnished the equivalent of US$300 million. Excluding repayments, the outstanding amount had risen to US$786 million in 1981, as major commitments to projects including agriculture, transportation, and electric power were made (chiefly by IDA, which accounted by 1981 for more than US$594 million of the outstanding total).

The Arab oil-producing states, as their balance of payments surpluses grew in the 1970s following increases in world petroleum prices, also became significant suppliers of development capital through bilateral loans and Arab international institutions. The largest of the latter was the Arab Fund for Economic and Social Development (AFESD), through which was proposed the 1976 program to develop Sudan as a breadbasket for the Arab world. The implementing agency, the Arab Authority for Agricultural Investment and Development (AAAID), was established in Khartoum, based on an agreement signed in November 1976 by twelve Arab states. After the mid-1970s, Saudi Arabia, one of the founders of AAAID, through its Saudi Development Fund became the largest source of investment capital, apparently convinced that Sudan's development could complement its own, especially in making up its large food deficits. Unfortunately, the ambitious plans for Sudan's becoming the Arab world's major food source faded by the mid-1980s into an economic nightmare as agricultural production declined sharply.

In 1977 the United States resumed economic (and military) aid to Sudan. This aid followed a ten-year lapse beginning with a break in diplomatic relations between the two countries in 1967, with relations restored in July 1972 (see United States, ch. 4). In 1977 the United States had become concerned about geopolitical trends in the region, particularly potential Libyan or Marxist Ethiopian attempts to overthrow the pro-Western Nimeiri government. In the five-year period 1977–81, United States economic aid amounted

135

to almost US$270 million, of which two-thirds was in the form of grants. By 1984, when the United States had become Sudan's largest source of foreign aid, the country's worsening economic and political situation, particularly Nimeiri's domestic policies with regard to the south and the imposition of the sharia (Islamic law) on society, caused the United States to suspend US$194 million of aid. In 1985, following Nimeiri's visit to Washington, the United States provided Sudan with food aid, insecticides, and fertilizers. After Nimeiri's overthrow in April 1985 and Sudan's failure to make repayments on loans, the United States discontinued non-food aid. The aid had been administered by the United States Agency for International Development (AID). It not only included direct funds for projects and project assistance through commodity imports (mainly wheat under the Food for Peace Program), but also generated local currency that was used to support general development activities. AID continued providing humanitarian relief assistance to distressed regions in Sudan through early 1991.

Britain also made substantial aid contributions to Sudan, notably the sum of US$140 million to the Power III Project in the 1980s (see Electric Power, this ch.). In January 1991, Britain suspended its development aid to Sudan, which had amounted to US$58 million in 1989, while continuing humanitarian aid. This policy change was caused by a number of factors, including alleged terrorist activities by Sudanese agents against Sudanese expatriates in Britain. In addition to Britain, France, West Germany, Norway, Japan, and other countries have provided significant economic or humanitarian aid to Sudan (Britain, West Germany, and the Netherlands also have been Sudan's main sources of imports). Japan is a major buyer of Sudanese cotton, while Sudan imports Japanese machinery. In early 1990, to ease Sudan's debt burden, the Danish government cancelled Sudan's outstanding debt totalling more than US$22.9 million. Other major financial assistance came from Arab countries, especially from Saudi Arabia (Sudan's largest importer) and Kuwait. By December 1982, Sudan owed the Persian Gulf states US$2 billion. Saudi Arabia's assistance after 1980 mainly took the form of balance of payments support and petroleum shipments, rather than project aid. The total amount of aid from Arab states dropped in 1988 to only US$127 million, the lowest figure since the late 1970s. Arab aid totaled US$215 million in 1985, US$208 million in 1986, and US$228 million in 1987. Sudan's support of Iraq in the 1991 Persian Gulf war alienated the Gulf states and Saudi Arabia, sharply curtailing their economic aid to Khartoum. The increasingly close ties between Sudan and Iran in the early 1990s also concerned the Gulf states and Saudi Arabia and was a factor in their diminished financial aid to Khartoum. Economic cooperation was initiated with Libya in the late 1980s, with Libya becoming Sudan's third largest supplier in 1989.

In mid-1991 the World Bank announced its decision to close its Khartoum office by December 31, 1991. The decision resulted from the deterioration in relations between Sudan and international monetary bodies following cessation of debt repayment by Khartoum to the World Bank and the IMF.

Among communist countries, prior to the collapse of communist regimes in the Soviet Union and Eastern Europe, China had been the most important provider of development funds. By 1971 it had furnished loans equivalent to US$82 million, and through 1981 an additional US$300 million was reported to have been made available. Sudan valued these loans because they were interest free and had long grace periods before repayments started. Economic cooperation with China continued into the 1980s. Sudan and China signed a trade cooperation protocol in March 1989, with technical agreements also renewed. A commercial protocol between the two countries was signed in April 1990. China remained a significant importer of Sudanese cotton in the mid-1980s, and Sudan imported about US$76 million in goods from China in 1988. Relations between Sudan and the Soviet Union improved markedly following Nimeiri's overthrow in 1985, but the overthrow did not result, as Khartoum had hoped, in Soviet economic assistance, but rather in a decrease in United States aid.

Prices, Employment, Wages, and Unions

Prices

The Ministry of Finance and Economic Planning's Department of Statistics compiled monthly data on consumer prices in Sudan based on approximately 100 items on sale in the capital area's three cities, Omdurman, Khartoum, and Khartoum North. This report contained two indexes covering the cost of consumer goods used by Sudanese having incomes below and above £Sd500 a year. At the beginning of the 1970s, annual price rises were moderate. From 1973 onward, the inflation rate grew because of continuing worldwide inflation, an increase in the money supply resulting from the central government's deficit financing and from borrowing by state corporations, shortages of consumer goods, and problems of supply caused by transport deficiencies. Late in the 1970s, increased private sector borrowing added to the pressures on prices. In the six-year period from 1972 to 1977, inflation increased at an average rate of almost 24 percent a year for the low-income group and

22 percent for the higher group. In 1979 the official rate was 30.8 percent and 33.6 percent for the low and high groups, respectively. The reported rates were somewhat lower in 1980: 25.4 and 26.3 percent, respectively.

A series of currency devaluations took place, beginning in 1979, as part of the new financing agreement with the IMF (see Balance of Payments, this ch.). The economic results of the devaluations did not meet expectations, however, leading by the late 1980s to resistance to IMF demands for further devaluations. The accompanying austerity measures during the 1980s included attempts gradually to remove subsidies on food and other products, reductions in public expenditures, real wages, and nonessential imports, as well as an effort to reinvigorate the export sector. Such efforts, however, had little impact on Sudan's economic viability as far as international financial lenders were concerned.

Annual inflation was estimated at 300 percent in mid-1991, with the market value of the Sudanese pound deteriorating at a constant rate. Sudan's debt burden, estimated at US$4 billion in 1981, rose to US$13 billion by mid-1990, with debt arrears to the IMF alone since 1984 totalling more than US$1.1 billion, a situation that led the IMF to threaten to expel Sudan unless it settled its debt arrears. In September 1990, the IMF adopted a Declaration of Noncooperation regarding Sudan, as a prelude to expulsion. In May 1991, an IMF delegation arrived in Khartoum for discussions with the government, which by then had repaid the IMF a token US$15 million and reaffirmed its determination to cooperate with the IMF. The IMF then postponed for six months its decision on whether to expel Sudan. The deterioration in Sudan's debt position also placed in doubt future World Bank lending to Sudan, with existing loans still secure.

Employment

The size of the country's economically active labor force has been difficult to estimate because of different definitions of participation in economic activity and the absence of accurate data from official sources, particularly the 1973 and 1983 censuses. In rural areas, large numbers of women and girls were engaged in traditional productive occupations, but apparently many have not been included in counts of the active work force.

The International Labour Organisation (ILO) estimated in 1980 that the work force was about 6 million persons, or approximately 33 percent of the population. This figure included about 300,000 unemployed. It also included the many male Sudanese working in other Arab states, a loss to Sudan that may have amounted to as much as 50 percent of its professional and skilled work force. The drop in world oil prices in the 1980s caused the Persian Gulf states to cut back drastically on their expatriate workers, leading in turn to increased unemployment in Sudan. In mid-1989 a total of 7,937,000 people were employed in Sudan, according to an ILO estimate. In the early 1990s, Sudan's employment situation was exacerbated by the 1991 Persian Gulf War, which resulted in the departure of the thousands of Sudanese workers based in Kuwait and Iraq, leaving many of their possessions behind. Sudan's support of Iraq also contributed to the departure of thousands of Sudanese workers from Saudi Arabia.

Unemployment figures were affected by the severe drought that spread throughout Sudan in the 1980s. In 1983–84, for example, several million people migrated from the worst hit areas in both the west and the east to Khartoum and other urban areas along the Nile. Many remained in these areas once the drought had eased, living in shanty towns and contributing to unemployment or underemployment in the cities. In addition, more than 1 million people from the south migrated to the north, as a result of the civil war and famine in these areas.

Agriculture was the predominant activity in Sudan, although its share of the labor force has gradually declined as other sectors of economic activity have expanded. In the 1955–56 census—the only complete count of the labor force for which data have been published (detailed results of the 1973 and 1983 censuses had not been released as of mid-1991)—almost 86 percent of those then considered as part of the work force were involved in agriculture, livestock raising, forestry, fisheries, or hunting. The Ministry of Finance and Economic Planning estimated that by 1969–70 the total had declined to somewhat less than 70 percent and that at the end of the 1970s the sector accounted for less than 66 percent. In mid-1989, the ILO estimated that about 4,872,000 people were employed in agriculture. Services, which included a government work force that grew about 10 percent a year in the 1970s, emerged as the second largest area of activity, encompassing an estimated 10.4 percent of those economically active in 1979–80, compared with 4.6 percent in 1955–56. Nonagricultural production—manufacturing, mining, electric power, and construction—accounted for 6.7 percent during 1979–80 and about 5.6 percent in 1955–56.

Wages

In 1991 reliable figures for wages in Sudan were difficult to obtain. Public sector wages have been generally higher than those of the privately employed, except in a few large private firms.

Until late 1974, when the Minimum Standard of Wages Order (Presidential Order No. 21) was issued, there had not been a minimum wage in the private sector, although in a few occupations such as stevedoring at Port Sudan, official wage orders had set certain minimums. The 1974 minimum, established at £Sd16.50 a month, was equivalent to the minimum entry wage for public sector jobs. It applied, however, basically only to workers in establishments having ten or more employees in the Khartoum area, Al Jazirah, and certain other urban centers. Its geographical limitations together with important exemptions—employees below the age of eighteen, all those in enterprises having fewer than ten workers, seasonal agricultural workers, and some others—excluded about three-quarters of all wage earners. Employers were allowed to raise wages that were below the minimum to the prescribed level in three steps to be achieved by October 1977. In 1979 the minimum wage was raised to £Sd28 a month, and a minimum daily rate of £Sd1.50 was established for unskilled workers.

In mid-1978 rising inflation and worker unrest led the government to inaugurate the Job Evaluation and Classification Scheme (JECS), through which a substantial two-stage increase in public sector wages was to be effected. Considerable discontent with gradings appeared to have arisen, and for many people, little improvement in salaries occurred. One of the problems reportedly was the misjudgments in the JECS reclassification process that resulted in commitment of all allocated funds for the program well before the program had been half completed. In early 1979, members of the domestic bank workers' union and hospital technicians, among others, carried out strikes, and in August the powerful 32,000-member Sudan Railway Workers' Union (SRWU) also walked out. The government promised SRWU members that they would be given the second half of the JECS raise, but the strike was ended by the use of armed troops. SRWU again went on strike in May–June 1981, in part also because of continued discontent with JECS actions. The strike, which was also ended by use of the military, was declared illegal and the union dissolved. Various leaders were arrested. The government then appointed a preparatory committee to reestablish the SRWU.

Unions

Trade union activity was banned by the Bashir government following its rise to power in the 1989 coup, and many union officials were imprisoned. Prior to 1989, the trade unions that were active were nevertheless under state control, most having been established in their latest incarnation by the government in 1971.

The labor union movement originated in 1946 with the formation by some Sudan Railways employees of the Workers' Affairs Association, the predecessor of the SRWU. Two years later the Trades and Tradesmen's Union Ordinance of 1948, which was based largely on the British model and the concepts of voluntary association and limited government intervention in union affairs, gave official sanction to unions. The 1948 ordinance permitted formation of unions by as few as ten individuals, and a proliferation of mostly small, ineffective bodies emerged. The major exception was the rail union, which, as an official body, became Sudan's wealthiest and most powerful union. In 1949 the workers' association helped form the national Workers' Congress, which in 1950 became the Sudan Workers Trade Unions Federation (SWTUF). Dominated by communists, the SWTUF was closely associated with the Sudanese Communist Party (SCP). The SWTUF failed to receive government recognition, and its interests and actions tended strongly to be along political lines. After national independence, the federation had frequent confrontations with the new government, including a successful general strike in October 1958. This strike was one of the factors that contributed to the military takeover of the government the following month (see The Abbud Military Government, 1958–64, ch. 1).

At the time of the 1958 coup, the SWTUF controlled roughly 70 percent of all labor union membership. The new military government repealed the 1948 ordinance, dissolved all unions, and detained many of the federation's leaders. Some union organization was again permitted after 1960 but it was prohibited for white-collar workers, and federations were not allowed. Upon restoration of the civilian government in 1964, the 1948 ordinance was reinstated, and the SWTUF reemerged. Union membership increased rapidly and had risen to about 250,000 workers in about 500 to 600 unions by 1970. Most were small (three-quarters had fewer than 200 members), financially weak, and generally not very effective. The few larger unions were in the public sector, led by the SRWU.

SWTUF leadership remained in communist hands. The SCP was allied with the group that carried out the military coup of May 1969, and the SWTUF and the unions were welcomed as partners in the proclaimed socialist struggle to better the conditions of the workers. Strikes, however, were prohibited by a presidential order issued shortly after the 1969 takeover. The relationship was abruptly ended after the abortive communist coup in mid-1971. The government dissolved the SWTUF and executed a number of its leaders.

Late in 1971, the government promulgated the Trade Unions Act, under which directives were issued in 1973 that established eighty-seven unions based on sectoral, occupational, and industrial lines. Somewhat more than half were ''employees' '' unions (for white-collar employees), and the rest were ''workers' '' unions (for blue-collar workers). The existing unions were variously merged into the specified groupings. The act contained measures to strengthen unionism, including a provision for compulsory dues and employer-paid time off to serve as union officials. The SWTUF was reinstituted for the ''workers' '' unions, and the Sudanese Federation of Employees and Professionals Trade Unions formed in 1975 for the white-collar group. Their representation of union interests was carried on within guidelines set by the government and the Sudan Socialist Union (SSU), the mass political party established by the government in 1972. In the late 1970s, they led strikes, which, although illegal, resulted in settlement of issues through negotiations with the government. The last major attempt by organized labor to strike occurred in June 1981, but the strike by the Sudan Railways Workers' Union was broken by the Nimeiri government, which arrested its leaders.

Prior to 1989, the SWTUF, in its weakened state, included forty-two trade unions, representing more than 1.7 million workers in the public and private sectors. The federation was affiliated with the International Confederation of Arab Trade Unions and the Organization of African Trade Union Unity.

Agriculture, Livestock, Fisheries, and Forestry

In the early 1990s, agriculture and livestock raising were the main sources of livelihood in Sudan for about 61 percent of the working population. Agricultural products regularly accounted for about 95 percent of the country's exports. Industry was mostly agriculturally based, accounting for 15 percent of GDP in 1988. The average annual growth of agricultural production declined in the 1980s to 0.8 percent for the period 1980–87, as compared with 2.9 percent for the period 1965–80. Similarly, the sector's total contribution to GDP declined over the years, as the other sectors of the economy expanded. Total sectoral activities, which contributed an estimated 40 percent of GDP in the early 1970s, had fluctuated during the 1980s and represented about 36 percent in 1988 (see table 6, Appendix). Crop cultivation was divided between a modern, market-oriented sector comprising mechanized, large-scale irrigated and rainfed farming (mainly in central Sudan) and small-scale farming following traditional practices that was carried on in the other

Experimental farm in Yambio, western Al Istiwai State
Courtesy Robert O. Collins
Cotton growing in Al Jazirah, where international funding
has helped rehabilitate irrigation systems
Courtesy Embassy of the Republic of Sudan, Washington

parts of the country where rainfall or other water sources were sufficient for cultivation.

Large investments continued to be made in the 1980s in
mechanized, irrigated, and rainfed cultivation, with their combined
areas accounting for roughly two-thirds of Sudan's cultivated land
in the late 1980s. The early emphasis on cotton growing on irrigated
land had decreased. Although cotton remained the most important crop, peanuts, wheat, and sugarcane had become major crops,
and considerable quantities of sesame also were grown (see table
7, Appendix). Rainfed mechanized farming continued to produce
mostly sorghum, and short-fiber cotton was also grown. Production in both subsectors increased domestic supplies and export
potentials. The increase appeared, however, to have been achieved
mainly by expanding the cultivated area rather than by increasing
productivity. To stimulate productivity, in 1981 the government
offered various incentives to cultivators of irrigated land, who were
almost entirely government tenants. Subsistence cultivators produced sorghum as their staple crop, although in the northerly,
rainfed, cultivated areas millet was the principal staple. Subsistence
farmers also grew peanuts and sesame.

Livestock raising, pursued throughout Sudan except in the extremely dry areas of the north and the tsetse-fly-infested area in
the far south, was almost entirely in the traditional sector. Because
livestock raising provided employment for so many people, modernization proposals have been based on improving existing practices and marketing for export, rather than moving toward the
modern ranching that requires few workers.

Fishing was largely carried out by the traditional sector for subsistence. An unknown number of small operators also used the country's major reservoirs in the more populated central region and
the rivers to catch fish for sale locally and in nearby larger urban
centers. The few modern fishing ventures, mainly on Lake Nubia
and in the Red Sea, were small.

The forestry subsector comprised both traditional gatherers of
firewood and producers of charcoal—the main sources of fuel for
homes and some industry in urban areas—and a modern timber
and sawmilling industry, the latter government owned. Approximately 21 million cubic meters of wood, mainly for fuel, were cut
in 1987. Gum arabic production in FY 1986–87 was about 40,000
tons. In the late 1980s, it became the second biggest export after
cotton in most years, amounting to about 11 percent of total exports.

Land Use

By 1991 only partial surveys of Sudan's land resources had been made, and estimates of the areas included in different land-use categories varied considerably. Figures for potentially arable land ranged from an estimate of 35.9 million hectares made in the mid-1960s to a figure of 84 million hectares published by the Ministry of Agriculture and Natural Resources in 1974. Estimates of the amount actually under cultivation varied in the late 1980s, ranging from 7.5 million hectares, including roughly 10 or 11 percent in fallow, to 12.6 million hectares.

Substantial variations also existed in land classified as actually used or potentially usable for livestock grazing. The ministry and the United Nations Food and Agriculture Organization (FAO) have classified about 24 million hectares as pastureland. The 1965 estimate of land use classified 101.4 million hectares as grazing land, and in 1975 an ILO–United Nations Development Programme (UNDP) interagency mission to Sudan estimated the total potential grazing land at between 120 million and 150 million hectares.

Forestland estimates also differed greatly, from less than 60 million hectares by staff of the Forestry Administration to about 915 million hectares by the Ministry of Agriculture and Natural Resources and the FAO (see Forestry, this ch.). Dense stands of trees covered only between 20 million and 24 million hectares of the total forestland. Differences in land classification may have been accounted for by use of some woodland areas for grazing and some traditional grazing lands for raising crops. Given the dearth of rainfall during the 1980s and early 1990s, the ecological damage from mechanized farming, and the steady march of desertification, discrepancies in these statistics had little meaning in 1991.

It was generally agreed, however, that in the late 1980s Sudan still had a substantial amount of land suitable for future cropping. The ILO–UNDP mission believed that two-thirds of the potential area for livestock grazing, however, was already in use. In addition to land suitable for cultivation and livestock grazing, Sudan also had about 76 million to 86 million hectares of desert. Additionally, an area of about 2.9 million hectares was covered by swamps and inland water, and about 280,000 hectares were occupied by urban settlements and other man-made features.

Land Tenure

The right to own property, to bequeath it to heirs, and to inherit it was established by the Permanent Constitution of 1973; this right was suspended in 1985. Sudan had long had a system of land registration through which an individual, an enterprise, or the government could establish title to a piece of land. Such registration had been extensive in northern Sudan, especially in Al

Khartum, Al Awsat, and Ash Shamali provinces. Before 1970 all other land (unregistered) belonged to the state, which held ownership in trust for the people, who had customary rights to it. In 1970 the Unregistered Land Act declared that all waste, forest, and unregistered lands were government land. Before the act's passage, the government had avoided interfering with individual customary rights to unregistered land, and in the late 1980s it again adhered to this policy.

The government owned most of the land used by the modern agricultural sector and leased it to tenants (for example, the Gezira Scheme) or to private entrepreneurs, such as most operators of large-scale mechanized rainfed farming. In the late 1980s, however, the great area of land used for pasture and for subsistence cultivation was communally owned under customary land laws that varied somewhat by location but followed a broadly similar pattern. In agricultural communities, the right to cultivate an area of unused land became vested in the individual who cleared it for use. The rights to such land could be passed on to heirs, but ordinarily the land could not be sold or otherwise disposed of. The right was also retained to land left in fallow, although in Bahr al Ghazal, Aali an Nil, and Al Istiwai there were communities where another individual could claim such land by clearing it.

Among the transhumant (see Glossary) communities of the north, the rights to cultivated land were much the same, but the dominant position of livestock in community activities had introduced certain other communal rights that included common rights to grazing land, the right-of-way to water and grazing land, the right to grass on agricultural land unless the occupier cut and stacked it, and the right to crop residues unless similarly treated. In the western savannas, private ownership of stands of *hashab* trees could be registered, an exception to the usual government ownership of the forests. But dead wood for domestic fuel and the underlying grass were common property. Water, a matter of greatest importance to stock raisers, was open to all if free standing, but wells that had been dug and the associated drinking troughs were private property and were retained by the digger season after season. In northern Sudan, especially in the western region where increasing population and animal numbers have placed pressure on the land, violations of customary laws and conflicts between ethnic groups over land rights have been growing. Resolution of these problems has been attempted by local government agencies but only on a case-by-case basis.

146

Control device for switching water flow to one of the many canals used for irrigation in Al Jazirah, south of Khartoum
Courtesy Embassy of the Republic of Sudan, Washington

Irrigated Agriculture

In 1991 Sudan had a large modern irrigated agriculture sector totaling more than 2 million hectares out of about 84 million hectares that are potentially arable. About 93 percent of the irrigated area was in government projects; the remaining 7 percent belonged to private operations. The Nile and its tributaries were the source of water for 93 percent of irrigated agriculture, and of this the Blue Nile accounted for about 67 percent. Gravity flow was the main form of irrigation, but about one-third of the irrigated area was served by pumps.

The waters of the Nile in Sudan have been used for centuries for traditional irrigation, taking advantage of the annual Nile flood. Some use of this method still continued in the early 1990s, and the traditional *shaduf* (a device to raise water) and waterwheel were also used to lift water to fields in local irrigation projects but were rapidly being replaced by more efficient mechanized pump systems. Among the first efforts to employ irrigation for modern commercial cropping was the use of the floodwaters of the Qash River and the Baraka River (both of which originate in Ethiopia) in eastern Sudan to grow cotton on their deltas (see fig. 4). This project was started in the late 1860s by the Egyptian governor and continued until interrupted by the turbulent period of the 1880s, leading to the reconquest of the country by the British in 1899. Cultivation was resumed in 1896 in the Baraka Delta in the Tawkar area, but in the Qash Delta it only resumed after World War I. Between 1924 and 1926, canals were built in the latter delta to control the flood; sandstorms made canals unfeasible in the Baraka. Between the 1940s and the 1970s, various projects were developed to irrigate land. In 1982 both deltas yielded only one crop a year, watered by the flood. Adequate groundwater, however, offered the eventual possibility of using pump irrigation from local wells for additional cropping or for supplementing any flood shortages.

The drought that affected Sudan in the 1980s was a natural disaster that had a crushing effect on the country's irrigation systems. In 1990–91, for instance, water was so scarce in the Tawkar area that for the first time in 100 years the crops failed.

As of 1990, the country's largest irrigation project had been developed on land between the Blue and White Nile rivers south of their confluence at Khartoum. This area is generally flat with a gentle slope to the north and west, permitting natural gravity irrigation, and its soils are fertile cracking clays well suited to irrigation. The project originated in 1911, when a private British enterprise, Sudan Plantations Syndicate, found cotton suited to the area and embarked on what in the 1920s became the Gezira Scheme, intended principally to furnish cotton to the British textile industry. Backed by a loan from the British government, the syndicate began a dam on the Blue Nile at Sannar in 1913. Work was interrupted by World War I, and the dam was not completed until 1925. The project was limited by a 1929 agreement between Sudan and Egypt that restricted the amount of water Anglo-Egyptian Sudan could use during the dry season. By 1931 the project had expanded to 450,000 hectares, the maximum that then could be irrigated by the available water, although 10,000 more hectares were added in the 1950s. The project was nationalized in 1950, and was operated by the Sudan Gezira Board as a government enterprise. In 1959 a new agreement with Egypt greatly increased the allotment of water to Sudan, as did the completion in the early 1960s of the Manaqil Extension on the western side of the Gezira Scheme. By 1990 the Manaqil Extension had an irrigated area of nearly 400,000 hectares, and with the 460,000 hectares eventually attained by the original Gezira Scheme, the combined projects accounted for half the country's total land under irrigation.

In the early 1960s, the government set up a program to resettle Nubians displaced by Lake Nubia (called Lake Nasser in Egypt), which was formed by the construction of the Aswan High Dam in Egypt. To provide farmland for the Nubians, the government constructed the Khashm al Qirbah Dam on the Atbarah River and established the Halfa al Jadidah (New Halfa) irrigation project. Located west of Kassala, this project was originally designed to irrigate about 164,000 hectares. In 1982 it was the only large irrigation project in the country that did not use the waters of the Blue Nile or White Nile. The resettlement was effected mainly after completion of the Khashm al Qirbah Dam in 1964. Part of the irrigated area was also assigned to local inhabitants. The main commercial crops initially introduced included cotton, peanuts, and wheat. In 1965 sugarcane was added, and a sugar factory having a design capacity of 60,000 tons was built to process it. The project enabled 200,000 hectares of land to be irrigated for the first time. Heavy silting as well as serious problems of drainage and salinity occurred. As a result, by the late 1970s the reservoir had lost more than 40 percent of its original storage capacity and was unable to meet the project water requirements. These problems persisted in the early 1990s.

The multipurpose Roseires Dam was built in 1966 and power-generating facilities were installed in 1971. Both the water and the power were needed to implement the Rahad River irrigation project located east of the Rahad River, a tributary of the Blue Nile. The Rahad entered the Blue Nile downstream from the dam, and during the dry season had an insufficient flow for irrigation purposes. Work on the initial 63,000 hectares of the project began in the early 1970s, the first irrigation water was received in 1977, and by 1981 about 80 percent of the prepared area was reported to be irrigated. (In May 1988, the World Bank agreed to provide additional funding for this and other irrigation projects.) Water for the project was pumped from the Blue Nile, using electric power from the Roseires plant, and was transported by an eighty-kilometer-long canal to the Rahad River (en route underpassing the Dindar River, another Blue Nile tributary). The canal then emptied into the Rahad above a new barrage that diverted the combined flow from the two sources into the project's main irrigation canal. Irrigation was by gravity flow, but instead of flat field flooding, furrow irrigation was used because it permitted more effective use of machinery.

In the 1920s, private irrigation projects using diesel pumps also had begun to appear in Al Khartum Province, mainly along the White Nile, to provide vegetables, fruit, and other foods to the capital area. In 1937 a dam was built by the Anglo-Egyptian condominium upstream from Khartoum on the White Nile at Jabal al Awliya to regulate the supply of water to Egypt during the August to April period of declining flow. Grazing and cultivated land along the river was flooded for almost 300 kilometers. The government thereupon established seven pump irrigation projects, partially financed by Egypt, to provide the area's inhabitants with an alternative to transhumance.

This irrigation project eventually proved successful, making possible large surpluses of cotton and sorghum and encouraging private entrepreneurs to undertake new projects. High cotton profits during the Korean War (1950–53) increased private interest along the Blue Nile as well, and by 1958 almost half the country's irrigated cotton was grown under pump irrigation. During the 1960s, however, downward fluctuations in world cotton prices and disputes between entrepreneurs and tenants led to numerous failures of pump irrigation projects. In 1968 the government assumed ownership and operation of the projects. The government established the Agricultural Reform Corporation for this purpose, and the takeover began that year with the larger estates. Subsequently, as leases expired, the corporation acquired smaller projects, until May 1970 when all outstanding leases were revoked. A considerable number of small pump operations that developed on privately owned land, chiefly along the main Nile but also on the Blue Nile, continued to operate.

Since the 1950s, the government has constructed a number of large pump projects, mostly on the Blue Nile. These have included the Junayd project on the east bank of the Blue Nile east of the Gezira Scheme. This project, with an irrigated area of about 36,000 hectares, went into operation in 1955 to provide an alternative livelihood for nomadic pastoralists in the area. It produced cotton until 1960, when about 8,400 hectares were converted to sugarcane. A sugar factory built to process the crop (with a potential capacity of 60,000 tons of sugar a year) opened in 1962. In the early 1970s, the Japanese-assisted As Suki project, also of 36,000 hectares, was established upstream from Sannar to grow cotton, sorghum, and oilseeds. In the mid-1970s, the government constructed a second project near Sannar of about 20,000 hectares. In addition to cotton and other crops such as peanuts, about 8,400 hectares of the area were devoted to raising sugarcane. The cane-processing factory, with a design capacity of 110,000 tons of sugar a year, opened in 1976. Several smaller Blue Nile projects added more than 80,000 additional hectares to Sudan's overall irrigated area during this time.

In the 1970s, when the consumption and import of sugar grew rapidly, domestic production became a priority, and two major pump-irrigated sugar plantations were established on the White Nile in the Kusti area. The Hajar Asalaya Sugar Project, begun in 1975, had an irrigated area of about 7,600 hectares. The sugar factory, completed in 1977, had a potential annual capacity of 110,000 tons. The Kinanah Sugar Project, which had almost 16,200 hectares under irrigation in 1981 and had a future potential of over 33,000 hectares, was one of the world's largest sugar-milling and refining operations. In 1985–86 production reached more than 330,000 tons a year. This project, first proposed in 1971, was beset with funding problems and overruns that increased overall costs from the equivalent of US$113 million estimated in 1973 to more than US$750 million when the plant opened officially in early 1981.

The Kinanah Sugar Project, unlike the country's four other government-owned sugar projects, was a joint venture among the governments of Sudan, Kuwait, and Saudi Arabia, and the Arab Investment Company, the Sudan Development Corporation, Kinanah Limited, and the AAAID, including local Sudanese banks. An initial trial run in the 1979–80 cane season produced 20,000 tons of sugar. Yield increased to an estimated 135,000 to 150,000 tons the following season. Production at the Hajar Asalaya factory did not get under way until the 1979–80 season because of cane and sugar-processing difficulties. Problems have also affected the other three state sugar factories, but as a result of proposed World Bank management, the output total of these four government operations for the 1984–85 season improved to nearly 200,000 tons. Output declined to 159,000 tons in 1985–86 because of the drought. In 1989 sugarcane production reached 400,000 tons.

Rainfed Agriculture

Cultivation dependent on rainfall falls into two categories. Most Sudanese farmers have always relied on rainfed farming. In addition to these traditional farmers, a large modern mechanized rainfed agriculture sector has developed since 1944–45, when a government project to cultivate the cracking clays of central Sudan started in the Al Qadarif area of Ash Sharqi Province, largely to meet the food needs of army units stationed in the British colonies in eastern Africa (present-day Kenya, Tanzania, and Uganda). An average of about 6,000 hectares a year was cultivated between 1945 and 1953, producing chiefly sorghum, under a sharecropping arrangement between the government and farmers who had been allocated land in the project. These estates proved costly, however, and in 1954 the government began encouraging the private sector to take up mechanized farming in the area, a policy that continued after Sudan gained independence in 1956. Under the new approach,

151

the government established several state farms to demonstrate production methods and to conduct research. Research activities have been very limited, however, because of staffing and funding problems, and the farms have been operated essentially as regular production units.

The private sector response was positive, and by 1960 mechanized farming had spread into other areas of the cracking clay zone in Ash Sharqi and Al Awsat provinces. The government set aside rectangular areas that were divided into plots of 420 hectares (later raised in places to 630 hectares) each. Half of these plots were leased to private farmers, the other half left in fallow. After four years, the originally leased land was to be returned to fallow and the farmer was to receive a new lease to an adjacent fallow area. When the demand for land grew faster than it could be demarcated, areas outside the designated project limits were taken over by private individuals. The four-year lease proved unpopular because it meant new investment in clearing land every four years, and apparently much of the worked land continued to be cultivated while fallow land was also placed under cultivation. By 1968 more than 750,000 hectares were being cultivated, of which it was estimated that more than 200,000 hectares constituted unauthorized holdings. The average agricultural production growth rate declined, however, from 2.9 percent in the period between 1965 and 1980, to 0.8 percent in the period between 1980 and 1987, the latest available figures. Reportedly, for the 1991–92 season, the Ministry of Agriculture and Natural Resources planned for about 7.3 million hectares of food crops to be planted, with about 1.6 million hectares planted in the irrigated sector and about 5.7 million hectares in the rainfed areas.

The investment requirements for mechanized farming favored prosperous cultivators, and eventually most farms came to be operated by entrepreneurs who raised capital through mortgageable property or other assets in the urban centers. Through arrangements with other individuals, these entrepreneurs frequently managed to control additional plots beyond the legal limit of two. Their ability to obtain capital also permitted them to abandon depleted land and to move into newly demarcated uncleared areas, a practice that had a deleterious impact upon the environment, deprived the indigenous inhabitants of work opportunities, and increased desertification. In 1968, to expand the operator base and to introduce more control over land allocation, crops, and farming methods, the government established the Mechanized Farming Corporation (MFC), an autonomous agency under the Ministry of Agriculture and Natural Resources. From 1968 through 1978, the IDA made three loans to the government to enable the MFC to provide technical assistance, credit for landclearing and machinery, and marketing aid to individual farmers and cooperative groups. The MFC also became the operator of state farms.

In the late 1970s, about 2.2 million hectares had been allocated for mechanized farming, and about 420,000 hectares more had been occupied without official demarcation. About 1.9 million hectares in all were believed to be under cultivation in any one season. Of the officially allocated land, more than 70 percent was held by private individuals. Private companies had also begun entering the field, and some allocations had been made to them. State farms accounted for another 7.5 percent. About 15 percent of the total allocated land was in MFC–IDA projects. The largest proportion of mechanized farming was in Ash Sharqi Province, 43 percent; the next largest in Al Awsat Province, 32 percent; and about 20 percent was in Aali an Nil Province. Mechanized farming had also been initiated in southern Kurdufan Province through a project covering small-scale farmers in the area of the Nuba Mountains, but under a different government program. Proposals also had been made for MFC projects using mechanized equipment in other areas of southern Kurdufan (some have already been tried) and southern Darfur provinces. There were serious feasibility problems in view of competition for land and conflicts with traditional farming practices, difficult soil conditions, and the probable negative effect on the large numbers of livestock of nomads.

Only a few crops had been found suitable for cultivation in the cracking clay area. Sorghum had been the principal one, and during the early 1980s it was planted on an average of about 80 percent of the sown area. Sesame and short-fiber cotton were also grown successfully but in relatively smaller quantities, sesame on about 15 percent of the land and cotton on about 5 percent. Soil fertility has reportedly been declining because of the continued planting of sorghum and the lack of crop rotation. Yields have apparently decreased, but in view of the area's greatly varying climatic conditions and the uncertain production data, definitive conclusions on trends appeared premature.

Livestock

In the early 1990s, drought caused a dramatic decline in livestock raising in Sudan, following a period in the early 1980s when livestock provided all or a large part of the livelihood of more than 40 percent of the country's population. Livestock raising was overwhelmingly in the traditional sector, and, although initial steps had been taken to improve productivity and develop market orientation, for the modern monetized economy the sector represented largely a potential asset. In 1983 Sudan's more than 50 million animals comprised the second largest national herd in Africa, next in size to that of Ethiopia. An FAO estimate in 1987 indicated that there were about 20.5 million cattle, 19 million sheep, 14 million goats, and 3 million camels. Other animals included 660,000 donkeys, 21,000 horses, a small number of pigs (kept by such non-Muslim peoples as the Nuba) and 32,000 chickens. By 1991 these numbers had been reduced by perhaps one-third by the drought of 1990–91; the August 1988 floods in the south, described as the worst in Sudan's history; and the ravages of civil war in the south. Poultry was raised mainly by farm families and villagers. A small modern sector consisted of limited government commercial operations and a few semicommercial private ventures.

Sudanese cattle are of two principal varieties: Baqqara and Nilotic. The Baqqara and two subvarieties constituted about 80 percent of the country's total number of cattle. This breed was found chiefly in the western savanna regions and in fewer, although significant, numbers farther to the east from Aali an Nil to Kassala in Ash Sharqi. The Nilotic, constituting approximately 20 percent of all cattle, were common in the eastern hill and plains areas of southeastern Al Istiwai, which were free of the tsetse fly, and in those parts of the Bahr al Ghazal and Aali an Nil lying outside the tsetse-fly zone. Because of periodic rinderpest epidemics, the total number of cattle was relatively small until about 1930, when it stood at an estimated 2 million. A vaccination program begun about that time and mass inoculations during the succeeding decades resulted in a great increase in numbers, which by 1970 had reached about 12 million.

In the vast areas used by pastoral herders (estimated to be 80 million to 100 million hectares), cattle husbandry was conducted in an economic, cultural, and social context that had evolved over generations. The system included an emphasis on increasing herd size as an investment for future family security. Small surpluses (usually bulls) were available for subsistence use, exchange, or sale for local consumption or export. Cattle were also used for marriage payments and among the Nilotes for rituals. Numbers of cattle also helped to establish or increase status and power in a social system in which cattle were the measure of wealth.

Most Nilotic cattle were kept by transhumant groups. Migrations, related to the wet and dry seasons, usually did not exceed 150 to 160 kilometers. The majority of the Baqqara strain of cattle belonged to the Baqqara Arabs (see Northern Arabized Communities, ch. 2). The latter were largely nomadic, but since at least

Market, or suq, *in Yambio, with townspeople engaged in bargaining*
Cattle suq *in Juba, capital of Al Istiwai State*
Courtesy Robert O. Collins

the early 1900s had had a settled base on which crop cultivation was practiced. The farmers, their relatives, or their agents moved the cattle over traditional migratory routes northward during the rainy season and southward to the area of the Bahr al Arab as the dry season progressed. Migrations in either direction might amount to 400 kilometers. The expansion of mechanized rainfed agriculture in the region used by the Baqqara, continued government efforts to enlarge the cultivated area, and pressures on the land from the growing population gradually reduced grazing areas. At the same time, traditional cultural forces brought about a steady increase in cattle numbers. The result was increasing overstocking and pasture depletion, until the outbreak of civil war in 1983 and the devastating droughts of the 1980s and early 1990s decimated not only the Nilotic herds but also livestock throughout Sudan. Many families and indeed whole ethnic groups who had traditionally survived on their cattle, sheep, goats, or camels, lost all of their herds and were forced to migrate to the Three Towns (Omdurman, Khartoum, and Khartoum North) in search of sustenance.

Sheep were herded chiefly by transhumants in Darfur and Kurdufan. Large numbers were found in the drier areas at greater elevations than the usual cattle zone. Several breeds were raised, but the predominant and preferred one was the so-called desert sheep, which had both good weight and good milk yield. Villagers in Al Awsat also raised large numbers of sheep, mostly on a nonmigratory basis. Fodder was obtained from crop residues on irrigated and rainfed farms and from vegetation along the rivers and canals. Goats, of which there were three principal breeds (desert, Nubian, and Nilotic), were found throughout the country south of the northern desert areas. They were raised mainly by sedentary families for milk and meat. Goat meat, although less popular than mutton, formed part of the diet of most families, particularly those having low incomes. Goat milk was an important source of protein, and many families in urban areas kept a few goats for their milk.

Camels were largely concentrated in the desert and subdesert regions of northern Darfur, northern Kurdufan, and southern Ash Sharqi. They were kept almost entirely by nomadic and seminomadic peoples, for whom the animal represented the preferred mode of transport. Camels were also important for milk and for meat. Camel ownership and numbers were sources of prestige in nomadic societies.

Fisheries

Sudan's total production of fish, shellfish, and other fishing products reached an estimated 24,000 tons per year in 1988, the latest available yearly figures. This figure compared with estimates of a potential yearly catch exceeding 100,000 tons. The principal source of fish was the Nile River system. In central and northern Sudan, several lakes and reservoirs have been formed by the damming of the river and its branches: the 180-kilometer section of Lake Nubia on the main Nile in Sudan and the reservoirs behind the Roseires and Sennar dams on the Blue Nile, the Jabal al Awliya Dam on the White Nile, and the Khashm al Qirbah Dam on the Atbarah tributary of the main Nile. These bodies of water accounted for about 11,000 tons of fish against a calculated potential of about 29,000 tons.

Production from Lake Nubia through 1979, the latest figures available in 1991, was only 500 tons a year, or about one-tenth of the estimated potential. Inhabitants around the lake, which had formed gradually in the 1960s, had no previous experience in fishing, and the first significant commercial exploitation of the lake's resources was undertaken by the government's Fisheries Administration. In 1973 a private company also started operations. In the mid- and late 1970s, an ice plant and a cold storage facility were built at Wadi Halfa with assistance from China. China also furnished thirty-five two-ton fishing vessels, a number of transport launches, and other fishing equipment. Cooling plants were constructed at Khartoum and Atbarah to hold fish that were brought from Wadi Halfa by railroad. Although ice was used in the shipments, substantial loss occurred, especially during the hotter months. To what extent fish production from the lake and availability to consumers were increased by these new facilities was not known in 1991.

The largest potential source of freshwater fish was southern Sudan, whose extensive river network and flooded areas in As Sudd were believed able to provide 100,000 to 300,000 tons annually on a sustained basis. Statistics on actual production were unavailable in 1991; much was consumed locally, although limited quantities of dried and salted fish were exported to Zaire where it was in great demand.

The country's second source of fish, the Red Sea coastal area, was relatively unexploited until the late 1970s. Annual production toward the end of the decade amounted to about 500 tons of fish, shellfish (including pearl oysters), and other marine life. In 1978 the British Ministry of Overseas Development began a joint project with the government Fisheries Administration to raise output by making boats, motors, and equipment available to fishermen. Included was an ice plant built at Sawakin to furnish local fishermen with ice for their catch. By 1982 the project was well advanced, and about 2,000 tons of fish were taken annually. A sustained catch of 5,000 tons might eventually be possible.

Forestry

Sudan has a large quantity of natural forest, much of which remained almost totally unexploited in 1991. Since the early 1900s, extensive areas of woodland and forest have been converted to agricultural use. Large amounts of land classifiable as woodland have also been cleared in the development of large-scale mechanized rainfed farming in Ash Sharqi and Al Awsat states, and smaller amounts in Aali an Nil and southern Kurdufan states. In the late 1970s, FAO estimated that the country's forests and woodlands totaled about 915,000 square kilometers, or 38.5 percent of the land area. This figure was based on the broad definition of forest and woodland as any area of vegetation dominated by trees of any size. It also included an unknown amount of cleared land that was expected to have forest cover again "in the foreseeable future." An estimate in the mid-1970s by the Forestry Administration, however, established the total forest cover at about 584,360 square kilometers, or 24.6 percent of the country's land area. More than 129,000 square kilometers (about one-quarter) of this amount were located in the dry and semiarid regions of northern Sudan. These forests were considered valuable chiefly as protection for the land against desertification, but they also served as a source of fuel for pastoral peoples in those regions. The continued population pressure on the land has resulted in an accelerated destruction of forestland, particularly in the Sahel, because charcoal remained the predominant fuel. The loss of forestland in the marginal areas of the north, accelerated by mechanized farming and by drought, resulted in a steady encroachment of the Sahara southward at about ten kilometers a year in the 1980s.

The productive forest extended below the zone of desert encroachment to the southern border. It included the savanna woodlands of the central and western parts of the country, which were dominated by various species of acacia, among them *Acacia senegal,* the principal source of gum arabic. Gum arabic was Sudan's second largest export product, accounting for 80 percent of the world's supply. It is nontoxic, noncalorific, and nonpolluting, having no odor or taste. It is used widely in industry for products ranging from mucilage (for postage stamps) to foam stabilizers to excipient in medicines and dietetic foods. In 1986–87 Sudan produced more than 40,000 tons marketed through the Gum Arabic Company. In the late 1980s, the drought severely curtailed production.

Fisherman with his nets on the Nile in northern Sudan
Port Sudan on the Red Sea, Sudan's major port
Courtesy Embassy of the Republic of Sudan, Washington

The principal area of productive forest and woodland, however, was in the more moist southern part of the country. Covering an area of more than 200,000 square kilometers and consisting mainly of broadleaf deciduous hardwoods, it remained largely undeveloped in 1990. Timber processed by government mills in the area included mahogany for furniture and other hardwoods for railroad ties, furniture, and construction. Domestic production of timber fell far short of local needs in the 1970s, and as much as 80 percent of the domestic requirement was met by imports.

Plantations established by the government Forestry Administration in the mid-1970s totaled about 16,000 hectares of hardwoods and 500 to 600 hectares of softwoods; most were in the south. They included stands of teak and in the higher elevations of the Imatong Mountains, exotic pines. Eucalyptus stands had also been established in the irrigated agricultural areas to serve as windbreaks and to supply firewood. A gradually increasing forest reserve had been developed, and by the mid-1970s it covered more than 13,000 square kilometers. Additional protection of forest and woodland areas was provided by several national parks and game reserves that encompassed 54,000 square kilometers in the mid-1970s.

Since 1983 the civil war has virtually halted forestry production in southern Sudan, which provided the majority of the country's forestry products. According to FAO estimates, however, in 1987 Sudan produced 41,000 cubic meters of sawed timber, 1,906,000 cubic meters of other industrial roundwood, and more than 18 million cubic meters of firewood. Each of these categories showed a substantial increase from production levels in the 1970s. The insatiable demand was for charcoal, the principal cooking fuel, and the one major forest product not dependent upon the south. Because wood of any kind could be turned to charcoal, the acacia groves of the Sahel have been used extensively for this purpose, with a resulting rapid advance of deforestation. To improve government forestry conservation and management policy, as well as the issue of land use, in 1990–91 plans were under way to establish a forestry resource conservation project, funded and cofinanced by several international development agencies and donors.

Manufacturing

The development of modern manufacturing received little direct encouragement in Sudan during the condominium period. British economic policies were aimed basically at expanding the production of primary products, mainly cotton, for export. Imports and traditional handicraft industries met the basic needs for manufactured goods. Indirectly, however, the vast Gezira Scheme cotton-growing project induced the construction of ginneries, of which more than twenty were in operation by the early 1930s. A secondary development was the establishment of several cottonseed oil-pressing mills. During World War II, small import substitution industries arose, including those manufacturing soap, carbonated drinks, and other consumer items. These operations did not survive the competition from imports after the war's end. Foreign private interests invested in a few larger enterprises that included a meat-processing factory, a cement plant, and a brewery, all opened between 1949 and 1952.

At independence the Sudanese government supported an industrial development policy to be effected through the private sector. To facilitate this process, Khartoum adopted the Approved Enterprises (Concessions) Act of 1956, to encourage private Sudanese and foreign investment. The act placed few restrictions on foreign equity holdings. By 1961, however, the government had concluded that the private sector lacked interest or funds to establish enterprises important to the national economy, and so it entered the manufacturing field. The first government project was a tannery opened that year, and this was followed in 1962 by a sugar factory. In 1962 Khartoum formed the Industrial Development Corporation (IDC) to manage government plants. During the decade, several additional government enterprises were built, including a second sugar factory, two fruit and vegetable canneries, a date-processing plant, an onion-dehydrating plant, a milk-processing plant, and a cardboard factory. During this time, the private sector also made substantial investment, which resulted in factories making textiles and knitwear, shoes, soap, soft drinks, and flour. Other private enterprises included printing facilities and additional oil-pressing mills. Among the largest private undertakings was the foreign-financed and foreign-built oil refinery at Port Sudan, which opened in 1964. Well over half the private sector investment during the decade came from foreign sources.

Government participation in the manufacturing sector increased dramatically after the 1969 military coup and the adoption of a policy aimed at placing the country's economic development in government hands, although private ownership continued. During 1970 and 1971, Khartoum nationalized more than thirty private enterprises. In 1972, however, to counter the drop in foreign private investment that followed, Nimeiri announced that private capital would again be accorded favorable treatment, and the government passed the Development and Promotion of Industrial Investment Act of 1972, containing even more liberal provisions than precoup legislation.

As the economy remained dependent on private capital, as well as capital investment from developed nations, the government incorporated further incentives for the favorable treatment of such capital in a 1974 revision of the industrial investment act and added provisions against arbitrary nationalization. Moreover, in 1972 Khartoum denationalized some enterprises nationalized earlier and returned them to their former owners under an arrangement for joint government-private ownership. One of the largest of these enterprises was the Bata Shoe Company, which was returned in 1978 as a reorganized joint company in which Bata held a 51 percent interest and the government 49 percent. The most successful such enterprise, however, was the Bittar Group, which in 1990 had become the largest undertaking in Sudan. Begun in the 1920s, nationalized in 1969 but returned to its owners in 1973, it has diversified into products ranging from exports of vegetable oils to imports of wheat, sugar, and insecticides. The firm has been active in a wide range of projects involving agriculture, electricity, and such industrial products as household and office equipment, soap, and detergents.

Throughout the 1970s, the government continued to establish new public enterprises, some state-owned, others in conjunction with private interests, and some having foreign government participation, especially by the Arab oil-producing states. The new plants included three sugar factories, among which was the Kinanah sugar-milling and refining factory; two tanneries; a flour mill; and more than twenty textile plants. A joint venture with United States interests built Sudan's first fertilizer plant south of Khartoum, which was in operation by 1986. Private investment continued, particularly in textiles. About 300 million meters of cloth were produced annually in the 1970s, but output fell to 50 million meters in 1985. In 1988 the textile industry functioned at about 25 percent of capacity. The latter figure reflected the effects of the civil war, the dearth of hard currency for spare parts to maintain machinery, and the debt crisis.

Since independence Sudan's modern manufacturing establishment has emphasized the processing of agricultural products and import substitution. The production of foodstuffs, beverages, and clothing has accounted for a large part of total output. Significant import substitution industries included cement, chemicals, and dry battery manufacture; glass-bottle-making; petroleum refining; and fertilizer production. In the late 1980s, estimates of the contribution of modern manufacturing to GDP varied from about 7 to 8 percent a year, including mining (compared to about 2 percent in 1956). Employment in the sector had risen during that period from

Craftsman engaged in jewelry making, Omdurman
Courtesy Embassy of the Republic of Sudan, Washington

possibly 9,000 in 1956 to 185,000 in 1977, including wage earners in government enterprises. Almost three-quarters of large-scale modern manufacturing was located in Al Khartum, attracted by market size, higher per capita income, better transportation and power infrastructure, and access to financial and government services.

Total manufacturing output, however, had not met expectation by the end of the 1970s and steadily declined in the 1980s. Overall output in some subsectors had grown as new facilities began operating, but the goal of self-sufficiency had generally not been attained. Shortages of domestic and imported raw materials, power failures, transportation delays, lack of spare parts, and shortages of labor ranging from qualified managerial staff and skilled workers to casual laborers had been drawbacks to effective operations and increased output. Losses of skilled labor and management to the Persian Gulf states have been particularly debilitating. In the 1980s, many factories operated below capacity—frequently at well under 50 percent of their potential. In some instances, low production also was related to poor project planning. For example, the government cannery at Kuraymah in Ash Shamali was already constructed when scientists found that the surrounding farming area could not produce the quantity of crops the plant could process.

163

The milk-processing facility at Babanusah south of Khartoum had a similar record of poor planning. Efforts to improve the transportation and power infrastructure, whose deficiencies have been major contributors to the manufacturing problems, and rehabilitation of existing plants were among the basic goals of the 1977–82 Six-Year Plan of Economic and Social Development (see Economic Development; Foreign Aid, this ch.). That plan was never effectively implemented. Some progress has been reported, but in 1990 the production problems faced earlier by manufacturing persisted.

Mining

In 1990 the mining industry accounted for less than 1 percent of the total GDP. A wide range of minerals existed in Sudan, but the size of reserves had not been determined in most cases. The discovery of commercially exploitable quantities of petroleum in the late 1970s offered some hope that the sector would play an increased role in the economy in the future (see Petroleum Use and Domestic Resources, this ch.). However, from February 1984, some months after concessions were allotted, oil exploration operations had been suspended in the south, where the largest deposits were located, as a result of the region's security problems. Nonhydrocarbon minerals of actual or potential commercial value included gold, chrome, copper, iron, manganese, asbestos, gypsum, mica, limestone, marble, and uranium. Gold had been mined in the Red Sea Hills since pharaonic times. Between 1900 and 1954, several British enterprises worked gold mines in the area and extracted a considerable quantity of the metal—one mine alone reportedly produced three tons of gold between 1924 and 1936. Gold also has been mined along the borders between Sudan and Uganda and Zaire, but not in commercially profitable amounts. During the 1970s, the government's Geological Survey Administration located more than fifty potential gold-producing sites in different parts of the country. Several joint ventures between the Sudanese Mining Corporation, a government enterprise, and foreign companies were launched in the 1980s; these undertakings produced gold at Gebeit and several other mines near the Red Sea Hills beginning in 1987. In 1988 about 78,000 tons of gold ore were mined in Sudan. In late 1990, Sudan and two French mining companies formed a joint venture company to exploit gold reserves in the Khawr Ariab wadi in the Red Sea Hills.

Chrome ore was mined in the Ingessana Hills in Al Awsat. In the late 1970s, output was reportedly more than 20,000 tons a year, of which more than four-fifths were produced by the Ingessana Hills Mines Corporation, a subsidiary of Sudanese Mining Corporation.

A private operation produced the remainder. The ore was exported, chiefly to Japan and Western Europe. In the 1980s, the establishment of ferrochrome processing facilities had been discussed
with Japanese interests, but the estimated 700,000 tons of reserves
were insufficient for profitable long-term operations. By 1983, when
the civil war brought a halt to all production in the Ingessana Hills,
chrome production had declined about 50 percent to only 10,000
tons per year. In 1988 production of chromium ore was estimated
at 5,000 metric tons. Asbestos had also been found in the Ingessana Hills area. It was reportedly of good commercial grade, and
mining possibilities were under study by a Canadian subsidiary
of the United States firm of Johns-Manville. A small pilot extraction plant had been built, but larger scale operations were dependent on locating adequate reserves and on the ending of the civil
war.

Large gypsum deposits, estimated to contain reserves of 220 million tons, were found along the Red Sea coast. Reportedly of high
purity, the ore was mined mainly north of Port Sudan. In the late
1980s, about 20,000 tons were produced annually, about 6,000 tons
by the Sudanese Mining Corporation and the remainder by private operations. Gypsum was used mostly in the production of cement. Limestone, found in substantial quantities in Sudan, was
mined both for use in making cement and for other construction
materials. Marble was also quarried for the latter purpose.

There has been some commercial mining of mica, exploitable
deposits of which had been located in Ash Shamali Province by
a UN mineral survey team between 1968 and 1972. The Sudanese
Mining Corporation produced about 1,000 tons of scrap mica in
FY 1978, but output reportedly slumped thereafter to about 400
tons annually. Manganese and iron ore, of which several large
deposits exist in different parts of the country, have been mined
at times but only on a small basis by international standards. There
were more than 500 million tons of iron ore deposits in the Fodik-
wan area of the Red Sea Hills, and beginning in the late 1980s
a project had been planned to produce between 120,000 and 200,000
tons a month. Exploitation of Sudan's mineral deposits, however,
depended in large part on foreign companies willing to undertake
such risks in the face of the country's mounting problems and on
international market factors.

Uranium ores have been discovered in the area of the Nuba
Mountains and at Hufrat an Nahas in southern Kurdufan. Mi-
nex Company of the United States obtained a 36,000-square-
kilometer exploratory concession in the Kurdufan area in 1977,
and the concession was increased to 48,000 square kilometers in

1979. Uranium reserves are also believed to exist near the western borders with Chad and Central African Republic. Another potential source of mineral wealth was the Red Sea bed. In 1974 officials established a joint Sudanese-Saudi Arabian agency to develop those resources, which included zinc, silver, copper, and other minerals. Explorations below the 2,000-meter mark have indicated that large quantities of the minerals are present, but as of 1990 no actual extraction had been undertaken.

Energy Sources and Supply

In 1990 the chief sources of energy were wood and charcoal, hydroelectric power, and imported oil. Wood and charcoal were principally used by households for heating and cooking. Substantial quantities of wood fuels, amounting to roughly one-fifth of the country's annual consumption, were also used by commercial operations—chiefly baking and brickmaking and, to a lesser extent, tobacco curing. Some use was also made of other vegetable matter including sugarcane bagasse, which met a significant part of the energy needs of the sugar mills, and cotton stalks, used locally by households. Consumption of wood and charcoal has continued to increase as the population has grown, and some concern has been voiced at the gradual depletion of forest and woodland resources serving the large towns. Overuse of the sparser vegetation in the semidesert grazing areas reportedly was resulting in some fuel deficiencies in those regions, as well as in desertification.

The country's hydroelectric potential has been only partially exploited. Major undeveloped hydropower sources existed at the several cataracts on the main Nile downstream from Khartoum. Natural gas was discovered in the early 1960s along the Red Sea coast in a fruitless search for petroleum. In the mid-1970s, further quantities were found during additional oil explorations, but development was not considered at the time to be commercially feasible. In October 1988, Sudan announced that natural gas production would start in one year; presumably this would come from the 85 billion cubic meters of gas reserves Chevron had earlier estimated. The 1979 and later petroleum discoveries in southern and southwestern Sudan added a new potential domestic energy source. However, these deposits to date have yielded little oil because petroleum companies, such as Chevron, had suspended oilfield explorations in these regions because of the civil war. Sudan had no known deposits of coal or lignite as of the early 1990s.

Electric Power

The only sizable area of the country having electric power

available to the public was the central region along the Blue Nile from Khartoum south to Ad Damazin. The central region in the early 1990s accounted for approximately 87 percent of Sudan's total electricity consumption. The area was served by the country's only major interconnected generating and distributing system, the Blue Nile Grid. This system provided power to both the towns and the irrigation projects in the area, including the Gezira Scheme. Another small, local, interconnected system furnished power in the eastern part of the country that included Al Qadarif, Kassala, and Halfa al Jadidah. The remaining customers were in fewer than twenty widely scattered towns having local diesel-powered generating facilities: Shandi, Atbarah, and Dunqulah in the north; Malakal, Juba, and Waw in the south; Al Fashir and Nyala in Darfur; Al Ubayyid and Umm Ruwabah in Kurdufan; a few towns along the White Nile south of Khartoum; and Port Sudan. About fifty other urban centers in outlying regions, each having populations of more than 5,000, still did not have a public electricity supply in 1982, the latest year for which statistical information was available. Rural electrification was found only in some of the villages associated with the main irrigation projects.

Approximately 75 percent of the country's total electric power was produced by the Public Electricity and Water Corporation (PEWC), a state enterprise. The remaining 25 percent was generated for self-use by various industries including food-processing and sugar factories, textile mills, and the Port Sudan refinery. Private and PEWC electricity generation increased about 50 percent in the 1980s, to an estimated 900 gigawatt hours in 1989 in attempts to counter frequent cuts in electric power. PEWC also handled all regular electricity distribution to the public. In 1989 PEWC power stations had a total generating capacity of 606 megawatts, of which about 53 percent was hydroelectric and the remainder thermal.

The largest hydroelectric plant was at Roseires Dam on the Blue Nile; it had a capacity of 250 megawatts. Other hydroelectric stations were located at the Sennar Dam farther downstream and at Khashm al Qirbah Dam on the Atbarah River; the latter was part of the small power grid in the Al Qadarif-Kassala area. The Sennar and Roseires dams were constructed originally to provide irrigation, Sennar in 1925 and Roseires in 1966. Electric-power generating facilities were added only when increasing consumer demands had made them potentially viable (Sennar in 1962 and Roseires in 1971), yet power generation in Sudan has never satisfied actual needs.

The Blue Nile Grid, in addition to its Roseires and Sennar hydroelectric plants, had thermal plants at Burri in eastern Khartoum, where work on a 40-megawatt extension began in 1986, and in Khartoum North, where a 60-megawatt thermal station began operation in 1985. In the late 1980s, two additional stations producing 40 to 60 megawatts each were under consideration for Khartoum North.

The demand for electricity on the Blue Nile system increased greatly in the late 1970s, and power shortages have been acute from 1978 onward. Shortages have been blamed in part on management inefficiency and lack of coordination between the PEWC and irrigation authorities and other government agencies. Demand continued to grow strongly during the 1980s as development projects were completed and became operational and the population of the Three Towns increased dramatically. New generating facilities were completed in 1986 under the Power III Project, almost doubling generating capacity in the Blue Nile Grid. The project included work on the Roseires units, funded by IDA, and on the Burri and Khartoum North installations, funded by the British Overseas Development Administration. In 1983, recognizing the need for more electricity, the government began seeking support for the Power IV Project to be funded by the World Bank, the African Development Bank, and the Federal Republic of Germany (West Germany) to bring the entire electrical system up to its full generating capacity. The plan was later scaled back from the initial cost of US$100 million and renamed Power V Project.

Petroleum Use and Domestic Resources

In 1982 roughly four-fifths of the nation's energy requirement for industry, modern agriculture, transportation, government services, and households (in addition to wood fuel, charcoal, and the like) was provided by imported petroleum and petroleum products. Approximately 10 percent of these imports were used to generate electricity. Foreign exchange costs for oil imports rose dramatically after 1973 and by 1988 amounted to almost 46 percent of earnings from merchandise exports. Dependence on external sources might lessen when the security situation permits Sudan's domestic petroleum resources to be exploited.

The search for oil began in 1959 in the Red Sea littoral and continued intermittently into the 1970s. In 1982 several oil companies were prospecting large concessions offshore and on land from the Tawkar area near the Ethiopian border to the northern part of the Red Sea Hills. No significant discoveries were reported. In 1974 Chevron, a subsidiary of Standard Oil Company of California,

Sennar Dam on the Blue Nile, one of Sudan's oldest dams and major source
of electric power for eastern Sudan
Courtesy Embassy of the Republic of Sudan, Washington
Waterworks at Maridi, west of Juba
Courtesy Robert O. Collins

169

began exploration of a 516,000-square-kilometer concession (later reduced to 280,000 square kilometers by voluntary relinquishment) in southern and southwestern Sudan. Drilling began in 1977, and the first commercial flow was obtained in July 1979 at Abu Jabirah in southern Kurdufan Province. In 1980 major finds were made at the company's Unity Field near Bentiu in Aali an Nil Province, where further drilling by early 1981 had brought in forty-nine wells having a combined flow of more than 12,000 barrels a day. The company has estimated this field's reserves at from 80 to 100 million barrels, but exploration farther south placed the reserves at more than 250 million barrels. Other oil companies—including some from the United States, Canada, and France—have also obtained concessions, and by 1982 almost one-third of Sudan had been assigned for exploration. Oil exploration and production have been hampered, however, by the almost total lack of infrastructure and by the civil war in the south of the country. Chevron had found small aircraft and helicopters essential for transport, the latter for moving portable rigs and equipment and for general use during the rainy season when all roads and locally constructed air strips were washed out.

The domestic processing of crude petroleum began in late 1964 when the Port Sudan oil refinery went into operation. The refinery, which was financed, built, and managed by the British Petroleum and Royal Dutch Shell companies—from July 1976 as a joint equal shareholding project with the government—had a capacity of about 21,440 barrels per day. Its capacity was well in excess of Sudan's needs at the time it was built, and refined products were exported. Local demand had quintupled by 1990, well beyond the plant's capacity. As a result, more than one-third of the gas oil (used in diesel motors and for heating) and well over two-fifths of the kerosene required for domestic use had to be imported. A substantial quantity of other products refined by the plant in excess of Sudan's own needs were exported.

The domestic petroleum discoveries led to intensive discussion within the government concerning the establishment of a new refinery. Southern Sudan pressed for construction near the oilfields in the south, but it was decided finally to locate the refinery at Kusti on the White Nile about 315 kilometers south of Khartoum. In August 1981, the White Nile Petroleum Company (WNPC) was set up by the central government as a subsidiary of the Sudanese National Oil Company to handle the undertaking. The government held a two-fifths share in WNPC, Chevron Overseas Petroleum Corporation another two-fifths, and the International Finance Corporation the remaining one-fifth. Plans called for a 550-kilometer pipeline to be built from the oilfields to the new refinery. By early 1982, however, the estimated costs of the refinery and pipeline had risen to at least the equivalent of US$1 billion as against an earlier project allotment of about one-third that figure.

The Kusti refinery was predicated on production for domestic consumption. Its estimated capacity (in early 1982) of between 15,000 and 25,000 barrels a day would meet only part of Sudan's overall requirements, however, and the quality of the petroleum would restrict economic production to certain products. Hence the Port Sudan refinery would have to continue operating. In view of the greatly increased cost estimates of the new plant, the World Bank in 1982 undertook a study of an alternative plan that might be more attractive to foreign capital. Under this plan, the proposed pipeline would run to Port Sudan, and an extension to the existing refinery would make it possible to export surplus refined products and even earn foreign-exchange credits. Contracts were let for the construction of the pipeline, but the government canceled them in September 1986. Further seismic studies were undertaken in the swamps (As Sudd) of Aali an Nil, but all of Chevron's exploration and development activities came to an abrupt end in February 1984 when guerrillas from the southern Sudanese insurgent group known as Anya Nya II attacked the main forward Chevron base across the Bahr al Ghazal River from Bentiu, killing four Chevron employees. Chevron immediately terminated its development program and, despite repeated demands by successive Sudanese governments, has refused to return to work its concession until the safety of its personnel can be guaranteed by a settlement of the Sudanese civil war. Total, the French oil company, shut down its operations several months later.

The Nimeiri government pressured foreign oil companies to resume exploration and drilling and hoped to encourage them to do so in part by forming the National Oil Company of Sudan (NOCS) in a joint venture with Saudi Arabian entrepreneur Adnan Khashoggi. After Nimeiri was overthrown, the new government dissolved NOCS but continued to press companies to renew work. As a result, Chevron stated in late 1987 that it would begin a sixty-day, two-well drilling program in southern Kurdufan in 1988, but postponed the work because of the spread of civil war. Several other foreign companies indicated an interest in petroleum exploration in 1988, following the completion of a three-year World Bank study of Sudan's hydrocarbon potential. The minister of energy and mining had announced in May 1987 that Sudan's confirmed oil reserves totaled 2 billion barrels, with an estimated 500 million barrels recoverable.

Transportation and Communications

Sudan's transport infrastructure in 1990 included an extensive railroad system that served the more important populated areas except in the far south, a meager road network (very little of which consisted of all-weather roads), a natural inland waterway—the Nile River and its tributaries—and a national airline that provided both international and domestic service. Complementing this infrastructure was Port Sudan, a major deep-water port on the Red Sea, and a small but modern national merchant marine. Additionally, a pipeline transporting petroleum products extended from the port to Khartoum (see fig. 6).

Only minimal efforts had been expended through the early 1980s to improve existing and, according to both Sudanese and foreign observers, largely inefficiently operated transport facilities. Increasing emphasis on economic development placed a growing strain on the system, and beginning in the mid-1970s a substantial proportion of public investment funds was allocated for transport sector development. Some progress toward meeting equipment goals had been reported by the beginning of the 1980s, but substantial further modernization and adequately trained personnel were still required. Until these were in place, inadequate transportation was expected to constitute a major obstacle to economic development.

Railroads

The country had two railroads. The main system, Sudan Railways, which was operated by the government-owned Sudan Railways Corporation, provided services to most of the country's production and consumption centers. The other railroad, the Gezira Light Railway, was owned by the Sudan Gezira Board and served the Gezira Scheme and its Manaqil Extension. Railroads dominated commercial transport, although competition from the highways has been increasing rapidly. The preeminence of the railroad system was based on historical developments that led to its construction as an adjunct to military operations, although the first line, built in the mid-1870s from Wadi Halfa to a point about fifty-four kilometers upstream on the Nile River, was initially a commercial undertaking. This line, which had not proved viable commercially, was extended in the mid-1880s and again in the mid-1890s to support the Anglo-Egyptian military campaigns against the Mahdiyah (see The Mahdiyah, 1884–98, ch. 1). Of little other use, it was abandoned in 1905.

The first segment of the present-day Sudan Railways, from Wadi Halfa to Abu Hamad, was also a military undertaking; it was built by the British for use in General Herbert Kitchener's drive against the Mahdiyah in the late 1890s. The line was pushed to Atbarah during the campaign and after the defeat of the Mahdiyah in 1898 was continued to Khartoum, which it reached on the last day of 1899. The line was built to 1.067-meter-gauge track specifications, the result apparently of Kitchener's pragmatic use of the rolling stock and rails of that gauge from the old line. This gauge was used in all later Sudanese mainline construction.

The line opened a trade route from central Sudan through Egypt to the Mediterranean and beyond. It became uneconomical, however, because of the distance and the need for transshipment via the Nile, and in 1904 construction of a new line from Atbarah to the Red Sea was undertaken. In 1906 the new line reached recently built Port Sudan to provide a direct connection between Khartoum and ocean-going transport.

During the same decade, a line was also built from Khartoum southward to Sannar, the heart of the cotton-growing region of Al Jazirah. A westward continuation reached Al Ubayyid, then the country's second largest city and center of gum arabic production, in 1911. In the north, a branch line that tied the navigable stretch of the Nile between the fourth and third cataracts into the transport system was built from near Abu Hamad to Kuraymah. Traffic in this case, however, was largely inbound to towns along the river, a situation that still prevailed in 1990.

In the mid- and late 1920s, a spur of the railroad was built from Taqatu Hayya, a point on the main line 200 kilometers southwest of Port Sudan, southward to the cotton-producing area near Kassala, then on to the grain region of Al Qadarif, and finally to a junction with the main line at Sannar. Much of the area's traffic, which formerly had passed through Khartoum, has since moved over this line directly to Port Sudan.

The final spurt of railroad construction began in the 1950s. It included extension of the western line to Nyala (1959) in Darfur Province and of a southwesterly branch to Waw (1961), southern Sudan's second largest city, located in Bahr al Ghazal Province. This work essentially completed the Sudan Railways network, which in 1990 totaled about 4,800 route kilometers.

Conversion of Sudan Railways to diesel fuel started in the late 1950s, but a few mainline steam locomotives continued in use in 1990, serving lines having lighter weight rails. Through the 1960s, the railroads essentially had a monopoly on transportation of export and import trade, and operations were profitable. In the early 1970s, losses were experienced, and, although the addition of new diesel equipment in 1976 was followed by a return to profitability, another

Figure 6. Transportation System, 1991

downturn had occurred by the end of the decade. The losses were attributed in part to inflationary factors, the lack of spare parts, and the continuation of certain lines characterized by only light traffic, but retained for economic development needs and for social reasons.

The chief cause of the downturn appeared to have been loss of operational efficiency. Worker productivity had declined. For example, repair of locomotives was so slow that only about half of the total number were usually operational. Freight car turnaround time had lengthened considerably, and the reported slowness of management to meet growing competition from road transport was also a major factor. The road system, although generally more expensive, was used increasingly for low-volume, high-value goods because it could deliver more rapidly—two or three days from Port Sudan to Khartoum, compared with seven or eight days for express rail freight and up to two weeks for ordinary freight. At the end of the 1980s, moreover, only 1 to 2 percent of freight trains arrived on time. The gradual erosion of freight traffic was evident in the drop from more than 3 million tons carried annually at the beginning of the 1970s to about 2 million tons at the end of the decade. The 1980s also saw a steady erosion of tonnage as a result of a combination of inefficient management, union intransigence, the failure of agricultural projects to meet production goals, the dearth of spare parts, and the continuing civil war.

Despite the rapidly growing use of roads, the railroads have remained of paramount importance because of their ability to move the large volume of agricultural exports at lower cost and to transport inland the increasing imports of heavy capital equipment and construction materials for development, such as requirements for oil exploration and drilling operations. Efforts to improve the rail system reported in the late 1970s and the 1980s included laying heavier rails, repairing locomotives, purchasing new locomotives, modernizing signaling equipment, expanding training facilities, and improving locomotive and rolling-stock repair facilities. One project would double-track the line from Port Sudan to the junction of the branch route to Sannar, thus in effect doubling the Port Sudan-Khartoum rail line. Substantial assistance has been furnished for these and other stock and track improvement projects by foreign governments and organizations, including the European Development Fund, the Development Finance Company, the AFESD, the International Development Association, Britain, France, and Japan. Implementation of much of this work has been hampered by political instability in the 1980s, debt, the dearth of hard currency, the shortage of spare parts, and import controls. Railroads were estimated in mid-1989 to be operating at less than 20 percent of capacity.

The Gezira Light Railway, one of the largest light railroads in Africa, evolved from tracks laid in the 1920s construction of the canals for the Gezira Scheme. At the time, the railroad had about 135 route kilometers of 1.6096-meter-gauge track. As the size of the project area increased, the railroad was extended and by the mid-1960s consisted of a complex system totaling 716 route kilometers. Its primary purpose has been to serve the farm area by carrying cotton to ginneries and fertilizers, fuel, food, and other supplies to the villages in the area. Operations usually have been suspended during the rainy season.

Roads

In 1990 Sudan's road system totaled between 20,000 and 25,000 kilometers, comprising an extremely sparse network for the size of the country. Asphalted all-weather roads, excluding paved streets in cities and towns, amounted to roughly 2,000 kilometers, of which the Khartoum-Port Sudan road accounted for almost 1,200 kilometers. There were between 3,000 and 4,000 kilometers of gravel roads located mostly in the southern region where lateritic road-building materials were abundant. In general, these roads were usable all year round, although travel might be interrupted at times during the rainy season. Most of the gravel roads in southern Sudan have become unusable after being heavily mined by the insurgent southern forces of the Sudanese People's Liberation Army (SPLA) (see Civil Warfare in the South, ch. 5). The remaining roads were little more than fair-weather earth and sand tracks. Those in the clayey soil of eastern Sudan, a region of great economic importance, were impassable for several months during the rains. Even in the dry season, earthen roads in the sandy soils found in various parts of the country were generally usable only by motor vehicles equipped with special tires.

Until the early 1970s, the government had favored the railroads, believing they better met the country's requirements for transportation and that the primary purpose of roads was to act as feeders to the rail system. The railroads were also a profitable government operation, and road competition was not viewed as desirable. In the mid-1930s, a legislative attempt had been made to prevent through-road transport between Khartoum and Port Sudan. The law had little effect, but the government's failure to build roads hindered the development of road transportation. The only major stretch of road that had been paved by 1970 was between Khartoum and Wad Madani. This road had been started under a United States aid program in 1962, but work had stopped in 1967 when Sudanese-United States relations were broken over the June 1967 Arab-Israeli War. United States equipment was not removed, however, and was used by government workers to complete the road in 1970.

Disillusionment with railroad performance led to a new emphasis on roads in a readjustment of the Five-Year Plan in 1973—the so-called Interim Action Program—and a decision to encourage competition between rail and road transport as the best way to

Warning that river had flooded the road
Courtesy Robert O. Collins
Relief truck of the Norwegian People's Aid near Kapoeta in eastern Al Istiwai
in the 1990 rainy season
Courtesy Roger Winter

improve services. Paving of the dry-weather road between Khartoum and Port Sudan via Al Qadarif and Kassala was the most significant immediate step; this project included upgrading of the existing paved Khartoum-Wad Madani section. From Wad Madani to Port Sudan, the road was constructed in four separate sections, each by different foreign financing, and in the case of the Wad Madani-Al Qadarif section, by direct participation of the Chinese. Other section contractors included companies from Italy, West Germany, and Yugoslavia. The last section opened in late 1980.

Other important road-paving projects of the early 1980s included a road from Wad Madani to Sannar and an extension from Sannar to Kusti on the White Nile completed in 1984. Since then the paved road has been extended to Umm Ruwabah with the intention to complete an all-weather road to Al Ubayyid. Paradoxically, most truckers in 1990 continued to pass from Omdurman to Al Ubayyid through the Sahelian scrub and the *qoz* (see Glossary) to avoid the taxes levied for use of the faster and less damaging paved road from Khartoum via Kusti.

A number of main gravel roads radiating from Juba were also improved. These included roads to the towns southwest of Juba and a road to the Ugandan border. In addition, the government built a gravel all-weather road east of Juba that reaches the Kenyan border. There it joined an all-weather road to Lodwar in Kenya connecting it with the Kenyan road system. All these improvements radiating from Juba, however, have been vitiated by the civil war, in which the roads have been extensively mined by the SPLA and the bridges destroyed. In addition, because roads have not been maintained, they have seriously deteriorated.

Small private companies, chiefly owner-operated trucks, furnished most road transport. The government has encouraged private enterprise in this industry, especially in the central and eastern parts of the country, and the construction of all-weather roads has reportedly led to rapid increases in the number of hauling businesses. The Sudanese-Kuwaiti Transport Company, a large government enterprise financed largely by Kuwait, began operations in 1975 with 100 large trucks and trailers. Most of its traffic was between Khartoum and Port Sudan. Use of road transport and bus services is likely to increase as paved roads are completed south of Khartoum in the country's main agricultural areas.

Inland Waterways

The Nile River, traversing Sudan from south to north, provides an important inland transportation route. Its overall usefulness, however, has been limited by natural features, including a number of cataracts in the main Nile between Khartoum and the Egyptian border. The White Nile to the south of Khartoum has shallow stretches that restrict the carrying capacities of barges, especially during the period of low water, and the river has sharp bends. Most of these southern impediments have been eliminated by Chevron, which as part of its oil exploration and development program dredged the White Nile shoals and established navigational beacons from Kusti to Bentiu. A greater impediment has been the spread of the water hyacinth, which impedes traffic. Man-made features have also introduced restrictions, the most important of which was a dam constructed in the 1930s on the White Nile about forty kilometers upriver from Khartoum. This dam has locks, but they have not always operated well, and the river has been little used from Khartoum to the port of Kusti, a railroad crossing 319 kilometers upstream. The Sennar and Roseires dams on the Blue Nile are without locks and restrict traffic on that river.

In 1983 only two sections of the Nile had regular commercial transport services. The more important was the 1,436-kilometer stretch of the White Nile from Kusti to Juba (known as the Southern Reach), which provided the only generally usable transport connection between the central and southern parts of the country. Virtually all traffic, and certainly scheduled traffic, ended in 1984, when the SPLA consistently sank the exposed steamers from sanctuaries along the river banks. River traffic south of Kusti had not resumed in mid-1991 except for a few heavily armed and escorted convoys.

At one time, transport services also were provided on tributaries of the White Nile (the Bahr al Ghazal and the Jur River) to the west of Malakal. These services went as far as Waw but were seasonal, depending on water levels. They were finally discontinued during the 1970s because vegetation blocked waterways, particularly the fast-growing water hyacinth. On the main Nile, a 287-kilometer stretch from Kuraymah to Dunqulah, situated between the fourth and third cataracts and known as the Dunqulah Reach, also had regular service, although this was restricted during the low-water period in February and March. Transport facilities on both reaches were operated after 1973 by the parastatal (mixed government and privately owned company) River Transport Corporation (RTC). Before that they had been run by the SRC, essentially as feeders to the rail line. River cargo and passenger traffic have varied from year to year, depending in large part on the availability and capacity of transport vessels. During the 1970s, roughly 100,000 tons of cargo and 250,000 passengers were carried annually. By 1984, before the Southern Reach was closed, the number of passengers had declined to less than 60,000 per year and the tonnage to less than 150,000. Although no statistics were available, the closing of the Southern Reach had by 1990 made river traffic insignificant.

Foreign economists have characterized the RTC's operations as inefficient, a result both of shortages of qualified staff and of barge capacity. The corporation had a virtual monopoly over river transport, although the southern regional government had established river feeder transport operations, and private river transport services were reported to be increasing until the resumption of the civil war. Despite its favored position, the RTC and its predecessor (SRC) experienced regular losses that had to be covered by government appropriations. In the late 1970s, the corporation procured new barges, pusher-tugboats, and other equipment in an effort to improve services, but this attempt proved useless because of the warfare that had continued from 1983.

Civil Aviation

In mid-1991 scheduled domestic air service was provided by Sudan Airways, a government-owned enterprise operated by the Sudan Airways Company. The company began its operations in 1947 as a government department. It has operated commercially since the late 1960s, holding in effect a monopoly on domestic service. In 1991 Sudan Airways had scheduled flights from Khartoum to twenty other domestic airports, although it did not always adhere to its schedules. It also provided international services to several European countries, including Britain, Germany, Greece, and Italy. Regional flights were made to North Africa and the Middle East as well as to Chad, Ethiopia, Kenya, Nigeria, and Uganda. The Sudan Airways fleet in 1991 consisted of thirteen aircraft, including five Boeing 707s used on international flights, two Boeing 737s and two Boeing 727s employed in domestic and regional services, and four Fokker F-27s used for domestic flights.

Sixteen international airlines provided regular flights to Khartoum. The number of domestic and international passengers increased from about 478,000 in 1982 to about 485,000 in 1984. Air freight increased from 6 million tons per kilometer in 1982 to 7.7 million tons per kilometer in 1984. As compared with the previous year, in 1989 passenger traffic on Sudan Airways fell by 32 percent to 363,181 people, reducing the load factor to 34.9 percent. By contrast, freight volume increased by 63.7 percent to 12,317 tons. At the end of 1979, Sudan Airways had entered into a pooling agreement with Britain's Tradewind Airways to furnish charter cargo service between that country and Khartoum under

*River steamers and barges were once major means of
transporting passengers and goods on the Nile.
Buffalo Cape on the Bahr al Ghazal River in Aali an Nil State, a river
station where steamers took on wood for fuel; village huts in background
Courtesy Robert O. Collins*

a subsidiary company, Sudan Air Cargo. A new cargo terminal was built at Khartoum.

Sudan Airways's operations have generally shown losses, and in the early 1980s the corporation was reportedly receiving an annual government subsidy of about £Sd500,000. In 1987 the government proposed to privatize Sudan Airways, precipitating a heated controversy that ultimately led to a joint venture between the government and private interests. Like the railroads and river transport operators, however, Sudan Airways suffered from a shortage of skilled personnel, overstaffing, and lacked hard currency and credit for spare parts and proper maintenance.

In the early 1980s, the country's civilian airports, with the exception of Khartoum International Airport and the airport at Juba, sometimes closed during rainy periods because of runway conditions. After the 1986 drought, which caused major problems at regional airports, the government launched a program to improve runways, to be funded locally. Aeronautical communications and navigational aids were minimal and at some airports relatively primitive. Only Khartoum International Airport was equipped with modern operational facilities, but by the early 1990s, Khartoum and seven other airports had paved runways. In the mid-1970s, IDA and the Saudi Development Fund agreed to make funds available for construction of new airports at Port Sudan and Waw, reconstruction and improvement of the airport at Malakal, and substantial upgrading of the Juba airport; these four airports accounted for almost half of domestic traffic. Because the civil war resumed, improvements were made only at Port Sudan. Juba airport runways were rebuilt by a loan from the European Development Fund, but the control tower and navigational equipment remained incomplete.

Marine Ports and Shipping

In 1990 Sudan had only one operational deep-water harbor, Port Sudan, situated on an inlet of the Red Sea. The port had been built from scratch, beginning in 1905, to complement the railroad line from Khartoum to the Red Sea by serving as the entry and exit point for the foreign trade the rail line was to carry. It operated as a department of SRC until 1974 when it was transferred to the Sea Ports Corporation, a newly established public enterprise set up to manage Sudan's marine ports. Facilities at the port eventually included fifteen cargo berths, sheds, warehouses, and storage tanks for edible oils, molasses, and petroleum products. Equipment included quay, mobile, and other cranes, and some forklift trucks, but much of the handling of cargo was manual. There were also a number of tugboats, which were used to berth ships in the narrow inlet.

During the early 1970s, port traffic averaged about 3 million tons a year, compared with an overall capacity of about 3.8 million tons. Exports were somewhat more than 1 million tons and imports about 2 million tons; about half of the latter was petroleum and petroleum products. By the mid-1970s, stepped up economic development had raised traffic to capacity levels. In 1985, however, largely as a result of the civil war, exports were down to 663 thousand tons (down 51 percent from the previous year), and imports were 2.3 million tons (down 25 percent from the previous year). Physical expansion of the harbor and adjacent areas was generally precluded by natural features and the proximity of the city of Port Sudan. However, surveys showed that use could be increased considerably by modernization and improvement of existing facilities and the addition of further cargo-handling equipment. In 1978, with the assistance of a loan from the IDA, work began on adding deep-water berths and providing roll-on/roll-off container facilities. A loan to purchase equipment was made by a West German group. The first phase was completed in 1982, and the second phase began in 1983, aided by a US$25 million World Bank credit. One of the major improvements has been to make the port more readily usable by road vehicles. Developed almost entirely as a rail-serviced facility, the port had large areas of interlacing railroad tracks that were mostly not flush with surrounding surfaces, thereby greatly restricting vehicular movement. Many of these tracks have been removed and new access roads constructed. Much of the cleared area has become available for additional storage facilities.

In the early 1980s, the Nimeiri government announced a plan to construct a new deep-water port at Sawakin, about twenty kilometers south of Port Sudan. Construction of a new port had long been under consideration in response to the projected growth of port traffic in the latter part of the twentieth century. A detailed study for the proposed port was made by a West German firm in the mid-1970s, and plans were drawn up for three general cargo berths, including roll-on/roll-off container facilities, and an oil terminal. Major funding for the port, known as Sawakin, was offered in 1985 by West Germany's development agency Kreditanstalt für Wiederaufbau and the DFC. After the Nimeiri government repeatedly postponed work on the port, the German government allocated the funds instead for purchase of agricultural inputs. Once work resumed, however, Sawakin port opened in January 1991, and was capable of handling an estimated 1.5 million tons of cargo a year.

A national merchant marine, Sudan Shipping Line, was established in 1962 as a joint venture between the government and Yugoslavia. In 1967 it became wholly government owned. From the initial two Yugoslav-built cargo vessels, the line had grown by the mid-1970s to seven ships, totaling about 52,340 deadweight tons. During 1979 and early 1980, eight more ships were added, including six built in Yugoslavia and two in Denmark. In 1990 the merchant marine represented a total of ten ships of 122,200 deadweight tons. The Yugoslav vessels were all multipurpose and included container transport features. The Danish ships were equipped with roll-on/roll-off facilities. Sailings, which had been mainly between Red Sea ports and northern Europe, were expanded in the late 1980s to several Mediterranean ports.

Pipelines

By the early 1970s, operational problems on the Port Sudan-Khartoum section of Sudan Railways had resulted in inadequate supplies of petroleum products reaching Khartoum and other parts of the country. In 1975 construction of an oil pipeline from the port to Khartoum was begun to relieve traffic pressure on the railroad. It was completed in mid-1976, but leaks were discovered and the 815-kilometer-long pipeline, laid generally parallel to the railroad, did not become operational until September 1977. As constructed, its capacity was 600,000 tons a year, but that throughput was only attained in mid-1981. In early 1982, steps were taken to add additional booster pumping stations to increase the rate to an annual throughput capacity of 1 million tons. The line carried only refined products, including gasoline, gas oil, kerosene, and aviation fuel obtained either from the refinery at the port or from import-holding facilities there. These fuels were moved in a continuous operation to storage tanks at Khartoum with some capacity offloaded at Atbarah. Rail tank cars released by the pipeline were reassigned to increase supplies of petroleum products in the western and southwestern regions of the country.

Communications

Domestic telecommunications in Sudan were sparse, and the system suffered from poor maintenance. In 1991 the country had only 73,000 telephones, two-thirds of which were in the Khartoum area. Telex was available in the capital. A domestic satellite system with fourteen ground stations, supplemented by coaxial cable and a microwave network, linked telephone exchanges and broadcast facilities within the country. Eleven cities had amplitude modulation (AM) radio stations, and Khartoum, Atbarah, and Wad Madani had television stations with broadcasts in Arabic seven hours nightly. The country had an estimated 6 million radio receivers and 250,000 television sets in 1991.

International telecommunications were modern and provided high-quality links to the rest of the world. A satellite ground station near the capital working with the International Telecommunications Satellite Organization's (Intelsat) Atlantic Ocean satellite permitted direct dialing of telephone calls between Sudan and Europe, North America, and parts of Africa. In addition, a second satellite ground station was linked to the Arab Satellite Organization's (Arabsat) pan-Arab communications network. The Arabsat network was used for live television broadcasts, news exchanges, and educational programming among the members of the League of Arab States (Arab League).

Finance

Banking

The traditional banking system was inherited from the Anglo-Egyptian condominium (1899–1955). When the National Bank of Egypt opened in Khartoum in 1901, it obtained a privileged position as banker to and for the government, a "semi-official" central bank. Other banks followed, but the National Bank of Egypt and Barclays Bank dominated and stabilized banking in Sudan until after World War II. Post-World War II prosperity created a demand for an increasing number of commercial banks. By 1965 loans to the private sector in Sudan had reached £Sd55.3 million.

Before Sudanese independence, there had been no restrictions on the movement of funds between Egypt and Sudan, and the value of the currency used in Sudan was tied to that of Egypt. This situation was unsatisfactory to an independent Sudan, which established the Sudan Currency Board to replace Egyptian and British money. It was not a central bank because it did not accept deposits, lend money, or provide commercial banks with cash and liquidity. In 1959 the Bank of Sudan was established to succeed the Sudan Currency Board and to take over the Sudanese assets of the National Bank of Egypt. In February 1960, the Bank of Sudan began acting as the central bank of Sudan, issuing currency, assisting the development of banks, providing loans, maintaining financial equilibrium, and advising the government.

There were originally five major commercial banks (Bank of Khartoum, An Nilein Bank, Sudan Commercial Bank, the People's

Cooperative Bank, and the Unity Bank) but the number subsequently grew. The public was dissatisfied with the commercial banks, however, because they were reluctant to lend capital for long-term development projects. Since the Nimeiri government decreed the 1970 Nationalization of Banks Act, all domestic banks have been controlled by the Bank of Sudan.

In 1974, to encourage foreign capital investment, foreign banks were urged to establish joint ventures in association with Sudanese capital. Banking transactions with foreign companies operating in Sudan were facilitated so long as they abided by the rulings of the Bank of Sudan and transferred a minimum of £Sd3 million into Sudan. Known as the "open door" policy, this system was partly a result of Nimeiri's disillusion with the left after the unsuccessful communist coup of 1971. Several foreign banks took advantage of the opportunity, most notably Citibank, the Faisal Islamic Bank, Chase Manhattan Bank, and the Arab Authority for Agricultural Investment and Development.

In addition, the government established numerous specialized banks, such as the Agricultural Bank of Sudan (1959) to promote agricultural ventures, the Industrial Bank of Sudan (1961) to promote private industry, the Sudanese Estates Bank (1966) to provide housing loans, and the Sudanese Savings Bank established to make small loans particularly in the rural areas. The system worked effectively until the late 1970s and 1980s, when the decline in foreign trade, balance-of-payments problems, spiraling external debt, the increase in corruption, and the appearance of Islamic banking disrupted the financial system.

Islamic Banking

The Faisal Islamic Bank, whose principal patron was the Saudi prince, Muhammad ibn Faisal Al Saud, was officially established in Sudan in 1977 by the Faisal Islamic Bank Act. The "open door" policy enabled Saudi Arabia, which had a huge surplus after the 1973 Organization of the Petroleum Exporting Countries (OPEC) increases in the price of petroleum, to invest in Sudan. Members of the Muslim Brotherhood and its political arm, the National Islamic Front, played a prominent role on the board of directors of the Faisal Islamic Bank, thus strengthening the bank's position in Sudan. Other Islamic banks followed. As a consequence, both the Ansar and Khatmiyyah religious groups and their political parties, the Umma and the Democratic Unionist Party, formed their own Islamic banks.

The Faisal Islamic Bank enjoyed privileges denied other commercial banks (full tax exemption on assets, profits, wages, and pensions), as well as guarantees against confiscation or nationalization. Moreover, these privileges came under Nimeiri's protection from 1983 onward as he became committed to applying Islamic doctrine to all aspects of Sudanese life. The theory of Islamic banking is derived from the Quran and the Prophet Muhammad's exhortations against exploitation and the unjust acquisition of wealth, defined as *riba*, or, in common usage, interest or usury. Profit and trade are encouraged and provide the foundation for Islamic banking. The prohibitions against interest are founded on the Islamic concept of property that results from an individual's creative labor or from exchange of goods or property. Interest on money loaned falls within neither of these two concepts and is thus unjustified.

To resolve this dilemma from a legal and religious point of view, Islamic banking employs common terms: *musharakah* or partnership for production; *mudharabah* or silent partnership when one party provides the capital, the other the labor; and *murabbahah* or deferred payment on purchases, similar in practice to an overdraft and the most preferred Islamic banking arrangement in Sudan. To resolve the prohibition on interest, an interest-bearing overdraft would be changed to a *murabbahah* contract. The fundamental difference between Islamic and traditional banking systems is that in an Islamic system deposits are regarded as shares, which does not guarantee their nominal value. The appeal of the Islamic banks, as well as government support and patronage, enabled these institutions to acquire an estimated 20 percent of Sudanese deposits. Politically, the popularity and wealth of Islamic banks have provided a financial basis for funding and promoting Islamic policies in government.

Foreign Trade and Balance of Payments
Foreign Trade

In 1989 Sudan's export earnings amounted to £Sd3,023.1 million and its imports £Sd5,373.4 million. Export earnings dropped to an estimated £Sd1,800 million in 1990, with imports remaining at the 1989 level. Agricultural products have dominated Sudanese exports since the condominium period, and in the 1980s they accounted for more than 90 percent of export receipts. Cotton, gum arabic, peanuts, sesame, and sorghum were the main commodities. Live animals; hides and skins; and peanut, cottonseed, and sesame products (oil and meal) constituted the more important remaining export items (see table 8, Appendix). Sudan has long been the world's second largest exporter of long-staple cotton, and cotton exports constituted more than 50 percent of total exports by value in the 1960s but declined to about 30 percent in the 1980s. Gum arabic was in second place until the 1960s when production of peanuts expanded to occupy that position. However, gum arabic returned to second place in the late 1980s. Sesame became the third most valuable export in the 1970s. Fluctuations have occurred in the earnings of these four principal commodities as the result of weather conditions, local price situations, and world market prices.

Foodstuffs and textiles were Sudan's largest imports by value at the start of national independence. These commodities held that position into the mid-1970s, when they were surpassed by increased imports of machinery and transport equipment as the government began an intensive drive for economic development. The share of foodstuffs and textiles declined by roughly one-half during the decade, from 40.5 percent in 1971 to less than 20 percent in 1979. In 1986 manufactured goods, including textiles, accounted for 20 percent of imports whereas wheat and foodstuffs represented about 15 percent. Machinery and transport equipment, which had accounted for about 22 percent of imports in 1970, averaged 40 percent between 1975 and 1978, reaching a high of 45 percent in 1976, and dropped to 25 percent in 1986, reflecting the slowdown of economic development (see table 9, Appendix).

Government plans for self-sufficiency through the development of import substitution industries achieved limited success in certain cases. Notable was the reduction in imports of refined petroleum products that resulted from the 1964 opening of the Port Sudan refinery. Substantial savings were made in foreign exchange expenditure until the rise in world crude petroleum prices after 1973. Crude oil and certain refined products accounted for only about 1 percent of import values in 1973 but had increased to more than 12 percent in 1986. Progress has been extremely slow in sugar production, and government factories were reported in the late 1970s to be meeting about one-third of the domestic demand. After its opening in 1980, the new Kinanah sugar mill and refinery, which alone had a rated capacity sufficient to replace most current sugar imports, helped in 1981 to increase overall sugar production to 71 percent of estimated consumption. Domestic textile production had also increased greatly from the 1960s, and the share of textiles in total imports had declined from about 20 percent at the end of the 1960s to less than 4 percent in 1980.

In the early condominium era, Egypt had been Sudan's main customer. The development of the Gezira Scheme, however, resulted in large-scale exports of cotton to Britain, which by the end of the 1920s was purchasing about 80 percent of Sudanese exports. Although development of the textile industry in other European countries gradually cut into Britain's share of cotton exports, at the start of World War II that country still was the destination of almost half of Sudan's total export trade and at the time of Sudanese independence continued to be the largest customer. During the 1960s, India, West Germany, and Italy emerged as major buyers; late in the decade Japan also became a major customer. In the late 1980s, Britain remained an important export destination. Other major customers were France, China, and Saudi Arabia. In 1989 Saudi Arabia was Sudan's main export market, buying an estimated 16.8 percent of Khartoum's exports, particularly sorghum and livestock. The United States, although not one of Sudan's largest purchasers, became a major customer in the latter 1980s, buying mainly cotton, gum arabic, and peanuts (see table 10, Appendix).

After the May 1969 coup, Khartoum took steps to expand trade with the Soviet Union and Eastern Europe. Exports to the Soviet Union rose dramatically in 1970 and 1971 as that country became Sudan's leading customer. After the abortive communist-led coup of 1971, however, relations deteriorated, and Soviet purchases dropped to almost nil. After 1985 overtures to improve economic relations with the Soviet Union met with little response. Economic ties with China improved in the mid- and late 1980s, with exports to Beijing reaching an estimated 7.3 percent of Khartoum's total exports in 1989, making it Sudan's fifth largest customer.

Sudan's imports were provided by a wide range of countries, led by Saudi Arabia in the late 1980s. In 1989, Saudi Arabia supplied nearly 14.1 percent of Sudan's total imports, with petroleum the chief import item. Britain was Sudan's main import source until 1980; in the late 1980s it became Khartoum's second largest provider, supplying an estimated 8.3 percent of the country's imports in 1989. Britain had well-established commercial and banking operations in Khartoum and a leading position in exporting manufactured goods, vehicles, tobacco, beverages, chemicals, and machinery to Sudan. Among the ten or twelve other top suppliers, the United States, West Germany (Germany after 1990), France, Italy, the Netherlands, China, and India were most significant. Most were also major export customers.

Through 1978 Iraq had been a prime source of Sudan's imports because it was the principal supplier of crude petroleum, a function that was taken over by Saudi Arabia in 1979 after Iraq cut off oil supplies because Sudan had backed Egypt in the latter's peace initiative with Israel. In the last years of the Nimeiri government, bilateral trade with Egypt was cut sharply but in April 1988, Sudan and Egypt signed a trade agreement valued at US$225 million.

In June 1991, Sudan ratified a US$300 million trade agreement with Egypt. Improved relations with Libya enabled Tripoli to become Sudan's third biggest importer in 1989. In January 1989, Sudan and Tripoli signed a US$150 million agreement for Sudan to buy Libyan crude oil. The two countries signed a trade pact in December 1989, with Sudan agreeing to purchase Libyan fuel, chemicals, fertilizer, cement, and caustic soda.

Balance of Payments

A reasonably accurate presentation of Sudan's balance of payments—the summary in money terms of transactions with the rest of the world—was hampered by what foreign economists considered understatements in official statistics of imports and public sector loans. The lack of reliable statistical information was a problem, but the effects on the economy of mismanagement, famine, and war were obvious. In the current account (covering trade, services, and transfer transactions), the trade balance throughout the two decades from 1960 to 1980 usually showed a deficit; only in 1973 was a relatively substantial surplus registered. After 1973 the trade balance was unfavorably affected by higher petroleum import costs and the greater costs of other imports that resulted from the worldwide inflation engendered by oil price increases. The impact on the balance of payments was especially serious because of its coincidence with the implementation after 1973 of an intensive development program that required greatly increased imports. The current account situation was not improved by the services sector (insurance, travel, and others), which regularly experienced a net loss, as did investment income. Transfers usually had a positive balance, but one insufficient to offset the usual deficit in trade and services. Net inflows and disbursement of foreign loans and other capital failed to cover the shortage in the current account, and the overall balance of payments was regularly in deficit (see table 11, Appendix).

The government from its earliest days had been forced to resort to external financing to cover balance of payments shortfalls. Deficits and debt service obligations were relatively insignificant until the mid-1970s. Particularly from 1974 to 1977, large-scale borrowing and new commitments were estimated at more than the equivalent of US$2.4 billion. At the end of 1979, outstanding public and publicly guaranteed debts (disbursed) totaled more than US$2.5 billion, of which almost US$1.8 billion was owed to governments, US$535 million to commercial lenders, and US$235 million to suppliers. In 1981 Sudan's debt burden was estimated at US$4 billion. Little control over borrowing was exercised within the government. The Ministry of Finance and Economic Planning officially had responsibility for contracting foreign loans, but such loans frequently had been authorized directly by Nimeiri. Many were relatively short-term and at interest rates too high for Sudan, considering its economic situation. Until the coup d'état of Colonel Umar al Bashir on June 30, 1989, there was little fiscal control over currency and imports, and imports tended to include a large number of luxury goods. After 1989 there was no improvement in Sudan's foreign debt situation, despite a reduction in government subsidies for bread, a 50-percent reduction of wheat imports, and the end of sugar importation, which was expected to save an estimated US$400 million annually. Despite these measures, total foreign debt rose in 1990 to US$13 billion, with debt liabilities, including principal and interest, estimated at US$980 million in 1988–89.

In 1978 Sudan failed to meet its obligations fully—debt service payments owed that year amounted to 17.9 percent of export earnings. It was apparent that it would also not meet its obligations in 1979, and so it sought relief from creditors. In late 1979, acting through the so-called Paris Club, a group of industrialized creditor countries including the United States, Japan, and nine West European states, Sudan rescheduled an estimated US$400 million to US$500 million of the debts guaranteed by Western export credit agencies. The agreed payments were to be made over a seven-year period commencing after a three-year grace period. Rescheduling of another US$600 million in loans and interest with more than 100 commercial banks—represented by the 5 main creditor banks—required a further two years; the agreement was signed at the end of 1981. Despite repeated reschedulings of Sudan's debt burden, both arrears and debt service payments continued to increase.

Since 1978 the government has undertaken various measures to improve the balance of payments situation. A 1979 devaluation of the overpriced Sudanese pound was carried out, reducing its value from the equivalent of US$2.87 to US$0.22. As of March 31, 1991, the official exchange rate was US$1 = £Sd4.50. Since then Sudan's economy has steadily weakened, as have its relations with the IMF and the Paris Club. In 1989 Sudan had repaid the IMF only a token US$15 million and continued to resist IMF demands for further economic austerity measures. Despite declarations by the Sudanese government that it was determined to cooperate with international lending organizations, in mid-1991 Sudan had made itself ineligible for debt relief because it was unable to service its debt.

*   *   *

Despite the problem of obtaining reliable and current information, a number of significant books and monographs have been published recently on various aspects of Sudan's economy. Among these is El Wathiq Kameir and Abrahim Kursany's *Corruption as the 'Fifth' Factor of Production in the Sudan,* which should be read in conjunction with the two books by Mansour Khalid, *Nimeiri and the Revolution of Dis-May* and *The Government They Deserve.* These books not only unravel corruption but also provide insightful analyses of Sudanese governments. Tim Niblock's *Class and Power in Sudan* covers the whole of the condominium and ends with the Nimeiri regime. Of more contemporary interest is the sound analysis of Sudan's economy in Medani M. Ahmed's *The Political Economy of Development in the Sudan.* A more recent work is a collection of essays, *Sudan since Independence;* several of these essays edited by Muddathir Abd al Rahim, Raphael Badal, Adlan Hardallo, and Peter Woodward pertain to the economy.

A very useful collection of essays is that edited by Ali Mohamed el Hassan, "Essays on the Economy and Society of the Sudan." More recent is a collection of essays on Sudan's economy edited by Paul van de Wel and Abdel Ghaffar Mohamed Ahmed, *Perspectives on Development in the Sudan.* Ali Abdel Gadir Ali's, *Some Aspects of Production in Sudanese Traditional Agriculture* has insightful comments on Sudan's economy. Siddiq Umbadda's *Import Policy in the Sudan, 1966-1976* and Mekki El Shibly's *Monetisation, Financial Intermediation, and Self-Financed Growth in the Sudan,* analyze the economy during the Nimeiri years. An assessment of Sudan's agricultural development is provided in Tony Barnett's and Abbas Abdelkarim's book, *Sudan: The Gezira Scheme and Agricultural Transition.* An important journal specifically devoted to the Sudan's economy, particularly during the Nimeiri regime, is *Sudan Journal of Economic and Social Studies.*

Statistical information can be found in the Annual Reports of the Bank of Sudan (especially the 1989 edition), but their statistical information becomes increasingly unreliable after the fall of the Nimeiri regime, reflecting the political instability. Moreover, after the coup of June 30, 1989, the regime became increasingly secretive. The Economist Intelligence Unit's *Country Report: Sudan,* published quarterly, provides valuable data about Sudan's economy, as does the chapter on Sudan in the annual Europa volume *Africa South of the Sahara.*

Finally, Islamic banking as a relatively new phenomenon in Sudan cannot be ignored because of its impact on the economy and the powerful political influence these financial structures are enjoying in contemporary Sudan. Joseph Schacht's *An Introduction to Islamic Law; Islamic Banking and Finance,* edited by Chibli Mallat; and the influential work by A. Mirakhour and Z. Iqbal, *Islamic Banking,* are useful works on the subject. (For further information and complete citations, see Bibliography.)

Chapter 4. Government and Politics

People's Palace in Khartoum, executive headquarters of the national government

IN MID-1991 SUDAN was ruled by a military government that exercised its authority through the Revolutionary Command Council for National Salvation (RCC–NS). The chairman of the fifteen-member RCC–NS and head of state was Lieutenant General Umar Hassan Ahmad al Bashir, who also served as prime minister, minister of defense, and commander in chief of the armed forces. The RCC–NS had come to power at the end of June 1989 as a result of a coup d'état that overthrew the democratically elected civilian government of Sadiq al Mahdi. Although the RCC–NS initially stressed that its rule was a transitional stage necessary to prepare the country for genuine democracy, it banned all political party activity, arrested numerous dissidents, and shut down most newspapers. Subsequently, members of the RCC–NS claimed that Western-style democracy was too divisive for Sudan. In place of parliament, the RCC–NS appointed committees to advise the government in specialized areas, such as one concerning the legal system to bring legislation into conformity with the sharia, or Islamic law.

The factors that provoked the military coup, primarily the closely intertwined issues of Islamic law and of the civil war in the south, remained unresolved in 1991. The September 1983 implementation of the sharia throughout the country had been controversial and provoked widespread resistance in the predominantly non-Muslim south. The Sudanese People's Liberation Movement (SPLM) and its military arm, the Sudanese People's Liberation Army (SPLA), were formed in mid-1983. They became increasingly active in the wake of President Jaafar an Nimeiri's abolition of the largely autonomous Southern Regional Assembly and redivision of the south, and as his program of Islamization became more threatening. Opposition to the sharia, especially to the application of *hudud* (sing., *hadd*), or Islamic penalties, such as the public amputation of hands for theft, was not confined to the south and had been a principal factor leading to the popular uprising of April 1985 that overthrew the government of Jaafar an Nimeiri. Although implementation of the sharia remained suspended for the next four years, northern politicians were reluctant to abolish Islamic law outright, whereas southern leaders hesitated to abandon armed struggle unless the legal system were secularized. The continuing conflict in the south prevented progress on economic development projects and eventually compelled the Sadiq al Mahdi government in the spring of 1989 to consider concessions on the applicability of sharia law as demanded by the SPLM.

On the eve of an historic government-SPLM conference to discuss the future status of Islamic law in Sudan, a group of military officers carried out a coup in the name of the newly constituted RCC-NS. Their intervention in the political process halted further steps toward a possible cancellation of the suspended but still valid sharia. Although the RCC-NS initially announced that the sharia would remain frozen, the government encouraged courts, at least in the north, to base decisions on Islamic law. SPLM leaders charged that the government was unduly influenced by Islamic political groups and announced that the SPLA would not lay down its arms and discuss political grievances until the government abrogated the sharia. Because neither the RCC-NS nor its southern opponents were prepared to compromise on the sharia, the military conflict continued in the south, where the government's authority was limited to the larger towns and the SPLA or other militias controlled most of the secondary towns and rural areas.

Although the RCC-NS banned all political parties following the 1989 coup, members of this ruling body have not concealed their personal and ideological ties to the National Islamic Front (NIF), the political arm of the Muslim Brotherhood. RCC-NS policy decisions on many social, as well as political and economic issues, reflected strong NIF influence. For example, the RCC-NS purged hundreds of army personnel, senior civil servants, and teachers perceived as being insufficiently Islamic, decreed that men and women must sit in separate sections on public buses, and forbade any Sudanese female to leave the country without the written consent of her father or legal male guardian. Finally, on New Year's Eve 1990, the government announced that the sharia would be applied in the north.

The RCC-NS policies aroused antagonism in the north as well as the south, and consequently political instability has continued to dominate Sudan. During 1990, for example, the Bashir government announced that at least two alleged coup attempts within the military had been foiled. In addition, there were several instances of antigovernment demonstrations being violently suppressed. Opposition politicians, international organizations, and foreign governments all accused the government of systematic human rights abuses in its efforts to quell dissent. Opposition to the Bashir government induced exiled leaders of banned political parties in the north and SPLA leaders in the south to meet on a number of occasions to work out a joint strategy for confronting the regime. Consequently, in mid-1991 the regime's stability seemed fragile and its political future uncertain.

Further clouding the regime's prospects for stability was the threat of famine in many parts of the vast country as a result of the drought, which had been sporadic throughout the 1980s and particularly severe since 1990, and of the continuing civil war. The Bashir government was preoccupied with the political ramifications of food shortages because it was acutely aware that riots by hungry Sudanese were one of the factors that had brought down the Nimeiri regime in 1985. Nevertheless, the government was determined that any food aid the country received not reach SPLA-controlled areas. The efforts to mix politics and humanitarian assistance angered foreign aid donors and international agencies, resulting in food shipment suspensions that have aggravated the food shortages.

Institutions of Government

Since obtaining independence from Britain on January 1, 1956, Sudan has had a political history marked by instability. The military first intervened in politics in November 1958 by overthrowing the parliamentary government of Prime Minister Abd Allah Khalil (see The Abbud Military Government, 1958–64, ch. 1). The ensuing regime of Major General Ibrahim Abbud lasted for six years before dissolving itself in the face of widespread popular opposition in 1964. The country then again experimented with civilian democratic government, which was terminated by a military coup in 1969. Colonel Jaafar an Nimeiri, leader of the junior officers who staged that coup, survived in power for sixteen years until overthrown by a military coup in 1985. The new government under Lieutenant General Abd ar Rahman Siwar adh Dhahab legalized political parties, scheduled elections, and handed over power to civilians in 1986. Sudan's third experiment in democratic rule was ended by yet another military coup on June 30, 1989.

The leaders of the 1989 military coup abolished all the existing executive and legislative institutions of government, suspended the constitution, arrested many prominent civilian politicians, banned all political parties and partisan political activity, and restricted freedom of the press. They established the Revolutionary Command Council for National Salvation, which was designated the legislative authority of the country. The chairman of the RCC–NS was designated as head of state. The RCC–NS also appointed a cabinet that served in many respects as the executive authority. Although the RCC–NS described its rule as transitional, pending the reestablishment of security and order throughout the country, as of mid-1991 the RCC–NS had not legalized political parties nor introduced permanent governmental institutions.

Revolutionary Command Council for National Salvation

In mid-1991 the RCC–NS remained the top decision-making body of the state. It consisted of fifteen members, all of whom were military officers. They were the original officers who had joined Bashir to carry out the 1989 coup. The most important members included Bashir, the chairman; Major General Az Zubair Muhammad Salih, the vice chairman and deputy prime minister; Major General At Tijani Adam at Tahir; Colonel Salah ad Din Muhammad Ahmad Karrar, a naval officer and chairman of the RCC–NS's economic committee; Colonel Muhammad al Amin Khalifa Yunis, chairman of the RCC–NS's peace and foreign relations committee; Colonel Bakri Hassan Salih; and Major Ibrahim Shams ad Din, commander of the NIF's youth movement. Two members, Brigadier General Uthman Ahmad Uthman, chairman of the RCC–NS's political committee, and Colonel Faisal Madani, were reportedly placed under house arrest in 1991 after they had tried to resign from the RCC–NS.

The RCC–NS had designated itself the legislative arm of government, but in practice it exercised some executive functions as well. Its chairman also served as prime minister and president of the republic. Although the RCC–NS had not publicized the rules and procedures governing its deliberations, most political affairs analysts believed government decisions were based on a majority vote of members rather than the ultimate authority of the chairman. The RCC–NS also had not drawn up any regulations pertaining to membership tenure or the selection of new members. The primary responsibility of the RCC–NS appeared to be preparing legislative decrees. Legislation was drafted in special committees, including committees for political issues, the economy, and foreign affairs, then placed before the RCC–NS for approval. In 1990 the RCC–NS created appointive civilian consultative councils to advise its committees. As of early 1991, five members of the RCC–NS also headed ministries.

The RCC–NS appointed a secretary general who was responsible for running the day-to-day affairs of the RCC–NS. The post of secretary general in the early 1990s went to a junior officer seconded to the RCC–NS. Colonel Abd al Mahmud was the first RCC–NS secretary general. He was replaced in June 1990 by Colonel Abd ar Rahim Muhammad Husayn.

The Presidency

The president served as head of state. As of early 1991, however, the RCC–NS had not defined the powers and duties of the office nor specified the term of office. The presidency was neither an elective nor an appointive position. In accordance with an RCC-NS decree, the chairman of the RCC-NS was designated the president of the republic. Since the 1989 coup, RCC-NS chairman Bashir, who was born in 1944, has been the president. At the time of the coup, Bashir had achieved only the rank of colonel. He was the commander of a paratroop brigade stationed at Al Mijlad in southern Sudan and had returned to Khartoum with 175 paratroopers only a few days prior to the coup. Bashir's earlier experience included military training in Egypt and Malaysia, and service on the frontline with the Egyptian armed forces during the October 1973 Arab-Israeli War. In the late 1970s, he was a military adviser in the United Arab Emirates. Soon after the coup, Bashir promoted himself to lieutenant general.

Council of Ministers

The RCC-NS appointed the Council of Ministers, or cabinet, which included civilian politicians and military officers. Cabinet composition varied, but in 1991 it included the prime minister; the deputy prime minister; some ministers of state and finance; and heads of about twenty other ministries. The main ministries included agriculture and natural resources, construction and public works, culture and information, defense, education, energy and mining, finance and economic planning, foreign affairs, health, higher education and scientific research, industry, interior, irrigation, justice, labor and social insurance, trade and cooperation, transport and communications, and welfare and social development.

Although the Council of Ministers was the designated executive arm of the government and a majority of ministers were civilians, in practice the council had no power independent of the RCC-NS. The prime minister, RCC-NS chairman Bashir, had authority to appoint and dismiss ministers, and he reshuffled the cabinet several times between 1989 and 1991. The important portfolios of defense and interior were held by RCC-NS members, and at least three other ministries were headed by RCC-NS officers. The civilian ministers could not undertake independent initiatives and had to obtain advance approval from the RCC-NS for any major policy decisions.

Parliamentary Government

The RCC-NS dissolved the elected legislature when it seized power in 1989. As of mid-1991, no plans had been announced for new elections or for the creation of a new representative body.

Nevertheless, Sudan's postindependence political history, characterized by alternating periods of parliamentary democracy and military rule, suggested that there was support for a popularly elected assembly. The country's first parliament, the Legislative Assembly, was established during the final years of British colonial rule, and the country's first multiparty elections were held in 1948. Subsequently, the Constituent Assembly drew up a transitional constitution that provided for a two-chamber legislature: an indirectly elected upper house, called the Senate, and a House of Representatives elected by direct popular vote. The British model of government was followed, that is, a parliamentary system in which the political party winning the most seats in the lower house formed the government. Multiparty elections for the House of Representatives were held in 1953 and 1958. The second parliament had been in session only a few months before being forcibly dissolved by a military coup. Parliamentary government was restored briefly between 1964 and 1969, during which time there were two multiparty elections for the House of Representatives.

Following the precedent set by the 1958 military coup, Nimeiri dissolved parliament and banned political parties when he seized power in May 1969. Five years later, in 1974, he permitted controlled elections for a new People's Assembly. In this and subsequent balloting, candidates had to be approved by the government, and persons with known or suspected ties to the banned political parties were barred from participation. The People's Assembly never functioned as an institution independent of the executive and was dissolved after Nimeiri's overthrow in April 1985. The first genuinely democratic parliamentary elections since 1968 were held in April 1986, but no political party won a majority of seats. During the next three years, six successive coalition governments were formed. The assembly was dissolved and political parties again banned following the June 30, 1989, military coup.

Constitutional Development

One of the first acts of the RCC–NS after seizing power was to abolish by decree the transitional constitution of 1985, drafted following the overthrow of the Nimeiri government to replace the 1973 Permanent Constitution. Bashir and other RCC–NS members initially promised that a constituent assembly would be convened to draw up a new constitution. During its first eighteen months, however, the RCC–NS government failed to address the issue of a constitution. Then in early 1991, in response to increasing criticism of its authoritarian and arbitrary rule, the RCC–NS announced the convening of a constitutional conference. Bashir invited civilian politicians, including those opposed to the government, to attend the conference and discuss without fear of reprisal legal procedures that might be set forth in a constitutional document. Although representatives of some banned political parties attended the constitutional conference in April, the conclave's lack of an electoral mandate, its government sponsorship, and a boycott by major opposition groups served to undermine the legitimacy of its deliberations.

The 1991 constitutional conference necessarily labored under a heavy historical legacy: drawing up a constitution acceptable to all elements of the country's diverse population has been an intractable political problem since Sudan became independent in 1956 with a temporary constitution known as the Transitional Constitution. The primary reason for this situation has been the inability of the country's major religious groups, the majority Muslims and the minority non-Muslims, to agree on the role of the sharia, or Islamic law. Islamic political groups, led by the Muslim Brotherhood, have insisted that any constitution must be based on the sharia. The non-Muslims have been equally insistent that the country must have a secular constitution. Despite the convening over the years of numerous committees, conferences, and constituent assemblies to discuss or draft a constitution, most Muslim and non-Muslim political leaders refused to compromise their views about the role of the sharia. The unresolved constitutional issue remained one of the major sources of disaffection in the predominantly non-Muslim south, where deep-seated fears of Islamization have been reinforced by the government's Islamic education policies during the Ibrahim Abbud military dictatorship (1958–64), Nimeiri's September 1983 introduction of the Islamic sharia by decree, and the failure since 1985 to remove the sharia as the basis of the legal system.

Regional and Local Administration

Relations between the central government and local authorities have been a persistent problem in Sudan. Much of the present pattern of center-periphery political relationships—local officials appointed by authorities in Khartoum—originated in the early part of the century. During most of the Anglo-Egyptian condominium period (1899–1955), the British relied upon a system called indigenous administration to control local governments in nonurban areas. Under this system, traditional tribal and village leaders—*nuzzar* (sing., *nazir*), *umada* (sing., *umda*), and shaykhs—were entrusted with responsibility for administrative and judicial functions within their own areas and received financial and, when necessary, military support from the central authorities. Following World War II, pressures arising from younger and better educated Sudanese led the British in 1951 to abandon administration by local rulers in favor of a system of local government councils. As they evolved under successive national administrations following independence in 1956, a total of eighty-four such councils were created and entrusted with varying degrees of community autonomy. This system, however, was plagued by problems of divided power, the councils being responsible to the minister of local government whereas provincial governors and district commissioners remained under the supervision of the minister of interior. Effectiveness varied from one local authority to another, but all suffered from inadequate finances and a shortage of trained personnel willing to serve in small, isolated communities. In the south, such problems were compounded when hundreds of colonial officials were replaced by Sudanese civil servants, almost all of whom were northerners. In many rural areas of Sudan, the system in the early years of independence was little different from the old indigenous administration dominated by the conservative, traditional elite, whereas in most cities the effectiveness of councils was seriously weakened by party politics.

The Abbud regime sought to end the dual features of this system through the 1961 Local Government Act, which introduced a provincial commissioner appointed by the central government as chairman of the provincial authority, an executive body of officials representing Khartoum. The 1961 law was not intended to be a democratic reform; instead, it allowed the central government to control local administration despite the existence of provincial councils chosen by local governmental and provincial authorities.

Soon after coming to power in the military coup of 1969, the Nimeiri government abolished local and regional government structures. The People's Local Government Act of November 1971 designed a pyramidal structure with local community councils at the base and progressively higher levels of authority up to the executive councils of the ten provinces. By 1980 community councils included an estimated 4,000 village councils, more than 800 neighborhood councils in cities and towns, 281 nomadic encampment councils, and scores of market and industrial area councils. In theory, membership on these local councils was based on popular election, but in practice the councils were dominated by local representatives of the Sudan Socialist Union, the only political party that Nimeiri permitted to function. Above the community councils was a second tier of local government structures that included 228 rural councils and 90 urban councils. A third tier consisted

People's Palace, Khartoum, executive center of government, seen from the Nile
Courtesy Embassy of the Republic of Sudan, Washington
Throne room and council house of an Azande chief, southern Sudan
Courtesy Robert O. Collins

205

of thirty-five subprovincial district councils, and at the apex were the province commissions, presided over by the province governor appointed from Khartoum.

Although there were some changes following Nimeiri's overthrow in 1985, the local government structures remained relatively intact. Parliament devolved more authority to community councils and reorganized the functions and powers of the province commissions. In February 1991, the RCC–NS instituted a major change in local government by introducing a federal structure. The federalism decree divided the country into nine states: Aali an Nil, Al Awsat, Al Istiwai, Al Khartum, Ash Shamali, Ash Sharqi, Bahr al Ghazal, Darfur, and Kurdufan. Generally, both the borders and names of the states are similar to the historical nine provinces of Sudan during the colonial period and early years of independence. The states were further subdivided into 66 provinces and 218 local government areas or districts. The RCC–NS appointed a governor, deputy governor, and council of ministers for each state. These officials were responsible for administration and economic planning in the states. They also appointed the province and district authorities in the states. The latter officials, for the most part the same persons who occupied local government posts before the federal structure was introduced, continued to be responsible for elementary and secondary education, health, and various government programs and services in the cities, towns, and villages (see fig. 7).

The Legal System

The administration of justice traditionally was regarded by arabized Sudanese and a number of southern ethnic groups as the most important function of government. In precolonial times supervision of justice was solely in the hands of the ruler. In the north, most cases were actually tried by an Islamic judge (qadi) who was trained in one of the Sunni (see Glossary) Islamic legal schools. Crimes against the government, however, were heard by the ruler and decided by him with the advice of the grand mufti, an expert in the sharia, who served as his legal adviser.

Although the Muslim influence on Sudanese law remained important, the long years of British colonial rule left the country with a legal system derived from a variety of sources. Personal law pertaining to such matters as marriage, divorce, inheritance, adoption, and family disputes was adjudicated in the sharia courts in the predominantly Muslim areas. Customary law, modified in varying degrees by the impact of the sharia and the concepts introduced by the British, governed matters of personal law in other areas of the country. Laymen, generally a chief or group of elders, presided over local courts. In addition to personal law, these courts, which numbered more than 1,000, heard cases involving land titles, grazing rights, and other disputes between clans and tribes.

The primary legal influence remained British because of the weight given to British legal precedents and because most of the lawyers and judges were British trained. After independence in 1956, much discussion took place on the need to reform or abrogate the system inherited from the British. A commission was preparing a revision of the legal system when Nimeiri and the Free Officers' Movement carried out the 1969 military coup against the elected civilian government (see The Nimeiri Era, 1969–85, ch. 1). The Nimeiri regime, which looked to Gamal Abdul Nasser's government in Egypt as a model, dissolved this commission and formed a new one dominated by twelve Egyptian jurists. In 1970 this commission unveiled a new civil code of 917 sections, copied in large part from the Egyptian civil code of 1949, with slight modifications based on the civil codes of other Arab countries. The next year draft commercial and penal codes were published.

This major change in Sudan's legal system was controversial because it disregarded existing laws and customs, introduced many new legal terms and concepts from Egyptian law without source material necessary to interpret the codes, and presented serious problems for legal education and training. The legal profession objected that the Sudanese penal code, which was well established and buttressed by a strong body of case law, was being replaced by the Egyptian code, which was largely transplanted from a French legal system entirely alien to Sudan. Following a 1971 abortive coup attempt against the Nimeiri government and increasing political disillusionment with Egypt, the minister of justice formed a committee of Sudanese lawyers to reexamine the Egyptian-based codes. In 1973 the government repealed these codes, returning the country's legal system to its pre-1970 common-law basis.

Following the suppression of a coup attempt in late 1976, Nimeiri embarked on a political course of "national reconciliation" with the religious parties (see National Reconciliation, ch. 1). He agreed to a principal Muslim Brotherhood demand that the country's laws be based on Islam and in 1977 formed a special committee charged with revising Sudan's laws to bring them into conformity with the sharia. He appointed Hassan Abd Allah at Turabi, secretary general of the Muslim Brotherhood, as chairman of the committee. Non-Muslims viewed the committee with suspicion, and two southern politicians who had agreed to serve on the commission rarely participated in its work. Turabi's committee drafted a total of seven

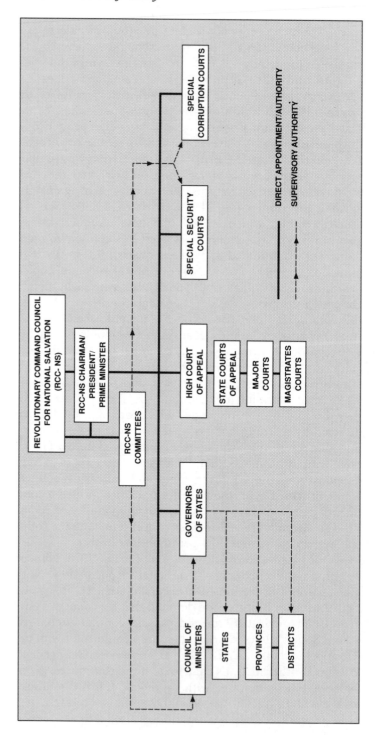

Figure 7. Organization of the Government, 1991

bills, which it sent to the People's Assembly for enactment. One of the proposed laws, the Liquor Prohibition Bill, prohibited the sale, manufacture, advertising, and public consumption of alcohol among Muslims. Another was the Zakat Fund Legislative Bill, which made mandatory the collection of a tax from Muslims for a social welfare fund administered separately from government accounts. The Sources of Judicial Decisions Bill called for repealing the section of the existing civil procedure code that permitted judges to apply the concept of "equality and good conscience" in the absence of a provision of law and provided that this be replaced by the Quran or the standards of conduct based on the words and practice of the Prophet Muhammad. The Turabi committee also called for the imposition of *hudud* and for bans on the payment of interest on loans.

During the next six years, only one of the Turabi committee's proposals, the law on *zakat,* was actually enacted. Following Turabi's appointment as attorney general in November 1981, however, Islamizing the legal system proceeded in earnest. This process culminated in the summer of 1983 with the establishment of a three-member committee that revised Turabi's earlier proposals. In September 1983, Nimeiri issued several decrees, known as the September Laws, that made the sharia the law of the land. In November the People's Assembly approved without debate legislation to facilitate the implementation of the sharia. These bills included the Sources of Judicial Decisions Bill, mentioned above, and a new penal code based on *hudud.*

The imposition of Islamic law was bitterly resented by secularized Muslims and the predominantly non-Muslim southerners. The enforcement of *hudud* punishments aroused widespread opposition to the Nimeiri government. Several judges who refused to apply the sharia were summarily dismissed. Their replacements, men with little or no legal training but possessing excessive zeal for the strict application of *hudud,* contributed to a virtual reign of terror in the court system that alienated many devout Muslims, including Sadiq al Mahdi, great-grandson of the religious ruler who defeated the British in 1885 (see The Khalifa, ch. 1). By early 1985, even Turabi believed it was time to disassociate the Muslim Brotherhood from Nimeiri's vision of Islamic law. He resigned as attorney general and was promptly arrested.

Following Nimeiri's overthrow in April 1985, imposition of the harshest punishments was stopped. Nevertheless, none of the successor governments abolished Islamic law. Both the transitional military government of General Siwar adh Dhahab and the democratic government of Sadiq al Mahdi expressed support for the sharia but criticized its method of implementation by Nimeiri. The complete abolition of the 1983 September Laws, however, remained a primary goal of the SPLM, which refused to end hostilities in the south until its demand was met. By early 1989, a reluctant Sadiq al Mahdi indicated his willingness to consider abrogation of the controversial laws. This process prompted his coalition partner, the NIF, organized by Turabi after Nimeiri's overthrow, to resign from the government in protest. Subsequently, Sadiq al Mahdi announced that the cabinet would consider on July 1, 1989, draft legislation repealing the September Laws and would meet with SPLM leaders to resolve peacefully the country's civil war.

The military coup of June 1989 occurred only twenty-four hours before the Sadiq al Mahdi government was scheduled to vote on rescinding the September Laws. Although the Bashir government initially retained the official freeze on implementation of those laws, it unofficially advised judges to apply the sharia in preference to secular codes. Turabi, who in 1983 had played an influential role in drafting the September Laws, was enlisted to help prepare new laws based on Islamic principles. In January 1991, Bashir decreed that Islamic law would be applied in courts throughout the north, but not in the three southern provinces.

Courts

Prior to Nimeiri's consolidation of the court system in 1980, the judiciary consisted of two separate divisions: the Civil Division headed by the chief justice and the Sharia Division headed by the chief qadi. The civil courts considered all criminal and most civil cases. The sharia courts, comprising religious judges trained in Islamic law, adjudicated for Muslims matters of personal status, such as inheritance, marriage, divorce, and family relations. The 1980 executive order consolidating civil and sharia courts created a single High Court of Appeal to replace both the former Supreme Court and the Office of Chief Qadi. Initially, judges were required to apply civil and sharia law as if they were a single code of law. Since 1983, however, the High Court of Appeal, as well as all lower courts, were required to apply Islamic law exclusively. Following the overthrow of Nimeiri in 1985, courts suspended the application of the harsher *hudud* punishments in criminal cases. Each province or district had its own appeal, major, and magistrates' courts. Serious crimes were tried by major courts convened by specific order of the provincial judge and consisted of a bench of three magistrates. Magistrates were of first, second, or third class and had corresponding gradations of criminal jurisdictions. Local magistrates generally advised the police on whether to prepare for a prosecution, determined whether a case should go to trial (and on what charges and at what level), and often acted in practice as legal advisers to defendants.

In theory the judiciary was independent in the performance of its duties, but since 1958 the country's various military governments have routinely interfered with the judicial process. For example, in July 1989 the RCC-NS issued Decree Number 3, which gave the president the power to appoint and dismiss all judges. Under the authority of this decree, Bashir dismissed scores of judges, reportedly because they were insufficiently committed to applying the sharia in their decisions, and replaced them with supporters of the NIF. One of the most extensive judicial firings occurred during September 1990, when more than seventy judges were dismissed. The effect of these actions was to make the judiciary responsible to the president.

In November 1989, the RCC-NS established special courts to investigate and try a wide range of violations, including particularly security offenses and corruption. The special security courts handled cases that dealt primarily with violations of the emergency laws issued by the RCC-NS. The special corruption courts initially investigated charges that the state brought against officials of the Sadiq al Mahdi government, but since 1990 they have dealt with cases of embezzlement, foreign-currency smuggling, and black market profiteering. Critics charged that there was a lack of due process in the special courts and that the regime used them as a means of silencing political opponents. Judges sitting in the special courts included both civilians and military officers.

Human Rights

International human rights organizations and foreign governments, including the United States, have reported that since the Bashir government came to power in 1989, it systematically engaged in a range of human rights abuses against persons suspected of dissident political activity (see Security Organizations, ch. 5). The Sudanese Human Rights Organization was forcibly dissolved in July 1989, and scores of politicians, lawyers, judges, and teachers were arrested. According to a February 1991 report by Amnesty International, arbitrary arrest continued to be frequent, at least 40 political prisoners with serious health conditions were not receiving medical treatment, more than 200 political prisoners had been detained for more than a year without charges, torture was routine, and some political prisoners were summarily executed after trials in which the accused were not afforded opportunities to present any defense.

Southern and Western Sudan

Southern Sudan

The three southern provinces of Al Istiwai, Bahr al Ghazal, and Aali an Nil were centers of opposition to Khartoum's authority since before independence. The first rebellion began in 1955 as a mutiny of southern troops who believed that the departure of the British would be followed by northern efforts to force arabization and Islamization on their region. The antigovernment movement gathered momentum after Sudan's independence in 1956 with the formation of opposition elements. The harsh treatment of southern civilians by northern armed forces and police caused a number of better educated southerners who served in government posts or were teachers to go into exile. Ultimately, in February 1962, many of these persons formed the Sudan Africa Closed Districts National Union. In April 1963, the group changed its name to the Sudan African National Union (SANU) and advocated outright independence for southern Sudan. Meanwhile, numerous less educated southern males, many of whom had been junior civil servants or former members of the Equatoria Corps, sought refuge in the bush and formed guerrilla bands, the Anya Nya, which began activities in 1963 (see Civil Warfare in the South; Paramilitary Groups, ch. 5). As the Anya Nya developed into an effective military force, it gradually succeeded in expelling central government officials from an increasing number of southern districts. In 1971, by which time Anya Nya controlled most rural areas, its military leaders formed a political organization, the Southern Sudan Liberation Movement (SSLM).

The Nimeiri regime recognized that the escalating civil strife in the south was a debilitating drain on the country's resources and a serious impediment to Sudan's economic development. In 1971 Nimeiri agreed to negotiate a compromise with the SSLM. Several sessions of mediated discussions culminated in peace negotiations in Addis Ababa, Ethiopia, in February and March 1972. Under the provisions of the Addis Ababa accords, the central government and the SSLM agreed to a cease-fire, and Khartoum recognized the regional autonomy of the three southern provinces. After signing the accord, Nimeiri issued a decree for the establishment of a Southern Regional Assembly. The assembly's members were elected in multiparty elections, the first of which was held in 1973, with a second election five years later. Throughout the 1970s, the Nimeiri government observed the Addis Ababa accords fairly faithfully, and the south's relative political freedom contrasted sharply with the authoritarian rule in the rest of the country.

The Addis Ababa accords eventually were undermined by the same factors that had fueled southern rebellion in the 1960s: fears that the north was determined to force arabization and Islamization upon the south. These fears were revived, beginning in the late 1970s, by the increasing influence of the Muslim Brotherhood over central government policies. In 1981 Nimeiri virtually abrogated the Addis Ababa accords by dissolving the Southern Regional Assembly. In addition to these major political developments, the general economic stagnation of the south, which by the early 1980s was plagued with high inflation, lack of employment opportunities, and severe shortages of basic goods, tended to reinforce southern suspicions of Khartoum.

After Nimeiri appointed Muslim Brotherhood leader Turabi as attorney general in November 1981, southern confidence in the central government's motives eroded rapidly. A mutiny among about 1,000 southern troops in February 1983 stimulated attacks on government property and forces throughout the region. By August a former colonel in the Sudanese army, John Garang, had been instrumental in forming the Sudanese People's Liberation Movement (SPLM). When Nimeiri imposed the sharia on the whole country one month later, further inflaming attitudes among non-Muslims in the south, the SPLM rebellion, coordinated by its newly formed military arm, the Sudanese People's Liberation Army (SPLA), turned into a full-scale civil war (see Sudanese People's Liberation Army, ch. 5). The intensification of fighting throughout 1984, and the SPLA's general success in expelling government forces from most rural districts and some towns were important factors contributing to Nimeiri's overthrow in 1985.

Unlike its predecessor, the SSLM, the SPLM sought, not secession from Sudan, but a solution based on a secular, democratic, and federal political system. Because one of the first acts of the transitional military government that overthrew Nimeiri was to suspend enforcement of the September Laws, Garang and other SPLM leaders initially were optimistic about resolving their grievances with Khartoum. The SPLM thus agreed to participate in negotiations with central government representatives and leaders of northern political parties. In 1986 SPLM leaders and several northern politicians met at Ethiopia's Koka Dam, where they signed an important declaration stating their common commitment to democracy. Nevertheless, the primary issue separating the SPLM from the northern parties—the role of the sharia—remained unresolved. Sadiq al Mahdi, whom Nimeiri had imprisoned for his criticism of the manner in which the 1983 laws had been implemented, as prime minister became reluctant to abrogate the sharia as the SPLM demanded.

Muhammad Uthman al Mirghani, head of the Democratic Unionist Party (DUP) and spiritual leader of the Khatmiyyah religious order, was one of the few northern politicians who recognized that ending the civil war and compromising on the issue of the sharia were inseparable. In November and December 1988, he met with Garang in Ethiopia and reached a tentative agreement that involved major government concessions with respect to the sharia. This agreement received the backing of many northern groups that wanted an end to the debilitating civil war. The NIF, however, strongly opposed the agreement and exerted considerable pressures on the Sadiq al Mahdi government to reject it.

Sadiq al Mahdi's temporizing on the Mirghani-Garang agreement sparked demonstrations in Khartoum by various labor unions and professional associations. Military officers who opposed continuation of the fighting in the south intervened in February 1989 to demand that the government seriously negotiate an end to the civil war. The military's memorandum to the cabinet provoked a political crisis that led Sadiq al Mahdi to form a new coalition government without NIF participation. This National Salvation government was dedicated to compromise with the SPLM on the basis of the Mirghani-Garang agreement. Accordingly, it set up a special committee of legal experts to draft legislation for the repeal of the September Laws.

The June 1989 coup made the Mirghani-Garang agreement a moot issue. Although the RCC–NS declared a unilateral cease-fire and announced its determination to settle the conflict in the south peacefully, its Islamic policies tended to alienate further, rather than to conciliate, the SPLM. Garang announced that the SPLA would continue the struggle but insisted that the SPLM was prepared to discuss a resolution of the civil war provided the government agreed not to enforce the sharia. Garang sent SPLM representatives to Ethiopia in August 1989 and to Kenya in December to discuss the war with RCC–NS representatives, but these meetings produced no results. The RCC–NS adopted the position that there could be no preconditions for peace talks. Consequently, the war continued, with the SPLA forces generally prevailing in military clashes with army contingents, especially in Al Istiwai, where support for the SPLM initially had been weak. In mid-1991 the government still held several important southern towns, including the largest cities of Juba and Yei in Al Istiwai, but they were besieged by the SPLA and could be resupplied only by air.

Western Sudan

Regional resentment of Khartoum was not limited to the south, but was present to varying degrees in other areas of Sudan, especially the western state of Darfur. Although the ethnically diverse people of Darfur were predominantly Muslim, more than 40 percent were not Arabs and generally felt more affinity with related groups in neighboring Chad than with Khartoum. The civil strife in Chad during the 1980s inevitably spilled over into western Darfur, exacerbating historical tensions between the non-Arab Fur and Zaghawa ethnic groups (see Chad, this ch.). The perception among many Fur that the RCC–NS encouraged and even armed militia among their enemies inspired guerrilla attacks on central government facilities and forces in Darfur. The general sense of antagonism toward the RCC–NS was reinforced by the drought and the near-famine conditions that have afflicted Darfur since 1984. Like its predecessors, the RCC–NS failed to cope with the social and economic consequences of the environmental disaster, a situation that increased alienation from the central government. By the early 1990s, much of Darfur was in a state of anarchy.

Political Groups

The RCC–NS banned all political parties following the 1989 coup and arrested several political leaders including the deposed prime minister, Sadiq al Mahdi. Nevertheless, all northern parties that existed at the time of the coup maintained their party structures outside the country or in southern areas controlled by antigovernment forces. Some banned political parties actually operated fairly openly in Khartoum and other urban centers. The National Islamic Front, whose leaders were considered to have close relations with several RCC–NS members, was particularly open. Both supporters and opponents of the regime asserted that in the past most government decisions were made by a secretive council of forty men whose members included both top military leaders and prominent figures in the NIF, a coalition dominated by the Muslim Brotherhood. In addition, several cabinet ministers belonged to the NIF. With the exception of the NIF, however, the precoup parties generally did not cooperate with the military government and were committed to its overthrow.

The RCC–NS attempted to broaden its legitimacy by meeting with members of the various opposition parties. Its first effort to reach out to the banned parties was to invite them to send representatives to a National Dialogue Conference, held in Khartoum in the autumn of 1989. Most of the parties sent delegates, but the

SPLM was conspicuously absent. The substantive results of the National Dialogue Conference were meager because the RCC–NS controlled the agenda and did not permit any criticism of its rule. Various meetings in 1990 and 1991 appeared to be aimed at coopting individuals rather than engaging in serious discussions about the country's government. The state-controlled media covered these meetings, but the participants rarely were prominent party leaders. In fact, Sadiq al Mahdi's Umma Party disassociated itself from contacts with the RCC–NS by announcing through its publications that the person with whom the RCC–NS met was not connected with the party. The DUP expelled two members for unauthorized contact with the government.

After the 1989 coup, the banned parties gradually coordinated a common opposition strategy. Northern political leaders initiated a dialogue with the SPLM that resulted in early 1990 in a formal alliance among the SPLM, the Umma Party, and the DUP. This grouping, known as the National Democratic Alliance (NDA), an organization in exile, most of whose leaders lived in Cairo, provided the Umma and other parties with access to valuable radio transmitting facilities in SPLM-controlled areas. The NDA was further strengthened when several high-ranking military officers whom the RCC–NS had dismissed from service in 1989 established informal contacts with it. The most prominent of these officers was Lieutenant General Fathi Ahmad Ali, who had served as armed forces commander in chief prior to Bashir's coup. In January 1991, the NDA proposed to establish a government in exile for the purpose of overthrowing the Bashir regime. General Ali was named head of the government and Garang his deputy. In March 1991, the NDA met in Ethiopia with representatives of military officers, professional associations, trade unions, and the Sudanese Communist Party to discuss ideas for organizing a national government.

Although all political parties remained officially banned in 1991, many precoup parties continued to operate underground or in exile. All the major Sudanese political parties in the north were affiliated with Islamic groups, a situation that has prevailed since before independence in 1956. Among the important religious organizations that sponsored political parties were the Ansar, the Khatmiyyah, and the Muslim Brotherhood. Although several secular parties had been set up between 1986 and 1989, except for the long-established Sudanese Communist Party and the Baath (Arab Socialist Resurrection) Party, none of these had effective organizations after the coup.

Khartoum International Airport, Sudan's major air center
Courtesy Embassy of the Republic of Sudan, Washington

Umma Party

During the last period of parliamentary democracy, the Umma Party was the largest in the country, and its leader, Sadiq al Mahdi, served as prime minister in all coalition governments between 1986 and 1989. Originally founded in 1945, the Umma was the political organization of the Islamic Ansar movement. Its supporters followed the strict teachings of the Mahdi, who ruled Sudan in the 1880s. Although the Ansar were found throughout Sudan, most lived in rural areas of western Darfur and Kurdufan. Since Sudan became independent in 1956, the Umma Party has experienced alternating periods of political prominence and persecution. Sadiq al Mahdi became head of the Umma and spiritual leader of the Ansar in 1970, following clashes with the Nimeiri government, during which about 3,000 Ansar were killed. Following a brief reconciliation with Nimeiri in the mid-1970s, Sadiq al Mahdi was imprisoned for his opposition to the government's foreign and domestic policies, including his 1983 denunciation of the September Laws as being un-Islamic.

Despite Sadiq al Mahdi's criticisms of Nimeiri's efforts to exploit religious sentiments, the Umma was an Islamic party dedicated to achieving its own Muslim political agenda for Sudan. Sadiq

217

al Mahdi had never objected to the sharia becoming the law of the land, but rather to the "un-Islamic" manner Nimeiri had used to implement the sharia through the September Laws. Thus, when Sadiq al Mahdi became prime minister in 1986, he was loath to become the leader who abolished the sharia in Sudan. Failing to appreciate the reasons for non-Muslim antipathy toward the sharia, Sadiq al Mahdi cooperated with his brother-in-law, NIF leader Turabi, to draft Islamic legal codes for the country. By the time Sadiq al Mahdi realized that ending the civil war and retaining the sharia were incompatible political goals, public confidence in his government had dissipated, setting the stage for military intervention. Following the June 1989 coup, Sadiq al Mahdi was arrested and kept in solitary confinement for several months. He was not released from prison until early 1991. Sadiq al Mahdi indicated approval of political positions adopted by the Umma Party during his detention, including joining with the SPLM and northern political parties in the National Democratic Alliance opposition grouping.

Democratic Unionist Party

The Democratic Unionist Party (DUP) was similarly based on a religious order, the Khatmiyyah organization. Ever since the Khatmiyyah opposed the Mahdist movement in the 1880s, it has been a rival of the Ansar. Although the Khatmiyyah was more broadly based than the Ansar, it was generally less effective politically. Historically, the DUP and its predecessors were plagued by factionalism, stemming largely from the differing perspectives of secular-minded professionals in the party and the more traditional religious values of their Khatmiyyah supporters. Muhammad Uthman al Mirghani, the DUP leader and hereditary Khatmiyyah spiritual guide since 1968, tried to keep these tensions in check by avoiding firm stances on controversial political issues. In particular, he refrained from public criticism of Nimeiri's September Laws so as not to alienate Khatmiyyah followers who approved of implementing the sharia. In the 1986 parliamentary elections, the DUP won the second largest number of seats and agreed to participate in Sadiq al Mahdi's coalition government. Like Sadiq al Mahdi, Mirghani felt uneasy about abrogating the sharia, as demanded by the SPLM, and supported the idea that the September Laws could be revised to expunge the "un-Islamic" content added by Nimeiri.

By late 1988, however, other DUP leaders had persuaded Mirghani that the Islamic law issue was the main obstacle to a peaceful resolution of the civil war. Mirghani himself became convinced that the war posed a more serious danger to Sudan than did any compromise over the sharia. It was this attitude that prompted him to meet with Garang in Ethiopia where he negotiated a cease-fire agreement based on a commitment to abolish the September Laws. During the next six months leading up to the June 1989 coup, Mirghani worked to build support for the agreement, and in the process emerged as the most important Muslim religious figure to advocate concessions on the implementation of the sharia. Following the coup, Mirghani fled into exile and he has remained in Egypt. Since 1989, the RCC–NS has attempted to exploit DUP factionalism by coopting party officials who contested Mirghani's leadership, but these efforts failed to weaken the DUP as an opposition group.

The Muslim Brotherhood

The Muslim Brotherhood, which originated in Egypt, has been active in Sudan since its formation there in 1949. It emerged from Muslim student groups that first began organizing in the universities during the 1940s, and its main support base has remained the college educated. The Muslim Brotherhood's objective in Sudan has been to institutionalize Islamic law throughout the country. Hassan Abd Allah at Turabi, former dean of the School of Law at the University of Khartoum, had been the Muslim Brotherhood's secretary general since 1964. He began working with Nimeiri in the mid-1970s, and, as his attorney general in 1983, played a key role in the controversial introduction of the sharia. After the overthrow of Nimeiri, Turabi was instrumental in setting up the NIF, a Brotherhood-dominated organization that included several other small Islamic parties. Following the 1989 coup, the RCC–NS arrested Turabi, as well as the leaders of other political parties, and held him in solitary confinement for several months. Nevertheless, this action failed to dispel a pervasive belief in Sudan that Turabi and the NIF actively collaborated with the RCC–NS. NIF influence within the government was evident in its policies and in the presence of several NIF members in the cabinet.

The Republican Brothers

A small but influential religious party in the early 1980s was the Republican Brothers. A Sufi shaykh, Mahmud Muhammad Taha, founded the Republican Brothers in the 1950s as an Islamic reform movement stressing the qualities of tolerance, justice, and mercy. Taha came to prominence in 1983 when he opposed Nimeiri's implementation of the sharia as being contrary to the essence of Islam. He was arrested and subsequently executed for heresy in January 1985. The execution of such a widely revered religious figure—Taha was seventy-six—aroused considerable revulsion in Sudan and was one of the factors that helped precipitate the coup against Nimeiri. Although the Republican Brothers survived the loss of its leader and participated in the political process during the parliamentary period, it has not been politically active since 1989.

Secular Political Parties

The two most important secular political parties in the north were the Sudanese Communist Party (SCP) and the Baath. The SCP was formed in 1944 and early established a strong support base in universities and labor unions. Although relatively small, the SCP had become one of the country's best organized political parties by 1956 when Sudan obtained its independence. The SCP also was one of the few parties that recruited members in the south. The various religiously affiliated parties opposed the SCP, and, consequently, the progression of civilian and military governments alternately banned and courted the party until 1971, when Nimeiri accused the SCP of complicity in an abortive military coup. Nimeiri ordered the arrest of hundreds of SCP members, and several leaders, including the secretary general, were convicted of treason in hastily arranged trials and summarily executed. These harsh measures effectively crippled the SCP for many years.

Following Nimeiri's overthrow, the SCP began reorganizing, and it won three seats in the 1986 parliamentary elections. Since the June 1989 coup, the SCP has emerged as one of the Bashir government's most effective internal opponents, largely through fairly regular publication and circulation of its underground newspaper, *Al Midan*. In November 1990, Babikr at Tijani at Tayyib, secretary general of the banned SCP, managed to escape from house arrest and flee to Ethiopia.

The Baath Party of Sudan was relatively small and sided with the Baath Party of Iraq in the major schism that divided this pan-Arab party into pro-Iraqi and pro-Syrian factions. The Baath remained committed to unifying Sudan with either Egypt or Libya as an initial step in the creation of a single nation encompassing all Arabic-speaking countries; however, the Baath's ideological reservations about the existing regimes in those two countries precluded active political support for this goal. The Nimeiri and Bashir governments alternately tolerated and persecuted the Baath. The RCC–NS, for example, arrested more than forty-five Baathists during the summer of 1990. Restrictions against the Baath were

eased at the end of year, presumably because Sudan supported Iraq
during the Persian Gulf War.

Sudanese People's Liberation Movement

Although based almost exclusively in the three predominantly
non-Arab southern states, the SPLM was the most important opposition force in Sudan (see Southern and Western Sudan, this ch.).
Most of its early members were ethnic Dinka, and until the late
1980s most recruits into its SPLA were of Dinka origin. The SPLM
was strongest where the largest number of Dinka resided, that is,
in Aali an Nil and Bahr al Ghazal. Both Nimeiri and Sadiq al Mahdi
had tried to exploit historical ethnic tensions between the Dinka
and other groups, such as the Nuer and Azande, as part of the
effort to contain the spread of the civil war. The RCC–NS, however,
tended to view all non-Muslims in the south as the same and in-
discriminately bombed non-Dinka towns and armed the Arab
militias that massacred civilians. The human rights group Africa
Watch reported in 1990 that the kidnapping, hostage-taking, and
other activities by militias in the south approached a reemergence
of slavery. The effect of RCC–NS policies was to strengthen the
appeal of the SPLM in non-Dinka areas, particularly the Azande
territory of western Al Istiwai. By 1991 almost one-half of the SPLA
forces were non-Dinka, although most of the higher-ranking officers
remained Dinka.

Information Media

Since independence the mass media have served as channels for
the dissemination of information supporting various political parties (during parliamentary periods) or official government views
(during the years of military rule). Radio, an important medium
of mass communication in the country's vast territory, has remained
virtually a government monopoly, and television broadcasting has
been a complete monopoly. The official Sudan News Agency
(SUNA), first established in 1971, distributed news about the country in Arabic, English, and French to foreign and domestic services.

Newspapers

Before the 1989 coup, Sudan had a lively press, with most political parties publishing a variety of periodicals. In Khartoum, twenty-
two daily papers were published, nineteen in Arabic and three in
English. Altogether, the country had fifty-five daily or weekly
newspapers and magazines. The RCC–NS banned all these papers
and dismissed more than 1,000 journalists. At least fifteen journalists, including the director of the Sudan News Agency and the

editor of the monthly *Sudanow,* were arrested after the coup. Since coming to power, the RCC–NS has authorized the publication of only a few papers and periodicals, all of which were published by the military or government agencies and edited by official censors. The leading daily in 1991 was *Al Inqadh al Watani* (National Salvation).

Radio and Television

Radio and television broadcasting were operated by the government. In 1990 there were an estimated 250,000 television sets in the country and about 6 million radio receivers. Sudan Television operated three stations located in Omdurman, Al Jazirah, and Atbarah. The major radio station of the Sudan National Broadcasting Corporation was in Omdurman, with a regional station in Juba for the south. Following the 1989 coup, the RCC–NS dismissed several broadcasters from Sudan Television because their loyalty to the new government and its policies was considered suspect.

In opposition to the official broadcast network, the SPLM operated its own clandestine radio station, Radio SPLA, from secret transmitters within the country and facilities in Ethiopia. Radio SPLA broadcasts were in Arabic, English, and various languages of the south. In 1990 the National Democratic Alliance began broadcasts on Radio SPLA's frequencies.

Foreign Relations

The 1989 coup accelerated the trend in Sudan's foreign policy of turning away from traditional allies, such as Egypt and the United States. This trend had begun following the overthrow of Nimeiri's government in 1985. As prime minister, one of Sadiq al Mahdi's foreign policy objectives was to ease the strain that had characterized relations with Ethiopia, Libya, and the Soviet Union during the latter years of Nimeiri's rule. Nevertheless, the country's need for foreign economic assistance to deal with the consequences of drought and civil war generally curtailed the extent to which foreign relations could be realigned.

The Persian Gulf crisis and subsequent war in 1991 caught Sudan in an awkward position. Although Khartoum's officially stated position was one of neutrality, the unofficial government position was one of sympathy for Iraq, stemming largely from a sense of appreciation for the military assistance Baghdad had provided since 1989. Sudan's failure to join the anti-Iraq coalition infuriated Saudi Arabia, which retaliated by suspending much-needed economic assistance, and Egypt, which responded by providing aid to opponents

*View of Khartoum, Sudan's capital, showing the Blue Nile
and the Blue Nile bridge
Courtesy Embassy of the Republic of Sudan, Washington*

of the Bashir regime. After the RCC–NS sent the deputy leader of the NIF to the Islamic Conference in Baghdad that Iraqi President Saddam Husayn organized in January 1991, Egypt withdrew its ambassador from Khartoum. The RCC–NS's efforts to maintain close relations with Iraq resulted in Sudan's regional isolation.

Egypt

In 1991 Sudan's relations with its most important neighbor were strained. This was partially a legacy of Cairo's close support of Nimeiri prior to 1985. Sudan was one of the few Arab countries that backed Egypt in 1979 after Anwar as Sadat had signed a separate peace agreement with Israel, and Nimeiri had taken a leading role in the early 1980s to help rehabilitate Egypt's position with the rest of the Arab world. Nimeiri was in Egypt en route home from a trip to the United States when his government was overthrown. Egyptian president Husni Mubarak granted Nimeiri political asylum and rejected Sudan's subsequent calls for his extradition. Beginning in 1986, relations gradually improved, and they were relatively normal by the time the Bashir coup occurred.

Relations with Egypt deteriorated steadily after the RCC–NS came to power. The Bashir regime was convinced that Egypt

223

supported opposition politicians, several of whom, including Mirghani, were granted political asylum; the NDA was also allowed
to operate in Egypt. Mirghani and other leaders, including Nimeiri,
issued regular criticisms of the government from the relatively safe
haven of Cairo. The RCC–NS responded by providing asylum to
Egyptian Islamic activists against whom were pending various
criminal charges and by encouraging NIF supporters residing in
Egypt to physically assault the organization's opponents. Relations
were further strained early in 1990 when the Egyptian government
invited a high-ranking SPLM delegation to Cairo. Even before the
Persian Gulf crisis erupted in August, Mubarak accused Sudan
of stationing Iraqi missiles on its soil and aiming them at the Aswan
High Dam, a charge strongly denied by the RCC–NS. Relations
only worsened after Sudan refused to join the Arab coalition against
Iraq. As of mid-1991, Egypt had not returned its ambassador to
Khartoum and was openly providing financial support to the DUP,
the SPLM, and other opposition groups.

Libya

Sudan's relations with Libya, its neighbor on the northwest, alter-
nated between extreme hostility and cordiality throughout the 1980s.
Nimeiri and Libyan leader Muammar al Qadhafi were especially
antagonistic toward each other. Nimeiri permitted the Libyan National Salvation Front to broadcast anti-Qadhafi diatribes from radio
transmitters located in Sudan. The Libyan government responded
by training anti-Nimeiri opposition forces in Libya and providing
financial and material support to the SPLM. Repairing relations
with Libya has been a goal of the transitional, parliamentary, and
military governments since 1985. The Sadiq al Mahdi government
permitted Libya to station some of its military forces in Darfur,
whence they assisted Chadian rebels in carrying out raids against
government forces in Chad. The expanding relations between
Sudan and Libya were not viewed favorably in Cairo, and in 1988,
apparently in response to pressures from Egypt and the United
States, the Sudanese government requested a withdrawal of the
Libyan forces.

Relations with Libya expanded again after the June 1989 coup.
Khartoum and Tripoli both expressed interest in an eventual unification of their nations. In July 1990, the Libyan-Sudanese joint
General Peoples' Committee held its first meeting, and the Councils of Ministers of the two countries met in a combined session.
Although a unity agreement was negotiated in 1990, the chief result
of these meetings was not political union but greater economic
cooperation. Libya and Sudan signed a trade and development

protocol that provided, among other things, for Libyan investment in agricultural projects in exchange for guaranteed access to Sudanese food supplies. The two countries also agreed to form a working committee to draft plans for easing travel restrictions between Darfur and the Al Khalij area on the Libyan side of the border. Later in 1990, Qadhafi made an official state visit to Khartoum. Although the Libyan leader expressed satisfaction with the progress made in relations between the two countries, he also lectured the RCC–NS on the inappropriateness of its close ties to the NIF.

Chad

Throughout the 1980s, relations with Chad, Sudan's neighbor on the west, were affected both by the civil strife in that country, which often spilled over into Darfur, and relations with Libya, which intervened in Chad's internal conflicts. At the time of the Bashir coup in June 1989, western Darfur was being used as a battleground by troops loyal to the Chadian government of Hissein Habré and rebels organized by Idris Deby and supported by Libya. Deby was from the Zaghawa ethnic group that lived on both sides of the Chad-Sudan border, and the Zaghawa of Darfur provided him support and sanctuary. Hundreds of Zaghawa from Chad had also fled into Sudan to seek refuge from the fighting. The RCC–NS was not prepared for a confrontation with Chad, which was already providing assistance to the SPLM, and thus tended to turn a blind eye when Chadian forces crossed into Darfur in pursuit of the rebels.

In May 1990, Chadian soldiers invaded the provincial capital of Al Fashir, where they rescued wounded comrades being held at a local hospital. During the summer, Chadian forces burned eighteen Sudanese villages and abducted 100 civilians. Deby's Patriotic Movement for Salvation (Mouvement Patriotique du Salut) provided arms to Sudanese Zaghawa and Arab militias, ostensibly so that they could protect themselves from Chadian forces. The militias, however, used the weapons against their own rivals, principally the ethnic Fur, and several hundred civilians were killed in civil strife during 1990. The government was relieved when Deby finally defeated Habré in December 1990. The new government in N'Djamena signaled its willingness for good relations with Sudan by closing down the SPLM office. Early in 1991, Bashir visited Chad for official talks with Deby on bilateral ties.

Relations with Other African States

Since 1983, Sudan's relations with its other African neighbors, Central African Republic, Ethiopia, Kenya, Uganda, and Zaire,

225

have been affected by the civil war in the south. These five countries hosted thousands of Sudanese refugees who had fled the fighting and provided various forms of assistance and/or sanctuary to the SPLM and SPLA. As of mid-1991, most of the border area with the Central African Republic, Kenya, Uganda, and Zaire was under SPLM control. The governments of Kenya and Uganda openly supported the SPLM's humanitarian organizations and facilitated the movement of international relief personnel and supplies into southern Sudan. The SPLM's most important foreign supporter, however, was the government of Colonel Mengistu Haile Mariam in Ethiopia. The Mengistu regime had provided military assistance, including facilities for training, to the SPLA and extensive political backing to the SPLM. In retaliation, Khartoum had allowed Ethiopian rebels to maintain facilities in Sudan, the Eritrean People's Liberation Front at Port Sudan, and the Tigray People's Liberation Front at Al Qadarif. As of mid-1991, it was not clear how the overthrow of the Mengistu regime would affect Ethiopia's relations with the SPLM and the Bashir government.

Relations with Other Arab States

Other than Egypt and Libya, Sudan's most important relations with Arab countries were with the oil-producing states of the Persian Gulf, in particular Kuwait, Saudi Arabia, and the United Arab Emirates. After 1974 these three countries became important sources of foreign economic assistance and private investment. During the economic crises of the 1980s, Saudi Arabia provided Sudan with military aid, concessionary loans, outright financial grants, and oil at prices well below the cost of petroleum in the international market. By 1990 foreign capital transfers had become the Sudanese government's most important source of revenue.

Despite its economic dependence, the Bashir regime refused to support the Saudi position during the Persian Gulf crisis of 1990–91. Other than the receipt of a small quantity of Iraqi military supplies, which the Bashir government used in its prosecution of the war in the south, its motive for its pro-Iraq stance remained obscure. In fact, relations between Baghdad and Khartoum, while correct, were limited in 1990. In the spring of that year, the Iraqi government had ignored official protests from Bashir and met with representatives of the banned Sudanese Baath Party and other opposition groups. The decision to side with Iraq adversely affected Sudan's relations with Saudi Arabia and its Arab allies. Riyadh retaliated by suspending all grants, project loans, and concessionary oil sales, measures that had a devastating impact on Sudan's budget and economy. After Iraq was defeated, Bashir and other

RCC–NS members tried to repair the damaged relations with Saudi Arabia and Kuwait, but as of mid-1991, these countries had not resumed their former largesse to Sudan.

United States

Sudan and the United States enjoyed generally close relations during the late 1970s and early 1980s. In fact, then-Vice President George Bush had paid an official visit to Khartoum only one month before Nimeiri's overthrow in April 1985, and Nimeiri himself was in Washington trying to obtain more United States aid when the mass demonstrations that culminated in his downfall erupted. Both the transitional military government and the parliamentary government viewed past United States support for Nimeiri suspiciously and were determined to end the de facto alliance that had developed after 1979. Because the most visible symbol of this alliance was Operation Bright Star, the biennial joint military exercises that had taken place partly on Sudanese territory, one of the first policy decisions was to terminate Sudan's participation in Operation Bright Star. Nevertheless, relations with the United States remained important while Sadiq al Mahdi was prime minister because Washington continued to be a significant donor of foreign aid.

This situation changed following the 1989 military coup. Washington terminated all economic assistance to Sudan in accordance with the provisions of a foreign assistance appropriations law that barred all United States assistance to a country whose democratically elected government had been overthrown by the military. Although this legislation included mechanisms for the Department of State to waive the provision, the Bush administration chose not to do so. The RCC–NS viewed the aid cut-off as an unfriendly gesture. Subsequently, when the United States continued to provide humanitarian assistance for the thousands of Sudanese being displaced by drought and civil war, administering this relief aid directly through the United States Agency for International Development, the RCC–NS accused Washington of interfering in the country's internal affairs. Khartoum's reluctance to cooperate with the humanitarian program prompted United States officials in early 1990 to criticize publicly the Bashir government for impeding the distribution of emergency aid and even confiscating relief supplies. These charges, which were echoed by the British, the French, and several international relief agencies, further antagonized the RCC–NS.

In this atmosphere, it was perhaps inevitable that Bashir would mistrust the motives of the United States when it proposed a peace initiative to end the civil war. In May 1990, after temporizing for several weeks, the RCC-NS rejected the United States proposals for a cease-fire. Khartoum's support for Iraq during the Persian Gulf war further strained relations between the two governments. Finally, in February 1991, the United States withdrew all its diplomatic personnel from Sudan and closed its embassy in Khartoum.

Relations with Other Countries

In 1991 Sudan was a member of several international organizations including the United Nations and its specialized agencies, the League of Arab States and the Organization of African Unity.

The policies of the RCC-NS, however, alienated all the European countries that traditionally had provided economic and humanitarian assistance to Sudan. Britain suspended several million dollars of grants and loans for development projects in January 1991 after the government released from prison five Palestinians who had been convicted of the 1988 terrorist murder of five Britons at a Khartoum hotel. Subsequently, London broke diplomatic relations as well. The twelve-member European Community issued a statement in February 1991 expressing its collective "shock and dismay" at Khartoum's failure to cooperate with nations and international organizations trying to assist Sudanese victims of drought and civil strife. The RCC-NS tried to counterbalance these deteriorating relations with expanded ties to such countries as China, Iran, Nigeria, and Pakistan. None of these countries, however, had the resources to replace the significant and needed aid that had dried up in the Arabian Peninsula, Europe, and North America.

* * *

Several excellent studies exist of Sudan's politics since independence in 1956 and up to the overthrow of the Nimeiri regime in 1985. There is a paucity, however, of published sources for the more recent years. The best overviews of pre-1985 political history are Peter Bechtold's *Politics in the Sudan since Independence,* Tim Niblock's *Class and Power in Sudan,* and Peter Woodward's *Sudan, 1898-1989: The Unstable State.* An excellent analysis of the movement to establish the sharia as the basis for Sudan's law is Carolyn Fluehr-Lobban's *Islamic Law and Society in the Sudan.* (For further information and complete citations, see Bibliography.)

Chapter 5. National Security

Sudan's national emblem, a prominent symbol in military insignia

SUDAN OCCUPIES A STRATEGICALLY SENSITIVE AREA of the African continent, and the nation's military establishment, developed during the period of British colonial administration, has remained influential in independent Sudan. Problems of domestic origin have, however, been the paramount sources of national security concern.

Sudan has experienced civil war during three-quarters of its existence as an independent nation. Historical divisions between the Arab-dominated north and the predominantly Black African, non-Muslim south spawned civil strife that was settled only in 1972, after about seventeen years. Open conflict broke out again in 1983 after President Jafaar an Nimeiri abrogated the peace accord by abolishing the Southern Regional Assembly, redividing the south into three regions, and imposing the sharia, or Islamic law, on the entire country. Since that time, the southern rebel forces, known as the Sudanese People's Liberation Army (SPLA), have gradually expanded the fighting, leaving the government forces in control of only a few key garrison towns of the south. Essentially a revolt among the Dinka and Nuer peoples, the largest groups in the south, the conflict has spread beyond the southern region to southern Darfur, southern Kurdufan, and southern Al Awsat states. The struggle has been complicated by the government policy of arming militias in communities opposed to the SPLA. As a result, local intercommunal conflicts have been exacerbated, and the civilian population has been victimized by violence and atrocities. Millions have been forced to flee their homes in the south to escape the fighting and avert starvation.

In spite of the pressures it faced in the south, the Sudanese military constituted the most stable institution in a nation beset by upheaval and economic crisis. Initially having a reputation for nonpartisanship, the armed forces were generally accepted as the guardians of the state when confidence in elected leaders faltered. Nimeiri, who came to power in a military coup d'état in 1969, was himself deposed by a group of officers in 1985. After a three-year period of civilian parliamentary government from 1986 to 1989, a group of middle-ranking officers again intervened to impose military rule. Aligned with the National Islamic Front (NIF), an Islamist (Muslim activist, also seen as fundamentalist) party, the new military clique purged the armed forces of potential dissenters, arrested suspected opponents, and introduced harsh internal security

231

controls. A politico-military militia, the Popular Defence Forces (PDF) was organized as an urban security force dedicated to the goals of the Islamist movement.

Its economy in a crippled condition, Sudan has been almost entirely dependent on help from other countries to equip its armed forces. After severing military ties with the Soviet Union in 1977, Sudan turned to Egypt, China, the West European countries, and the United States for arms. In most cases, these purchases were financed by Saudi Arabia and other moderate Arab states. The reluctance of Western nations to supply weapons and munitions that could be used to support military operations in the south and the new military leaders' alienation from other Middle Eastern countries have made it increasingly difficult to procure arms and matériel.

The Sudanese armed forces, numbering about 71,000 in the early 1990s, were responsible for both internal and external security. Most troops were deployed to defend against SPLA attacks and contain the southern insurgency. Their effectiveness was impaired by poor morale and shortages of functioning weapons and essential supplies. Most of the armored vehicles, artillery, and aircraft from the Soviet Union were more than twenty years old and no longer serviceable as a result of lack of maintenance and spare parts.

In addition to the questionable effectiveness of its armed forces, Sudan faced other security problems. Sudan had on its borders two states equipped with Soviet arms: Ethiopia on the east and Libya on the northwest. Although each of these states constituted a potential threat, it was the seemingly unwinnable war in the south and the growing unpopularity of a military leadership fueled by strong Islamism that were the dominant national security issues.

The Military in National Life

The warrior tradition has played an important part in the history of Sudanese society, and military involvement in government has continued in modern Sudan. Although Sudan inherited a parliamentary government structure from the British, the Sudanese people were accustomed to a British colonial administration that was inherently military in nature. British officers held high administrative positions in both the provincial and central governments. At independence Sudan faced difficult problems that few believed could be solved by untested parliamentary rule in a country fragmented by competing ethnic, religious, and regional interests. It seemed natural to turn to a national institution like the army that could address these problems through a system of centralized enforcement and control.

Development of the Armed Forces

The military force that eventually became the Sudanese army was established in 1898, when six battalions of black soldiers from southern Sudan were recruited to serve with Britain's General Herbert Kitchener in his campaign to retake Sudan (see Reconquest of Sudan, ch. 1). In the succeeding thirty years, no fewer than 170 military expeditions were sent to establish order, halt intertribal warfare, and restrain occasional messianic leaders, mostly in Darfur in the west.

During the period of the Anglo-Egyptian condominium (1899–1955), participation of southerners in northern units of the Sudanese armed forces was all but eliminated. The British had developed a policy of administrative separation of the Muslim-dominated northern Sudan and the mostly non-Muslim south, where the separate Equatoria Corps commanded by British officers was maintained (see The Anglo-Egyptian Condominium, 1899–1955, ch. 1). Sudanese troops in the north were commanded largely by Egyptian and British commissioned officers until an anti-British mutiny in 1924, apparently incited by Egyptian officers, caused Egyptian troops and units to be sent home. In 1925 local forces were designated the Sudan Defence Force (SDF), and the Sudanese assumed an increasing share of responsibility for its command.

After 1900 the British sought to develop an indigenous officer class among educated Sudanese, mostly from influential northern families. Consequently, the SDF came to be viewed as a national organization rather than as an instrument of foreign control. The prestige of the 20,000-man SDF was enhanced by its outstanding performance in World War II against numerically superior Italian forces that operated from Ethiopia. In the decade between the end of World War II and Sudan's independence, the SDF did not grow significantly in size, but Sudanese assumed increasingly important posts as British officers were reassigned or retired. Sudanese officer candidates were screened and selected, but Sudanization of the armed forces in practice meant their arabization. The underdeveloped education system in the south produced few qualified candidates, and most lacked fluency in Arabic, the lingua franca of the armed services. The British had hoped to use the recruitment of southerners into the army after World War II to spur their integration into Sudanese national life.

On the eve of independence, in 1955, the SDF's Equatoria Corps—made up almost entirely of southern enlisted men but increasingly commanded by northerners as the British withdrew—

mutinied because of resentment over northern control of national politics and institutions. Northern troops were sent to quell the rebellion, and the Equatoria Corps was disbanded after most of its men went into hiding and began what became a seventeen-year struggle to achieve autonomy for the south.

At independence in 1956, Sudan's 5,000-man army was regarded as a highly trained, competent, and apolitical force, but its character changed in succeeding years. To deal with the southern insurgency, the army expanded steadily to 12,000 personnel in 1959, and it leveled off at about 50,000 in 1972. After independence, the military—particularly the educated officer corps—lost much of its former apolitical attitude; soldiers associated themselves with parties and movements across the political spectrum.

Role in Government

On four occasions since independence, the Sudanese armed forces have stepped in to overthrow civilian political institutions and impose a period of military rule. In some instances, the military leadership introduced a measure of stability and renewal. The military enjoyed an advantage because they were accepted by the people as a balancing element against domination by one of the major social, political, or religious groupings that contested for civilian political power. The view of the military as an institution free from specific ethnic or religious identification raised expectations that the armed forces could achieve what civilian politicians could not. Almost invariably, however, the military leaders found themselves unskilled in dealing with the country's chronic economic problems and the chaotic conditions caused by civil war. Accustomed to wielding authority, the military regimes tended to become increasingly authoritarian. Major government initiatives foundered because they were imposed inflexibly with little regard for practical possibilities and the interests affected.

The military's first intervention in Sudanese politics occurred in November 1958, hardly three years after independence. Civilian politicians appeared unable to cope with economic distress and the insurrection in the south. Major General Ibrahim Abbud, the armed forces commander, led the coup. Although the action was apparently planned in concert with leading politicians who envisaged a short military rule, Abbud remained in power until 1964. Initially popular in comparison to the heads of the fractious, stalemated first civilian governments, Abbud was forced to step down when antiregime demonstrations rocked Khartoum. In spite of increasingly dictatorial methods, Abbud had been unable to impose economic order or bring an end to the fighting in the south.

The army remained a pillar of support for the civilian regime that followed, and senior military officers continued to serve in political appointments (see Return to Civilian Rule, 1964–69, ch. 1). A number of field-grade officers, however, some of whom had been linked to Abbud's ouster, had little loyalty to the political system and were impatient with the consensus-oriented civilian government. Disgruntled over the stalemate in the civil war, the intractable economic situation, and official repression of leftist and pan-Arab organizations, a small group calling itself the Free Officers' Movement took control in 1969. At its head was Jafaar an Nimeiri, then a colonel.

From 1969 until 1971, a military government—the Revolutionary Command Council (RCC), composed of nine young officers and one civilian—exercised authority over a largely civilian cabinet. The RCC represented only a faction within the military establishment. Initially, it followed radical policies in cooperation with the Sudanese communists, carrying out nationalizations, escalating the war in the south, violently repressing the Ansar politico-religious sect, and suppressing democratic institutions. More than 300 high-ranking officers who had been influential in previous governments were arrested or removed from the army when they refused to support the policies of Nimeiri and the RCC. Only one general officer was retained. Later, differences within the RCC between those officers with nationalist sympathies and leftist-oriented officers guided by the well-organized Sudanese Communist Party precipitated a communist-led coup attempt in 1971. Officers heading loyal units resisted the leftist takeover, enabling Nimeiri to survive and regain control (see Revolutionary Command Council, ch. 1).

After the RCC was dissolved in late 1971, the country was technically no longer ruled by a military government. Nimeiri's mounting prestige forged him a broader base of support than he had achieved during the RCC years. Over the next decade, the military establishment remained Nimeiri's major constituency and source of power and was, accordingly, well represented in the government. Military men were appointed to head important ministries, to undertake major domestic and international missions, and to assist in the founding and staffing of the country's sole political party, the Sudan Socialist Union (SSU). Defense ministers (who were general officers) served concurrently as secretaries general of the SSU. The National Security Council, whose members were generally military officers, served as an important arena for framing political and economic policies. Eighteen seats in the largely powerless People's Assembly were reserved for armed forces personnel. Nimeiri justified the predominance of military personnel in the upper echelons of government by pointing out that they represented the most disciplined organization in Sudan and that, in a country riven by partisanship, the military as an institution was motivated by nationalist convictions.

Although military officers remained prominent in the government, by the early 1980s Nimeiri increasingly acted as if the armed forces were an instrument of his personal political dictates rather than the source of his political power. The armed forces gave the support necessary for Nimeiri to survive numerous coup attempts (some by dissatisfied military elements), but the special relationship between Nimeiri and his high command seriously eroded. In an extraordinary move in 1982, Nimeiri retired General Abd al Majid Hamid Khalil—vice president, minister of defense, commander in chief of the armed forces, secretary general of the SSU, and generally regarded as the heir apparent—along with twenty-two other top-ranking officers.

Following the purge, Nimeiri assumed personal command of the armed forces and for a time held the defense portfolio in the cabinet. In 1983 large numbers of southern troops mutinied, and civil war broke out again after Nimeiri's centralist and Islamist policies had increased southern alienation. Nimeiri's increasingly arbitrary actions also drove away his traditional sources of support, and the armed forces were of little help as resistance to his policies mounted in the form of massive demonstrations and strikes.

While Nimeiri was en route home from a visit to Washington in 1985, he was deposed in a bloodless coup led by Minister of Defence Lieutenant General Abd ar Rahman Siwar adh Dhahab. The new leadership formed a Transitional Military Council of fifteen officers to govern the country for a one-year period until civil authority could be restored. The council fulfilled its purpose when elections were held in April 1986 and a civilian government took office.

Coalition governments in the established pattern of Sudanese politics ruled from 1986 to 1989 under Prime Minister Sadiq al Mahdi. The government forces were unable to bring the southern insurrection under control, and Sadiq al Mahdi's relations with the military were often stormy. In September 1986, the commander in chief of the armed forces and the chief of the general staff were forcibly retired along with about twenty other officers. In February 1989, the army leadership presented Sadiq al Mahdi with an ultimatum, demanding that he make the coalition government more representative and that he bring the civil war to an end. In June 1989, Sadiq al Mahdi's government was overthrown in a coup led by Colonel Umar Hassan Ahmad al Bashir, a paratroop officer stationed in the south. Bashir headed a ruling Revolutionary Command Council for National Salvation (RCC-NS) of fifteen officers, mostly of middle rank (see Revolutionary Command Council for National Salvation, ch. 4). The RCC-NS justified its action by citing the neglect of the armed forces by the Sadiq al Mahdi government and its failure to reverse the deteriorating economic situation and reestablish security in the south. Bashir was head of state, prime minister, commander in chief of the armed forces, and minister of defense. The vice chairman of the RCC-NS, a major general, was named deputy prime minister. Other officers held the key domestic security portfolios of minister of interior, minister of justice, and attorney general.

Like preceding military regimes, Bashir's government was initially welcomed as bringing an end to a period of political turbulence and paralysis of action. It was soon revealed, however, to be linked to the more orthodox Muslim elements of the Muslim Brotherhood and the National Islamic Front (NIF) political party. Its violent suppression of political expression and cruel treatment of suspected opponents had a disillusioning effect. It dismissed or retired the army commander and 27 other generals composing the senior leadership, and up to 500 other officers. In April 1990, the RCC-NS executed twenty-eight officers, including senior officers removed by the junta, to put down a threatened coup against the regime. The RCC-NS's ruthless action had the effect of intimidating potential opposition.

The harshness displayed by the Bashir military government and its incompetence in dealing with Sudan's economic difficulties had by the close of 1990 alienated nearly all governments to which it could turn for help. The Bashir junta justified its intervention as the only alternative to civilian mismanagement. Unlike other military governments, however, it followed policies that were highly partisan, bearing the distinct ideological imprint of the NIF and the Muslim Brotherhood.

The Armed Forces in Sudanese Society

When the British attempted to forge an indigenous officer class before World War II, most Sudanese officers came from upper and middle-class urban families that enjoyed inherited wealth and prestige. After that time, greater numbers were drawn from the emerging class of merchants and civil servants inhabiting urban areas where formal elementary and secondary education was more easily obtainable. Officer cadets, who had to possess a fourth-year secondary school certificate, were chosen on the basis of performance in a series of written and oral competitive examinations. A requirement that cadets possess a good knowledge of Arabic had long eliminated many southerners educated in English who otherwise might have qualified. It was estimated that only 5 to 10 percent of all Sudanese officer cadets in 1981 were southerners.

The quality of incoming officers, extremely high during the pre-independence period, was thought to have been lowered by the increased size of the army—particularly during the 1968–72 surge in personnel strength. The Sudanese Communist Party, which had become entrenched in the universities and trade unions during the 1960s, contributed to the emergence of a generation of officers that was predominantly anti-Western. Many officers received their initial training from Soviet advisers. After the revolt against Nimeiri in 1971, in which some communist officers were implicated, retribution fell on many of the officers with leftist leanings. The officer corps became increasingly conservative at a time when Nimeiri himself was stressing nationalism for Sudan. The military faction that deposed Nimeiri in 1985 was not distinguished by any particular political orientation, although as individuals its members maintained links with all the important social, religious, and ethnic groups.

In spite of the linkage of the Bashir junta to the NIF and Nimeiri's earlier Islamization program, it was generally believed that among career officers no more than 5 percent were dedicated to Muslim activism. Most officers were modern in outlook, of middle-class and urban backgrounds, and inclined to be nonsectarian.

In the armed forces as a whole, the political and ethnic makeup was influenced by historical factors. From the time of the Anglo-Egyptian condominium, many nomadic peoples of northeastern Sudan had served in the military, as had members of the Khatmiyyah politico-religious sect. By the 1980s, however, Sudanese from the northeast and the Nile Valley were estimated to constitute no more than 20 percent of the military, although they continued to be well represented in the officer corps. Many officers had ties to the Khatmiyyah group and to the Mirghani family and were supporters of the Democratic Unionist Party. Under the Bashir government, northerners continued to dominate the senior leadership, although numerous sensitive positions were held by officers with origins in the south. A general who was a Dinka led one of the brigades active in the fighting against the Dinka-led SPLA.

In the early 1980s, it was estimated that members of the Ansar politico-religious group and other Sudanese from Darfur and Kurdufan provinces accounted for approximately 60 percent of the army's enlisted manpower. The Ansar and other western Sudanese might have been even more numerous in the uniformed services had not recruitment restrictions been imposed during the Nimeiri regime, when these groups were perceived to be among the major sources of opposition to the national leadership.

The presence in the armed forces of non-Muslim black southerners has been a source of contention in Sudan since the condominium period. Until after World War II, southerners were recruited for service only in the Equatoria Corps and rarely served alongside northern Sudanese. Recruitment was suspended after the 1955 mutiny in the south, and when it was resumed the following year, southern volunteers were required to serve in the north under northern officers. The rebellion in the south discouraged southerners from joining the armed forces until the 1972 settlement.

As part of the Addis Ababa accords ending the civil war, 6,000 of the former Anya Nya (named after a tribal poison) guerrillas were to be integrated gradually into the national army's Southern Command to serve with 6,000 northerners. By including southern officers in the top echelon of the Southern Command, the two forces appeared to have meshed successfully. In 1982 it was estimated that southerners outnumbered northerners 7,000 to 5,000 in the Southern Command, but there were relatively few southerners stationed in the north, and none held important positions. Nimeiri's decision the following year to transfer southern troops to the north because of his doubts over their loyalty to the central government was resisted by the southerners and was one of a number of factors that triggered the renewal of the civil war.

External Security Concerns

The largest nation in Africa, Sudan has a common frontier with eight other countries. It occupies a strategic location on the continent. Its capital, Khartoum, is situated at the junction of the White Nile and the Blue Nile. Via its port on the Red Sea, Port Sudan, the nation is linked to the Arab countries of the Middle East. To the south, it is adjacent to the tropical lake country of central Africa. In the west, it is exposed to recurrent conflict among Chadian factions and potential contention with Libya. Even under stable conditions, it would be impracticable for Sudan to devote sufficient military force to ensuring the security of its entire periphery. Fortunately, few problems have arisen necessitating a strong military presence along the boundaries with Egypt, Kenya, Central African Republic, and Zaire. Threats to the stability of the border area have generally been confined to Chad on the west, Ethiopia on the east, and, to a lesser degree, Uganda in the south.

Relations between Sudan and Egypt have varied but in general in the 1970s and 1980s were characterized by differences over such matters as use of the Nile waters. Egypt subscribed to a stable, militarily viable Sudan because it regarded Sudanese territory as providing depth to its own strategic defenses, buffering it from potential threats emanating from sub-Saharan Africa. The border between Egypt and Sudan was unguarded except for minimal policing to discourage smuggling and drug trafficking.

Sudan's Darfur Province contiguous with Chad was unstable during most of the 1980s. The instability resulted from the combination of Chadian combatants operating from bases on Sudanese territory, Libyan troops and Libyan-supported units of the Islamic Legion crossing the border in search of rebels, and fighting among Arab and non-Arab ethnic groups (see Chad, ch. 4). Arms were easily available in the border zone. Conceivably, Libya might desist from further interference in Darfur following the victory—gained with Libyan help—of the Chadian rebels under Idris Deby in December 1990.

The 1,600-kilometer border between Ethiopia and Sudan was also disturbed; both nations provided each other's insurgents with military assistance and sanctuary. In the northeast, the Sudanese government supported the Eritrean People's Liberation Front operating from Sudanese territory at Port Sudan. The Tigray People's Liberation Front was also given facilities at Al Qadarif. Ethiopia retaliated by providing the SPLA insurgents in the south with supplies and bases. Sudan periodically accused Ethiopia of carrying out bombing raids against the estimated 100,000 Eritrean refugees living in camps and villages in eastern Sudan.

A comparable situation prevailed on Sudan's border with Uganda. In 1986 and 1987, the president of Uganda, Yoweri Museveni, accused Sudan of allowing its territory to be used as a haven in cross-border attacks by 3,000 members of the former Ugandan army loyal to the deposed dictator, Idi Amin Dada. Sudan, in turn, charged that SPLA units were receiving aid from Uganda. In mid-1990, the Sudanese government announced that an agreement had been reached providing for the establishment of border security posts and that each country would prohibit its territory from being used for hostile attacks against the other.

Civil Warfare in the South

Except for a period of tenuous peace between 1972 and 1983, Sudan has been the scene of armed rebellion in the south since before the nation became independent in 1956. The second stage of the Sudanese civil war entered its ninth year in 1991. The protracted struggle pitting the mostly Muslim north against the adherents of indigenous faiths and of Christianity in the south has

One of about 200 burnt-out huts in Yei; destruction of homes was a common form of reprisal during the civil war in southern Sudan.
Courtesy Robert O. Collins

resulted in hundreds of thousands of deaths—mostly noncombatants—and has forced millions to flee the south in search of food and escape from violence. The rebel forces controlled most of the rural areas of the south as of mid-1991, besieging the government troops holding the major towns. Both sides were guilty of violence against civilians, but the government's policy since 1985 of arming undisciplined tribal militia bands was responsible for the most flagrant cruelties.

First Civil War, 1955–72

In August 1955, five months before independence, southern troops of the Equatoria Corps, together with police, mutinied in Torit and other towns. The mutinies were suppressed although some of the rebels were able to escape to rural areas. There they formed guerrilla bands but, being poorly armed and organized, presented no extensive threat to security. The later emergence of a secessionist movement in the south led to the formation of the Anya Nya guerrilla army, composed of remnants of the 1955 mutineers and recruits among southern students. Active at first only in Al Istiwai, Anya Nya carried its rebellion to all three southern provinces between 1963 and 1969. In 1971 a former army lieutenant, Joseph Lagu, united the ethnically fragmented guerrilla bands in support of a new political movement, the Southern Sudan Liberation Movement (SSLM). The war ended in March 1972 with an agreement between Nimeiri and Lagu that conceded to the south a single regional government with defined powers.

Renewed Civil Warfare, 1983–

Under the terms of the 1972 peace settlement, most of the Anya Nya fighters were absorbed into the national army, although a number of units unhappy with the agreement defected and went into the bush or took refuge in Ethiopia. Angry over Sudan's support for Eritrean dissidents, Ethiopia began to provide help to Sudan's independent rebel bands. The rebel forces gathered more recruits among the Dinka and Nuer people, the largest groups in the south, and eventually adopted the name of Anya Nya II.

Those original Anya Nya who had been absorbed into the army after the 1972 peace accord were called upon to keep the guerrillas in check and at first fought vigorously on behalf of the national government. But when in 1983 Nimeiri adopted policies of redividing the south and imposing Islamic law, the loyalty of southern soldiers began to waver. Uncertain of their dependability, Nimeiri introduced more northern troops into the south and attempted to transfer the ex-guerrillas to the north. In February 1983, army units in Bor, Pibor Post, and Pochala mutinied. Desertions and mutinies in other southern garrisons soon followed.

In mid-1983 representatives of Anya Nya II and of the mutinous army units meeting in Ethiopia formed the Sudanese People's Liberation Army (SPLA). John Garang, a Dinka Sudanese, was named its commander and also head of the political wing, the Sudanese People's Liberation Movement (SPLM). The southern forces in rebellion failed to achieve full unity under Garang, and, in a struggle for power, the dissident units composed of elements of Anya Nya II were routed by Garang's forces. The defeated remnants, still calling themselves Anya Nya II, began to cooperate with the national army against the SPLA.

Still scarcely an effective fighting force, the SPLA relied at first on ambushes of military vehicles and assaults on police stations and small army posts, mainly in the Nuer and Dinka areas of Aali an Nil Province and northern and eastern Bahr al Ghazal Province. An SPLA attempt to invade eastern Al Istiwai in early 1985 was met with stiff resistance by the army and government militias. But by 1986 the SPLA was strong enough to hold the important town of Rumbek in southern Bahr al Ghazal for several months and was also able to press an attack against Waw, the provincial capital.

During 1987, the SPLA took Pibor Post and Tonga in Aali an Nil, and by the beginning of 1988, it had captured a number of towns on the Ethiopian border and near the White Nile. Advancing northward into Al Awsat Province, it held Kurmuk and Qaysan for a time in late 1987.

The SPLA was opposed by many communities in Al Istiwai Province where the Dinka and Nuer were not popular. The national army was assisted by a militia of the Mundari people, but the SPLA was gradually able to consolidate its position in eastern Al Istiwai. By 1988 the SPLA controlled the countryside around Juba, the major southern city, besieging at least 10,000 government troops, who were virtually cut off from supplies except for what could be delivered by air. During a general offensive in early 1989, the SPLA captured Torit and other strategic towns of eastern Al Istiwai. From May to October 1989, an informal truce prevailed. After the conflict resumed, the areas being contested were principally in western and central Al Istiwai, focusing on the government garrisons at Juba and Yei (see fig. 8). The fighting often consisted of ambushes by the more lightly armed but mobile guerrillas against government convoys moving supplies from the north. With captured weapons and arms imported from Ethiopia and other African countries, the SPLA was increasingly capable of conducting orthodox warfare employing artillery and even armored vehicles, although its forces still avoided conventional engagements against government units.

Anya Nya II began to crumble in 1987, many units and their commanders deserting to the SPLA. But since 1985, the government had been encouraging the formation of militia forces in areas where opposition to the Dinka- and Nuer-dominated SPLA was strongest. These militias were soon playing a major role in the fighting and were partly responsible for the ravages that the civilian population had been forced to endure. The arming of tribal groups inflamed existing intercommunal conflicts and resulted in the deliberate killing of tens of thousands of noncombatants and a vast displacement of civilians.

Millions of villagers were forced from their homes as a consequence of the fighting and the depredations of militias, the SPLA, and Anya Nya II. Devastation of northern Bahr al Ghazal by the roving *murahalin* (Arab militias) forced large numbers of destitute people to evacuate the war zone in 1986 and 1987, many of them making their way to northern Sudan to escape starvation. Raiding decreased in 1988 and diminished further in 1989 as a result of depopulation of the land and a stronger SPLA presence in northern Bahr al Ghazal. Nevertheless, the migrations continued because of the severe food shortage. Almost 1 million southerners were believed to have reached Khartoum in 1989, and hundreds of

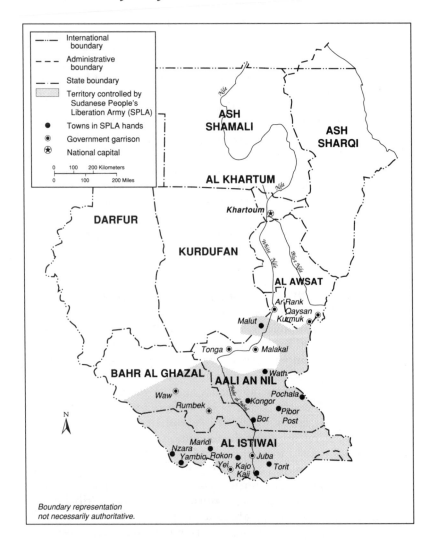

Figure 8. The Civil War in Southern Sudan, Spring 1991

thousands had appeared in other towns and cities. About 350,000 Sudanese refugees were registered in Ethiopia in 1989, at least 100,000 were in Juba, and 28,000 crossed into Uganda to escape the fighting in southern Al Istiwai.

Sudanese People's Armed Forces

The armed forces of the national government, known as the Sudanese People's Armed Forces (SPAF), were believed to have a total personnel strength of about 71,500 in 1991. The army numbered about 65,000 officers and enlisted men. The navy had perhaps 500, and the air force and air defense command each had a complement of about 3,000.

General Bashir, the chairman of the RCC–NS and head of state since the coup of June 1989, was also supreme commander of the armed forces and minister of defense. A colonel at the time of the coup, Bashir subsequently assumed the rank of lieutenant general. The SPAF chief of staff, Lieutenant General Ishaq Ibrahim Umar, was in immediate command of the armed forces. The general staff included deputy chiefs of staff for operations, administration, and logistics, who also held the rank of lieutenant general. The commander of the air force, the commander of air defense command, division commanders, and most military governors held the rank of major general. A retired major general was appointed minister of state for defense affairs to serve as Bashir's deputy in the Ministry of Defence (see fig. 9). The actual responsibilities and influence of senior officers depended greatly on their political status, ethnic affiliation, and other factors in addition to their positions in the chain of command.

Army

The army was basically a light infantry force in 1991, supported by specialized elements. Operational control extended from the headquarters of the general staff in Khartoum to the six regional commands (central, eastern, western, northern, southern, and Khartoum). Each regional command was organized along divisional lines. Thus, the Fifth Division was at Al Ubayyid in Kurdufan (Central Command), the Second Division was at Khashm al Qirbah (Eastern Command), the Sixth Division was assigned to Al Fashir in Darfur (Western Command), the First Division was at Juba (Southern Command), and the Seventh Armored Division was at Ash Shajarah near Khartoum (Khartoum Command). The Airborne Division was based at Khartoum International Airport. The Third Division was located in the north, although no major troop units were assigned to it. Each division had a liaison officer attached to general headquarters in Khartoum to facilitate the division's communication with various command elements.

This organizational structure did not provide an accurate picture of actual troop deployments. All of the divisions were understrength. The Sixth Division in Darfur was a reorganized brigade with only 2,500 personnel. Unit strengths varied widely. Most brigades were composed of 1,000 to 1,500 troops. Each battalion varied in size from 500 to 900 men, and a company might have

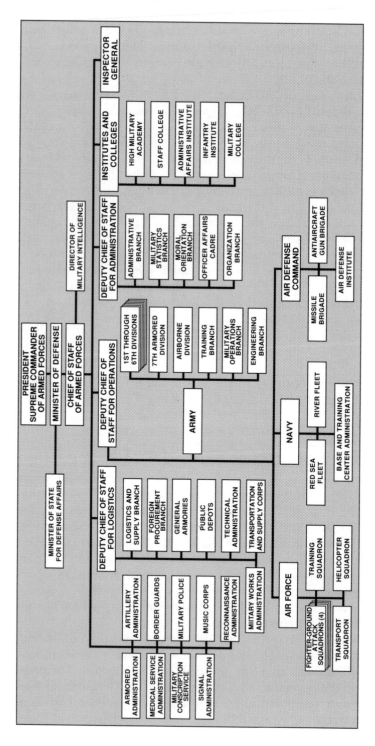

Figure 9. Organization of the Armed Forces, 1991

as few as 150 and as many as 500. In the south, the First Division was supplemented by a number of independent brigades that could be shifted as the requirements of the conflict dictated. According to *The Military Balance, 1991–1992,* the main army units were two armored brigades, one mechanized infantry brigade, seventeen infantry brigades, one paratroop brigade, one air assault brigade, one reconnaissance brigade, three artillery regiments, two anti-aircraft artillery brigades, one engineering regiment, and one special forces battalion.

The army did not have its own general headquarters but functioned under the immediate control of the deputy chief of staff for operations. Headquarters and training facilities were maintained in or near the national capital area for most of its specialized corps. These included the armored, artillery, signal, and medical service administrations; the transportation and supply corps; and the engineering branch. Among other support elements were the military police and the border guards.

The Sudanese army's inventory of armaments and equipment was extremely varied, reflecting its shifting military relations with other nations in a position to supply arms. At different times, Britain, the Soviet Union, China, the United States, Libya, and Egypt have been important sources of weaponry (see Foreign Military Assistance, this ch.). Much of the equipment delivered to Sudan, particularly from the Soviet Union, was obsolescent, and maintenance has been seriously deficient. Because Sudan had been deprived of support from a number of countries and was unable to afford foreign exchange to pay for needed spare parts, much of the existing stock of arms was believed to be inoperable. The army was virtually immobilized at times for lack of fuel and ammunition.

During the 1970s, the bulk of the army's armored strength consisted of T–54 and T–55 medium tanks delivered by the Soviet Union early in the decade. About seventy Chinese Type 62 light tanks were also delivered in 1972. During the early 1980s, this equipment was supplemented by M–41, M–47, and M–60A3 tanks produced in the United States. Most of the Soviet tanks were believed to be unserviceable, and only the M–60A3 tanks were considered to be up-to-date. The Sudanese army also had a mixed collection of armored personnel carriers (APCs), armored reconnaissance vehicles, and other wheeled fighting vehicles. The most modern of these were 36 M–113 APCs and 100 Commando-type armored cars from the United States, and 120 Walid APCs from Egypt (see table 12, Appendix).

Artillery pieces included a number of guns and howitzers mostly of United States and Soviet origin. All of the artillery was towed with the exception of 155mm self-propelled howitzers acquired from France in 1981. The army's modest antitank capability was based on the jeep-mounted Swingfire guided-wire missile, manufactured in Egypt under British license.

Air Force

The air force has been largely dependent on foreign assistance since its inception in 1957, when four primary trainer aircraft were delivered by Egypt. The British provided most aircraft and training (some in Sudan and some in Britain) before 1967. After that time, Soviet and Chinese advisers and technicians assumed a supportive role, and their equipment became the foundation for the Sudanese air force in the 1970s. These aircraft included Soviet-built MiG-17 and MiG-21 fighter-bombers and Chinese-built J-5 (essentially the same as the MiG-17) and J-6 (practically identical to the Soviet MiG-19) fighter-bombers. Seven Northrop F-5Es and two F-5Fs were delivered by the United States beginning in 1981, but plans to acquire additional F-5s never materialized because funds were not available. Libya transferred five Soviet MiG-23s in 1987.

As of 1990, combat aircraft were organized into two fighter-ground attack squadrons (one with the nine F-5s and the other with ten J-5s), and one fighter squadron with J-6s. A second fighter squadron of MiG-21s and MiG-23s was listed, although it was believed that as of 1991 all of the MiGs were nonoperational with the exception of one MiG-23. The combat squadrons were armed with Soviet Atoll and American Sidewinder air-to-air missiles. Sudan had no bomber force. In 1986 it was reported that Libyan Tu-22 bombers had been used against rebel positions in the south. Other bombing attacks were carried out by transport planes (see table 13, Appendix).

The actual state of readiness of the combat arm of the air force was uncertain, but it was believed that much of the equipment was not in serviceable condition owing to a shortage of parts and inadequate maintenance. Pilot proficiency training was limited by fuel shortages that kept aircraft grounded. A small contingent of Chinese technicians assisted with maintenance and pilot training. A few training aircraft were also supplied by the Chinese. The air force had been of little value in providing air cover for ground operations in the south. The SPLA boasted that its shoulder-fired surface-to-air missiles (SAMs) had brought down many aircraft,

claiming that several jet fighters had been destroyed, as well as a number of helicopters and transports.

The transport arm of the air force was of central importance in maintaining supply links with beleaguered southern garrisons. The single transport squadron received six C-130H Hercules transports from the United States in 1978 and 1979. Although one was damaged by an SPLA missile in 1987, the five aircraft still operational in 1991 provided airlift capability essential to government garrisons in the south. The air force also had two Canadian-built DHC-5D Buffalo transports and two Soviet An-12 heavy cargo transports, as well as four smaller Casa C-212 Aviocars from Brazil.

The air force had a number of unarmed helicopters available for ground support operations against the southern rebels, although it was estimated that as many as 50 percent were not in flying condition. The newest helicopter models were French-designed SA-330 Pumas assembled in Romania and Agusta/Bell 212s manufactured in Italy.

The two main bases of the air force were at Khartoum International Airport and Wadi Sayyidna Air Base north of Omdurman. The air force also had facilities at civilian airports, including those at Atbarah, Al Fashir, Juba, Malakal, Al Ubayyid, Port Sudan, and Wad Madani.

Air Defense Command

The air defense command maintained its headquarters at Port Sudan and was commanded by a major general. A secondary command post was at Omdurman. One of its two brigades was equipped with antiaircraft guns and the other was armed with SAMs (see table 14, Appendix). The three battalions of SAMs had been introduced to provide high- and medium-altitude air defense for Port Sudan, Wadi Sayyidna, and Khartoum. In the absence of Soviet technicians who had serviced the missiles and associated radar during the 1970s, the SA–2 systems were considered to be nonoperational.

The second air defense brigade was deployed to provide tactical air defense in the Western Command and Southern Command. In addition to Vulcan 20mm self-propelled guns supplied by the United States, it was equipped with a variety of weapons whose operational status was uncertain. Fire control and acquisition radar for the Vulcan and other systems was provided by the United States, Egypt, and France. The vulnerability of Sudanese air defenses was exposed in 1984 when a Libyan Tu-22 bomber was able to overfly much of the country in daylight, dropping bombs in the vicinity of the national radio station at Omdurman at a time of tension between Nimeiri and Qadhafi.

Navy

The navy, formed in 1962, was the smallest branch of the country's military establishment. Its personnel strength was uncertain but was estimated at 500 officers and men. Headed by a brigadier general from headquarters in Port Sudan, the service was responsible for coastal and riverine defense and for deterring smuggling along the Red Sea coast. A Nile River patrol unit was based at Khartoum.

The navy was formed originally around a nucleus of four armed coastal patrol boats provided by Yugoslavia. Subsequently, river patrol boats, landing craft, and auxiliary vessels were also obtained from Yugoslavia, and a Yugoslav training staff was on hand until 1972. In 1975 the Yugoslav patrol boats were replaced by two seventy-ton patrol craft and four ten-ton patrol craft transferred from Iran and armed with machine guns. In 1989 four new 19.5-ton riverine fast patrol craft armed with 20mm and 7.62mm machine guns were delivered by Yugoslavia for operations on the White Nile. The purpose of the new craft was to protect river convoys of supplies and troops to the south. The operational status of the two large patrol craft was regarded as uncertain in 1990. The general standard

National Security

of efficiency of the navy was considered to be inadequate as a consequence of a lack of maintenance and spare parts. Most auxiliary vessels had drifted into a state of total disrepair (see table 15, Appendix).

The navy was assigned two Casa C–212 aircraft, operated by air force crews, which had a limited capacity to carry out maritime reconnaissance over the Red Sea. The airplanes were unarmed.

Personnel

The Sudanese armed forces have not been the source of any strain on the nation's manpower resources. In 1990 there were an estimated 5,600,000 males between the ages of 15 and 49, of whom 3,400,000 were fit for military service. The number reaching the military age of eighteen annually was approximately 273,000. The United States Arms Control and Disarmament Agency (ACDA) estimated that, as of 1989, only 2.5 persons per 1,000 of population were in the armed forces. Among Sudan's neighbors, corresponding figures were Egypt 8.7 per 1,000, Ethiopia 5.0 per 1,000, and Libya 21.0 per 1,000.

In the first years after independence, recruitment notices reportedly attracted ten applicants for each vacancy. Poorer Sudanese, particularly westerners and southerners, were attracted to the armed forces in great numbers. Not all could be accommodated, so that selection of enlisted men was fairly strict, based on physical condition, education, and character of the applicant. Although the adult literacy rate in Sudan was then estimated to be no more than 20 percent, enlisted personnel were required to have some ability to read and write. The recruit enlisted for three years, and if his record remained good, he could reenlist for further three-year periods until he had served a total of twenty years, at which time he was retired with the highest rank he had attained. Soldiers who received technical training could be obliged to sign an understanding that they would remain on active duty for nine years.

There were reports as of the late 1980s that the morale of the army had suffered because soldiers from other areas of Sudan disliked assignment to the south, where they faced an interminable war in which they had no personal interest and in which a military victory seemed unattainable. Newer recruits, many from the west, felt isolated and threatened in the besieged garrison towns. Large numbers of government troops whose homes were in the south had reportedly deserted to the SPLA, their motivation for continuing the struggle against the insurgency drained by food shortages and lack of needed supplies. Both under the Sadiq al Mahdi government and immediately after the June 1989 coup, the leadership

251

announced that conscription would be introduced to permit an expansion of the government's efforts in the south, but the rate of enlistments had apparently remained high enough so that it had not been necessary to impose a draft. It was possible that, in the light of widespread economic distress, the army was still regarded as a means of escape from poverty.

Pay rates of both officers and noncommissioned officers generally have been equal to or better than those of civilians of comparable status. Base pay was extremely low by United States standards; a colonel received the equivalent of about US$150 a month in 1990. Military personnel were, however, entitled to extensive additional benefits. Housing was provided for senior personnel commensurate with their office and rank, and generous housing allowances were provided for others. Free medical care was provided to all armed forces personnel and their families. Although the country was suffering from a food scarcity, essential goods were available at commissaries at subsidized prices. Items severely rationed in the civilian economy, such as tea, coffee, sugar, and soap, as well as bread produced by military bakeries, could be purchased at low prices and resold at a considerable profit. This trade offered a welcome supplement to the incomes of the junior ranks. Officers outside Khartoum usually held second jobs. Enlisted personnel were likely to set themselves up as small farmers or traders with profits from the resale of rationed goods. Officers of field grade and above could purchase imported automobiles free of duty; higher-ranking officers were assigned full-time cars and drivers. Gasoline was also available at low prices. In addition, senior officers had numerous opportunities to travel abroad at government expense.

Retirement income was virtually as high as the active duty salary, and most of the privileges of military service continued.

The behavior of government soldiers in the south and in the areas where the SPLA was active was the subject of critical reports by Amnesty International, Africa Watch, and other international human rights groups. Amnesty International described numerous incidents in which the army was responsible for the deliberate killing or mistreatment of civilians from ethnic groups suspected of supporting the SPLA. Very few SPLA prisoners of war were held by the government; many cases were documented of captured SPLA fighters, including wounded, being executed without trial.

Few if any prosecutions resulted in connection with the alleged violations. The United States Department of State has confirmed Amnesty International's conclusion that the Sadiq al Mahdi government appeared to condone human rights abuses by the military, citing the cases of generals who received promotions after service in areas where atrocities occurred. There was limited evidence of a shift in attitude by the Bashir government after it assumed power in 1989. Two of the implicated generals were forced to retire from government service, and some soldiers were relieved, although not disciplined, after a series of revenge killings and other violations against civilians in Waw.

Although the Bashir government had announced its intention of purging the armed services of women after it came to power in 1989, large-scale dismissals did not take place. As of 1991, it was reported that about 2,000 women were in uniform, 200 of them officers through the rank of lieutenant colonel. The women were assigned to a range of military duties in the medical service as nurses, dietitians, and physical therapists, and in administration, translation, military intelligence, communications, and public affairs.

Training

The SPAF established numerous institutions for training its military personnel. Foreign military observers believed that the training offered was of a professional caliber within the limitations of available resources. The Military College at Wadi Sayyidna, near Omdurman, had been Sudan's primary source of officer training since it opened in 1948. A two-year program, emphasizing study of political and military science and physical training, led to a commission as a second lieutenant in the SPAF. In the late 1970s and early 1980s, an average of 120 to 150 officers were graduated from the academy each year. In the late 1950s, roughly 60 graduated each year, peaking to more than 500 in early 1972 as a result of mobilization brought on by the first southern rebellion. Students from other Arab and African countries were also trained at the Military College, and in 1982 sixty Ugandans were graduated as part of a Sudanese contribution to rebuilding the Ugandan army after Amin's removal from power. It was announced in 1990 that 600 members of the National Islamic Front's associated militia, the Popular Defence Forces (PDF), had been selected to attend the Military College to help fill the ranks of the officer corps depleted by resignations or dismissals (see Paramilitary Groups, this ch.).

The Military College's course of study, while rigorous, was reportedly weak in scientific and technical instruction. Junior officers were, however, given opportunities to continue their education at the University of Khartoum. Many officers also studied abroad. It was estimated that at least 50 percent had received some schooling in Egypt. Others were sent to the United States, Britain (pilots and mechanics), Germany (helicopter pilots), and Middle Eastern countries. Most high naval officers had been trained at the Yugoslav naval academy; other naval officers were detailed for training in the states of the Persian Gulf. Opportunities for training abroad were greatly curtailed, however, as a result of international disapproval of the policies of the Bashir government.

Since the early 1970s, the Staff College in Omdurman has graduated fifty-five to sixty majors and lieutenant colonels annually with masters' degrees in military science. Officers from other Arab countries—Jordan, Kuwait, and the United Arab Emirates—attended, as well as some Palestinians. Since 1981 the High Military Academy in Omdurman, a war college designed to prepare colonels and brigadier generals for more senior positions, offered a six-month course on national security issues. The academy was commissioned to produce strategic analyses for consideration by the Bashir government.

In addition to the academies, the SPAF also operated a variety of technical schools for junior and noncommissioned officers, including infantry, artillery, communications, ordnance, engineering, and armored schools, all in the vicinity of Khartoum. An air force training center at Wadi Sayyidna Air Base was constructed with Chinese help to train technicians in aircraft maintenance, ground control, and other skills. In the army, recruitment and basic training of enlisted personnel were not centralized but were the responsibility of each division and regional command.

Uniforms, Ranks, and Insignia

Before 1970 the highest officer grade in the rank structure was that of *fariq* (equivalent to a lieutenant general), but new grades were added when Nimeiri became a general and, later, a field marshal. As of 1991, however, there were no officers higher than lieutenant general, and only five, including Bashir, at that rank (see fig. 10).

The army service uniform was dark green, with insignia of rank displayed in gold on shoulder boards. It differed only slightly from police officer uniforms, which were another shade of green with black shoulder boards. A green beret was standard in the army except for airborne units, which wore red berets. The police wore black berets. Officers of field grade and above frequently wore service caps. The air force uniform was blue, although the insignia of rank were the same as for the army. The standard naval uniform was white with blue shoulder boards.

Defense Costs

The civil war in the south had a devastating impact. Not only were military operations in the south a great expense, but the economy was disrupted by the fighting, and perhaps 3 million persons were displaced from or within the war zones. Because of secrecy restrictions dating from the June 1967 Arab-Israeli War, no substantial information on the defense budget was released publicly or provided to the People's Assembly, which, however, had been suspended in 1989. Various official and unofficial estimates of the size of defense expenditures and the burden imposed on the economy by the military establishment have differed widely. A United States government agency estimated the defense budget at US$610 million in 1989, representing 7.2 percent of gross national product (GNP—see Glossary). The Sudanese government has estimated the cost of conducting the war at about US$1 million a day.

Although the specific components of military spending were not available, it was known that the principal category of the defense budget was personnel-related costs. Most large purchases of arms had been financed with credits from the supplying countries. Financial assistance from other countries, principally the Arab oil-producing states of the Persian Gulf, had made these credit purchases possible. Arms imports had fallen since the resumption of the civil war in 1983, as a result of the unwillingness of Western countries to supply weapons that could be used in the hostilities, and of subsequent cutbacks in financial aid from the Middle East. The total amount of funds for military procurements available through loans, grants, direct purchases, and barter arrangements was not made public.

Paramilitary Groups

Various militia groups, supplied and supported by the government, have served as important adjuncts to the armed forces in the fighting in the south. Beginning in 1983, when the first militias were formed under Nimeiri, the government increasingly relied on the militias to oppose the SPLA. The militias were given arms and ammunition but usually operated independently of the army. No reliable data were available on the size of militia forces, although it has been roughly estimated that 20,000 men participated in militia activities at one time or another.

The Anya Nya II group, formed among southern mutineers from the army (after first splitting off from the rebel movement and obtaining weapons and training from the SPAF), was a major factor in the war between 1984 and 1987. Predominantly from the Nuer, the second largest ethnic group in the south, Anya Nya II fought in rural areas of Aali an Nil on behalf of the government. Anya Nya II emerged as a significant factor in the war in that province, disrupting SPLA operations and interfering with the movement

COMMISSIONED OFFICERS

SUDANESE RANK	MULAZIM THANI	MULAZIM AWWAL	NAQIB	RAID	MUQADDAM	AQID	AMID	LIWA	FARIQ	FARIQ AWWAL	MUSHIR[1]
ARMY, AIR FORCE, AND NAVY											
U.S. ARMY AND AIR FORCE RANK TITLES	2D LIEUTENANT	1ST LIEUTENANT	CAPTAIN	MAJOR	LIEUTENANT COLONEL	COLONEL	BRIGADIER GENERAL	MAJOR GENERAL	LIEUTENANT GENERAL	GENERAL	GENERAL OF THE ARMY/AIR FORCE
U.S. NAVY RANK TITLES	ENSIGN	LIEUTENANT JUNIOR GRADE	LIEUTENANT	LIEUTENANT COMMANDER	COMMANDER	CAPTAIN	COMMODORE	REAR ADMIRAL	VICE ADMIRAL	ADMIRAL	FLEET ADMIRAL

ENLISTED PERSONNEL

SUDANESE RANK	MUSTAJIDD	JUNDI	WAKIL ARIF	ARIF	RAQIB	RAQIB AWWAL	MUSAID		MUSAID AWWAL	NO RANK
ARMY, AIR FORCE[2], AND NAVY[2]	NO INSIGNIA	NO INSIGNIA	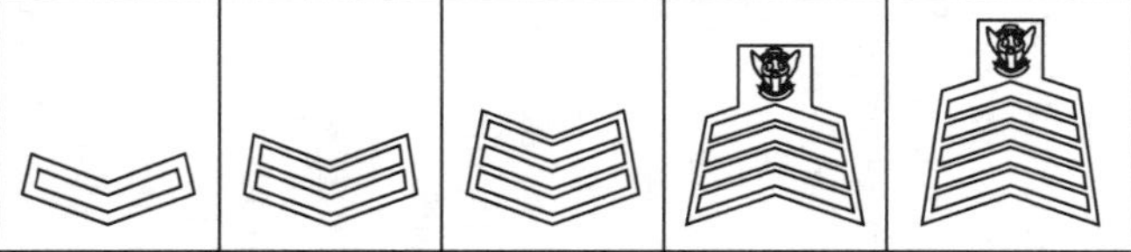						INSIGNIA NOT KNOWN	
U.S. ARMY RANK TITLES	BASIC PRIVATE	PRIVATE	PRIVATE 1ST CLASS	CORPORAL	SERGEANT	STAFF SERGEANT	SERGEANT 1ST CLASS	MASTER SERGEANT	1ST SERGEANT/SERGEANT MAJOR	COMMAND SERGEANT MAJOR/SERGEANT MAJOR OF THE ARMY
U.S. AIR FORCE RANK TITLES	AIRMAN BASIC	AIRMAN	AIRMAN 1ST CLASS	SENIOR AIRMAN/SERGEANT	STAFF SERGEANT	TECHNICAL SERGEANT	MASTER SERGEANT		SENIOR MASTER SERGEANT	CHIEF MASTER SERGEANT/CMSGT OF THE AIR FORCE
U.S. NAVY RANK TITLES	SEAMAN RECRUIT	SEAMAN APPRENTICE	SEAMAN	PETTY OFFICER 3D CLASS	PETTY OFFICER 2D CLASS	PETTY OFFICER 1ST CLASS	CHIEF PETTY OFFICER		SENIOR CHIEF PETTY OFFICER / MASTER CHIEF PETTY OFFICER	FLEET FORCE MASTER CHIEF PETTY OFFICER / MASTER CHIEF PETTY OFFICER OF THE NAVY

Note: [1] Army rank only. [2] Color not known.

Figure 10. Military Ranks and Insignia, 1991

of SPLA recruits to the Ethiopian border area for training. Anya Nya II units were structured with military ranks and were based near various army garrisons. The government assisted the group in establishing a headquarters in Khartoum as part of regime efforts to promote Anya Nya II as an alternative southern political movement in opposition to the SPLA. Eventually, however, SPLA military success led to a decline in morale within Anya Nya II and induced major units, along with their commanders, to defect to the SPLA beginning in late 1987. By mid-1989, only one Anya Nya II faction remained loyal to the government; it continued its close relations with the government after the Bashir coup and retained its political base in Khartoum.

Some of the most devastating raids and acts of banditry against the civilian population were perpetrated by the militias known as *murahalin,* formed among the Rizeiqat, Rufaa al Huj, Misiriyah, and other groups, all members of the cattle-raising Baqqara Arab nomad tribes in Darfur and Kurdufan. These Arab communities traditionally competed for pasture land with the Dinka of northern Bahr al Ghazal and southern Kurdufan. Raiding by the *murahalin* between 1985 and 1988 precipitated a vast displacement of Dinka civilians from Bahr al Ghazal. Although already armed, the *murahalin* were given arms and ammunition and some covert training by the SPAF. Some joint counterinsurgency operations also took place in conjunction with government forces. According to Amnesty International, the raids carried out by the *murahalin* were accompanied by the deliberate killing of tens of thousands of civilians; the abduction of women and children, who were forced into slavery; the looting of cattle and other livestock; and the burning of houses and grain supplies. By late 1988, the growing presence of the SPLA reduced the threat of the *murahalin* against villages and cattle camps. Moreover, the devastation was so severe that little was left to plunder. Dinka refugees moving north to escape famine were still exposed to militia attacks, however.

The Rizeiqat *murahalin* were responsible for one of the worst atrocities of the war when, in retaliation for losses suffered in an engagement with the SPLA, more than 1,000 unarmed Dinka were massacred at the rail junction of Ad Duayn, most of them burned to death. The tactics of the Misiriyah *murahalin* were similar to those of the Rizeiqat; their ambushes of refugees and attacks on villagers in northeastern Bahr al Ghazal were among the most murderous and destructive of any perpetrated by the militia groups. The government armed the Rufaa al Huj as a militia in 1986, after the SPLA appeared in southern Al Awsat Province to recruit followers among the non-Arab peoples of the area. In the early months of 1987, combined operations by the SPAF and the Rufaa al Huj militia against non-Arab populations in retaliation for the SPLA offensive resulted in many atrocities.

The government also armed as militias a number of southern non-Arab tribes opposed to the SPLA. In 1985 members of the Mundari in Al Istiwai, who were hostile to the Dinka because of their ruthless behavior, were recruited to help counter the growing SPLA threat in that province. Most of the Mundari dissociated themselves from the militia, however, as the presence of the SPLA strengthened in Al Istiwai. In Bahr al Ghazal, the government formed a militia concentrated around Waw, and established a training base for it there. Hostile relations with the Dinka in the area spawned considerable violence, culminating in massacres in August and September 1987 among Dinka who had taken refuge in Waw.

In February 1989, Sadiq al Mahdi proposed that the *murahalin* militias be institutionalized into popular defense committees. Although the armed forces apparently went ahead with the formation of some such committees, the proposals were strongly opposed by other political groups in Khartoum, who feared that the *murahalin* would become a factional fighting unit loyal to Sadiq al Mahdi's Umma Party.

In October 1989, the Bashir government promulgated the Popular Defence Act, whose original purpose seemed to be to proceed with the plan of the previous government to give legitimacy to the militias as auxiliaries of the SPAF. The government established a new paramilitary body, the Popular Defence Forces (PDF), to promote the political objectives of the government and the NIF. This action did not, however, result in the disappearance of the existing militias. The PDF was under the command of a brigadier general of the army, and its recruits were armed with AK-47 assault rifles. According to the government, the weapons would be stored in army depots and distributed only when needed.

Both men and women ostensibly were enrolled on a voluntary basis, although some coercion was reported. Military officers and civil servants at all levels were also recruited, particularly those wishing to demonstrate their loyalty to the Islamic activist movement. Membership in the PDF was required for admission to a university and for most significant positions in northern society.

The original period of training was to be for up to three months, and refresher training could last up to fifteen days a year. In June 1990, the government held a graduation for the second PDF training class, numbering 1,287 persons. According to the chief of the PDF, more than ten PDF camps would be located in various parts of the country; each camp would be capable of training three groups of 5,000 a year. The government's target was a PDF personnel of 150,000, but independent observers doubted that this goal could be achieved with available resources or that the PDF would assume more than a marginal role in maintaining internal security.

Foreign Military Assistance

Sudan lacked a reliable source of military matériel as of mid-1991, even though the country faced a severe shortage of equipment and of support items. Most of its weaponry of Soviet design was more than twenty years old and could be kept operational only with the limited help provided by Libya and China. As a result, most of the Soviet tanks, artillery, missiles, and aircraft were not in serviceable condition. Western suppliers were unwilling to provide arms for use against the southern insurgents. Military credits previously available from Saudi Arabia and the countries of the Persian Gulf had been cut off as a reaction to Sudan's continued support of Iraq, following Iraq's 1990 invasion of Kuwait. Egypt, normally an important source of both equipment and training, had severely curtailed its cooperation with the Bashir government. Some assistance, particularly in the form of munitions, had been provided by Iraq, but this help had ended in August 1990. Although Libya and China continued to provide some military items, the supply from China was limited by the strict financial terms imposed by the Beijing authorities.

Except for a production line for small caliber ammunition, Sudan has never had an arms industry. Consequently, foreign sources for weapons, equipment, ammunition, and technical training have been indispensable. After independence British advisers helped train the Sudanese army and air force, and British equipment predominated in the ground forces. Relations between the government in Khartoum and London were periodically strained, however, and after the June 1967 Arab-Israeli War, diplomatic and military ties were severed. Military links with the United States and the Federal Republic of Germany (West Germany) were also broken for a time.

The breach with the Western nations was followed by a period of close military cooperation with the Soviet Union between 1968 and 1971. Sudan benefited from the Soviet Union's first significant military assistance program in a sub-Saharan Africa country. By 1970 it was estimated that there were 2,000 Soviet and East European technical advisers in the country. About 350 Sudanese received training in the Soviet Union and other communist countries. Soviet assistance corresponded with a dramatic growth in the

Sudanese armed forces from 18,000 in 1966 to nearly 50,000 by 1972. The bulk of the equipment used by the ground and air forces throughout the 1970s and until the early 1980s was of Soviet origin, including tanks, artillery, and MiG combat aircraft.

Vulnerabilities resulting from overreliance on one arms supplier became obvious when relations with the Soviet Union cooled considerably following the coup attempt against Nimeiri in 1971. Soviet and East European military advisers were expelled from Sudan for a year. After relations were repaired, previously arranged deliveries of tanks were completed and a new purchase of combat aircraft was negotiated. Military agreements with the Soviet Union remained in force until 1977, but Sudan began to pursue a policy of diversifying its arms sources. When Moscow promised extensive military aid to the revolutionary regime in neighboring Ethiopia, the Sudanese government expelled all ninety Soviet military advisers and ordered the military section of the Soviet embassy in Khartoum closed.

After its relations with the Soviet Union chilled again, Sudan turned to China, which supplied the SPAF initially with light weapons and later delivered fighter aircraft and light tanks. As of the mid-1980s, about fifty Chinese advisers provided maintenance support for tanks and aircraft, including Soviet equipment previously supplied, and trained Sudanese pilots and aircraft mechanics.

Military cooperation with Britain resumed in 1973, although it was confined mainly to training and instruction at the Military College and the armored, infantry, and signals schools. Yugoslavia assisted in founding the Sudanese navy; for more than a decade it provided all of the vessels and the bulk of officer and technical training. The Yugoslav naval support program was not renewed in 1972, however, because of frustrations the Yugoslavs had encountered in accomplishing their mission. In 1989 four more river craft were acquired from Yugoslavia, and subsequently a Yugoslav delegation was reported to have visited Khartoum to discuss a revival of training assistance.

The purchase of weapons from Western countries was financed largely by oil-rich Arab states that were pleased to see Soviet influence in Sudan ended. Arab financial assistance, especially from Saudi Arabia, was instrumental in the purchase in 1977 of six C-130 Hercules transport aircraft from the United States, estimated to cost US$74 million, and two Buffalo transports from Canada. Saudi assistance was also credited for Sudan's acquisition of ten light helicopters and as many as 4,000 vehicles from West Germany. In addition, Saudi Arabia in 1980 supplied the SPAF with seventy used American-built M–41 and M–47 tanks from its reserve inventory.

Until 1985 Sudan maintained its closest military ties with Egypt. Under a twenty-five-year defense agreement signed in 1976, the two countries established a joint defense council, a joint general staff organization, and a permanent military committee to implement decisions of the joint council and the staff organization. Since 1986 Egypt has provided Egyptian-manufactured Swingfire anti-tank missiles, Walid armored personnel carriers, ammunition, and other equipment to Sudan. Although Sadiq al Mahdi declared his intention to abrogate the defense pact in order to meet a key SPLA condition for peace, Bashir reaffirmed the pact after his takeover in 1989. The internal repressions of the new government and Sudan's refusal to condemn the Iraqi invasion of Kuwait in 1990, however, produced discord between the two nations, and Egypt rejected appeals from Sudanese leaders for additional military aid.

Until 1976 United States military aid to Sudan was negligible, consisting primarily of training in the United States for a small number of Sudanese officers. Soon after officially agreeing in November 1976 to provide Sudan with selected arms, the United States sold Sudan transport aircraft financed by Saudi Arabia, followed several years later by F–5 combat airplanes. Believing that Sudan was threatened by neighboring Ethiopian and Libyan forces heavily armed by the Soviet Union, Washington adopted a growing role in Sudan's security. Between fiscal year (FY—see Glossary) 1979 and FY 1982, military sales credits rose from US$5 million to US$100 million. Subsequent aid was extended on a grant basis. In addition to aircraft, United States aid consisted of APCs, M–60 tanks, artillery, and Commando armored cars. United States grant aid reached a peak of US$101 million in FY 1982; at the time, this amount constituted two-thirds of all United States military assistance to sub-Saharan Africa. Between the inception of the program in 1976 and its virtual termination in 1986, military grants and sales credits to Sudan totaled US$154 million and US$161 million, respectively. Sudan granted the United States naval port facilities at Port Sudan and agreed to some airport prepositioning rights for military equipment for contingent use by the United States Central Command. Sudanese and United States forces participated in joint maneuvers designated Operation Bright Star in 1981 and 1983.

When civil war again erupted in the south in 1983, military grants and credits from the United States dropped abruptly, and in 1985 Sudan terminated Operation Bright Star. After FY 1987, no assistance was extended with the exception of less than US$1 million annually for advanced training for Sudanese officers and training in the maintenance of previously supplied equipment. Military aid was formally suspended in 1989 under a provision of the United States Foreign Assistance Act prohibiting assistance to countries in arrears on interest payments on previous loans. In March 1990, the United States also invoked a provision of the act barring assistance to regimes overthrowing a democratic government.

According to a survey by ACDA of sources of arms imported by Sudan, Sudan obtained about US$350 million in military arms and equipment between 1983 and 1988. The United States was the largest supplier, accounting for US$120 million. China and France each provided US$30 million and Britain US$10 million. About US$160 million came from unidentified sources, probably largely from Egypt and Libya, and as purchases from other Western suppliers financed by Arab countries.

Sudanese People's Liberation Army

The SPLA was formed in 1983 when Lieutenant Colonel John Garang of the SPAF was sent to quell a mutiny in Bor of 500 southern troops who were resisting orders to be rotated to the north. Instead of ending the mutiny, Garang encouraged mutinies in other garrisons and set himself at the head of the rebellion against the Khartoum government. Garang, a Dinka born into a Christian family, had studied at Grinnell College, Iowa, and later returned to the United States to take a company commanders' course at Fort Benning, Georgia, and again to earn advanced economics degrees at Iowa State University.

By 1986 the SPLA was estimated to have 12,500 adherents organized into twelve battalions and equipped with small arms and a few mortars. Recruits were trained across the border in Ethiopia, probably with the help of Ethiopian army officers. By 1989 the SPLA's strength had reached 20,000 to 30,000; by 1991 it was estimated at 50,000 to 60,000. Many members of the SPLA continued their civilian occupations, serving in individual campaigns when called upon. At least forty battalions had been formed, bearing such names as Tiger, Crocodile, Fire, Nile, Kalishnikov, Bee, Eagle, and Hippo.

In addition to Garang, who as commander in chief adopted the rank of colonel, other senior officers included a field commander, a chief of staff, and a chief of staff for administration and logistics. Most of these officers, as well as zonal commanders, held the rank of lieutenant colonel; battalion commanders were majors or captains. Promotion was based on seniority and the number of battles fought. Consequently, most of the senior leadership and field

SPLA soldier guarding
a cattle vaccination program
near Kapoeta, June 1988
Courtesy Roger Winter

SPLA-built bridge on road between
Kapoeta and Torit in
eastern Al Istiwai, 1990
Courtesy Roger Winter

commanders were members of the Dinka group. Others were from the Nuer and Shilluk groups. Members of some other groups from Al Istiwai were given commands to help win over members of their groups.

The SPLA claimed that its arms came from captured government stocks or were brought by troops deserting from the SPAF. It admitted to having received a considerable amount of support and matériel from Libya before 1985 because of Libya's hostility toward Nimeiri and its desire to see him overthrown. It denied receiving arms from Ethiopia, although it operated from bases in Ethiopia, and outside observers believed that that country furnished the bulk of the SPLA's weaponry. The government's claims that the SPLA had Israeli advisers and received equipment from Israel were generally discounted. Its small arms included Soviet, United States, and German assault rifles. According to *The Military Balance, 1991-1992*, the SPLA also had 60mm mortars, 14.5mm antiaircraft guns, and Soviet SA-7 shoulder-fired SAMs. Other sources claimed that the SPLA had captured or otherwise acquired howitzers, heavier mortars, BM-21 truck-mounted rocket launchers, jeep-mounted 106mm antitank recoilless rifles, and about twenty armored vehicles. It had a supply of land mines that were widely used.

Amnesty International and Africa Watch have cited deliberate killings by the SPLA of SPAF and militia prisoners captured in combat, and of civilians believed to be informers or opposed to the insurgency movement. Although about 300 government troops were being held by the SPLA as of mid-1989, there were reports that after the capture of Bor, surrendering soldiers, possibly numbering in the hundreds, were shot. Indiscriminate SPLA rocket and mortar attacks on government-held towns resulted in many civilian casualties.

State of Internal Security

A population divided among nearly 600 ethnic groups and tribal units and a conspicuous split between a largely Arab population in the north and black, non-Muslim southerners meant that Sudan's government had a high potential for instability. Political movements based on these regional, tribal, religious, and socioeconomic divisions have been responsible for numerous breakdowns of authority. Nimeiri's autonomy solution for the south in 1972 ended the first civil war. His decision in 1981 to abolish the Southern Regional Assembly and the later redivision of the south into three regions, however, revived southern opposition and helped to reignite the southern insurgency. Dissatisfaction with Nimeiri's rule also grew in the north as economic distress became more acute. The 1985 military coup that ousted Nimeiri was preceded by massive demonstrations in Khartoum triggered by price increases of food staples. The traditional political parties that dominated civilian politics reemerged in 1986 after a year of transitional military rule. Most parties continued to reflect sectarian loyalties rather than to promote national interests. Unable to function effectively through shifting political coalitions and unable to end the war in the south, civilian authority was again overturned, to be replaced by the authoritarian rule of Bashir on June 30, 1989.

The new military government immediately invoked emergency legislation banning strikes and other work stoppages as well as unauthorized political meetings. Political parties and trade unions were dissolved and their property frozen or seized. Leading members of the main political parties were arrested, as were senior members of the Sudan Bar Association and other prominent figures thought to be unfriendly to the new regime. More than 100 trade unionists were detained, while others were dismissed from the civil service, the army, and the police.

Although some political prisoners had been released by early 1990, evidence of continued opposition to the military government brought harsh repressive measures. In December 1989, a prominent physician was sentenced to death (later commuted to imprisonment) for organizing a doctors' strike. Another doctor was sentenced to fifteen years' imprisonment. In March 1990, the government announced that it had crushed a coup conspiracy, arresting prominent members of the Umma Party and military officers. Less than a month later, the regime alleged that it had discovered another coup plot among the military and executed twenty-eight high-ranking officers whom it claimed were implicated.

Although the military government was widely unpopular, its ruthless suppression of any manifestation of discontent appeared to have frightened the internal opposition into silence. A number of exiled politicians active in the previous Sadiq al Mahdi government announced the formation of an opposition organization, the National Democratic Alliance, in early 1990. The SPLA radio station in Ethiopia allotted broadcasting time to the alliance, but the group, brought together by political expediency, had difficulty organizing effective opposition to the Bashir regime. Former armed forces chief of staff, Lieutenant General Fathi Ahmad Ali, was among the exiled dissidents and became head of the National Democratic Alliance. Military purges, however, had left the majority of active officers silent for fear of dismissal and loss of their commands. Infiltration of informers into the SPAF made any form of dissident activity risky. Curfews were imposed, and detachments of troops guarding bridges and other key points minimized the possibility of military action to topple the regime. At the Khartoum International Airport, the Airborne Division, which was considered loyal to the government, was available at short notice to help repel a coup attempt.

The presence of as many as 1 million refugees from southern Sudan in the vicinity of Khartoum was potentially destabilizing, but the refugees were weak and too divided into ethnic and regional groups to be a political threat. Student groups had in the past been involved in demonstrations that contributed to the downfall of unpopular governments, but the loyalty of the majority of students was uncertain.

The small communist movement, with considerable support among educated Sudanese and involvement in student and union organizations, was among the opposition elements to the Bashir government. The Sudanese Communist Party (SCP) played an important role in the first years of Nimeiri's rule but was harshly suppressed and forced underground after participation in the unsuccessful coup against Nimeiri in 1971. Although Nimeiri's campaign of reconciliation with his political opponents in 1977 enabled some prominent SCP members to resurface, communists arrested for organizing strikes and demonstrations comprised the largest single group of political prisoners. The SCP's role in the urban demonstrations of 1985 contributed to Nimeiri's overthrow. The SCP became active in parliamentary politics in 1986 but was among the political groups banned by the Bashir regime. It joined with other parties in underground opposition to the military government. Several communists were rounded up and detained without charge after the 1989 coup, allegedly for instigating a protest against the government among students at the University of Khartoum.

Internal Security Agencies

Apart from in the south, domestic order in Sudan was a shared responsibility of the military, the national police force, and security organs of the Ministry of Interior. Martial law was in effect in government-controlled areas of the south and in some northern areas as well.

Sudan Police Force

The Sudan Police Force (SPF) had its beginnings in 1898 when a British army captain was placed in the central administration for police duties, and thirty British army officers directly responsible to him were detailed to organize provincial police establishments. The arrangement proved overly centralized, however, and complete decentralization of police control was introduced in 1901. As great differences arose in the standards and performance of the police in the various provinces, a modified form of administrative control by the central authorities was decreed in 1908, with the provincial governors retaining operational control of the forces. The SPF was officially established by the British in 1908 and was absorbed by the Sudanese government on independence in 1956.

It was technically and economically impractical for the police to cover the entire area of Sudan; therefore, a system of communal security was retained for more than seventy years. The central government gave tribal leaders authority to keep order among their people. They were allowed to hire a limited number of "retainers" to assist them in law enforcement duties. This system was finally abolished by the Nimeiri government in the early 1970s.

Under Nimeiri, command and administration of the SPF was modified several times. The police were responsible to the minister of interior until 1979, when the post of minister of interior was abolished and various ministers were made responsible for different areas of police work. This arrangement proved unwieldy, however, and the Police Act of 1979 instituted a unified command in which the head of the force reported directly to the president. After Nimeiri's fall, the cabinet position of minister of interior was restored, and the director general of police was made responsible to him.

Central police headquarters in Khartoum was organized into divisions, each commanded by a police major general. The divisions were responsible for criminal investigations, administration, training, public affairs, passport control, immigration, and security affairs. The main operational elements were the traffic police and the riot police. The 1979 legislation brought specialized police units, such as that of the Sudan Railways, under the authority of the SPF headquarters. The Khartoum headquarters maintained liaison and cooperation with the International Criminal Police Organization (Interpol) and with agencies involved in combating international drug traffic.

The government's new system of administration delegated many powers to the regional level, but law enforcement outside major urban areas remained provincially oriented. Thus, the national police establishment was subdivided into provincial commands, which were organized according to the same divisions found in the national headquarters. Local police directors were responsible to provincial police commissioners, who in turn were responsible to the SPF director general in Khartoum. Each provincial command had its own budget.

The SPF expanded from roughly 7,500 officers and men at independence in 1956 to approximately 18,000 in 1970 and 30,000 by the mid-1980s. Except for the south where internal security in government-held areas was the responsibility of military and security organs, the police establishment was distributed roughly in proportion to population density but was reinforced in areas where there was a likelihood of trouble. In some places, the police were too thinly scattered to provide any real security. It was reported that there were no police stations along the Nile from the town of Wadi Halfa on the Egyptian border south to Dunqulah, a distance of about 300 kilometers. Elsewhere in the north, police posts could be staffed by as few as two police with insufficient transport or communications equipment to patrol their district. Efforts to control smuggling were apparently the responsibility of the armed forces and the security authorities.

Police officer cadets usually received two years of training at the Sudan Police College near Khartoum. The institution was equipped to provide theoretical and practical instruction; it also served as a training school for military personnel who required police skills in their assignments. In addition to recruit training, the college offered instruction in aspects of criminal law, general police duties, fingerprinting, clerical work, photography, and the use of small arms. Enlisted recruits usually underwent four months of training at provincial headquarters. Although not numerous, women served in the SPF in limited capacities. They were generally assigned to administrative sections, to juvenile delinquency matters, or to criminal cases in which female Sudanese were witnesses or defendants. The Bashir government announced plans to remove women from the police, but, according to one report, a number of women were actually promoted to higher positions because of the mass firing of senior male police officers.

Provincial police had traditionally enjoyed good relations with the community, but during the Nimeiri regime many people regarded them more as the object of fear than as a source of security. The police were said to have acted appropriately—firmly but with restraint—during civil demonstrations in the first half of the 1980s. Since the resumption of civil war in 1983, serious abuses of human rights have not generally been attributed to the police, as they have been to the armed forces, government militias, and security organizations. Police treatment of persons under arrest could be harsh. Police patrols in Khartoum have harassed or beaten people occasionally without apparent motive. Public order campaigns in Khartoum, often targeting southern refugees, could result in roundups of thousands charged with illegal street vending or

Police post near Yei, western Al Istiwai State
Police force in Maridi
Courtesy Robert O. Collins

269

loitering. In urban areas police reportedly often acted against refugees, stealing from them and beating them for minor infractions. Refugees seldom had recourse to the legal system when attacked by the police. The police were known to have inflicted floggings summarily for drinking alcohol or for curfew violations. Brutality increased after the 1989 coup, but roundups and floggings declined somewhat after officials of the Bashir government promised closer supervision of the police.

Security Organizations

The Sudanese internal security and intelligence apparatus evolved into a feared and hated institution after Nimeiri came to power in 1969. During the period of Revolutionary Command Council rule (1969–71), the military intelligence organization was expanded to investigate domestic opposition groups. After the council was abolished, the organization's responsibilities focused on evaluating and countering threats to the regime from the military. It also provided a 400-man Presidential Guard.

The Office of State Security was established by decree in 1971 within the Ministry of Interior. The new agency was charged with evaluating information gathered by the police and military intelligence; it was also responsible for prison administration and passport control. The sensitive central security file and certain other intelligence functions were, however, maintained under the president's control. In 1978 the presidential and Ministry of Interior groups were merged to form the State Security Organisation (SSO). Under the direction of Minister of State Security Umar Muhammad at Tayyib, a retired army major general and close confidant of the president, the SSO became a prominent feature of the Nimeiri regime, employing about 45,000 persons and rivaling the armed forces in size. This apparatus was dismantled in 1985.

According to the United States Department of State's *Country Reports on Human Rights Practices for 1990*, government surveillance, which was previously rare, became intense after the 1989 coup. Efforts were made to prevent contact between Sudanese and foreigners. Civilians, especially suspected dissidents, were harassed, church services were monitored, and activities of journalists were closely supervised. Neighborhood "popular committees" used their control over the rationing system to monitor households.

The Bashir government created a new security body. Generally referred to as "Islamic Security" or "Security of the Revolution," it was under the direct control of a member of the RCC–NS. Its purpose was to protect the Bashir regime against internal plots and to act as a watchdog over other security forces and the military.

It quickly became notorious for indiscriminate arrests of suspected opponents of the regime and for torturing them in its own safe houses before turning them over to prison authorities for further detention. A similar organization, Youth for Reconstruction, mobilized younger Islamic activists.

Criminal Justice System

The Sudanese criminal code embodied elements of British law, the penal code of British colonial India, and the Egyptian civil code (see The Legal System, ch. 4). In 1977 Nimeiri formed a committee, dominated by the Muslim Brotherhood, to revise the legal code according to the sharia (Islamic law). In September 1983, the Nimeiri government introduced a version of the sharia prescribing harsh corporal punishments for such crimes as murder, theft, drinking alcohol, prostitution, and adultery. These "September Laws," sometimes known as *hudud* (sing., *hadd,* penalty prescribed by Islamic law) provided for execution, flogging, amputation, and stoning as modes of punishment for both Muslims and non-Muslims. During the final twenty months of Nimeiri's rule, at least ninety persons convicted of theft had their hands amputated. The military and civil governments succeeding Nimeiri between 1985 and 1989 suspended the September Laws. Progress on a new Islamic penal code to replace the September Laws was delayed by the legislature pending a constitutional assembly that would include the SPLA. Although flogging, consisting normally of forty lashes, was limited to offenses involving sex or alcohol, it was often inflicted summarily. In 1989 the RCC–NS extended flogging as a punishment for a much wider range of offenses. Extreme *hudud* sentences such as amputations were not handed down, however, and many *hudud* sentences imposed under the Sadiq al Mahdi government were converted to jail terms and fines.

In the regular criminal court system, extensive guarantees of due process were prescribed for accused persons. These courts consisted of a panel of three judges. The judicial process involved a police or magistrate's investigation and an arrest warrant preceding the arrest. Trials were held in public except when the accused requested a closed trial. The accused had to be brought before a court within forty-eight hours of arrest, informed of the charges, and provided with access to an attorney of the accused's choice. There were legal aid services for the poor, but, because resources were limited, legal aid was apportioned to those facing serious charges and those most in need. Bail was permitted except in some capital cases. Defendants had the right to speak, to present evidence on their own behalf, and to appeal judgments through a series of courts from the magistrate level to the High Court of Appeal.

Under the state of emergency imposed by the Sadiq al Mahdi regime in 1987, the government had wide powers in areas declared to be emergency zones to arrest and preventively detain for an indefinite period anyone suspected of contravening emergency regulations. Military personnel could not be arrested by civilian authorities, nor was there provision for judicial review of actions by the armed forces. The Sadiq al Mahdi government declared emergency zones in the southern and western areas of the country and used the detention powers on people suspected of sympathy with the rebellion.

On seizing power in 1989, the RCC–NS declared a state of emergency for the whole of Sudan and granted itself broad powers. The government initially detained more than 300 people without warrants, including many prominent political and academic figures, journalists, alleged leftists, and trade unionists. About sixty judges who petitioned against the government's action were also detained. Many of the original detainees were released within several months, but they were replaced by others. There were an estimated 300 to 500 detainees at the close of 1990; some reports claimed as many as 1,000 detainees.

After the 1989 coup, the regular civilian courts continued to handle ordinary criminal offenses, including theft and some capital crimes, although the court system was seriously backlogged and the judiciary was less independent of the executive than previously. After experimenting with various forms of special courts, the RCC–NS established special security courts in November 1989. These courts were formed by the military governors of the regions and the commissioner of the national capital. The courts had three-member panels of both military and civilian judges. They tried persons accused of violating constitutional decrees, emergency regulations, and some portions of the criminal code, notably drug crimes and currency violations. The new security courts did not extend normal protections to the accused. Attorneys were permitted to sit with defendants but were not permitted to address the courts. Sentences imposed by the courts were to be carried out immediately, with the exception that death penalties were to be reviewed by the chief justice and the head of state. The special security courts gained a reputation for harsh sentences. Two defendants convicted of illegal possession of foreign currency and another convicted of drug smuggling were executed and others were sentenced to death for similar crimes, although the sentences were not carried out.

Trial in Tambura, western Al Istiwai State, with stolen goods (honey in cans) and judges in foreground, accused on the right
Courtesy Robert O. Collins

In areas of the south affected by the war, normal judicial procedures could not be applied and civil authorities were made redundant by the application of the state of emergency. Units of the armed forces and militias ruled by force of arms, and in many cases the accused were summarily tried and punished, especially for offenses against public order. In war-torn southern Kurdufan the government authorized a system of justice administered by village elders, and a similar system was reportedly in effect in areas controlled by the SPLA.

Incidence of Crime

The widespread instability and clashes between ethnic groups arising from the civil war were accompanied by breakdowns of law and order in many parts of the country. Killings, rapes, and thefts of personal possessions, food, and livestock were committed by various militia groups and frequently by the SPLA and the government armed forces as well. Large areas of Sudan became depopulated as a result of the fighting and migrations in search of safety. The availability of weapons contributed to the prevalence of banditry, especially along the Chad, Zaire, and Uganda borders. In the western province of Darfur, the police wielded little authority, and lawlessness prevailed. Smuggling was also common, particularly along the Ethiopian border.

The collapse of security in many areas was not fully reflected in available statistics on crime, although some indications of the pattern of criminality did emerge. According to the most recent data reported by Sudan to Interpol covering the year 1986, more than 135,000 criminal offenses were recorded, reflecting a rate of 650 crimes per 100,000 of population. More than 1,000 homicides occurred, and 3,300 sex offenses were registered, including 600 rapes. There were 7,300 serious assaults. The more than 100,000 thefts of various kinds constituted by far the most common category of crime. They included armed robbery (33,000 cases), breaking and entering (22,500), theft under aggravated circumstances (1,900), and automobile theft (1,500). There were 15,000 cases of fraud and 3,600 drug infractions.

Sudan was not a major international narcotics marketplace. Most narcotics consumed in Sudan consisted of marijuana grown in the eastern part of the country. Penalties for narcotics use were similar to those for alcohol and could include flogging. In nearly all categories except narcotics violations, Sudan reported more offenses than Egypt, a country with more than twice the population. This discrepancy may be accounted for by more accurate police records on the extent of criminal activity or by different definitions of the offenses reported to Interpol.

Sudanese authorities claimed to have solved more than 70 percent of most forms of robbery and theft and 53 percent of all crimes reported. Only 25 percent of homicides, 40 percent of general sex offenses, and 32 percent of rape cases were recorded as solved.

Prison System

General supervision of the Sudan Prison Service was carried out by the director general of prisons, who was responsible for the country's central prisons and reformatories. Provincial authorities managed detention centers and jails in their administrative jurisdictions. The central prisons were Kober in Khartoum North, Shalla in Al Fashir, Darfur State, and Port Sudan on the Red Sea. It was reported that there were about 140 local prisons and detention centers in the early 1990s.

Prison conditions were generally poor. Treatment of prisoners varied widely, however. Some were restricted by shackles, whereas others were allowed to return home at night. There were persistent reports of beatings and other forms of mistreatment, including torture, of detainees and other political prisoners in the central penal institutions, although these were apparently inflicted by security officials and not regular prison guards. After reports appeared that detainees of the Bashir government were being subjected to torture, Amnesty International was allowed to visit a select group of prisoners at Kober, where prison conditions were reputed to be the best in Sudan. Facilities at the large prison at Port Sudan were spartan. Although treatment was not brutal, extreme heat contributed to the harsh living conditions. The most primitive conditions were said to be at Shalla. In general, political prisoners welcomed transfer to prison to escape physical abuse from security personnel.

Although conditions at prison hospitals were described as fair, a number of political prisoners complained of being denied treatment for medical problems. Trade unionists arrested after the 1989 coup and held at Kober Prison submitted a protest alleging the denial of family visits and of adequate medical treatment, while challenging the legal grounds for their arrests. In retaliation, the government transferred many of them to Shalla Prison, 600 kilometers from Khartoum. The Sudanese regime's violations of the civil rights of its citizens in 1991 continued to be a source of concern not only to members of the opposition in Sudan but also to the international community in general.

* * *

Details on military units and equipment are available from *The Military Balance* published annually by the International Institute for Strategic Studies in London. Further information on the sources of Sudan's arms can be found in *Forecast International/DMS Market Intelligence Report: Middle East and Africa*. Reports by two international human rights organizations give accounts of the conflict in the south, the role of various militia groups, and the abuses committed by all of the fighting units, especially against the civilian population. These are Amnesty International's *Sudan: Human Rights Violations in the Context of Civil War*, published in 1989, and Africa Watch's *Denying "The Honor of Living": Sudan, A Human Rights Disaster*, published in 1990.

The Southern Sudan by Douglas H. Johnson provides a concise account of the fighting in the south through 1988. The section on Sudan by Gwynne Dyer in *World Armies* includes an abbreviated history of the Sudanese armed forces until 1983. Articles by John O. Voll in *Current History* in 1986 and 1990 discuss the record of military regimes in Sudan as alternatives to civilian government.

United States-Sudanese military relations are recounted in Jeffrey A. Lefebvre's "Globalism and Regionalism: U.S. Arms

Transfers to Sudan" in *Armed Forces and Society*. Information on the criminal courts system and the record of the Bashir government with respect to judicial processes and human rights can be found in the annual *Country Reports on Human Rights Practices* published by the United States Department of State. (For further information and complete citations, see Bibliography.)

Appendix

Appendix

Table 1. *Metric Conversion Coefficients and Factors*

When you know	Multiply by	To find
Millimeters	0.04	inches
Centimeters	0.39	inches
Meters	3.3	feet
Kilometers	0.62	miles
Hectares (10,000 m²)	2.47	acres
Square kilometers	0.39	square miles
Cubic meters	35.3	cubic feet
Liters	0.26	gallons
Kilograms	2.2	pounds
Metric tons	0.98	long tons
....	1.1	short tons
....	2,204	pounds
Degrees Celsius	9	degrees Fahrenheit
(Centigrade)	divide by 5 and add 32	

Table 2. *Population Distribution and Density by Province, 1983*

Province	Population	Density [1]
Aali an Nil	1,471,540	6.8
Al Awsat	4,026,668	28.3
Al Istiwai	1,406,181	5.3
Al Khartum	1,802,299	85.5
Ash Shamali	1,067,098	2.2
Ash Sharqi	2,208,199	6.5
Bahr al Ghazal	2,265,510	10.6
Darfur	3,093,660	6.8
Kurdufan	3,074,797	8.1
SUDAN	20,415,952 [2]	8.6

[1] Inhabitants per square kilometer.
[2] Adjusted total population in 1983 was 21,593,000.

Source: Based on information from Sudan, Ministry of Finance and Economic Planning, Department of Statistics, *1983 Preliminary Census Results,* Khartoum, 1984, passim; and Sudan, Ministry of Finance and Economic Planning, Department of Statistics, Khartoum, unpublished data.

Table 3. Population of Major Towns, Census Years 1973 and 1983

Town	1973	1983
Al Qadarif	66,465	119,002
Al Ubayyid	90,073	139,446
Kassala	99,652	142,909
Khartoum	333,906	476,218
Khartoum North	150,989	341,155
Omdurman	n.a.	526,284
Port Sudan	132,632	212,741
Wad Madani	106,715	141,065

n.a.—not available.

Source: Based on information from Sudan, Ministry of Finance and Economic Planning, Department of Statistics, *1983 Preliminary Census Results,* Khartoum, 1984, passim.

Table 4. Enrollment, Teachers, and Institutions by Level of Education, 1985–86

Level	Enrollment	Teachers	Institutions
Preprimary [1]	235,943	5,569	4,003
Primary [2]	1,766,738	50,389	7,009
Secondary			
General [2]	542,788	21,970	n.a.
Teacher training [1]	3,444	479	n.a.
Vocational [2]	23,150	1,280	n.a.
Total secondary	569,382	23,729	n.a.
Universities and higher			
institutes [1]	37,367	2,165	n.a.

n.a.—not available.
[1] 1985 figures.
[2] 1986 figures.

Source: Based on information from "Sudan—Statistical Survey," *The Middle East and North Africa, 1991,* London, 1990, 801.

Table 5. Government Budget, 1983–84, 1984–85, and 1985–86 [1]
(in millions of Sudanese pounds) [2]

	1983–84	1984–85	1985–86
Revenues			
Direct taxes	404.5	300.5	351.6
Indirect taxes	839.9	984.6	1,222.6
Other	224.6	200,4	216.2
Total revenues	1,469.0	1,485.5	1,790.4
Expenditures			
Ordinary budget			
Defense and security	260.6	462.0	473.1
Economic services	74.3	196.0	208.0
Social services	69.9	160.8	182.0
Loan repayments	212.0	118.0	465.4
Provincial governments	270.3	360.5	557.0
Other	755.6	1,214.9	1,492.8
Total ordinary budget	1,642.7	2,512.2	3,378.3
Development budget			
Agricultural sector	135.4	139.1	96.3
Industrial sector	119.2	110.1	74.6
Transportation and communications	67.6	52.1	57.9
Services sector	59.4	54.3	32.5
Other	101.4	97.4	107.8
Total development budget	483.0	453.0	369.1
Total expenditures	2,125.7	2,965.2	3,747.4

[1] Years ending June 30.
[2] For value of the Sudanese pound—see Glossary.

Source: Based on information from "Sudan—Statistical Survey," *The Middle East and North Africa, 1991,* London, 1990, 799.

Table 6. Gross Domestic Product by Sector, 1985-86 to 1988-89 [1]
(in percentages)

Sector	1985-86	1986-87	1987-88	1988-89
Agriculture	32.0	34.0	32.0	36.0
Commerce	22.0	15.0	15.0	n.a.
Transportation and communications	10.0	11.0	11.0	n.a.
Manufacturing and mining	10.0	7.0	8.0	8.2
Construction	4.0	5.0	6.0	4.6
Electricity and water	n.a.	n.a.	n.a.	1.8
Government services	10.0	n.a.	n.a.	11.5
Other services	12.0	26.0	25.0	37.8
TOTAL [2]	100.0	100.0	100.0	100.0

n.a.—not available; included in other categories.
[1] Years ending June 30.
[2] At factor cost. Figures may not add to totals because of rounding.

Table 7. Principal Crops, 1986-88
(in thousands of tons)

Crop	1986	1987	1988
Cassava (manioc) [1]	80	80	65
Cotton, seed	413	546 [1]	394 [2]
Cottonseed [1]	271	300	290
Cotton lint [1]	150	174	130
Dates [2]	120	125	120
Mangoes [2]	128	130	128
Millet	285	153 [1]	550 [1]
Peanuts (in shell)	379	434	527 [1]
Sesame seed	216	258	278 [1]
Sorghum (durra)	2,282	1,300	4,640 [1]
Sugarcane	4,500	5,000	4,500
Tomatoes [2]	155	160	158
Watermelons [2]	130	127	125
Wheat	199	157	181 [1]
Yams [2]	116	118	120

[1] Unofficial estimate.
[2] Food and Agriculture Organization estimate.

Source: Based on information from "Sudan—Statistical Survey," *The Middle East and North Africa, 1991,* London, 1990, 798.

Table 8. Principal Exports, 1986–89
(in millions of Sudanese pounds) *

Commodity	1986	1987	1988	1989
Cotton	366.7	455.2	978.4	1,348.8
Sesame	58.8	134.8	269.0	333.3
Gum arabic	141.7	267.1	281.6	313.0
Sorghum (durra)	n.a.	248.8	106.7	297.1
Sheep and lambs	66.8	42.9	124.5	192.5
Other	199.2	348.3	530.2	538.4
TOTAL	833.2	1,497.1	2,290.4	3,023.1

n.a.—not available.
* For value of the Sudanese pound—see Glossary.

Table 9. Principal Imports, 1986–89
(in millions of Sudanese pounds) *

Commodity	1986	1987	1988	1989
Manufactured goods	481.4	1.0	1,042.6	1,178.5
Petroleum and petroleum products	292.6	7.9	1,044.6	1,082.2
Machinery and equipment	405.7	4.9	776.1	826.4
Transportation equipment	n.a.	368.9	507.8	786.6
Chemicals	342.9	248.1	500.9	399.1
Wheat and flour	120.5	199.6	402.2	412.8
Other	687.2	312.5	497.9	687.8
TOTAL	2,402.2	2,612.9	4,772.1	5,373.4

n.a.—not available.
* For value of the Sudanese pound—see Glossary.

Table 10. *Principal Trading Partners, 1987–89*
(in percentages)

Country	1987	1988	1989
Exports			
Egypt	17.2	17.2	n.a.
Saudi Arabia	n.a.	n.a.	16.8
Italy	10.7	10.7	7.4
Soviet Union	n.a.	8.0	n.a.
Japan	7.4	7.4	10.9
Thailand	7.0	7.0	8.0
China	n.a.	n.a.	7.3
Britain	n.a.	n.a.	6.5
France	4.7	4.7	n.a.
Imports			
United States	12.1	6.6	n.a.
Saudi Arabia	10.4	11.8	14.1
Britain	10.0	9.3	8.3
Netherlands	6.5	6.4	5.3
Japan	6.2	n.a.	n.a.
Libya	n.a.	n.a.	6.0
Italy	6.0	5.6	n.a.
West Germany	n.a.	5.9	5.8

n.a.—not available.

Table 11. Balance of Payments, 1986–88 [1]
(in millions of United States dollars)

	1986	1987	1988
Merchandise exports (f.o.b.) [2]	326.8	265.0	427.0
Merchandise imports (f.o.b.)	− 633.7	− 694.8	− 948.5
Trade balance	306.9	− 429.7	− 521.5
Exports of services	228.8	192.2	171.6
Imports of services	− 272.8	− 323.1	− 341.3
Balance on goods and services	− 350.9	− 560.6	− 691.2
Private unrequited transfers (net)	− 89.3	133.7	216.3
Government unrequited transfers (net)	244.2	194.6	117.0
Current account balance	− 17.4	− 232.4	− 358.0
Long-term capital (net)	− 110.4	− 235.7	63.1
Short-term capital (net)	15.1	322.4	5.0
Capital account balance	− 95.3	86.7	68.1
Errors and omissions (net)	− 89.4	− 185.3	7.5
Valuation changes (net)	− 83.1	− 142.6	44.7
Exceptional financing (net)	248.0	295.4	287.1
Changes in reserves	− 37.6	− 178.3	49.5

[1] Figures may not add because of rounding.
[2] f.o.b.—free on board.

Source: Based on information from "Sudan—Statistical Survey," *The Middle East and North Africa, 1991*, London, 1990, 800.

Table 12. Major Army Equipment, 1991

Type and Description	Country of Origin	In Inventory
Main battle tanks		
T-54/55	Soviet Union	200
Type 59	China	10
M-60A3	United States	20
Light tanks		
Type 62	China	70
Armored reconnaissance vehicles		
AML-90	France	6
Saladin	Britain	15
Ferret	-do-	50
BRDM 1/2	Soviet Union	30
Armored personnel carriers		
BTR-50/152	-do-	40
OT-62/64	Czechoslovakia	30
M-113	United States	36
V-100/150 Commando	-do-	80
Walid	Egypt	100
Artillery		
M-101, 105mm	United States	18
Model 56, 105mm	-do-	6
D-74, 122mm	-do-	4
M-1938, 122mm	-do-	24
Type 54/D-30, 122mm	Soviet Union/ China	42
M-46/Type 59-1, 130mm	-do-	27
D-20, 152mm	Soviet Union	4
M-114A1, 155mm	United States	12
AMX Mk F-3, 155mm, self- propelled	France	6
Multiple rocket launchers		
BM-21, 122mm	Soviet Union	4
Antitank weapons		
Swingfire guided-wire missiles	Egypt	4
M-1942 76mm guns	Soviet Union	18
M-1944 100mm guns	-do-	20
B-10 82mm recoilless rifles	-do-	30
M-40A1 106mm recoilless rifles	United States	100
Mortars		
M-43, 120mm	Soviet Union	12
AM-49, 120mm	-do-	24

Source: Based on information from *The Military Balance, 1991–1992*, London, 1991, 119.

Table 13. *Major Air Force Equipment, 1991*

Type and Description	Country of Origin	In Inventory
Fighter ground attack aircraft		
F–5E/F	United States	9
J–5	China	10
J–6	-do-	9
Fighter aircraft		
MiG-21 [1]	Soviet Union	8
MiG-23 [2]	-do-	3
J-6	China	6
Counterinsurgency aircraft		
BAC-167 Mk Strikemaster [1]	Britain	3
BAC Jet Provost Mk 55	-do-	3
Transport aircraft		
C–130H Hercules	United States	5
An–24	Soviet Union	5
DHC–5D Buffalo	Canada	2
C–212 Aviocar	Brazil	4
EMB–110P	-do-	6
F–27 Friendship	Netherlands	1
Falcon 20/50 executive jet	France	2
Maritime reconnaissance aircraft		
Casa C–212 Aviocar	Brazil	2
Helicopters		
AB–212	Italy	11
IAR/SA–330 Puma	France/ Romania	15
Mi-4	Soviet Union	4
Mi-8	-do-	14
Mi-24 (armed)	-do-	2
Training aircraft		
MiG-15U	-do-	4
MiG-21U	-do-	4
JJ-5	China	2
JJ-6	-do-	2

[1] Nonoperational.
[2] One operational.

Source: Based on information from *The Military Balance, 1991–1992,* London, 1991, 119; and Forecast International/DMS Market Intelligence Report, *Middle East and Africa,* Greenwich, Connecticut, 1990.

Table 14. Major Air Defense Equipment, 1991

Type and Description	Country of Origin	In Inventory
Antiaircraft guns		
M-167 Vulcan, 20mm	United States	n.a.
M-163 Vulcan, 20mm, self-propelled	-do-	n.a.
ZU-23-2, 37mm	Egypt	n.a.
M-1939/Type 63, 37mm	China	120
L-60 Bofors, 40mm	Sweden	60
KS-12, 85mm	Soviet Union	n.a.
KS-19, 100mm	-do-	n.a.
Surface-to-air missiles		
SA-2 high altitude, radar-guided	-do-	18 launchers
SA-7 man-portable, short-range	-do-	n.a.
Redeye	United States	n.a.

n.a.—not available.

Source: Based on information from *The Military Balance, 1991–1992,* London, 1991, 119.

Table 15. Major Naval Equipment, 1991

Type and Description	Country of Origin	In Inventory
Patrol craft		
Coastal, 70 tons (from Iran), each with one Oerlikon 20mm gun	West Germany	2
Sewart, 10 tons (from Iran), each with one 12.7mm machine gun	United States	4
Inshore (river operations) type 15, 19.5 tons, each with one Oerlikon 20mm gun and two 7.62mm machine guns	Yugoslavia	4
Amphibious craft		
Sobat (DTM-221) LCU, 410 tons	-do-	2

Source: Based on information from *Jane's Fighting Ships, 1991–92,* Coulsdon, Surrey, United Kingdom, 1991, 512–13.

Bibliography

Chapter 1

Abbas, Mekka. *The Sudan Question.* London: Faber and Faber, 1952.

Abdin, Hasan. *Early Sudanese Nationalism, 1919–1925.* Khartoum: Khartoum University Press, 1985.

Ajayi, J.F. Ade (ed.). *General History of Africa, 6: Africa in the Nineteenth Century until the 1880s.* Berkeley: University of California Press, 1989.

Albino, Oliver. *The Sudan: A Southern Viewpoint.* London: Oxford University Press, 1970.

Alier, Abel. *Southern Sudan: Too Many Agreements Dishonoured.* Exeter, Devon, United Kingdom: Ithaca Press, 1990.

Allen, T. *Full Circle?: An Overview of Sudan's "Southern Problem" since Independence.* Manchester, United Kingdom: International Development Center, Manchester University, 1986.

Arkell, A.J. *A History of the Sudan from the Earliest Times to 1821.* (2d ed., rev.) London: Athlone Press, 1961.

Arou, Mom K.N., and B. Yongo-Bure. *North-South Relations in the Sudan since the Addis Ababa Agreement.* Khartoum: Institute of African and Asian Studies, 1989.

Asad, Talal. *The Kababish Arabs: Power, Authority, and Consent in a Nomadic Tribe.* New York: Praeger, 1970.

Baclal, R.K. "The Rise and Fall of Separatism in Southern Sudan," *African Affairs* [London], 75, No. 301, October 1976, 463–74.

Barbour, K.M. "The Sudan since Independence," *Journal of Modern African Studies,* 18, No. 1, March 1980, 73–97.

Barnett, Tony. *The Gezira Scheme: An Illusion of Development.* London: Frank Cass, 1977.

Bates, D. *The Fashoda Incident of 1898: Encounter on the Nile.* Oxford: Oxford University Press, 1984.

Bechtold, Peter K. *Politics in the Sudan: Parliamentary and Military Rule in an Emerging African Nation.* New York: Praeger, 1976.

Beshir, Mohamed Omer. *Revolution and Nationalism in the Sudan.* New York: Barnes and Noble, 1974.

_____. *The Southern Sudan: Background to Conflict.* New York: Praeger, 1968.

_____. *The Southern Sudan: From Conflict to Peace.* New York: Barnes and Noble, 1975.

Butt, Audrey. *The Nilotes of the Sudan and Uganda.* (Ethnographic

Survey of Africa, East-Central Africa, Pt. 4.) London: International African Institute, 1964.

Collins, Robert O. *King Leopold, England, and the Upper Nile, 1899-1909.* New Haven: Yale University Press, 1968.

_____. *Land Beyond the Rivers: The Southern Sudan, 1898-1918.* New Haven: Yale University Press, 1971.

_____. *Shadows in the Grass: Britain in the Southern Sudan, 1918-1956.* New Haven: Yale University Press, 1983.

_____. *The Waters of the Nile: Hydropolitics and the Jonglei Canal, 1900-1988.* Oxford: Clarendon Press, 1990.

Collins, Robert O., and Francis Mading Deng. *The British in the Sudan, 1898-1956: The Sweetness and the Sorrow.* Stanford: Hoover Institution Press, 1984.

Crawford, O.G.S. *The Fung Kingdom of Sennar: With a Geographical Account of the Middle Nile Region.* New York: AMS Press, 1978.

Crowder, Michael (ed.). *The Cambridge History of Africa, 8: From c. 1940 to c. 1975.* Cambridge: Cambridge University Press, 1984.

Cunnison, Ian. *Baggara Arabs: Power and the Lineage in a Sudanese Nomad Tribe.* Oxford: Clarendon Press, 1966.

Daly, Martin W. *British Administration and the Northern Sudan.* Leiden, Netherlands: Brill, 1979.

_____. *Empire on the Nile: The Anglo-Egyptian Sudan, 1898-1934.* Cambridge: Cambridge University Press, 1986.

_____. *Imperial Sudan: The Anglo-Egyptian Condominium, 1934-56.* Cambridge: Cambridge University Press, 1991.

_____. *Modernization in the Sudan: Essays in Honour of Richard Hill.* New York: Lilian Barber Press, 1985.

De Medeires, F. "The Peoples of the Sudan: Populations." Pages 119-39 in I. Hrbek (ed.), *General History of Africa, 3: Africa from the Seventh to the Eleventh Century.* Berkeley: University of California Press, 1988.

Deng, Francis Mading. *Tradition and Modernization: A Challenge for Law among the Dinka of the Sudan.* (2d ed.) New Haven: Yale University Press, 1987.

Deng, Francis Mading, and Martin W. Daly. *"Bonds of Silk": The Human Factor in the British Administration of Sudan.* East Lansing: Michigan State University Press, 1989.

Deng, William. *The Problem of Southern Sudan.* London: Oxford University Press, 1963.

Duncan, J.S.R. *The Sudan's Path to Independence.* Edinburgh: William Blackwood, 1957.

Eprile, Cecile. *War and Peace in the Sudan, 1955-1972.* London: David and Charles, 1974.

Evans-Pritchard, Edward E. *The Azande: History and Political Institutions.* Oxford: Clarendon Press, 1971.

———. *The Nuer.* Oxford: Oxford University Press, 1940.

Ewald, Janet J. *Soldiers, Traders, and Slaves: State Formation and Economic Transformation in the Greater Nile Valley, 1700-1885.* Madison: University of Wisconsin Press, 1990.

Fabunmi, L.A. *The Sudan in Anglo-Egyptian Relations, 1800-1956.* London: Longman, 1960.

Fage, J.D. (ed.). *The Cambridge History of Africa, 2: From c. 500 B.C. to A.D. 1050.* Cambridge: Cambridge University Press, 1978.

Fluehr-Lobban, Carolyn. "Law in the Sudan: History and Trends since Independence," *Africa Today,* 28, No. 2, 1981, 69-77.

Gray, Richard (ed.). *The Cambridge History of Africa, 4: From c. 1600 to c. 1790.* Cambridge: Cambridge University Press, 1975.

Gresh, Alain. "The Free Officers and the Comrades: The Sudanese Communist Party and Nimeiri Face-to-Face, 1969-1971," *International Journal of Middle East Studies,* 21, 1989, 393-409.

Gurdon, Charles. *Sudan in Transition: A Political Risk Analysis.* (Special Report Series, No. 226.) London: Economist Intelligence Unit, 1986.

Hale, Sondra. "Sudan Civil War: Religion, Colonialism, and the World System." Pages 157-84 in Suad Joseph and Barbara L.K. Pillsbury (eds.), *Muslim-Christian Conflicts: Economic, Political, and Social Origins.* Boulder, Colorado: Westview Press, 1978.

Hasan, Yusuf Fadl. "The Penetration of Islam in the Eastern Sudan." Pages 112-23 in I.M. Lewis (ed.), *Islam in Tropical Africa.* (2d ed.) Bloomington: International African Institute in association with Indiana University Press, 1980.

Henderson, Kenneth David Druitt. *Sudan Republic.* New York: Praeger, 1965.

Hill, Richard. *Egypt in the Sudan, 1820-1881.* London: Oxford University Press, 1959.

Holt, P.M. "Egypt, the Funj, and Darfur." Pages 14-57 in Richard Gray (ed.), *The Cambridge History of Africa, 4: From c. 1600 to c. 1790.* Cambridge: Cambridge University Press, 1975.

———. "Islamic Millenarianism and the Fulfillment of Prophecy: A Case Study." Pages 335-48 in Ann Williams (ed.), *Prophecy and Millenarianism: Essays in Honour of Marjorie Reeves.* Harlow, Essex, United Kingdom: Longman, 1980.

———. *The Mahdist State in the Sudan, 1881-1898: A Study of Its Origins, Development, and Overthrow.* Oxford: Clarendon Press, 1958.

———. "The Nilotic Sudan." Pages 327-44 in P.M. Holt, Ann K.S. Lambton, and Bernard Lewis (eds.), *The Cambridge History of Islam, 2: The Further Islamic Lands, and Islamic Society and*

Civilization. Cambridge: Cambridge University Press, 1970.

Holt, P.M., and Martin W. Daly. *A History of the Sudan: From the Coming of Islam to the Present Day*. (4th ed.) London: Longman, 1986.

Holt, P.M., Ann K.S. Lambton, and Bernard Lewis (eds.). *The Cambridge History of Islam, 2: The Further Islamic Lands, and Islamic Society and Civilization*. Cambridge: Cambridge University Press, 1970.

Hrbek, I. (ed.). *General History of Africa, 3: Africa from the Seventh to the Eleventh Century*. Berkeley: University of California Press, 1988.

Ibrahim, H.A., and B.A. Ogot. "The Sudan in the Nineteenth Century." Pages 356–75 in J.F. Ade Ajayi (ed.), *General History of Africa, 6: Africa in the Nineteenth Century until the 1880s*. Berkeley: University of California Press, 1989.

Johnson, D.H. "Judicial Regulation and Administrative Control: Customary Law and the Nuer, 1898–1954," *Journal of African History* [London], 27, No. 1, 1986, 59–78.

Joseph, Suad, and Barbara L.K. Pillsbury (eds.). *Muslim-Christian Conflicts: Economic, Political, and Social Origins*. Boulder, Colorado: Westview Press, 1978.

Khalid, Mansour. *The Government They Deserve: The Role of the Elite in Sudan's Political Evolution*. London: Kegan Paul, 1990.

_____. *Nimeiri and the Revolution of Dis-May*. London: Kegan Paul, 1985.

Khalid, Mansour (ed.). *John Garang Speaks*. London: Kegan Paul, 1987.

Kirwan, L.P. "A Contemporary Account of the Conversion of the Sudan to Christianity," *Sudan Notes and Records* [Khartoum], 20, No. 2, 1937, 289–95.

Kopietz, Hans-Heino, and Pamela Ann Smith. "Egypt, Libya and the Sudan." Pages 502–63 in Michael Crowder (ed.), *The Cambridge History of Africa, 8: From c. 1940 to c. 1975*. Cambridge: Cambridge University Press, 1984.

Lapidus, Ira M. *A History of Islamic Societies*. Cambridge: Cambridge University Press, 1989.

Lees, Francis, and Hugh C. Brooks. *The Economic and Political Development of the Sudan*. Boulder, Colorado: Westview Press, 1977.

Lesch, Ann Mosely. "Confrontation in the Southern Sudan," *Middle East Journal*, 40, No. 3, Summer 1986, 410–28.

Lewis, I.M. (ed.). *Islam in Tropical Africa*. (2d ed.) Bloomington: International African Institute in association with Indiana University Press, 1980.

Long, David E., and Bernard Reich (eds.). *The Government and Politics of the Middle East and North Africa.* Boulder, Colorado: Westview Press, 1980.

Mahdi, Mandour el. *A Short History of the Sudan.* London: Oxford University Press, 1965.

Mahmoud, Mahgoub El-Tigani. "The Mahdist Correctional System in the Sudan: Aspects of Ideology and Politics," *Africa Today,* 28, No. 2, 1981, 78–86.

Marlowe, John. *A History of Egypt and Anglo-Egyptian Relations, 1800–1956.* (2d ed.) Hamden, Connecticut: Archon Books, 1965.

Marsot, Afaf Lutfi S. *Egypt in the Reign of Muhammad Ali.* Cambridge: Cambridge University Press, 1984.

Mawut, L.L. *Dinka Resistance to Condominium Rule, 1902–1932.* Khartoum: Khartoum University Press, 1983.

Mercer, Patricia. "Shilluk Trade and Politics from the Mid-Seventeenth Century to 1861," *Journal of African History* [London], 12, No. 3, 1971, 407–26.

Minear, Larry. *Humanitarianism under Siege.* Trenton, New Jersey: Red Sea Press, 1990.

Moorehead, Alan. *The White Nile.* New York: Harper and Row, 1960.

Niblock, Tim. *Class and Power in Sudan: The Dynamics of Sudanese Politics, 1898–1985.* Albany: State University of New York Press, 1987.

O'Ballance, Edgar. *The Secret War in the Sudan: 1955–1972.* Hamden, Connecticut: Archon Books, 1977.

O'Fahey, R.S. "Slavery and the Slave Trade in Dar Fur," *Journal of African History* [London], 14, No. 1, 1973, 29–43.

O'Fahey, R.S., and J.L. Spaulding. *Kingdoms of the Sudan.* (Studies in African History Series.) London: Methuen, 1974.

Paul, A. *A History of the Beja Tribes of the Sudan.* London: Frank Cass, 1971.

Rahim, Muddathir Abdel. *Changing Patterns of Civilian-Military Relations in the Sudan.* Uppsala, Sweden: Scandinavian Institute of African Studies, 1978.

_____. *The Development of British Policy in the Southern Sudan, 1899–1947.* Khartoum: Khartoum University Press, 1968.

_____. *Imperialism and Nationalism in the Sudan: A Study in Constitutional and Political Development, 1899–1956.* Oxford: Clarendon Press, 1969.

Reich, Bernard. "Democratic Republic of the Sudan." Pages 339–57 in David E. Long and Bernard Reich (eds.), *The Government and Politics of the Middle East and North Africa.* Boulder, Colorado: Westview Press, 1980.

Salih, Kamal Osman. "The Sudan, 1985–89: The Fading Democracy," *Journal of Modern African Studies* [London], 28, No. 2, 1990, 199–224.

Sanderson, Lilian Passmore. "Education in the Southern Sudan: The Impact of Government-Missionary-Southern Sudanese Relationships upon the Development of Education During the Condominium Period, 1898–1956," *African Affairs* [London], 79, No. 315, April 1980, 157–70.

Santandrea, Stefano. *A Tribal History of the Western Bahr al-Ghazal.* Bologna, Italy: Editrice Nigrizia, 1964.

Scott, P. "The Sudan People's Liberation Movement (SPLM) and Liberation Army (SPLA)," *Review of African Political Economy* [Sheffield, United Kingdom], No. 33, 1985, 69–82.

Shibeika, Mekki. *British Policy in the Sudan, 1882–1902.* Oxford: Oxford University Press, 1952.

———. *The Independent Sudan.* New York: Robert Speller, 1959.

Shinnie, P.L. "Christian Nubia." Pages 556–88 in J.D. Fage (ed.), *The Cambridge History of Africa, 2: From c. 500 B.C. to A.D. 1050.* Cambridge: Cambridge University Press, 1978.

———. *Medieval Nubia.* Khartoum: Sudan Antiquities Service, 1954.

———. *Meroe: A Civilization of the Sudan.* (Ancient Peoples and Places Series.) London: Thames and Hudson, 1967.

Smith, Ian R. *The Emin Pasha Relief Expedition, 1886–1890.* London: Oxford University Press, 1972.

Spaulding, Jay. *The Heroic Age in Sinnar.* East Lansing: African Studies Center, Michigan State University, 1985.

Sylvester, Anthony (pseud.). *Sudan under Nimeiri.* (2d ed.) London: Bodley Head, 1977.

Theobald, A.B. *The Mahdiya: A History of the Anglo-Egyptian Sudan, 1881–1899.* London: Longman, 1951.

Thomas, Graham F. *Sudan: Death of a Dream.* London: Darf, 1990.

Trigger, B.G. "Languages of the Northern Sudan: A Historical Perspective," *Journal of African History* [London], 7, No. 1, 1966, 19–25.

Trimingham, J. Spencer. *Islam in the Sudan.* London: Oxford University Press, 1949.

Van Gerven, Dennis P., David S. Carlson, and George J. Armelagos. "Racial History and Bio-Cultural Adaptation of Nubian Archaeological Populations," *Journal of African History* [London], 14, No. 4, 1973, 555–67.

Voll, John O. *Historical Dictionary of the Sudan.* (African Historical Dictionaries, No. 17.) Metuchen, New Jersey: Scarecrow Press, 1978.

Voll, John O., and Sarah Potts Voll. *The Sudan: Unity and Diversity in a Multicultural State*. Boulder, Colorado: Westview Press, 1985.
Wai, Dunstan M. *The African-Arab Conflict in the Sudan*. New York: Africana, 1981.
_____. "Pax Britannica and the Southern Sudan," *African Affairs* [London], 79, No. 316, July 1980, 375–95.
_____. "The Sudan: Domestic Politics and Foreign Relations under Nimeiry," *African Affairs* [London], 78, No. 312, July 1979, 297–317.
Wai, Dunstan M. (ed.). *The Southern Sudan: The Problem of National Integration*. London: Frank Cass, 1973.
Waller, John H. *Gordon of Khartoum: The Saga of a Victorian Hero*. New York: Atheneum, 1988.
Warburg, Gabriel. *Islam, Nationalism, and Communism in a Traditional Society: The Case of Sudan*. London: Frank Cass, 1978.
_____. "The Sharia in Sudan: Implementation and Repercussions, 1983–1989," *Middle East Journal*, 44, No. 4, Autumn 1990, 624–37.
Wendorf, Fred (ed.). *Contributions to the Prehistory of Nubia*. Dallas: Southern Methodist University Press, 1968.
Williams, Ann (ed.). *Prophecy and Millenarianism: Essays in Honour of Marjorie Reeves*. Harlow, Essex, United Kingdom: Longman, 1980.
Woodward, Peter. *Condominium and Sudanese Nationalism*. Totowa, New Jersey: Barnes and Noble, 1979.
_____. "Nationalism and Opposition in the Sudan," *African Affairs* [London], 80, No. 320, July 1981, 379–88.
_____. "The South in Sudanese Politics, 1946–1956," *Middle Eastern Studies* [London], 16, No. 3, October 1980, 178–92.
_____. "Sudan after Numeiri," *Third World Quarterly* [London], 7, No. 4, 1985, 958–72.
_____. *Sudan, 1898–1989: The Unstable State*. Boulder, Colorado: Rienner, 1990.
Woodward, Peter (ed.). *Sudan since Nimeiri*. London: School of Oriental and African Studies, University of London, 1986.

(Various issues of the following publication were also used in the preparation of this chapter: *Sudan Notes and Records* [Khartoum].)

Chapter 2

El Agraa, Omer, Adil M. Ahmad, Ian Haywood, and Osman M. El Kheir. *Popular Settlements in Greater Khartoum*. London: International

Institute for Environment and Development, 1985.

Ahfad University College. *Ahfad University College.* Omdurman, Sudan: 1990.

Ali, Mohamed Adham. *Development and Problems of Girls' Education in Northern Sudan, 1: A History of Girls' Education.* (No. 113.) Khartoum: Economic and Social Research Council, 1983.

Alier, Abel. *Southern Sudan: Too Many Agreements Dishonoured.* Exeter, Devon, United Kingdom: Ithaca Press, 1990.

Barbour, K.M. *The Republic of the Sudan: A Regional Geography.* London: University of London Press, 1961.

Bayoumi, Ahmed. *The History of Sudan Health Services.* Nairobi: Kenya Literature Bureau, 1979.

Bechtold, Peter K. "More Turbulence in Sudan: A New Politics This Time?" *Middle East Journal,* 44, No. 4, Autumn 1990, 579-95.

Cloudsley, Anne. *Women of Omdurman: Life, Love, and the Cult of Virginity.* New York: St. Martin's Press, 1984.

Collins, Robert O. *The Waters of the Nile: Hydropolitics and the Jonglei Canal, 1900-1988.* Oxford: Clarendon Press, 1990.

Dareer, Asma el. *Woman, Why Do You Weep? Circumcision and Its Consequences.* London: Zed Press, 1982.

Deng, Francis Mading. *Cry of the Owl.* New York: Barber Press, 1989.

_____. *The Dinka of the Sudan.* New York: Holt, Rinehart, and Winston, 1972.

_____. "War of Visions for the Nation," *Middle East Journal,* 44, No. 4, Autumn 1990, 596-609.

Evans-Pritchard, Edward E. *The Nuer.* Oxford: Oxford University Press, 1940.

Farah, Abdel Aziz M., Osman el M. Nur, and Taj el A. Eawi (eds.). *Aspects of Population Change and Development in the Sudan.* (Proceedings of Second National Population Conference, April 26-28, 1982.) Khartoum: Khartoum University Press, 1982.

Fluehr-Lobban, Carolyn. "Islamization in Sudan: A Critical Assessment," *Middle East Journal,* 44, No. 4, Autumn 1990, 610-23.

Kilgour, Mary C. "Refugees and Development: Dissonance in the Sudan," *Middle East Journal,* 44, No. 4, Autumn 1990, 638-48.

Lebon, J.M.G. *Land Use in the Sudan.* Bude, Cornwall, United Kingdom: Geographical Publications, 1965.

Lienhardt, Godfrey. *Divinity and Experience: The Religion of the Dinka.* New York: Oxford University Press, 1987.

Lightfoot-Klein, Hanny. *Prisoners of Ritual: An Odyssey into Female Genital Circumcision in Africa.* New York: Harworth Press, ca. 1989.

The Middle East and North Africa, 1991. London: Europa, 1990.

Mills, L.R. *Population and Manpower in the Southern Sudan.* Geneva: International Labour Organisation, 1977.

Omdurman Ahlia University. *Omdurman Ahlia University.* Omdurman, Sudan: 1990.

Othman, M. Abdalghaffar. *Current Philosophies, Patterns, and Issues in Higher Education.* Khartoum: Khartoum University Press, 1988.

Population of the Sudan: A Joint Project on Mapping and Analysing the 1983 Population Census Data. Wad Madani, Sudan: Population Studies Center, Faculty of Economics and Rural Development, University of Gezira, 1984.

Saghayroun, Atif A. Rahman, Abdel-Aziz Farah, Samira Amin Ahmed, and Al Haj Hamed Mohamed Kheir (eds.). *Population and Development in the Sudan: The Quest for a National Policy.* (Proceedings of Third National Population Conference, October 10–14, 1987, Khartoum.) Khartoum: National Population Committee, 1988.

Sanderson, Lilian Passmore, and Neville Sanderson. *Education, Religion, and Politics in Southern Sudan, 1899–1964.* London: Ithaca Press, 1981.

Squires, Herbert Chavasse. *The Sudan Medical Service: An Experiment in Social Medicine.* London: Heinemann Medical Books, 1958.

Sudan. Ministry of Culture. *Sudan Facts and Figures.* Khartoum: 1974.

_____. Ministry of Finance and Economic Planning. Department of Statistics. *1983 Preliminary Census Results.* Khartoum: 1984.

Trimingham, J. Spencer. *Islam in the Sudan.* London: Oxford University Press, 1949.

United States. Embassy in Khartoum. ''Health and Medical Information.'' Khartoum: 1990.

Wahab, A.A. ''Rain Day Averages, 1921–1950,'' *Sudan Meteorological Service* [Khartoum], 2, 1957, passim.

Wai, Dunstan M. *The African-Arab Conflict in the Sudan.* New York: Africana, 1981.

Wai, Dunstan M. (ed.). *The Southern Sudan: The Problem of National Integration.* (Cass Library of African Studies, No. 152.) London: Frank Cass, 1973.

Warburg, Gabriel R. ''The Sharia in Sudan: Implementation and Repercussions, 1983–1989,'' *Middle East Journal,* 44, No. 4, Autumn 1990, 624–37.

Waterbury, John. *Hydropolitics and the Nile Valley.* Syracuse, New York: Syracuse University Press, 1979.

(Various issues of the following publication were also used in the preparation of this chapter: *Sudan Journal of Population Studies* [Khartoum], 1987–91.)

Chapter 3

Abd al Rahim, Muddathir, Raphael Badal, Adlan Hardallo, and Peter Woodward (eds.). *Sudan since Independence: Studies of the Political Development since 1956.* Brookfield, Vermont: Gower, 1986.

Africa South of the Sahara, 1992. (21st ed.) London: Europa, 1991.

Ahmed, Medani M. *The Political Economy of Development in the Sudan.* (African Seminar Series, No. 29.) Khartoum: Institute of African and Asian Studies, University of Khartoum, 1987.

Ali, Ali Abdel Gadir. *Some Aspects of Productivity in Sudanese Traditional Agriculture: The Case of the Northern Province.* Khartoum: Economic and Social Research Council, National Council for Research, 1977.

————. *The Sudan Economy in Disarray: Essays on the Crisis.* Khartoum: Ali Abdel Gadir Ali (distributed in the United Kingdom by Ithaca Press), 1985.

Bank of Sudan. *Annual Report of the Bank of Sudan, 1989.* Khartoum: 1989.

Barnett, Tony, and Abbas Abdelkarim. *Sudan: The Gezira Scheme and Agricultural Transition.* London: Frank Cass, 1991.

The Cambridge Encyclopedia of the Middle East and North Africa. (Ed., Trevor Mostyn.) New York: Cambridge University Press, 1988.

Hassan, Ali Mohamed el (ed.). *Essays on the Economy and Society of the Sudan.* Khartoum: Economic and Social Research Council, National Council for Research, 1978.

Kameir, El Wathiq, and Ibrahim Kursany. *Corruption as the 'Fifth' Factor of Production in the Sudan.* (Research Report No. 72.) Uppsala, Sweden: Scandinavian Institute of African Studies, 1985.

Khalid, Mansour. *The Government They Deserve: The Role of the Elite in Sudan's Political Evolution.* London: Kegan Paul, 1990.

————. *Nimeiri and the Revolution of Dis-May.* London: Kegan Paul, 1985.

Mallet, Charles (ed.). *Islamic Banking and Finance.* (Occasional Series.) London: School of Oriental and African Studies, University of London, 1988.

The Middle East and North Africa, 1991. London: Europa, 1990.

Mirakhour A., and Z. Iqbal. *Islamic Banking.* (Occasional Paper Series, No. 49.) Washington: International Monetary Fund, 1985.

Niblock, Tim. *Class and Power in Sudan: The Dynamics of Sudanese Politics, 1898-1985.* Albany: State University of New York Press, 1987.

Schacht, Joseph. *An Introduction to Islamic Law.* Oxford: Clarendon Press, 1964.

Shibly, Mekki el. *Monetisation, Financial Intermediation, and Self-Financed Growth in the Sudan (1960/61-1979/80).* Khartoum: Development Studies and Research Centre, Faculty of Economic and Social Studies, University of Khartoum, 1984.

Umbadda, Siddiq. *Import Policy in Sudan, 1966-1976.* Khartoum: Development Studies and Research Centre, Faculty of Economic and Social Studies, University of Khartoum, 1984.

Van de Wel, Paul, and Abdel Ghaffar Mohamed Ahmed (eds.). *Perspectives on Development in the Sudan: Selected Papers from a Research Workshop in The Hague, July 1984.* (Organized by Joint Programme of Research and Teaching in Regional and Rural Development and Planning of Institute of Social Studies, The Hague and Development Studies and Research Center, University of Khartoum.) The Hague: Institute of Social Studies, 1986.

World Radio TV Handbook, 1991. (Ed., Andrew G. Sennitt.) (Hvidovre,) Denmark: Billboard, 1990.

(Various issues of the following publications were also used in the preparation of this chapter: Economist Intelligence Unit, *Country Report: Sudan* [London], 1989-91; *Middle East Economic Digest* [London]; and *Sudan Journal of Economic and Social Studies* [Khartoum].)

Chapter 4

Africa Watch. *Denying "The Honor of Living": Sudan, A Human Rights Disaster.* New York: 1990.

Amnesty International. *Report on the Human Rights Situation in Sudan.* London: 1991.

Bechtold, Peter K. "More Turbulence in Sudan: A New Politics This Time?" *Middle East Journal,* 44, No. 4, Autumn 1990, 579-95.

_____. *Politics in the Sudan since Independence.* New York: Praeger, 1977.

_____. "The Sudan since the Fall of Numayri." Pages 367-89 in Robert O. Freedman (ed.), *The Middle East from the Iran-Contra Affair to the Intifada.* Syracuse, New York: Syracuse University Press, 1991.

Benavides, Gustavo, and Martin W. Daly (eds.). *Religion and*

Political Power. Albany: State University of New York Press, 1989.

Cudsi, Alexander. "Islam and Politics in the Sudan." Pages 36–55 in James P. Piscatori (ed.), *Islam in the Political Process.* Cambridge: Cambridge University Press, 1983.

Daly, Martin W. "Islam, Secularism, and Ethnic Identity in the Sudan." Pages 83–97 in Gustavo Benavides and Martin W. Daly (eds.), *Religion and Political Power.* Albany: State University of New York Press, 1989.

Deng, Francis Mading. "War of Visions for the Nation," *Middle East Journal,* 44, No. 4, Autumn 1990, 596–609.

Duffield, Mark. "Absolute Distress: Structural Cases of Hunger in Sudan," *Middle East Report,* No. 166, September-October 1990, 4–11.

Economist Intelligence Unit. *Country Report: Sudan,* 3. London: Economist, 1990.

_____. *Country Report: Sudan,* 1. London: Economist, 1991.

Esposito, John L. "Sudan in the Politics of Islamic Revivalism." Pages 187–203 in Shireen T. Hunter (ed.), *The Politics of Islamic Revivalism: Diversity and Unity.* Bloomington: Indiana University Press, 1988.

_____. "Sudan's Islamic Experiment," *Muslim World,* 76, Nos. 3–4, July-October 1986, 181–202.

Europa Annual, 1990. London: Europa, 1989.

Fluehr-Lobban, Carolyn. *Islamic Law and Society in the Sudan.* London: Frank Cass, 1987.

_____. "Islamization in Sudan: A Critical Assessment," *Middle East Journal,* 44, No. 4, Autumn 1990, 610–23.

Freedman, Robert O. (ed.). *The Middle East from the Iran-Contra Affair to the Intifada.* Syracuse, New York: Syracuse University Press, 1991.

Hooglund, Eric. "The Other Face of War," *Middle East Report,* No. 171, July-August 1991, 3–12.

Hunter, Shireen T. (ed.). *The Politics of Islamic Revivalism: Diversity and Unity.* Bloomington: Indiana University Press, 1988.

Ibrahim, Riad. "Factors Contributing to the Rise of the Muslim Brethren in Sudan," *Arab Studies Quarterly,* 12, Nos. 3–4, Summer-Fall 1990, 33–53.

The Impact of the Gulf Crisis on Developing Countries. (Briefing Paper Series.) London: Overseas Development Institute, March 1991.

Kilgour, Mary. "Refugees and Development: Dissonance in the Sudan," *Middle East Journal,* 44, No. 4, Autumn 1990, 638–48.

Lesch, Ann Mosely. "Khartoum Diary," *Middle East Report,* No. 161, November-December 1989, 36–38.

Lusk, Gill. "Sense of Unreality," *Middle East International* [London], No. 389, December 7, 1990, 16–17.

_____. "Sudan: No Answer to War or Famine," *Middle East International* [London], No. 391, January 11, 1991, 18.

_____. "Sudan Changing Tune," *Middle East International* [London], No. 399, May 3, 1991, 19.

Mahmoud, Fatima Babiker. *The Sudanese Bourgeoisie.* London: Zed Press, 1984.

The Middle East and North Africa, 1990. London: Europa, 1989.

Nduru, Moyiga Korokoto. "Food Politics," *New African* [London], No. 279, December 1990, 17.

Niblock, Tim. *Class and Power in Sudan: The Dynamics of Sudanese Politics, 1898-1985.* Albany: State University of New York Press, 1987.

O'Brien, Jay. "Sudan's Killing Fields," *Middle East Report,* No. 161, November–December 1989, 32–35.

Perlez, Jane. "Islamic Politics Drive Away Allies of the Sudan," *New York Times,* November 7, 1990, A17.

Piscatori, James P. (ed.). *Islam in the Political Process.* Cambridge: Cambridge University Press, 1983.

Press, Robert M. "Shadowy Ruling Council Guides Sudan to Fundamentalist Goals," *Christian Science Monitor,* November 20, 1990, 8.

_____. "Sudanese Military Regime Faces Growing Opposition," *Christian Science Monitor,* October 23, 1990, 5.

Rondinelli, Dennis. "Administrative Decentralization and Economic Development: The Sudan Experiment with Devolution," *Journal of Modern African Studies,* 19, No. 4, 1981, 595–624.

Rouleau, Eric. "Sudan's Revolutionary Spring," *MERIP Reports,* No. 135, September 1985, 3–9.

Smith, Gayle. "George Bush in Khartoum," *MERIP Reports,* No. 135, September 1985, 25–26.

"Sudan: The Great Hunger," *Africa Confidential* [London], 31, No. 22, November 9, 1990, 4.

Taha, Mahum Muhammad. (Trans., Abdullah Ahmed an Naim.) *Second Message of Islam.* Syracuse, New York: Syracuse University Press, 1987.

Voll, John O. "Political Crisis in Sudan," *Current History,* 89, No. 546, April 1990, 153–56, 178–80.

Warburg, Gabriel. *Egypt and the Sudan: Studies in History and Politics.* Totowa, New Jersey: Frank Cass, 1985.

_____. "The Sharia in Sudan: Implementation and Repercussions, 1983-1989," *Middle East Journal,* 44, No. 4, Autumn 1990, 624–37.

Woodward, Peter. *Sudan, 1898-1989: The Unstable State.* Boulder, Colorado: Rienner, 1990.

World Radio TV Handbook, 1991. (Ed., Andrew G. Sennitt.) Hvidovre, Denmark: Billboard, 1990.

Yongo-Bure, Benaiah. "Sudan's Deepening Crisis," *Middle East Report,* No. 172, September-October 1991, 8-13.

Chapter 5

Abdelkarim, Abbas, Abdallah el-Hassan, and David Seldon. "The Generals Step In," *MERIP Reports,* No. 135, September 1985, 19-24.

Africa Contemporary Record: Annual Survey and Documents, 1987-1988. (Eds., Colin Legum and Marion E. Doro.) New York: Africana, 1989.

Africa Watch. *Denying "The Honor of Living": Sudan, A Human Rights Disaster.* New York: 1990.

Amnesty International. *Sudan: Human Rights Violations in the Context of Civil War.* London: 1989.

_____. *Sudan: Imprisonment of Prisoners of Conscience.* London: 1990.

Bechtold, Peter K. *Politics in the Sudan: Parliamentary and Military Rule in an Emerging African Nation.* New York: Praeger, 1976.

Berkeley, Bill. "War Without End," *New Republic,* No. 3, 877, May 8, 1989, 14-15.

Cater, Nick. "A Step Backwards?" *Africa Report,* 34, No. 5, September-October 1989, 32-35.

_____. "Sudan's Mr. Tough Guy," *New African* [London], 264-65, September-October 1989, 11-12.

Defense and Foreign Affairs Handbook. (Ed., George R. Copley.) Washington: Perth, 1989.

Dyer, Gwynne. "Sudan." Pages 541-44 in John Keegan (ed.), *World Armies.* Detroit: Gale Research, 1983.

Fluehr-Lobban, Carolyn. *Islamic Law and Society in the Sudan.* London: Frank Cass, 1987.

Forecast International/DMS Market Intelligence Report. *Middle East and Africa.* Greenwich, Connecticut: Defense Marketing Services, 1990.

Gurdon, Charles. *Sudan in Transition: A Political Risk Analysis.* (Special Report Series, No. 226.) London: Economist Intelligence Unit, 1986.

Jamal, Sadia. "Under Bashir's Boot," *New African* [London], No. 274, July 1990, 9-10.

Shia (from Shiat Ali, the Party of Ali)—A member of the smaller of the two great divisions of Islam. The Shia supported the claims of Ali and his line to presumptive right to the caliphate and leadership of the Muslim community, and on this issue they divided from the Sunni (*q.v.*) in the first great schism within Islam. Later schisms have produced further divisions among the Shia over the identity and number of imams (*q.v.*). Shia revere Twelve Imams, the last of whom is believed to be in hiding.

the Sudan—Historical term for the geographical region stretching across Africa from Cape Verde on the Atlantic coast to the Ethiopian plateau in the east between about 8° and 16° north latitude; characterized by savanna and semiarid steppe. Term derived from Arabic *bilad as sudan* (literally, land of the blacks). Not to be confused with Sudan, the country.

Sudanese pound (£Sd)—Until May 1992, Sudanese currency consisted of 1,000 millimes = 100 piasters = 1 Sudanese pound. As of March 31, 1991, the official exchange rate was US$1 = £Sd1.30; from February 1985 to October 1987, the official exchange rate was set at US$1 = £Sd2.50. The Sudanese pound was gradually being replaced by the dinar (*q.v.*).

sudd—Barrier or obstruction; with lower case the term designates clumps of aquatic vegetation that block the Nile channel; with upper case, the term is used loosely for the entire White Nile swamps.

Sunni (from sunna meaning "custom," giving connotation of orthodoxy in theory and practice)—A member of the larger of the two great divisions of Islam. The Sunnis supported the traditional method of election to the caliphate and accepted the Umayyad line. On this issue they divided from the Shia (*q.v.*) in the first great schism within Islam.

Three Towns—Sudanese reference to the cities of Khartoum, Khartoum North, and Omdurman. Located in close proximity to the juncture of the White Nile and Blue Nile rivers, they form a single metropolitan area.

transhumant—Transhumance is the seasonal movement of livestock along well-established routes by herders or by an ethnic group as a whole.

umudiyah (pl., *umudiyat*)—Formerly a political division under an *umda,* encompassing a number of villages in the case of sedentary peoples or a section of a tribe in the case of nomadic peoples. Among nomadic or seminomadic peoples, several such divisions constituted a *naziriyah* (*q.v.*).

World Bank—Informal name used to designate a group of three affiliated international institutions: the International Bank for Reconstruction and Development (IBRD), the International Development Association (IDA), and the International Finance Corporation (IFC). The IBRD, established in 1945, has as its primary purpose the provision of loans to developing countries for productive projects. The IDA, a legally separate loan fund but administered by the staff of the IBRD, was set up in 1960 to furnish credits to the poorest developing countries on much easier terms than those of conventional IBRD loans. The IFC, founded in 1956, supplements the activities of the IBRD through loans and assistance designed specifically to encourage the growth of productive private enterprises in the less developed countries. The president and certain senior officers of the IBRD hold the same positions in the IFC. The three institutions are owned by the governments of the countries that subscribe their capital. To participate in the World Bank group, member states must first belong to the International Monetary Fund (IMF—*q.v.*).

Index

AAAID. *See* Arab Authority for Agricultural Investment and Development

Aali an Nil (province/state), 48, 63, 93, 206; agriculture in, 153, 158; civil war in, 242–43; Dinka in, 80, 87, 93, 221; land tenure in, 146; militias in, 255; opposition of, to Islamization, 212; Sudanese People's Liberation Army presence in, 50

Aba Island, 42

Abbas I, 16

Abbud, Ibrahim, xxiv, 35–36

Abbud government (*see also* Supreme Council of the Armed Forces), xxiv, 36–37, 199, 234; arabization under, xxiv, 37; civil war under, 234; economy under, 37, 234; education under, 37, 203; government dissolved by, 37; Islamization under, 203; missionaries expelled by, xxiv, 37; opposition to, 36, 37, 234; problems in, 36, 234; promises of, 36; southern policies of, 36–37, 204, 234

Abd al Latif, Ali, 29; exiled, 29

Abd al Qadir al Jilani, 104

Abd al Wahab, Ahmad: in coup of 1958, 35–36; as member of Ansar, 36

Abu Hamad, 23; rail transportation to, 173

Abu Jabira, 170

Abu Klea. *See* Abu Tulayh

Abu Tulayh (Abu Klea), 20

ACDA. *See* United States Arms Control and Disarmament Agency

acquired immune deficiency syndrome (AIDS), 119

Ad Damazin irrigation project, 131

Addis Ababa accords (1972), xxv, 85, 212, 242, 264; abrogated, 213, 231, 239; signed, 46, 52; terms of, 44–46, 239

AFESD. *See* Arab Fund for Economic and Social Development

African-Arab relations. *See* north-south division

African Development Bank, 168; agricultural credit from, xxviii

African heritage (*see also* south; southerners), 3, 94

Africa Watch, 17, 221, 252, 264

Agricultural Bank of Sudan, 186

agricultural production, 134, 135; decline of, 49; growth of, 142, 152

agricultural products (*see also* cotton), 118, 162; dates, 35; millet, 64, 144; peanuts, xxvi, 63, 64, 144, 149, 150, 187, 188; as percentage of exports, 142; sesame, xxvi, 63, 64, 144, 153, 187, 188; sorghum, xxvi, 63, 144, 150, 151, 153, 187; wheat, 144, 149, 188

Agricultural Reform Corporation, 150

agricultural sector: in drought, xxv; as percentage of gross domestic product, xxvi

agriculture (*see also* livestock raising), xxvi, 127; in Al Jazirah, 12; commercial xxvi, 64; under five-year plans, 130; forests converted to, 158; loans for, 49, 135; as public enterprise, 128; share of labor force, 139, 142; subsistence, 144; traditional, 128, 142

agriculture, irrigated, 129, 142, 144, 147–51; in Al Jazirah, 63; area for, 147; for cotton, 148; in Khashm al Qirbah, 63

agriculture, mechanized, 144, 151–52; area cultivated, 153; operators of, 152, 153

agriculture, rainfed, 129, 142, 144, 151–53; mechanized, 151, 156, 158; traditional, 151

Ahfad University College, 116

Ahmose I, 4

AID. *See* United States Agency for International Development

AIDS. *See* acquired immune deficiency syndrome

air defense command, 250; headquarters, 250; matériel of, 250; number of personnel in, 245; state of readiness of, 250

air force, 248–49; aircraft of, 248; bases, 249; helicopters of, 249; insignia of, 254; matériel of, 248; number of personnel in, 245; ranks of, 254; state of, 248; training in, 248; transport arm of, 249; uniforms of, 254

airports, 182, 245, 249, 266

232, 260–61; investment from, 162; military assistance from, 259; relations with, 226–27; training of military officers in, 253–54

Arab Fund for Economic and Social Development (AFESD), 49, 135, 175

Arab heritage (*see also* Arabs; north), 3; claimed by Nubians, 10–11

Arabia, 14; Nubian trade with, xxiii, 10

Arabian Peninsula, 66

Arabic, 69, 85; classical, 71; colloquial, 70–71; Juba, 71–72; as language of government, 71; as language of instruction, xxx, 71, 111, 118; as language of mass media, 71, 185, 221, 222; as language of military, 233, 238; as lingua franca, 69, 70, 233; Modern Standard, 70, 71; in Nubia, 8; as official language, xxvi, 31, 32, 46, 57, 71; in south, 31, 32; varieties of, 70–72

Arab Investment Company, 151

Arab-Israeli War (1973), 201

arabization: under Abbud, xxiv, 37; of armed forces, 233; under Bashir, xxx; under British, 27; as cause of civil war, xxx; facilitated by intermarriage, 9, 11; facilitated by Islam, 11; fears of, 213; of Jaali, 73; of Nile River Valley, 71; of Nubians, 74; of south, xxiv, 85, 212

Arab League. *See* League of Arab States

Arab nationalism, 34

Arabs, xxiii, 9–11; Christian, 72; differences among, 57, 74; distribution of, 72; early contact of, with Nubians, 9–10; Egypt ruled by, 10; influence of, on Nilotes, 80; invasion of Nubia by, 9; and Meroe, 6; nationalist movement among, 29; nomadic, 73, 74, 75, 78, 89–91; as percentage of population, xxvi, 72; privileged position of, in Nubia, 10–11; racial background of, 86; sedentary, 73, 74, 75; siege of Dunqulah by, 9; slaves used by, 10, 86; as tenants, 92; tribal conflicts among, 73–74; tribes of, 73, 74

Arabsat. *See* Arab Satellite Organization

Arab Satellite Organization (Arabsat), 185

archaeological exploration, 3–4

armed forces (*see also* military; *see also under* *individual branches*), 244–55, 255, 265; Arabic in, 233, 238; arabization of, 233; under Bashir, 231, 253; desertion from, 251; development of, 233–34;

ethnic groups in, 238; human rights abuses by, 252, 273; internal security operations of, 268; literacy rate in, 251; under Nimeiri, 236; nomads in, 238; personnel in, 232, 245, 259–60; political groups in, 238; purged, 231, 236, 265; racial segregation in, 239; role of, in foreign policy, xxxi; role of, in government, 234–37; in south, 273

army, 245–48; Anya Nya incorporated into, 46; armored strength of, 247; artillery of, 248; economic problems of, 18; headquarters of, 247; indigenous officers in, 233, 237–38; insignia of, 254; morale of, 251; mutiny by, 29, 32, 35, 43, 213, 234, 236, 242, 262; number of personnel in, 234, 245; operational control of, 245; opposition to British officers in, 233; opposition of, to Sadiq al Mahdi government, 39; organizational structure of, 245; origins of, 233; purged, 198, 265; ranks of, 254; recruitment, 254; Southern Command, 239; southern officers in, 239; support units of, 247; training, 254; training facilities of, 247; uniforms of, 254; units of, 247; unit strengths of, 245–47

Ar Rusayris. *See* Roseires Dam

asbestos, 165

Ashigga Party, 30

ashraf, 73

Ash Shajarah, 245

Ash Shamali (province/state), 206; Arabs in, 72; land registration in, 146; refugees in, 67

Ash Sharqi (province/state), 63, 206; agriculture in, 152, 153, 158; refugees in, 67

Asia, 18

As Saltana az Zarqa. *See* Black Sultanate

As Sudd, xxv, 62–63, 64, 65, 157; oil prospecting at, 171

As Suki irrigation project, 150

Assyria, 5

Aswan, 21

Aswan High Dam, 65, 149; resettlement of Nubians near, 74, 148–49

Atbarah, 23, 66, 157; airport, 249; electric generation in, 167; rail transportation from, 173; television station in, 222

Atbarah River, 65, 74, 149

Sudan: A Country Study

Lake Fajarial, 62
Lake Nasser. *See* Lake Nubia
Lake No, 62
Lake Nubia, 63, 65, 148-49; fishing in, 144, 157
lakes, 157
Lake Shambe, 62
Lake Victoria, 65
landownership, 145-46; customary, 146; by state, 146
land registration, 145
land tenure, 92, 145-46; under Anglo-Egyptian condominium, 24; hired labor for, 92; wages for workers in, 92
land use, 144-45; cultivation, 145; forest, 145; grazing, 145; pasture, 145
languages (*see also under individual languages*), 69-72; acquisition of, by migrants, 69; Afro-Asiatic, 69-70; differences among, 57; distribution of, 69-71; lingua francas, 69, 70; in Meroe, 6; multilingualism, 69, 70; Niger-Kurdufanian, 69, 70; Nilo-Saharan, 69, 70; number of, xxvi, 69, 70; as political instrument, 69; of south, xxvi, 58; as symbol of identity, 69
League of Arab States (Arab League), 185, 228
legal system (*see also* sharia), 206-11; under Anglo-Egyptian condominium, 24; British influence on, 207; customary, 206-7; Egyptian influence on, 207; Islamization of, 209; precolonial, 206; problems in, 207; revisions of, 207-9
Legislative Assembly, 30, 202; boycott of elections for, 30; elections for, 30
Libya, 232, 261; aid from, xxviii, xxxi; Bashir's visit to, xxxi; desire for union with, 220, 224; economic cooperation with, 137, 224-25; matériel from, 247, 248, 259, 262; relations with, xxxi, 190, 222, 224-25, 239, 240, 250; support of, for Sudanese rebels, 224, 264; trade with, 190
Libyan Desert, 58
Libyan National Salvation Front, 224
limestone, 165
lineages: minimal, 91-92; in nomadic society, 90-91, 93; ruling, 93
Liquor Prohibition Bill, 209
literacy: encouraged by church, 8; rate, 111, 251
livestock, 153-56; camels, 154, 156; cattle, 154-56; effects of drought on, 153,

154; export of, 187; goats, 154, 156; number of, 154; sheep, 154, 156
livestock raising (*see also* agriculture), xxvi, 146; in Darfur, 64; methods of, 144; traditional, 153; work force in, 139, 142
loans, 185
Local Government Act (1961), 204
location, 239

Madani, Faisal, 200
Madi people, 83; religion of, 107
Mahdi (*see also* Ansar; Mahdist movement; Mahdiyah), xxiv, 105, 217; background of, 18; death of, 20; exile of, 19; family of, 73; jihad of, xxiv, 19; Muhammad Ahmad ibn as Sayyid Abd Allah revealed as, xxiv, 18; self-proclaimed Mahdi, xxiv, 106; theology of, 19, 20
Mahdi, Abd ar Rahman al, 30, 34, 35
Mahdi, Al Hadi al (imam), 36, 39, 40, 42
Mahdi, Sadiq al (elder), 36
Mahdi, Sadiq al (younger), xxiv, xxv, xxxii, 36, 40, 46, 51, 209; amnesty granted to, 47; arrested, 215, 217, 218; exiled to Egypt, 42; meeting of, with Nimeiri, 47
Mahdi al Muntazar, Al. *See* Mahdi
Mahdi government, 39, 128, 197; agreement of, with Sudanese People's Liberation Movement, xxv, 210; coalitions of, xxv, 40, 51-52, 214, 217, 218, 236; corruption in, 51; dissolved, 51, 52; ethnic groups under, 221; factionalism in, 51; foreign policy under, 222; foreign relations under, 227; goals of, 39; human rights abuses under, 252-53; legal charges against, 211; military under, 236; militias under, 258; nomads under, 91; opposition to, 39; overthrown, xxv, 40, 53, 236-37; priorities of, 51; sharia under, 209-10, 213-14; state of emergency under, 272
Mahdist movement (*see also* Mahdi; Mahdiyah), xxiv, 19, 57, 106; as threat to regional stability, xxiv
Mahdist uprisings: under Anglo-Egyptian condominium, 24
Mahdiyah (*see also* Mahdi; Mahdist movement), 18-23, 172; established, 20; purged, 21; sharia under, 21
Mahjub, Abd al Khaliq, 40, 42; deported, 42

322

production, 171; resources, xxvi, 168–71; use, 168–71

PEWC. *See* Public Electricity and Water Corporation

physicians, 118, 119

Pibor Post, 242, 243

pipelines, 184; capacity of, 184; problems on, 184

plain of the Sudan, 58

Pochala, 242

police, 266–70; actions of, 268–70; administration of, 265, 267; communal, 267; distribution of, 268; insignia of, 254; mutiny by, 241; under Nimeiri, 267; number of, 268; organization of, 267; origins of, 266–67; purged, 265; ranks of, 254; responsibilities of, 268; training of, 268; uniforms of, 254; units of, 267; women in, 268

Police Act (1979), 267

political development, 26, 27

political instability, 199

political parties: banned, xxviii, 36, 41, 197, 198, 199, 202, 215, 265, 266; under Bashir government, xxviii, 197, 198, 199, 202, 215; factions in, 50; under Khatim government, 37; under Nimeiri government, 42, 202; religious, 207; representing south, 37; revival of, 50–51; secular, 220–21; underground activities of, 216

Popular Defence Act (1989), xxix, 258

Popular Defence Forces (PDF), 258; camps, 258–59; created, xxxii, 232; membership in, 116, 258; number of personnel in, 258, 259; training of, 258; training of military officers from, 253

population (*see also* ethnic groups; *see also under individual ethnic groups*), 67–69; under age eighteen, 68; Arabs as percentage of, xxvi, 72; Azande as percentage of, 81; birth rate, 67, 82; Christians as percentage of, 85, 100; death rate, 67, 68; density, 6, 68; destruction of, under the Khalifa, 23; Dinka as percentage of, 87; distribution of, xxvi; family planning, 68; fertility rate, 68; growth rate, 67; infant mortality, 67; life expectancy, 68; Muslims as percentage of, 100; Nilotes as percentage of, 78; in 1983, 67; in 1990, xxvi, 67; Nubian, 74; projected, 67–68; rural, 68; urban, xxvi, 68; West Africans as percentage

of, 77; work force as percentage of, 138, 142

ports, 182–84; capacity of, 183; facilities, 182–83; traffic in, 183

Port Sudan, xxxi, 25, 26, 30, 74, 172, 182–83, 250; air defense command in, 250; airport, 182, 249; built, 182; electric generation in, 167; improvements in, 183; navy in, 250; oil refinery, 170, 171, 188; port facilities, 182–83; rail transportation to, 173; United States facilities in, 261

Port Sudan Prison, 274, 275

Power Project: III, 136, 168; IV, 168; V, 168

Presbyterians, 27

presidency, 200–201

Presidential Guard, 270

press: Arabic used in, 71; restrictions on, 199

price controls, xxvii

prices, 137–38

prime minister, 33

prisoners: political, 266, 274; treatment of, 274–75

prison system, 274–75

private sector: enterprises controlled by, 128, 161; investment, 131; irrigated agriculture in, 129; loans to, 185

professional associations, 37, 47, 216; banned, 42; demonstrations by, 214

Public Electricity and Water Corporation (PEWC), 167

public sector: earnings, 131; enterprises controlled by, 128; investment, 130–31, 132; wages, 139

Qadhafi, Muammar al: state visit by, xxxi, 225

Qadiriyah brotherhood, 104

Qallabat, 21

Qash Delta, 62; cotton cultivation in, 148

Qash River, 62, 63

Qaysan, 243

qoz, 61, 64, 178

Quran, 9, 70, 116, 187

Quraysh people, 10

Rabak, 131

radio, 185, 221, 222; receivers, 222; stations, 222

military assistance from, 261–62; relations with, 35, 227–28, 259; technical assistance from, 34, 35, 176; trade with, 189
United States Agency for International Development (AID), 136, 227; Food for Peace Program, 136
United States Arms Control and Disarmament Agency (ACDA), 251, 262
United Tribes Society (*see also* White Flag League): founded, 29
Unity Bank, 186
universities: admission to, 116, 258; support of, for Sudanese Communist Party, 220, 238
University of Cairo, 114
University of Juba, 88, 114
University of Khartoum, 110, 219; antigovernment protests in, 37; Arabic as language of instruction in, 71, 118; English as language of instruction in, 71, 111, 118; enrollment, 114; faculty dismissed from, 118; training of military officers in, 253
Upper Egypt. *See* Egypt, Upper
Upper Nile, 16
Upper Nile Province (*see also* Aali an Nil), 27, 44
uranium, 165; concession, 165–66
urban areas: administration of, 46; controlled by government forces, 43; migration to, 74, 84; population of, 68; services in, 89
urbanization, 57
Uthman, Uthman Ahmad, 200

Verona Fathers, 27
villages: class structure in, 92; land tenure in, 92; officials in, 92

Wadai (Chad), 77
Wadi Halfa, 20, 23, 157
Wadi Sayyidna Air Base, 249, 250, 254
Wad Madani, 249
wages, 139–40; minimum, 140; public sector, 139
Wahhabi Muslims, 14
water: under Nile Waters Agreement, 148; for nomads, 61
Waw, 118; airport, 182; atrocities against civilians in, 39; civil war in, 242, 258; electric generation in, 167
Wawat, 4
West Africans, 77–78; origins of, 77; as

percentage of population, 77; as tenants, 92
West Germany. *See* Federal Republic of Germany
western Sudan, 61, 215; government control of, xxix; geography of, 61; topography of, 61
WFP. *See* United Nations World Food Programme
White Flag League (*see also* United Tribes Society), 29
White Nile, xxv, 4, 57, 62, 63, 64, 65, 90; drainage of, 64; Southern Reach, 179, 180
White Nile Basin, 17
White Nile Petroleum Company, 170
Wingate, Sir Reginald, 24
Wolseley, Lord Garnet Joseph, 20
women: associations of, 42; circumcision of, 99, 100; in labor force, 138; in Mahdist movement, 19; as military officers, 253; raiding for, 88; responsibilities of, 98–99; restrictions on, 99; segregation of, 99; in south, 100; work by, outside the home, 99; *zar* cult of, 99
workers: remittances from, 134–35
Workers' Affairs Association, 141
Workers' Congress, 141
work force, 138–39; in agriculture, 139; as percentage of population, 138
World Bank, xxvi, 49, 138; credit from, 183; credit denied by, xxvii, 137; grant from, xxvii–xxviii; loans from, 127, 135, 149, 168
World Health Organization, 119
World War II, 25; Sudan Defence Force in, 30, 233

Yambio, 66
Yei, 214; civil war in, 243
Yohannes IV, 21
Youth for Reconstruction, 271
Yugoslavia: aid from, 127, 178; joint ventures with, 184; matériel from, 250; military assistance from, 250, 260; training of military officers in, 253–54

Zaghawa people, 75–76, 215, 225; government efforts to destroy, xxxiii; location of, 75
Zaire, 225–26, 239, 273
Zakat Fund Legislative Bill, 209
zar cult, 99
Zubayr, Rahman Mansur az, 19

Published Country Studies

(Area Handbook Series)

550-65	Afghanistan	550-87	Greece
550-98	Albania	550-78	Guatemala
550-44	Algeria	550-174	Guinea
550-59	Angola	550-82	Guyana and Belize
550-73	Argentina	550-151	Honduras
550-169	Australia	550-165	Hungary
550-176	Austria	550-21	India
550-175	Bangladesh	550-154	Indian Ocean
550-170	Belgium	550-39	Indonesia
550-66	Bolivia	550-68	Iran
550-20	Brazil	550-31	Iraq
550-168	Bulgaria	550-25	Israel
550-61	Burma	550-182	Italy
550-50	Cambodia	550-30	Japan
550-166	Cameroon	550-34	Jordan
550-159	Chad	550-56	Kenya
550-77	Chile	550-81	Korea, North
550-60	China	550-41	Korea, South
550-26	Colombia	550-58	Laos
550-33	Commonwealth Caribbean, Islands of the	550-24	Lebanon
550-91	Congo	550-38	Liberia
550-90	Costa Rica	550-85	Libya
550-69	Côte d'Ivoire (Ivory Coast)	550-172	Malawi
550-152	Cuba	550-45	Malaysia
550-22	Cyprus	550-161	Mauritania
550-158	Czechoslovakia	550-79	Mexico
550-36	Dominican Republic and Haiti	550-76	Mongolia
550-52	Ecuador	550-49	Morocco
550-43	Egypt	550-64	Mozambique
550-150	El Salvador	550-35	Nepal and Bhutan
550-28	Ethiopia	550-88	Nicaragua
550-167	Finland	550-157	Nigeria
550-155	Germany, East	550-94	Oceania
550-173	Germany, Fed. Rep. of	550-48	Pakistan
550-153	Ghana	550-46	Panama

550-156	Paraguay	550-53	Thailand
550-185	Persian Gulf States	550-89	Tunisia
550-42	Peru	550-80	Turkey
550-72	Philippines	550-74	Uganda
550-162	Poland	550-97	Uruguay
550-181	Portugal	550-71	Venezuela
550-160	Romania	550-32	Vietnam
550-37	Rwanda and Burundi	550-183	Yemens, The
550-51	Saudi Arabia	550-99	Yugoslavia
550-70	Senegal	550-67	Zaire
550-180	Sierra Leone	550-75	Zambia
550-184	Singapore	550-171	Zimbabwe
550-86	Somalia		
550-93	South Africa		
550-95	Soviet Union		
550-179	Spain		
550-96	Sri Lanka		
550-27	Sudan		
550-47	Syria		
550-62	Tanzania		

on many complex and controversial meanings; in general,
however, it indicates that particular descendant of the House
of Ali who is believed to have been God's designated repository
of the spiritual authority inherent in that line. The identity of
this individual and the means of ascertaining his identity have
been the major issues causing divisions among Shia.

International Monetary Fund (IMF)—Established along with the
World Bank (*q.v.*) in 1945, the IMF is a specialized agency
affiliated with the United Nations and is responsible for stabilizing international exchange rates and payments. The main
business of the IMF is the provision of loans to its members
(including industrialized and developing countries) when they
experience balance of payments difficulties. These loans frequently carry conditions that require substantial internal economic
adjustments by the recipients, most of which are developing
countries.

jazirah—Peninsula or island; with upper case, term refers to the
cultivated lands south of Khartoum between the Blue Nile and
the White Nile.

jizzu—Located in the area of 16° north latitude in northwest Darfur
and in Chad; region beyond the semidesert where the late rains
produce a combination of grass and herbaceous plants in winter
such that camels and sheep can graze without additional water
supply.

khalwa—Small Islamic rural school that stressed memorization of
the Quran and provided some instruction in the reading and
writing of Arabic.

naziriyah (pl., nazuriyat) —Formerly, among nomadic and seminomadic Arab groups, an administrative and local court under
a *nazir*, comprising several *umudiyat* (*q.v.*). A *naziriyah* included either an entire tribe or a section of a large tribe.

qoz—General term used for sand dunes.

Sahel—A narrow band of land bordering the southern Sahara,
stretching across Africa. It is characterized by an average annual rainfall of between 150 and 500 millimeters and is mainly suited to pastoralism.

sharia—Traditional code of Islamic law, both civil and criminal,
based in part on the Quran. Also drawn from the hadith (*q.v.*);
the consensus of Islamic belief (*ijma;* i.e., consensus of the
authorities on a legal question); and analogy (*qiyas;* i.e., an
elaboration of the intent of law).

shaykh—Leader or chief. Word of Arabic origin used to mean either
a political or a learned religious leader. Also used as an
honorific.

Glossary

dinar—Sudanese unit of currency introduced in May 1992 to replace the Sudanese pound (*q.v.*). One dinar was worth ten Sudanese pounds.

fiscal year (FY)—An annual period established for accounting purposes. The Sudanese fiscal year extends from July 1 to the following June 30.

gross domestic product (GDP)—A value measure of the flow of domestic goods and services produced by an economy over a period of time, such as a year. Only output values of goods for final consumption and intermediate production are assumed to be included in the final prices. GDP is sometimes aggregated and shown at market prices, meaning that indirect taxes and subsidies are included; when these indirect taxes and subsidies have been eliminated, the result is GDP at factor cost. The word *gross* indicates that deductions for depreciation of physical assets have not been made. Income arising from investments and possessions owned abroad is not included, only domestic production. Hence, the word *domestic* is used to distinguish GDP from gross national product (*q.v.*).

gross national product (GNP)—The gross domestic product (*q.v.*) plus net income or loss stemming from transactions with foreign countries, including income received from abroad by residents and subtracting payments remitted abroad to nonresidents. GNP is the broadest measurement of the output of goods and services by an economy. It can be calculated at market prices, which include indirect taxes and subsidies. Because indirect taxes and subsidies are only transfer payments, GNP is often calculated at factor cost by removing indirect taxes and subsidies.

hadith—Tradition based on the precedent of the Prophet Muhammad's words and deeds that serves as one of the sources of Islamic law.

hafr (pl., *hafri*)—An excavated water reservoir fed by rainfall.

imam—A word used in several senses. In general use and lowercased, it means the leader of congregational prayers; as such, it implies no ordination or special spiritual powers beyond sufficient education to carry out this function. It is also used figuratively by many Sunni (*q.v.*) Muslims to mean the leader of the Islamic community. Among Shia (*q.v.*) Muslims, the word takes

_____. *Sudan: Threats to Stability.* (Conflicts Studies Series, No. 173.) London: Institute for the Study of Conflict, 1985.

(Various issues of the following publications were also used in the preparation of this chapter: *Africa Confidential* [London]; *African Defence Journal* [Paris]; *Africa Report;* *Economist* [London]; Economist Intelligence Unit, *Country Reports* [London]; Joint Publications Research Service, *Near East and South Asia; Keesing's Record of World Events* [London]; *Middle East International* [London]; *Middle East Journal; New African* [London]; *New York Times;* and *Washington Post.*)

Jane's Fighting Ships, 1991-92. (Ed., Richard Sharpe.) Coulsdon, Surrey, United Kingdom: Jane's International Group, 1991.

Johnson, Douglas H. *The Southern Sudan.* London: Minority Rights Group, 1988.

LeFebvre, Jeffrey A. "Globalism and Regionalism: US Arms Transfers to Sudan," *Armed Forces and Society,* 17, No. 2, Winter 1991, 211-27.

Lesch, Ann Mosely. "Confrontation in the Southern Sudan," *Middle East Journal,* 40, No. 3, Summer 1986, 410-28.

The Middle East Military Balance, 1986. (Eds., Aharon Levran and Zeev Eytan.) Boulder, Colorado: Westview Press, 1987.

The Military Balance, 1990-1991. London: International Institute for Strategic Studies, 1990.

The Military Balance, 1991-1992. London: International Institute for Strategic Studies, 1991.

Nabie, Isata, and John Prendergast. "A Land Divided," *Africa Report,* 35, No. 4, September-October 1990, 58-61.

Rouleau, Eric. "Sudan's Revolutionary Spring," *MERIP Reports,* No. 135, September 1985, 3-9.

"Sudan." Pages 951-80 in *Africa South of the Sahara, 1990.* London: Europa, 1989.

"Sudan: The Viewpoint from the South," *Africa Confidential* [London], 30, No. 23, November 17, 1989, 1-2.

United States. Arms Control and Disarmament Agency. *World Military Expenditures and Arms Transfers, 1989.* Washington: GPO, 1990.

_____. Department of State. *Country Reports on Human Rights Practices for 1989.* (Report submitted to United States Congress, 101st, 2d Session, House of Representatives, Committee on Foreign Affairs, and Senate, Committee on Foreign Relations.) Washington: GPO, 1990.

_____. Department of State. *Country Reports on Human Rights Practices for 1990.* (Report submitted to United States Congress, 102d, 1st Session, Senate, Committee on Foreign Relations, and House of Representatives, Committee on Foreign Affairs.) Washington: GPO, 1991.

Voll, John O. "Political Crisis in Sudan," *Current History,* 89, No. 546, April 1990, 153-56, 179-80.

_____. "The Sudan after Nimeiry," *Current History,* 85, No. 511, May 1986, 213-16, 231-32.

Wai, Dunstan M. *The African-Arab Conflict in the Sudan.* New York: Africana, 1981.

Woodward, Peter. *Sudan, 1898-1989: The Unstable State.* Boulder, Colorado: Rienner, 1990.